D1477767

Documenting Eighteenth Century Satire: Pope, Swift, Gay, and Arbuthnot in Historical Context

Documenting Eighteenth Century Satire:
Pope, Swift, Gay, and Arbuthnot
in Historical Context

By

Pat Rogers

CAMBRIDGE
SCHOLARS

P U B L I S H I N G

Documenting Eighteenth Century Satire:
Pope, Swift, Gay, and Arbuthnot in Historical Context,
by Pat Rogers

This book first published 2012

Cambridge Scholars Publishing

12 Back Chapman Street, Newcastle upon Tyne, NE6 2XX, UK

British Library Cataloguing in Publication Data
A catalogue record for this book is available from the British Library

ISBN (10): 1-4438-3211-1, ISBN (13): 978-1-4438-3211-3

For Keith Thomas

TABLE OF CONTENTS

ACKNOWLEDGMENTS

For permission to quote from materials in their care, I wish to thank the Centre for Buckinghamshire Studies; Devon Record Office; the Museum of Rural Life; and the National Archives.

Several portions of the book have appeared, in most cases in a substantially different form, as follows: Chapter One, *Modern Philology*, 79 (1982): 304-08; Chapter Two, *Times Literary Supplement*, 19 October 2007, 13-15; Chapter Three, *TLS*, 14 November 2008, 15-17; Chapter Four, *The Enduring Legacy: Tercentenary Essays on Alexander Pope*, ed. G..S. Rousseau and P. Rogers (Cambridge University Press, 1988; 2010), 187-98; Chapter Five, *Arion*, 3rd series, 12 (2005): 19-31; Chapter Eight, *Modern Language Review,* 99 (2004): 875-88; Chapter Nine, *Yearbook of English Studies*, 18 (1988): 41-50; Chapter Ten, *Literature and History,* 14 (2005): 14-36; Chapter Eleven, *British Journal for Eighteenth Century Studies,* 28 (2005): 83-95; Chapter Twelve, *Orthodoxy and Heresy in Eighteenth-Century Society,* ed. R. Hewitt and P. Rogers (Lewisburg: Bucknell University Press, 2002), pp. 112-33.

Students of the subject will easily recognize the degree of my indebtedness to a host of editors, historians and literary scholars. Among those whose work I have quarried and who have died since I first envisaged the possibility of this book are Ragnhild Hatton, Maynard Mack, David Nokes, David Underdown, Aubrey Williams and David Woolley. Their achievement lives on.

The dedication reflects my longstanding debt to Keith Thomas, whose work has opened up so many corners of the British past. He may be surprised, but I hope gratified, to find that this extends to the world of the eighteenth-century satirists.

SHORT TITLES

Anecdotes	Joseph Spence, *Observations, Anecdotes, and Characters of Books and Men*, ed. J. M. Osborn. 2 vols. Oxford: Clarendon Press, 1966.
Ault, *New Life*	Norman Ault, *New Light on Pope*. London: Methuen, 1949.
Carswell, *Bubble*	John Carswell, *The South Sea Bubble*. Stroud: Sutton, 2001.
Defoe, *Tour*	Daniel Defoe, *A Tour thro' the Whole Island of Great Britain*, in *Writings on Travel, Discovery and History*, ed. J. McVeagh. 4 vols. London: Pickering and Chatto, 2001.
Gay, *Letters*	John Gay, *Letters*, ed. C.F. Burgess. Oxford: Clarendon Press, 1966.
Gay, *Poetry and Prose*	John Gay, *Poetry and Prose*, ed. V.A. Dearing and C.E. Beckwith. 2 vols. Oxford: Clarendon Press, 1974.
Howson, *Thief-Taker*	Gerald Howson, *Thief-Taker General: The Rise and Fall of Jonathan Wild*. London: Hutchinson, 1970.
Journal to Stella	Jonathan Swift, *Journal to Stella*, ed. H. Williams. 2 vols. Oxford: Clarendon Press, 1948.
Mack, *Life*	Maynard Mack, *Alexander Pope: A Life*. New Haven: Yale University Press, 1985.
Memoirs of Scriblerus	*The Memoirs of the Extraordinary Life, Works, and Discoveries of Martinus Scriblerus*, ed. C. Kerby-Miller. New York: Oxford University Press, 1988.
Paulson, *Hogarth*	Ronald Paulson, *Hogarth*. 3 vols. New Brunswick: Rutgers University Press, 1991.
Pope *Corr*	*The Correspondence of Alexander Pope*, ed. G. Sherburn. 5 vols. Oxford: Clarendon Press, 1956.

Pope *Prose*   *The Prose Works of Alexander Pope*, vol. 1, ed.
                      N. Ault. Oxford: Blackwell, 1936; vol. 2, ed. R.
                      Cowler. Hamden, CT: Archon Books, 1986.

Swift *Corr*   *The Correspondence of Jonathan Swift*, ed. D.
                      Woolley. 4 vols. Frankfurt: Peter Lang, 1999-
                      2005.

Swift *Poems*   *The Poems of Jonathan Swift*, ed. H. Williams.
                      3 vols. Oxford: Clarendon Press, 1958.

Swift *Prose*   *The Prose Works of Jonathan Swift*, ed. H.
                      Davis et al. 14 vols. Oxford: Basil Blackwell,
                      1939-68.

TE   *The Twickenham Edition of the Poems of
                      Alexander Pope*, ed. J. Butt et al. 11 vols.
                      London: Methuen, 1938-68.

Tilley   Morris P. Tilley, *A Dictionary of Proverbs in
                      England in the Sixteenth and Seventeenth
                      Centuries*. Ann Arbor: University of Michigan
                      Press, 1950.

INTRODUCTION

The major English satirists of the eighteenth century continue to stimulate readers, and every year they provoke a great deal of valuable critical and scholarly work. We have had important studies devoted to Swift, Pope and Gay, though perhaps Swift is alone in retaining the full share of undergraduate courses in literature that writers of this stamp once claimed. At the same time the long neglected polymath Dr John Arbuthnot seems ready to emerge from the shadows, with an edition of his letters by Angus Ross in 2006 and a political biography by the same scholar scheduled for publication shortly. However, little has been done in recent years to consider the work of the Scriblerian group as a whole.[1]

It is also the case that criticism of this group, as of authors at large, has tended to step back a little from basic archival research. Students have preferred to follow a theoretical or ideological approach, often with great profit. Some general works on satire, too, have illuminated key eighteenth-century texts. Among such books we might instance *The Difference Satire Makes* (2001) by Fredric V. Bogel, as well as *Satire: A Critical Re-Introduction* (1994) by Dustin Griffin and *The Literature of Satire* (2004) by Charles A. Knight. Bogel develops a sophisticated theory of the genre, analyzing what he terms a "double structure" which bridges the rhetorical gap between satirist and satiric object. His examples range from Ben Jonson and Dryden to Byron, but the most detailed exploration is conducted around the main Augustan writings, notably Swift's poems and *The Beggar's Opera*. Both Griffin and Knight pay a good deal of attention to the same authors, with especially close attention to *The Dunciad* on the part of Knight. However, the most influential commentator has probably been Claude Rawson, with a succession of books revealing his interest in the twin notions evoked in the title of his collected essays, *Satire and Sentiment 1650-1830* (1994). All readers must feel a debt of gratitude to these critics. But we owe a comparable debt to editors, biographers and scholars who have done so much to open up the personal and historical context of Scriblerian authorship.[2]

While this book does not propound a general theory of satire, the essays do make some modest effort to establish a praxis. Of course, it is never enough merely to collect inert "background" facts. The more important task concerns the *use* we make of such material. We need to discriminate, for instance, between what could potentially be relevant and what actually does help us to gauge the tone, intention and methods of a particular satire. Each chapter seeks to illustrate the means by which external evidence can support internal clues to enhance our understanding of some representative texts. This approach will never produce a single unquestioned "meaning," but it can strengthen the grounds for reading the work in certain ways and sometimes for excluding another interpretation. Does it matter if we pick up on every small allusion? *Gulliver's Travels* survives even though we know little more about the precise targets of its satire than we did a hundred years ago, except in limited areas, and we may well be missing a number of contemporary in-jokes that contemporaries would have spotted. But there is always the chance that rediscovery of topical references will take us further into the work, as in the case of *The Dunciad* and of several poems by Swift.

In fact, the opportunities for first-order research, drawing on unpublished or unexamined sources, have never been greater. The marvellous expansion of electronic aids has made it possible to track down almost instantaneously troves of material which were once very difficult to locate, and in some cases even to transcribe these documents straight into a personal computer. Such material offers up immense possibilities to those studying topics such as Augustan satire, which deal chiefly with historically determined issues. Exploration in this field need not confine itself to the discovery of sources and analogues, though such things still have their critical uses. Rather, the new finds may help us to understand individual works more completely by providing a whole *raison d'être* for their composition, and supplying clues to hidden meanings within the text. One aim of this book is to encourage fresh research which will reveal unsuspected richness in books we thought we already understood – which in the case of these satirists may include items as familiar as *Gulliver's Travels*, *The Rape of the Lock* and *The Beggar's Opera*. Another aim is to draw attention to less well known works by Scriblerian authors, in the belief that closer examination may uncover a new richness that has been occluded, partly by our own ignorance of the elements that went into their making – now that these elements are more easily detected by the kind of study enabled by modern electronic tools.

General agreement exists that, since the time of Aristophanes, Horace and Juvenal, satire has been among the most historically conditioned of literary genres. However, we need to be clear about the consequences for criticism. Not every stray allusion to a topical affair carries great significance: many of the incidental details about Pope's dunces were unknown to most contemporaries, and explaining a single reference will seldom change our overall view of *The Dunciad.* Nevertheless, in combination such buried facts will occasionally supply a vital clue to the workings of this poem. In these chapters I attempt to find documentary evidence which helps to explain the wider themes of a given text, and which will make possible a fuller interpretation of its procedures.

Obviously, there is a great deal more going on in the works of the Scriblerian group than a mere transcription of actuality. They contain elements of the fantastic, the mysterious, the surreal, the romantic, the supernatural, the hyperbolic, the grotesque, the ludic – even the magical at times. We encounter most of these things in *The Rape of the Lock* alone. They constitute the ingredients that Margaret Doody considers basic to fiction, and that have been eclipsed in the reign of what she calls "compulsory realism" in the eighteenth and nineteenth century.[3] Swift and his friends did not know they were supposed to follow such a path, and they were not compulsory realists. What does mark off their writings from the bourgeois novel, say, is a willingness to stretch the truth of everyday existence for satiric effect, and in this respect their heir is not Richardson or Austen but Dickens. But they liked to start from the observable, and their work grows much more intelligible as soon as we excavate the roots of their invention, often buried in the humus of history and invisible to a modern eye. Swift's Partridge is not the "real" astrologer John Partridge: Pope's Curl is not the historic publisher Edmund Curll; and Gay's Peachum is not the actual thief-taker, Jonathan Wild. Nevertheless, the better we know these people the less likely we are to misjudge the thrust of the satire in which they appear.

In line with these considerations, the book has been planned to range across different modes of satire, in poetry, prose and drama. It covers some of the best known works of eighteenth-century British literature. For example, a new focus is offered on *The Rape of the Lock* and on poems by Swift, challenging some earlier interpretations. The meaning of *The Beggar's Opera* is reappraised in the light of fresh information. A major reassessment of *The Dunciad* involves consideration of several elements previously neglected, most notably the role of City of London politics. In addition the book deals with less familiar but important texts of the age, including Gay's *Trivia,* Pope's *Epistle to Miss Blount,* and Swift's poem on *Sid Hamet.* Along with these come works which have been unduly neglected for the most part, despite considerable literary merit: these include Pope's *Duke upon Duke* and Swift's *The Bubble.* The best of Pope's prose works rival his poetry in wit, daring and invention, as Chapter 6 may suggest. One chapter concerns a poem, still virtually unknown, that surfaced in the 1970s, and it offers the first full interpretation and edition of this item, written by Gay and/or Pope. Another describes a previously unsuspected hoax, almost certainly perpetrated by the Scriblerians, concerning the quest for the longitude. Yet another finds an unsuspected, but close, link between poems by Pope and Pushkin. Several, including Chapters 5, 6 and 13, uncover a topographical element behind the satire. All the studies expose fresh materials, which have not applied to the text in question before now, and seek to offer new insights into modes of Augustan satire.

While each work is considered in its own terms, a number of common issues arise and cross-references naturally emerge. Thus, historical events such as the South Sea Bubble recur, while the use that the satires made of London life appears in several chapters, as do consistent targets of the satirists, such as the rascally publisher Curll and the politician Nicholas Lechmere. One item deals with Swift's response to extreme prophets and another with Pope's handling of the same issue. Commonality is also found in some of the devices and techniques explored, for example the use of proverbial idiom in five of the studies. The target works were all written in the short period from 1710 to 1728 (disregarding the revised version of *The Dunciad*), and they took off from one specific milieu.[4] Probably each of the four writers knew something of them before they reached print.[5] These narrow origins make it all the more remarkable that the satire should remain so potent after three hundred years.

The sources used include numerous unpublished documents, such as wills, inventories, estate deeds, settlements, marriage contracts, criminal records and private correspondence, drawn from a number of repositories. But not all materials that have been neglected exist in manuscript form: others lie hidden in plain sight, overlooked among the bulky files of contemporary newspapers, magazines and pamphlets. Most of these have not been quarried heavily, if at all, before now. Chapter 1 finds a concealed occasion for a poem by Swift, while Chapters 10 and 11 delve at length into the criminological and political background of works by Gay and Pope. Chapter 12 supplies a longer perspective, by relating *The Dunciad* to a pervasive tradition of millenarian thought. In other cases the contextual material explored in the chapters is drawn from literary motifs and conventions of the period. Thus Chapters 8 and 9 investigate the mode of popular balladry as it was reinvented for Scriblerian purposes.

Three of the longest items have never been published in any form. Four more are heavily revised and expanded, with new documentation. Four others have been reordered and brought up to date. The three remaining chapters are corrected and lightly revised versions. The material previously published appeared in general collections or in literary and scholarly journals – two in the 1980s, others in 2003-2008. None of the chapters has appeared in previous books, other than two items that came out in collections I edited. They follow the broad chronological order in which the works under review were written. All have been chosen to support a single case with regard to "documenting" literature of the past.

Notes

[1] One book that partially bucks this trend is Dustin Griffin's comparative study of the relations between Swift and Pope, published in 2010. See the Select Bibliography at the end of the book (p. 299).

[2] Among the most important contributions are the correspondence of Swift and Pope edited by (respectively) David Woolley and George Sherburn; the Twickenham edition of Pope's poetry by John Butt and others; the lives of these writers by Irvin Ehrenpreis and Maynard Mack; the letters of Arbuthnot, edited by Angus Ross; and biographies of Gay by David Nokes and Lady Mary Wortley Montagu by Isobel Grundy. For fuller details, see the Select Bibliography, pp 243-5.

[3] Margaret Anne Doody, *The True Story of the Novel* (New Brunswick, NJ, 1995).

[4] The only text considered in detail here which Swift wrote while working apart from his Scriblerian friends in Dublin is *The Bubble*, discussed in Chapter 9. Even this has a limited "Irish" context, since it deals with an event whose epicentre was London.

[5] An exception may be the earliest item, Swift's poem on "Sid Hamet," as this was written before Pope and Gay joined the circle of friends. Equally Swift's absence in Ireland may have meant that he remained unaware of works such as Gay's *Trivia* and Pope's *Full and True Account* until they appeared in print.

CHAPTER ONE

THE ROD OF MOSES AND THE WAND OF THE PROPHET: SWIFT'S POEM ON "SID HAMET"

On 4 October 1710, Jonathan Swift reported to Stella that he had sent a "lampoon" to be printed. This can be identified as an attack on the recently ousted chief minister, Lord Godolphin, called "The Virtues of Sid Hamet the Magician's Rod," which Swift had begun on 26 September. He worked on the poem for more than week, and found it "very slow" work. It was published by John Morphew, a "trade publisher," by 14 October and according to the author the poem was "cried up to the skies."

As noted by Harold Williams, the name of the hero is based on Lord Treasurer Godolphin's given name together with the supposed narrator of *Don Quixote* (Swift *Poems*, 1: 131-5; *Journal to Stella*, 1: 30, 41, 59).[1] Sidney Godolphin (1645-1712), created first Earl in 1706, held the post of lord treasurer throughout the earlier years of Queen Anne's reign, with the moderate Whig ministry in place from 1702. He managed the monetary side of the War of Spanish Succession while Marlborough conducted military operations, and acquired a reputation as a financial wizard. After the ill-fated impeachment of Dr Henry Sacheverell in 1710, Godolphin lost his grip on power. The Tories came to the fore under the leadership of Robert Harley, shortly to make Swift his principal agent of publicity. Godolphin was forced out of office in August 1710, shortly before the Tories gained an overwhelming victory in the general election. The poll was actually going on around the time Swift wrote his work – voting began in the City of London, for example, on 9 October. To that extent the lampoon may be regarded as a kind of electioneering pamphlet.

I

The method of the poem hinges on one particular event and utilizes other aspects of Godolphin's career. For some time the queen had shilly-shallied over dismissing Godolphin, and it was only after a number of confusing signals that she sent him her celebrated letter of 7 August 1710, demanding his resignation in return for a pension of £4,000 per annum: "I desire that, instead of bringing the staff to me, you will break it, which I believe will be easier to us both."[2] Humiliatingly, the message was conveyed to the lord treasurer by a groom in the service of the master of the horse. In fact he never received any of the promised pension before his death two years later, though Anne did not cease to consult Godolphin privately. Swift refers to this episode specifically in lines 79-80 of "Sid Hamet":

> Dear Sid, then why wer't thou so mad
> To break thy Rod like naughty Lad?

But in fact the staff of office traditionally carried by each lord treasurer had been in question throughout the entire poem, which offer a series of riffs on the basic theme of rods. To break the staff, as Macaulay remarks in describing this episode, was a sign of renunciation of office.

Irvin Ehrenpreis, who denies Swift's poem "the least claim to literary merit, much though its author valued it," describes the work in these terms: "Rods celebrated in scripture, myth, and fiction are compared with Godolphin's white staff of office."[3] We need also to recall that Swift's own relations with Godolphin had deteriorated. When he arrived in England in September he got a frosty reception, "altogether short, dry, and morose," from the former minister – not wholly unexpected in the circumstances. At this, Swift had determined to even the score: "I am come home rolling resentments in my mind," he told Stella on 10 September. He intended to print his lampoon "for revenge on a certain great person." The poem created a great deal of interest, not least among leading figures in Swift's circle such as Harley and the Earl of Peterborough; but most readers believed that its author was Matthew Prior, a misconception which both writers appear to have enjoyed. A few days after publication, Swift was able to inform Stella that the verses "run prodigiously" (Swift *Corr* 1: 291; *Journal to Stella*, 1: 6, 13, 36, 60, 65).

In addition to recent events, the text of "Sid Hamet" harks back to earlier phases of Godolphin's career. The rod carried by "Our great Magician", Sid Hamet, was made of "honest *English* Wood," but it was then "Metamorphos'd by his Grasp" and grew into a hissing, stinging asp (5-14) – a reversal of the story told in Exodus concerning the rod of Moses. Next Swift invokes a witch's broomstick, calling up the same image of a sabbath held at midnight that Pope used in his *Epistle to a Lady* (*TE* 3.ii: 69). He follows that with a divining rod, which here detects not water but precious minerals (21-34). In this case Sid's "Magick *Rod*" enabled him to detect deposits of gold ore in Scotland: this supplies a hit at the way in which the Union was sold to the two parliaments by the ministry in 1707, and the bribery of Scottish leaders in which Godolphin had allegedly engaged. The rod also permitted him to pick out a likely "*Cully*," or mark, off whom he could make money. He could likewise wield his staff like the caduceus of Mercury (the "opiate Rod" of Hermes, mentioned in *Paradise Lost*, 11: 133) to scatter opium over "the *British* Senate" (40), that is deceive parliament. Here Swift may be thinking of the malfeasance and jobbery which, Tory critics alleged, had permitted City men and contractors to profit from the war.

As well as dowsing, Godolphin's white staff is adapted to fishing for greedy placemen, who would do his bidding at Westminster. In this capacity as an angler's rod, it provides a perfect instrument of corruption: "He caught his Fish, and sav'd his Bait" (48). After this the stick transforms into a conjurer's wand, used to create a magic circle. Sid was able to make an especially large circle, into which he took "mischievous Spirits," but "when th' enchanted Rod was broke,/ They vanish'd in a stinking Smoak" (57-8). The meaning is plain: while at the centre of power Godolphin drew into his orbit a number of worthless agents and instruments of his policy, who disappeared as soon as he fell from grace. When Swift wrote the poem, most of the old ministry had resigned, though it was still impossible for Harley to get rid of Godolphin's coadjutor, the Duke of Marlborough himself. On 20 September the *Journal* lists for Stella some of "the removals," including leading figures such as Lord Somers and Henry Boyle: "I am almost shocked at it, though I did not care if they were all hanged" (*Journal to Stella*, 1: 24).

In the next section of his poem Swift contrasts Sid's rod with the sceptre of Agamemnon in the *Iliad*, barren of leaves once its wood was severed from the tree, "As *Homer* tells us o'er and o'er" (69) – most obviously at the moment when Achilles swears on it and then throws it on the floor in his quarrel with the Greek king in the first book of the poem. Inversely the lord treasurer's wand proves fruitful, shooting out "Golden Boughs, and Golden Fruit" (72), resembling the apples of the Hesperides. It was transmitted to him through "the Hero's line" (62) as an heirloom, just as the sceptre of Agamemnon was handed down to him from ancestors (*Iliad* 2: 101-8, where however it is made clear that Hephaestus, or Vulcan, had forged the staff in bronze). These lines glance at the insinuation that Godolphin owed his power to his connection with the Churchill family – his son had married in 1698 the eldest daughter and heiress of the Duke and Duchess of Marlborough, with £5,000 of her dowry provided by Princess (later Queen) Anne. This is not the only canard to which Swift's poem lends credence. At its conclusion, he distorts the actual sequence of events by suggesting that Godolphin should have kissed the rod and returned it to his mistress (81), that is knuckled under (Tilley R156), whereas in truth he was simply doing the queen's bidding. Swift knew this perfectly well: on 9 September, shortly before composing "Sid Hamet," he had written to Archbishop William King and described how in response to the instructions he had received Godolphin "broke his Staff, and flung the Pieces in the Chimney, desiring Mr. Smith [the chancellor of the exchequer, who was present] to be Witness that he had obeyed the Queen's Commands" (Swift *Corr*, 1: 291).

When Swift writes that Godolphin chose "to break [his] Rod like naughty Lad" (80), we can hardly fail to hear a contrast with the end of *The Tempest*. There of course Prospero abjures his rough magic, and declares, "I'll break my staff," voluntarily renouncing his supernatural powers along with his legitimate rule. Against this Godolphin appears as a usurper like Antonio, brought to book by the true monarch, who strips him of his unearned influence. Reacting to his dismissal like a badly behaved schoolboy, he deserves to feel the master's cane – or "rod," as it was normally called when wielded by the most famous disciplinarian of the age, Dr Richard Busby of Westminster school. Pope allots Busby a speech in Book 4 of *The Dunciad,* uttered by a spectral form holding in its hand "the Virtue of the dreadful wand" (*TE* 5: 355). The note to this line ran, "A Cane usually born by Schoolmasters, which drives the poor Souls about like the wand of Mercury."

According to "Sid Hamet," the minister would have done better to turn his staff into "a *Newmarket* Switch" (84). This alludes to Godolphin's interest in horse racing, along with his estate and stables close to the town – more of the minister's ill-gotten gains, from Swift's point of view.[4] A riding-rod, according to *OED*, was "a stick or switch carried in the hand when riding." Instead Sid has made it into a "Rod for [his] own Breech" (84) – a form of self-chastisement (Tilley R153). Its next incarnation may be "a *Rod in Piss*" (86), a punishment in store (Tilley R157). We know very well the sanction that many Tories envisaged for the former lord treasurer: they wanted to see him impeached – but the queen would never have contemplated such a thing. With this flurry of proverbial usages, the poem completes its denunciation of Godolphin – and by implication the whole Whig ministry - as a party of corrupt tricksters, analogous to "the conj'ring Tribe" of strolling mountebanks and cheating illusionists. In this light "Sid Hamet" has more artistic coherence, and more political edge, than we have previously realised.

Ehrenpreis contends that the weight of allusion caused Swift his problems in writing the poem. "Most of the rhythms are doggerel," he asserts, "the language is generally clumsy; the tone, erratic. The images are more mean than homely, and the wit is palpably forced. Almost inevitably the end limps and sounds awkward, though Swift tries as usual for a hammerblow." The critic's dislike of "Sid Hamet" may go back to an underlying thread he discerns, that is "a dense unintentionally phallic imagery, suggesting that Swift was symbolically castrating a father figure."[5] This reading seems farfetched, insofar as the staffs which provide Swift's analogues were all familiar in scripture, literature, mythology and folklore, and none was created for the purpose by the poet. The force of the ending is lost unless we take account of the build-up of coarse proverbial usages in the latter stages of the work. By this means Swift effects a swerve to a new sense of his key word – the rod of punishment, which should now be exercised on Godolphin himself. Last, like all previous commentators, Ehrenpreis missed two elements vital to the design.

The first of these is a wide-ranging current of allusion to the staff both of Moses and of his brother Aaron (often interchangeable in subsequent exegesis, Jewish and Christian alike). This constitutes the key image, set in motion at the very start:

> The *Rod* was but a harmless Wand,
> When *Moses* held it in his hand,
> But soon as e'er he *lay'd it down*,
> 'Twas a devouring Serpent grown.   (1-4)

The lines allude to a scene in Exodus 4:2-4, which editors have annotated. But although Swift does not mention other episodes, a reader in his day would automatically recall familiar passages from the scriptures, where the rod is seen as the symbol of Moses' authority over the Israelites. They would remember incidents, too, where the staffs of both Moses and Aaron exercise miraculous power during the plagues, akin to that of the "magicians" (e.g. Exodus 7-8), following an instruction for Aaron from Moses to cast down his rod before Pharaoh so that it becomes a serpent. In Numbers 20: 11, the brothers strike the rock to produce water for the congregation to drink; and of course Moses parts the Red Sea with his staff in Exodus 14. Finally, as related in the book of Numbers 17: 1-17, Moses prophesies that Aaron's rod will "[bring] forth buds, and [bloom] blossoms" – compare *Sid Hamet*: "*Sid*'s Scepter, full of Juice, did shoot / In golden Boughs, and golden Fruit" (71-2). The trope was used by another poet in the same year, in a savage attack on the Whig Junto which also implicated Godolphin:

> On his right Hand was old *Vulpone* plac'd,
> With Wealth, and ev'ry Thing but *Merit* grac'd:
> A Man whose Arts, and undiscover'd Wiles,
> Had vested him with wrong'd *Britannia*'s Spoils;
> And whose all powerful and commanding Wand,
> Like *Aaron*'s, had distress'd and vex'd the Land.[6]

We should look in vain for any Lawrentian sense of phallic power as Swift takes over the biblical text. Moses and Aaron use their staffs to ward off evil and defeat the oppressive empire of Pharaoh, casting out plagues, producing life-giving nourishment from the desert, and helping the Israelites to freedom. By contrast Godolphin does the exact opposite: he acts like a conjuror rather than a prophet, and he produces rich pickings for himself in the form of "Juice", gold to augment the family coffers. By his misuse of the emblem of his authority, he betrays the beneficent empire of the queen, embodied in the "honest *English* Wood" of the white staff. All in all, Godolphin becomes the antitype of Moses, standing as the leader who misleads his people and undermines the authority vested in him. Unlike the prophet, he uses hocus-pocus to delude his followers. Moreover, as we have seen, the rod's power to "divine" (31) suggests another form of staff – one indeed that was popularly known as a Mosaical rod.

Satirists generally try to limit the range of allusions. But Swift could not restrict the scope of his opening reference: his first readers simply knew too much about the subject.

II

A second layer of implication is present in "Sid Hamet." It has passed unobserved that Swift took his title, and several leading ideas for the poem, from a topical story in the periodical press. This appeared in nos. 4 and 9 of a new *Tatler*-style journal called *The Visions of Sir Heister Ryley,* which ran for about a year: its author was the projector Charles Povey.[7] He was a man of considerable energy and initiative, whose career has not been very fully studied. In an age of projectors, he became notorious as the most ingenious of all company promoters. His Laputan schemes included a fire-bomb, that is extinguisher, and a new coin of gold and silver "to give in exchange for South-Sea stock and Paper Money" (Read's *Weekly Journal,* 19 November 1720).

The ostensible theme of Povey's journal is the need for a reformation of manners, particularly in the area of sexual behavior. However, a titillating quality in the stories printed may point to the real sales appeal of the *Visions.* Of the two issues in question, the first introduced a French pseudo-prophet, James Aymar. The second was headed "The Continuation of the Virtue of *James Aymar*'s Wand," and described how the cheat met his downfall. Povey mentions the wand's "virtue" several times in the text. These issues are dated, respectively, 28 August and 8 September 1710. They concern Jacques Aimar-Vernai, a peasant from Dauphiné, who became prominent around 1692 and set off a fierce debate on the alleged powers of the divining rod. He claimed that he could track murderers and thieves with the aid of his rod. Aimar became the centre of widespread debate for a time, involving Nicolas Malebranche and more tangentially Antoni van Leeuwenhoek among others, but the episode had dropped out of sight for some years. Interest in England was kindled once more by the French prophets, who operated in England from 1706.[8] Most people would have remembered at least the outline of Aymar's story and the controversy it sparked.

The vigour of the analogies set out in "Sid Hamet" is much increased if we recall Povey's two papers. In the transcription which follows, the text is taken from the collected edition "printed for the author" and sold by a variety of tradesmen and tradeswomen. No date is supplied on the title page, but the volume almost certainly appeared soon after the final number of the journal on February 21, 1710[/11].

From my House in St. James's Square, August 25.
They who assert. That in such a Polite Age as this, it is mere trifling to attempt to impose upon the World. have in some respect, Reason on their side; but all things considered they do not argue right. There are a great many more private Persons at present than formerly, ho are able to resist the Force, and stop the Course of Illusion. I own it, but withal reply, our Age is as easie to be impos'd upon as any whatsoever. And after what we have seen concerning an Explication of the Apocalypse,[9] we have no reason to say that the World is grown more cunning now a-days. In truth, it is not; all the Delusions which tickle Men's Fancies, go down glib with them. They are not asham'd when they are convinc'd that they have been overseen: neither have they the less respect for them who have out-witted them; and they cry out as loud as ever against those who have not faith enough to be deluded; a pretty instance whereof we have in the Case of *James Aymer* [sic], a Frenchman, who pretended to find out all the Faults and Actions of Men, be they never so secret, only by the Moon of a pretended Wand, which he always carryed about him. Never did any thing make a greater Noise, or occasion the Writing of so many Books about the

Miracles this Person was said to do. I am certainly informed that several Politicians in the Court of *France* thought at first, that by the Virtue of this Wand they should in a short time gain great Advantages over their Enemies the Allies: but it is evident they were mightily disappointed in their Expectation. Should I enlarge upon the Story; the single History of this Matter only would fill a whole Volume, and perhaps expose the People of *France* to more contempt than all the Writings of our Historians have done. It's true, if *James Aymar* could have made his Pretensions good, it might have gain'd the King many Signal Victories: For then that Prince could have told what his Enemies had consulted in their Councils against him, long before they were capable of pulling their Designs into Execution: Nay, he could have told by Virtue of this Wand, whether a Battle or a Siege would have turned to Honour, or have proved fatal to his Affairs. . .

Struck by the potential opened up by the wand, the author decides to make his readers "a little merry":

If this great Prophet had been a true one. it might have carried the Reformation of Manners throughout the whole world, more effectively than the Missionaries with all their Art and Pains have hitherto done: For should such a Man be seated on the Stage of this Terrestrial Globe; Jealousie, that Pest of a married Life, would soon be banish'd all humane Society. Neither the *Italians* nor the Eastern Nations would then have occasion to set Guards over their Wives, or watch them with *Argus*'s Eyes themselves; each Man would trust to their Honesty, and they need but bring them to the Test of the Wand, and the Men would not only free themselves from wracking Cares, which too often hasten their Ruin; but they would perceive themselves under the Necessity of maintaining their Conjugal Vow, if they had any value for their own Reputation. The being call'd to the Court and appearing before a Prince, would strike less Horror into the Mind of the Guilty, than the Arrival of an *Abaris*.[10] The greatest number of Offences, the most dangerous Sins, such I mean, as are committed under the hopes that they'll never rise up to their publick Shame; would be entirely suppress'd by thinking on the Wand.

At this point the author quotes a short passage from one of Horaces's odes,[11] and launches into an argument that "this Wand would be of wonderful Advantage to the World, it would ease the Publick of the Funds it is obliged to establish for the Maintenance of Foundlings: For it would discover those who are their Parents, and force them to maintain them themselves: Besides, it would enhaunce the Fear of the evil Consequence; which Dread is such a restraint upon Incontinency, that without it there would be more frequent and more scandalous Acts of Uncleanness committed."

After this bawdy episode, Sir Heister brings himself up with a jerk to the events in hand:

> But to come a little closer to the Matter. I shall relate a Passage or two concerning the pretended Virtue of *James Aymar's* Wand. The Prior of the Charter House of *Ville neuve* in *Avignon,* travell' d through *Orange* with *James Aymar,*[12] by whose Assistance he pretended to discover several Boundaries of Land that were lost; but by chance he was made use of upon another Occasion. Three Days before, A Child was laid at the Gate of the Convent of the Capuchins:[13] The Rector of the Hospital desired James *Aymar* to discover who did it. To this he readily consented, came to the Capuchin's Gate, where the Child had been laid, and in the View of a great Multitude, took the Way which the motion of his Wand directed to, and went to a Village of the County of *Venaisin,* nam'd *Camaret,* and from thence into a Farm-House, which he said positively was the Place where the Child was born. I forgot to tell you that in the way, he met with a Man on Horseback, and that by the motion of his Wand, he discover'd that he was the Father of the Foundling. The Judge of the Place, either of his own accord, or at the Sollicitation of some Persons concerned, desired James *Aymar,* and these who set him to work, to make no farther Enquiry, and that he would cause the Child to be taken home again, which was accordingly done. The Conclusion of this notable Story, with an Account how *James Aymar's* Wand came to lose its admirable Virtue, and the Disappointment many of the People of *France* met with, upon the Discovery of the Cheat, must be reserv'd to fill up part of another Paper.

So ends the first issue relating to Aymar's wand.

III

Two weeks later, a second paper embellishes on the theme:

> *From my House in* St. James's Square, September 7
> *The Continuation of the Virtue of* James Aymar's *Wand.*
> Many of the People *of France* were so prejudiced in favour of this Impostor, that they made him do things which he never thought of, and found out Reasons to excuse him when he did not succeed. He impos'd on the Publick by the appearance of a simple and rustick Air, and speaking only the Gibberish of his Country; but he was in the bottom nothing less than what he appeared to be. The Motion of his Wand was the Cause of the Illusion. The People saw the forked Stick turn so dexterously in his Hand, that they did not perceive the insensible Motion of his Fist, which determined it to turn forcibly and quick, by the Spring which he gave to his Wand.[14] Besides his apparent natural Plainness, he affected to be devout, went often to Confession, every Day to Mass, and shewed other external

Tokens of a great Sense of Religion; and affirmed that he had very
carefully preserved his Virginity, without which (as he said) he could not
succeed with his Wand. He would not walk in the Streets in the Day-time,
for fear, as he said, of being murdered by Thieves and Pick-Pockets. But
all this was only, because the Night served better for his Tricks.

Yet, however ridiculous Aymar might appear, he did not want admirers
among the people:

Some wanted to know when a Peace would be concluded; others were very
desirous to be informed how many Victories the King should get the next
Campaign. Some ask'd him whether he could not discover the Thieves,
who were guilty of such a Robbery, at such a time, in such a Place, &c.
Others were eager to be certified, whether such a Saint was not the true
one, rather than that of another Parish, which bragg'd of having him also.
Others brought Relicks to him, to know whether they really belong'd to
such a Saint. A Young Silk-Weaver, who was contracted, gave him two
Crowns to know whether the Woman he was contracted to had her Maiden
Head or no. Those who shard the Profit took care to bring Grist to the Mill,
and made them pay the Money before hand. Such a Man as this at *London,*
with his Wand, would be a certain Gain, and an inexhaustible Mine[15] for
those who should have a Share in the Profit; since it is well known that
several of our Petty-Conjurors,[16] who do not pretend to perform a
thousandth Part of the Miracles attributed to *James Aymar;* gain to
themselves considerable Estates, by the good Opinion that the well
disposed People of *Great Britain* have of them. If this Trade of the Wand
had gone on in *France,* the Persons who suspected others, and those who
were suspected, would have strove who should pay him best. He would
have got Money out of the Husbands and Wives, the Gallants and their
Mistresses. The Wand would not have moved but for those who gave
most.[17] I believe that if the Mystery of these sorts of pretended Prodigies
could be discovered, we should find that there is a Combination of People
always at the Head of the Plots, who, upon the first broaching of the Cheat
abroad, go about and boast of an extraordinary Talent, and endeavour
under-hand to establish the Belief of it; witness the late *French* Prophets.
But there are some Cheats who have no need of Emissaries; the Credulity
of the Publick is a sufficient Preparation for their acting the Imposture. . .

At this point the author announces that he will "proceed to shew the full
Discovery of the Cheat of this Wand," as it is "well worth Observation":

. . .The Court of *France* hearing of the great Miracles performed by Virtue
of the said Wand in several Provinces ordered *James Aymar* to be sent for
to *Paris,* to make some of his Experiments before the Prince of *Conde,*
whose extraordinary Abilities proved fatal to the Impostor and his

Followers, and soon pull'd down the Trophies set up by the Partisans of *James Aymar.* This poor *Ignoramus* was so wretchedly baffled in the Tryal he made of shewing his Art in the Palace of *Conde,* that his Reputation became a Bankrupt for ever. The Publick was made acquainted with all the Transactions, and it was in vain to plead Uncertainties in the Case; since it was by order of that Great Prince that the World was informed of the Cheat. Nevertheless all this would not do with some People, but they were for assigning some Reason for the Miscarriages of the Wand; among these was M. *Vallemont,* who has lately publish'd, *A Treatise concerning the Secret Philosophy of the Diviner's Wand.*[18] That Author goes about to explain, how the Peasant of *Dauphine* might be mistaken in the Tryal of his Skill before the Prince, though he had really the Power and Gifts of which he boasted. This sort of Philosophers, as well as the Unfolders of Prophecies, (for both of them are of the same Stamp) are a kind of Enthusiasts, who will never own themselves to have been in the wrong; and who, though they are convinc'd of the Falsity of the things they have advanc'd, treat with a haughty Air those Men of sound Judgment who will not espouse their whimsical Notions.

And so to the climax of the case:

But notwithstanding what this and other Authors wrote to support the Credit of the Wand, and keep the Delusion on foot; *James Aymar* himself at last confessed to the Prince of *Conde,*[19] that he knew nothing of all that had been attributed to him, and that what he had hitherto done was to gain the Pence. Whereupon the Prince ordered him to retire as soon as possible to his own Village, because being no Longer under his Protection, the People whom he had accus'd would stop him. I had forgot to mention one thing which was more especially remarkable in this Story: The Magistrates of the City of *Lyons* had such a mighty Veneration for the Miracles done by the Wand, that they caused an innocent Man to be put to a cruel Death upon the bare Impeachment of this Impostor; and many other Acts of Injustice of the like Nature were committed in several other Provinces of the Kingdom.[20]

Aymar stands here as a type of the false conjuror, deluding people by the dexterous motion of his wand. There are hints of the political theme drawn out by Swift: "our Petty-Conjurers," a phrase used by Povey, is highly relevant to Swift's view of statecraft. The appeal of a flashy magician to the get-rich-quick mentality is equally well conveyed. Finally, Aymar is shown predicting the date of the peace, a matter of widespread concern in 1710. We need to keep in mind another fact: the term "wand" has lost currency except in relation to a conjuror's spells, but in this period it was regularly used in the sense of a staff of office, such as the lord treasurer's white rod.

Swift, of course, had a marked addiction to mock astrology; apart from the Partridge papers involving "Isaac Bickerstaff," a recent example can be found in his "Famous Prediction of Merlin, the British Wizard" (1709). The Aymar papers were a real gift to him. Out of the hints supplied by Povey, he builds up an allegory of politics as a rascally trade carried on by "dexterous" showground illusionists. No doubt he recalled the scare over French prophets in 1707; but the direct occasion for this attack on the impostures of statesmen was provided by both articles in *The Visions of Sir Heister Ryley*. A number of verbal parallels reinforce the effect, not to mention the title, drawn by Swift from the heading to Povey's second paper. *The Visions* gave Swift a starting point and a model: the notorious Aymar served as the type of a charlatan and cheat. First described as a Wand" (1), a term Povey uses no less than twenty-two times, the staff of office is reduced in "Sid Hamet" to the level of a conjuror's prop. Equally, the "trial" that Aymar underwent in Condé's palace may suggest an event which did most to bring down Godolphin, that is the arraignment of Sacheverell by the peers in Westminster Hall. Certainly his banishment by the prince parallels Godolphin's dismissal: the clear implication is that the minister will be exposed when the enquiries into the financial management of the war are concluded. Meanwhile he deserves to be cudgelled like a common thief. G.M. Trevelyan once regretted the fact that the queen "chose to dismiss the Treasurer as a squire would discharge a cheating bailiff."[21] That is exactly how Tory polemicists attempted to portray the nature of the transaction.

By this means Swift implicitly aligns Godolphin with notorious rogues of the age. Even the title, with its punning reference to "virtue," carries an underlying reference to the claims of quacks and astrologers – an association the Scriblerian group liked to make in political satires. The magical potency of the white staff, in conjuring up the perquisites of wealth and power, shows up the lack of true virtue – moral value – in its owner. According to manuals of black magic, the conjuror should take a rod of hazel and recite a prayer of consecration, invoking the powers of darkness to endow the wand with the "virtue of the rods of Jacob, of Moses and of the mighty Joshua.'[22] Nowadays conjurors are people who perform in theatres or at children's parties: Swift recalls a time, only a very few generations back, when people genuinely believed that the black arts (or even, misused, white magic) could be enlisted to assist in Satan's campaign. For Swift, we might say, politics was itself a sort of black art. It is no news that the Scriblerian group interested themselves in folklore, superstitions and popular beliefs (see also Chapter 12). What emerges here is Swift's ability to harness such things to develop his view of Godolphin as a charlatan on the level of James Aymar.

All this is an aspect of the satire Ehrenpreis and all other commentators have almost entirely missed.[23] The suggestion that the poet was conducting a symbolic castration of a father must fall on two counts: first, Swift leaves out the bawdy element so prominent in Sir Heister's papers, and second, Sid Hamet is envisaged as all too potent in the use of his weapon. If we read the poem as outlined here, a riddling and obscure thrust of rhetoric becomes intelligible, once the contemporary model has been identified. "Do you like *Sid Hamet's Rod?* Do you understand it all?", Swift wrote to Stella a few weeks later (*Journal to Stella,* 1: 110). It is unlikely that she did, in the fullest sense, unless by some chance the "visions" of Sir Heister Ryley had filtered through to Dublin. She would, however, have known just what to make of the rod of Moses and Aaron.

Notes

[1] The most fully annotated text of the poem appears in Frank H. Ellis, ed., *Poems on Affairs of State,* 7 vols (New Haven: Yale University Press, 1963-75), 7: 473-91.

[2] *The Letters and Diplomatic Instructions of Queen Anne,* ed. Beatrice Curtis Brown (London: Cassell, 1935), p. 305. The next day Anne informed the Duke of Marlborough that Godolphin's behaviour had made it impossible for her to "let him keep the white staff any longer; and therefore I orderd him this morning to break it."

[3] Irvin Ehrenpreis. *Swift: The Man, the Works and the Age,* 3 vols (London: Methuen, 1962-83), 2: 388. A useful discussion is that of A.B. England, "The Subversion of Logic in some Poems of Swift," *Studies in English Literature 1500-1900,* 15 (1975): 413-16.

[4] He would sneer at Godolphin's knowledge of horse-racing in *Examiner* no. 27, on 1 February 1711: see *Swift vs. Mainwaring: The Examiner and the Medley,* ed. Frank H. Ellis (Oxford: Clarendon Press, 1985), p. 217. Reporting to William King on the lord treasurer's dismissal, he writes, "A letter was sent to him by the Groom of the Queen's Stables, to desire he would break his Staff" (Swift *Corr,* 1: 291).

[5] Ehrenpreis, *Swift,* 2: 588.

[6] *A Collection of Poems, for and against Dr. Sacheverell* (London, 1710), p. 32.

[7] For the most up-to-date account of Povey (1651?-1743), inventor and speculator, see the entry by Mark G. Spencer in *The Oxford Dictionary of National Biography.* The material in F.B. Relton, *An Account of the Fire Insurance Companies. . .also of Charles Povey* (London: Swan Sonnenstein, 1893), may be supplemented by P.G.M. Dickson, *The Sun Insurance Office 1710-1960* (London: Oxford University Press, 1960), pp. 17-31. For Povey's relevance to *Gulliver's Travels,* see my essay, "Gulliver and the Engineers," in *Eighteenth-Century Encounters* (Brighton: Harvester, 1985, pp. 11-28 (20-2).

[8] Citations from the reprint in volume form (1711), pp. 13-15, 33-6. On the prophets, see Hillel Schwartz, *The French Prophets: The History of a Millenarian Group in Eighteenth-Century England* (Berkeley: University of California Press, 1980).

[9] The circumstances underlying this passage are set out by James Sutherland, "John Lacey and the Modern Prophets," in *Background for Queen Anne* (London: Methuen, 1939), pp. 36-74: see also Schwartz, pp. 72-112. The episode concerns the arrival of so-called French prophets in England, chiefly between 1706 and 1708 (see Sutherland, p. 59, for the nature of the apocalypse foretold). A noisy campaign was waged in newspapers and pamphlets over the merits of this new sect: the most distinguished contributor was perhaps Dr Edmund Calamy. Swift was in England for long periods during the controversy and must have been aware of the claims and counterclaims. His Partridge papers may owe something to this vociferous exchange. Defoe alludes to the episode in *The Review*.

[10] A priest of Apollo, in Greek mythology, who was made invisible by the golden arrow on which he rode through the air and who gave oracles.

[11] Povey supplies a remarkably free paraphrase of the final ode in the last book of Horace's *Odes* (4: 15). I have not traced the source, which would seem to resemble a metrical psalter in its technique.

[12] Venaissin Comté was at this date still ceded, along with Avignon, to the Pope. It surrounded the small principality of Orange on the east bank of the Rhone. Villeneuve-les-Avignon lies on the opposite bank.

[13] Franciscans.

[14] Cf. Swift, "Sid Hamet's Rod," lines 11-12: "Would hiss and sting, and roll, and twist, / By the mere virtue of his fist."

[15] Cf. "Sid Hamet's Rod," lines 21-34, esp. 27-8: "As ready was the wand of Sid / To bend where golden mines were hid."

[16] Cf. "Sid Hamet's Rod," line 49: "Sid's brethren of the conjuring tribe."

[17] Cf. "Sid Hamet's Rod," lines 31-4: "And by a gentle bow divined / How well a cully's purse was lined: / To a forlorn and broken rake, / Stood without motion, like a snake."

[18] Pierre Le Lorrain de Vallemont (1649-1721) attached to later editions of his *La Physique Occulte* (1693) an appendix entitled "Traité de la Baguette divinataire." An English translation of another work by this physician and savant, under the title of *Curiosities of Nature and Art,* had appeared in 1707. This may have drawn renewed attention to the divining rod.

[19] Henri-Jules de Bourbon, Prince de Condé (1645-1709), son of "le grand Condé."

[20] The episode in Lyons had taken place as far back as 1692. Aymar's later history is unknown.

[21] "Anne treated Godolphin even at worse at parting than Victoria treated Gladstone. She refused to see him at all; she sent him no message of kindness or gratitude, but merely an order to break the White Staff of his office. On such an occasion it would have been well if the sovereign. . .had remembered old and long service, and in this case still older private friendship" (G.M. Trevelyan, *England under Queen Anne: The Peace and the Protestant Succession* (London: Collins, 1963), p. 89).

[22] A.E. Waite, *The Book of Ceremonial Magic* (London: Ryder, 1911), p. 163. For the background concerning magical spells and conjuration, see Keith Thomas, *Religion and the Decline of Magic* (Harmondsworth: Penguin 1978), esp. pp. 252-300.

[23] Another of the poem's most salient images, that of the divining rod, would have carried many relevant associations to contemporary readers. In August 1722 the enterprising Edmund Curll advertised a forthcoming book entitled *Occult Philosophy: or an Historical Treatise of the Diving Rod*. Unfortunately this work, which must have been a translation of de Vallemont, never emerged, but that was probably not owing to the lack of a market. For the use of diving rods to locate treasure, see Thomas, *Religion*, p. 362.

CHAPTER TWO

FAMILY PLOTS IN *THE RAPE OF THE LOCK*

Family and kinship hover everywhere behind the text of *The Rape of the Lock*. Just as the Compsons, the Snopeses and the Sutpens in Faulkner's Yoknapatawpha carry with them a burden of generations gone before, so the characters in the *Rape* trail clouds of dynastic history. Of course, the work moves far beyond any literal biography of the "real life" characters; but at its inner core the *Rape* dramatizes relationships forged within the recusant community in early modern England. Many documents, scattered in archives around England, illustrate the strategies which older Catholic houses adopted to survive in a cold political and economic climate.[1]

As most people know, Alexander Pope claimed that he received a commission for his poem in order to defuse a family quarrel, occasioned by an assault on Arabella Fermor by Robert, seventh Baron Petre. Later the author reported:

> The stealing of Miss Belle Fermor's hair, was taken too seriously, and caused an estrangement between the two families, though they had lived so long in great friendship before. A common acquaintance and well-wisher to both, desired me to write a poem to make a jest of it, and laugh them together again. It was with this view that I wrote my *Rape of the Lock*, which was well received and had its effect in the two families.
>
> (*Anecdotes* 1: 44-5)

The motive looks a little suspect, and the consequences might prove less benign than the account pretends. Pope's acquaintance was John Caryll, a member of an old Sussex family, and one of his longest-lasting friends.

From the very start the *Rape* bore a dedication to Caryll in its opening verses. The earliest two canto version (1712) disguised him as "C--", and even when the poem was expanded in 1714, the name was not spelt out in full, though Pope told his friend he was "strangely tempted to have set your name at length, as well as I have my own [for the first time]; but I remembered your desire you formerly express'd to the contrary" (Pope *Corr*, 1: 210). This did not happen until after the death of both Pope and Caryll, when the line would become "This Verse to *Caryll*, Muse! is due."

Despite this, all readers close to events, and many outside the immediate family circle, would have found little trouble in decoding so transparent a cipher. It looks as if Caryll would have preferred Pope to keep his poem out of general circulation, and one can well understand why. In May 1712, just as the first version appeared, he wrote anxiously to the poet:

> But where hangs the Lock now? (tho' I know that rather than draw any just reflection upon your self, of the least shadow of ill-nature, you would freely have suprest one of the best of Poems.) I hear no more of it -- will it come out in Lintot's Miscellany or not? I wrote to Lord Petre upon the subject of the Lock, some time since, but have as yet had no answer.
>
> (Pope *Corr*, 1: 142)

Some one less hell-bent on scoring a literary triumph might have picked up the note of concern in these words, and the half-hidden desire to have the *Rape* kept under wraps. But Pope had already committed himself.

Many factors explain Caryll's reluctance to appear too conspicuously, but some uneasiness proceeded simply from his own relation to the Petres: his grandfather had married the young Baron's great-aunt. Moreover, until Lord Petre came of age in 1710, three years after succeeding to the title as seventh Baron, Caryll acted as his guardian. This connection has been long established, as has the fact that the model for the blustering "Sir Plume" in the poem, Sir George Browne, had family links with both Arabella and Caryll.[2] However, the intricacies of relationships within the close-knit Catholic community went very much further, since these clans thinly dispersed among the gentry and aristocracy had intermarried with great regularly ever since the Reformation. The principal fact we have missed is that the Fermors and the Petres had formed a marital tie not far in the past - just two generations back on one side, three on the other. Consequently, the long existing "great friendship" had its basis in a shared family history.

I

It turns out that Arabella and the real-life Baron were related quite closely by marriage. A step or two nearer, and they would have fallen into the forbidden degrees prescribed by their church. In 1628 Lucy Fermor (*c*.1607-79), sister of Arabella's great-grandfather, had wed William Petre (1602-77), brother of the third Baron, and great-uncle of the current peer.[3] To exemplify the involutions caught up in the match, this William was also the brother of Catherine Petre, John Caryll's grandmother. While one marriage does not produce a coherent family network, the situation possessed features that made for a high level of relatedness. Whereas the

Petres had been ennobled by James I, the Fermors of Tusmore never advanced beyond a knighthood. Arabella was of course a commoner, along with the rest of her immediate line. However, both sides of the marriage belonged to the recusant community of the Thames Valley, which had preserved its distinctive identity through many travails. As John Bossy has shown, this sizeable group supplied a convenient corridor for papal missions into the Midlands.[4] A prominent example was afforded by the Stonors, whose living representatives were well known to Pope: it was they who had once given the martyr Edmund Campion and his colleague Robert Parsons refuge at their house, which survives in a beautiful wooded setting among the Chiltern hills. Inevitably, the Stonor genealogy meshes into that of the Brownes, the Blounts and others close to events satirically replayed in *The Rape of the Lock*. As a result, when Lucy married William, the transaction served to cement a number of existing ties, and to enhance the unity of a beleaguered minority.

We can trace without difficulty the Fermor line, whose genealogy may be comically transmogrified in the last canto of the *Rape*. There Pope describes a "deadly Bodkin" the heroine draws with reference to its use by her "great great Grandsire," his widow, "her infant Grandame" and her mother. Plotting these on Arabella's line of descent, the first can be identified as Sir Richard Fermor, who died in 1643. His wife, Cornelia Cornwallis, later in life became deranged, and in 1646 Lucy petitioned the House of Lords concerning "Dame Cornelia Farmer, widow," who had been "distempered with lunacy." She was placed in the custody of Henry Withypole. The trouble went back much earlier: in 1617 Cornelia had been accused of shooting a gentleman in the right side of his body.[5] Richard and Cornelia were the parents of William Petre's bride in 1628. As noted, the groom was the son of the second Baron Petre, and brother of the third, from whom the current lord descended. William Petre died in 1677, aged seventy-four, while Lucy survived for two more years. Her husband had been educated at Oxford and the Inner Temple, and published at St Omer a translation of the *Flos Sanctorum* of the Jesuit Pedro de Ribadeneira (1669). A short coach-ride from Ingatestone, the Petres' family home in Essex, lay Stanford Rivers, where the couple had their residence, bestowed on them in the marriage settlement. However, William clung to his royalist allegiance even when parliament granted the estate to the Earl of Essex in 1645. Somehow he hung on to the house as well as the manorial rights through the civil war and its aftermath. Among five children born to the couple, the eldest was William (1630-88), whose offspring later occupied Bellhouse, part of the Stanford Rivers property. Two generations on, another William Petre married a sister of the third Earl of Derwentwater, the Jacobite leader beheaded on Tower Hill in 1716.

Originally from a mercantile background in Wales, the Fermors had been established at Somerton in Oxfordshire since the mid 1500s. At the start of the next century they acquired the nearby estate of Tusmore, located in the gentle folds of Flora Thompson country between Bicester and Brackley. Since his eldest son John had already died, Sir Richard was succeeded by Lucy's second brother Henry. The line then passed down through Henry (d. 1673), his son Richard (d. 1684) and his grandson Henry, who became Arabella's father. Her mother was Helen or Eleanor Browne, descended from the old Catholic gentry. A first cousin of Sir George Browne, she had among her immediate ancestors the families of Pope's Berkshire friends and neighbours, Blounts of Mapledurham and Englefields of Whiteknights, near Reading.

When Henry Fermor died in 1703, he bequeathed his household property in St James's, London to his wife, whereas the property at Tusmore went to his eldest son James. There is no reference to Arabella, but the executors were given discretion to apply funds towards the portions of Henry's sister Frances or his daughters.[5] Frances died unmarried in 1720, leaving money to her brother Richard, her four married sisters and her goddaughter Henrietta, Arabella's cousin. Again the prime beneficiary was James, but he survived only two more years. His will shows some of the financial difficulties which the family were now experiencing. The ultimate legatee is his eldest son, another Henry, while other family members are mentioned - but not Arabella.[6]

After this the Fermors held Tusmore for almost a century, but in the 1760s they put up a new mansion to a design by Robert Mylne and the last vestiges of the old house which Arabella knew perished by fire in 1837. Any animosity the family once held against the author of *The Rape of the Lock* had now dissipated, for in the park they erected a temple of peace dedicated to Pope.In 1720 James Fermor was forced to sell the estate of Halton, near Wendover, which the family had acquired on the marriage of his ancestor Thomas in 1571. (His will mentions money borrowed at interest from Captain Dayroll, a sign of the times.) It was bought for a considerable sum, perhaps approaching £20,000, in trust for Francis Dashwood, a boy of twelve who would later achieve fame as a politician and alleged founder of the Hell Fire Club at Medmenham Abbey. A protestant, Dashwood was able to halve the taxes which the Fermors had been paying on the estate. Documents survive naming James's mother, uncle, brother and sister Henrietta to guarantee the transfer of the manor and advowson, but as a married woman Arabella was by now off the family radar and she nowhere figures in the deeds. Out of the proceeds from selling Halton, the Fermors planned to reduce debts and supply the needs of their women members not otherwise provided for. One of the executors was Robert Dormer of Rousham, not very far from Tusmore, a close friend of his fellow gardener Alexander Pope.[7]

As the eldest among the Fermor girls, Arabella had only one surviving sister outside the conventual life, namely Henrietta, the sixth of them. A few years earlier, the second daughter Winifred entered the Benedictine nunnery at Dunkirk while the third, Mary, had now begun the process of joining her. Both the Carylls and the Petres served as major figures in the foundation of this convent, and the coats of arms of each family appeared in the stained glass windows overlooking its cloister. As first lady abbess, the founders appointed in 1663 none other than Mary Caryll, the daughter of Catherine Petre and so John's aunt: this post she held right up to her death in August 1712. John kept in regular correspondence with her throughout this period, and Abbess Mary could hardly have been unaware of the scandal which broke around her family in the last months of her life. Other members of the community at this date included one of John's nieces, along with his daughter, also Mary, who had taken the name Romana when she made her vows in 1708. Meanwhile Mary Frances Fermor herself was professed at Dunkirk in April 1713, and would live to succeed as abbess in her turn. As a novice just about to consecrate herself to God, she surely felt distraught if she heard of the publicity surrounding her sister. Pope had turned the faint whispers of a family secret into an insistent murmur, audible far beyond the secluded halls of English recusants.[8]

Arabella's unremarkable later history takes little time to recount. On the rebound from Lord Petre, maybe, she married Francis Perkins of Ufton within a few months of the appearance of the augmented *Rape*. As Pope told Martha Blount late in 1714, with his tongue in his cheek, "My Acquaintance runs so much in an Anti-Catholic Channel, that it was but tother day I heard of Mrs Fermor's being Actually, directly, and consummatively, married" (Pope *Corr*, 1: 269). We know from a settlement made after the marriage in June 1715, surviving in the Ufton manuscripts, that Arabella's jointure amounted to £4,500.[9] Perkins belonged to another Catholic family in the adjoining county of Berkshire: his mother was a daughter of Augustine Belson of Brill, one of the most conspicuous recusants in the area. The Perkins clan had been under scrutiny for their heterodox beliefs since the time of the Elizabethan spymaster Sir Francis Walsingham. Together the couple had six children. When Francis died in 1736, the bulk of the estate went in trust, but along with £52.10.0 for her immediate maintenance he did "bequeath unto my Loving Wife All her Wearing Apparell Gold watch and Jewels and her dressing Plate with the Furniture of her Closet and Chamber" - an appropriate legacy, perhaps, for one who had inspired the character of Belinda.[10] One of the trustees, Sir Henry Englefield, now owned the estate at Whiteknights: he was a first cousin of the Blount sisters, Martha and Teresa, and of course well known to Pope. Arabella died in 1738, and six years later her sister Henrietta, named in probate as a spinster of St George's, Hanover Square, followed her. Within a generation her sons managed to squander the family fortune: by 1780 large holdings of land in Berkshire and Wiltshire had gone, and only Ufton was left.

II

So much for the Fermor connection. On the side of the Petres, the narrative is simpler. After the death of the third Baron (brother of William Petre), the line continued through three of his sons. William, the fourth in line, was accused of high treason by Titus Oates and died in the Tower. The sixth Baron, Thomas, was Robert's father, and passed on the title at his death in 1707. His will recited an agreement from 1699, to which one party was Henry Browne, who later succeeded as fifth Viscount Montagu, while another was William Petre of Belhouse (a direct descendant of Lucy Fermor). However, the main purpose of the agreement and the will was to set up John Caryll together with Sir Edward Southcote as joint administrator and executor, as well as guardian of the heir Robert Petre and his sister. Sir Edward lived at Writtle, not far off: he was a brother of the Benedictine priest, Thomas Southcote, and father of the well-known gardener, Philip Southcote, pioneer of the *ferme ornée*. A sister had married John Stafford-Howard, an outlaw because of his service at the Jacobite court, and a member of the perennially suspect Howard family. Lord Petre also made provision for his wife and daughter, both named Mary.[11]

When Robert wrote his own will a few years later, some of this pattern repeated itself. After his spat with Arabella, and even before the first version of the *Rape* appeared, the new Baron had embarked on his pitifully brief marriage. The bride was Catherine Walmesley, an heiress just two months past her fifteenth birthday. Her father Bartholomew had been a colonel in the army of James II who had spent several years at the court of St Germains. He was accused of hosting a meeting to foment a rebellion at his home, Dunkenhalgh, near Accrington, which today has been converted into a hotel. At this Catholic stronghold in mid-Lancashire, lands were granted on behalf of James to sympathizers, and informers alleged that the group had built up a stock of arms. After her father's death in early 1702 Catherine passed with two sisters into the guardianship of a relative, Sir William Gerrard, who had himself been arrested along with Bartholomew in 1694 for plotting rebellion. Both men were acquitted when no witness appeared against them, but little doubt exists that Walmesley served as one of the underground agitators for the Stuart cause. Catherine became sole heiress with the death of her only brother Francis. This was the background of the girl who entered the Petre family just as Pope brought out his poem.

The baron's marriage settlement, dated 19 July 1712, survives in a huge roll at the Devon Record Office, along with many Petre documents.[12] Seven sheets of discoloured parchment unfurl like a worn-out hall-mat, with the final attachment signed and sealed by those involved - perhaps the first time that Catherine used her new family seal. The "indenture sexpartite" actually names fourteen individuals among the six parties deputed to act as trustees, executors and administrators. At the top of the tree stood the Duke of Leeds and the Duke of Beaufort, high church protestants with some links to the current ministry. In fact the octogenarian Leeds, better known from his time as Lord Treasurer under Charles II as the Earl of Danby, would die "of convulsions" just seven days after the indenture was signed. It was not a good omen for the marriage. Next in line come Lord Carteret, a leading politician from the 1720s to the1740s, and Lord Stawell. Most of the others named were Catholics, and some known Jacobites: a sprinkling of Lancashire gentry represent Catherine's side, as trustees of her father's will.[13] A John Caryll appears, but this is not Pope's friend (the baron's former guardian), rather his son and heir. The arrangements cover a wide array of properties stretching from Essex to Somerset and Devon. As with other legal documents, the phraseology textualizes with stuttering emphasis the social reach of the family – a statement heavily inflected here by its religious connections. In the circumspect way of these things, provision was made for Catherine on her husband's death, an eventuality which came to pass eight months later, and for any son. The widow was to receive an annuity of £2,000 and Lord Petre's posthumously born son would get £300 until he was sixteen, £700 after that.

By far the most striking feature of this elaborate document is the revelation that Catherine brought no less than £55,000 to the marriage: out of this £5,000 had already been paid and £50,000 was "paid or well and sufficiently secured." (By contrast, we recall, Arabella's portion amounted to £4,500; Mary Petre, the baron's sister, was to have only £2,000.) This immense sum, presumably including money from the Petres, was fit for a duchess: Sarah Churchill might have settled for less in a daughter-in-law. The entire document supplies fine print for the marriage articles, drawn up on the wedding day four months earlier. An inevitable poignancy hangs over its hopeful clauses, by which the family planned to cement a great union of Catholic lineage and Catholic money. At the end of *The Rape of the Lock*, Belinda disarms the Baron by throwing snuff in his face, "Just where the Breath of Life his Nostrils Drew," and he retreats in comic confusion: "Sudden, with starting Tears each Eye o'erflows, / And the high Dome re-ecchoes to his Nose." In his last words to the heroine, he proclaims, "Nor think, to die dejects my lofty Mind; / All that I dread, is leaving you behind!"(5: 81, 85-6, 99-100). These phrases had one meaning when the poem first came out in 1712; but Pope's decision to leave them there two years later appears insensitive. The real-life baron had gone, and all his manors, messuages, lands and tenements were now held in trust for a teenage widow and her fatherless infant.

III

By the time that the expanded version of the *Rape* went into print, Queen Anne and her ministry were both on their last legs. It was a time of feverish political threats and fears. A year later the first major Jacobite rising took place, and the family circle represented in Pope's story entered a period of deep anxiety. Caryll, who could be called a dynastic Jacobite, saw many of his relatives take up arms for the Pretender: among these, several were caught and suffered confiscation of their properties. Actually, his own estate at West Grinstead was sequestrated in 1715, and he moved to his other house at Ladyholt. Some of the family decamped to France. In terms of the dispersal of Catholic estates, it was the most malign episode since the Reformation. Four Walmesleys were out in the struggle: as Paul Monod has observed, this kind of turnout "testified to the fact that the '15 in Lancashire was a family affair."[14] With such a crisis widely felt to be imminent, the last thing the Catholic community wanted was to have its private ructions exposed to the general gaze. "I have made a star of. . .Mrs. Fermor," Pope once wrote, punning on the climactic scene at the end of the *Rape* (Pope *Corr*, 2: 293).. What his co-religionists most wanted at this juncture was to be left in decent obscurity. Instead, he had emblazoned the name of a friend and leader of the community, next to Belinda's, in the first four lines of the poem.

Within a year of his wedding the Baron died of smallpox, leaving his young wife pregnant with a son born posthumously less than three months later. This son, who became eighth baron on his birth, subsequently married the daughter of the ill-fated Earl of Derwentwater. Catherine's portion had originally been set in her father's will as £4,000, to be augmented if her sisters predeceased her, a sum less than Arabella brought with her; but now by the terms of the marriage settlement, stoked up by the Petres' lawyers, she had her annuity. In the event her elder brother and two sisters died without issue, and the great family estates in Lancashire and Yorkshire all came to her. Her settlement shows that Catherine could anticipate a secure future, even if the Petres suffered misfortune. Understandably she became something of a catch, and the rumour got abroad that she might be a suitable bride for the Old Pretender. According to the *Complete Peerage,* "she seems to have gone over to the Continent to be looked at. According to Father [Thomas] Southcott, she 'was so rich that it would be a fine thing'." But this prospect horrified the Earl of Mar, the Pretender's advisor, who called Southcott "a great romancer": James Edward decided that Lady Petre's rank was insufficient, and looked elsewhere.[15] A letter from the Pretender's mother, Mary of Modena, thanks Catherine for the offer of £1,000 for his use. During her widowhood Catherine wrote numerous letters to John Caryll, a sign of her complete integration into the extended family. When she eventually did remarry, she chose the scion of another old papist family in southern England, the future Lord Stourton – whose great-grandmother had been a Petre. In a legal document from 1734, the new husband is named as "Hon. Chas. Stourton Walmesley of Dunken Hall, esq." Money had talked again, but in time it all came back to the Petres.

The Baron only just had time to complete his will, signed on 20 and 21 March 1713, for he died on the very next day. As with most Petre wills, the document begins with a pious preamble, made more touching here by the testator's recognition of his bodily sickness. Generous provision is made to confirm and augment previous settlements for his mother and sister, with Catherine named as executrix. Unhappily some of these provisions were nullified when Mary followed her brother to the grave just three weeks later, aged about nineteen: in her own will she would leave her "dear sister Petre" just one thing – "my Gold Cross". Again the estate is left in the hands of trustees, namely Edward Southcott, Caryll and a third individual. Since the testator knows that his wife is "enseint or with child," he makes provision for the child, depending on its gender when born. The Baron appoints as residuary legatee William Petre of Bellhouse and his heirs: however, it is made clear that no one may "evict molest interrupt or disturb" his female relatives in the peaceable enjoyment of their entitlements, on pain of severe consequences. (The women were debarred by the strict settlement from inheriting directly.) Robert refers to his "dear and loving wife," and refers to her poignantly as one "for whom I cannot doe too much." The will names Catherine as executrix, but as she was still only sixteen administration was granted to Caryll and Southcott, allowing them to oversee the terms of the will *durante minori* (sic) *aetatis dictae Executricis.*[16]

Once more we see the central role Caryll played in family affairs. Whatever he felt about the way private matters had been aired in the first version of the *Rape*, he surely harboured even more mixed emotions when the new poem appeared with further damaging content, and his inadequately concealed name still in place at its head. His former ward was now dead, along with the remaining blood relative (Mary), and his new charge was a young widow with a fatherless baby. No one, to my knowledge, has commented on the propriety of Pope's choice in reissuing the poem, with fresh barbs, given all these circumstances. The Petres and even the Fermors may have had an opinion about that.

When the *Rape* came out, individuals close to the action would call to mind a long history of amicable relations between various branches of the extended family. Thus, in 1640 Mary Caryll married into another prominent Sussex line, the Gages: a settlement was made with the first Henry Fermor as one party, and Edmund Plowden as another - the Plowdens were intertwined with Petres, Blounts, Englefields, Perkinses, and Stonors among others. However, the immediate tie here derived from a marriage between Francis Plowden and Mary Fermor two generations earlier. A document from 1656 concerns an action for "recovery" of the manor of Halton estate, that is a legal fiction by which entailed property could be transferred between two parties. The principals were William Petre esquire (Lucy's husband) and Edmund Plowden, while the two vouchees were Henry and Richard Fermor, that is Lucy's brother and nephew.[17] Up and down the country, record offices preserve such tokens of Catholic solidarity. In settlements and bequests, a minority under threat of near-extinction sought to hold on to what it had, and to protect its valued resources from any onslaughts from outside.

Apart from their importance in revealing the way landed estates were distributed, family wills cast a different sidelight on *The Rape of the Lock*, since they enshrine, too, the disposition of small household goods. Objects like those which make up so intimate a part of the texture of Pope's verse crop up regularly. Thus Caryll's uncle Edward Bedingfield (the intermediary Pope used with Lord Petre and Arabella) bequeathed to his nephew Henry Eyre his "fine picktooth case of Staned Ivory garnisht with gold," desiring him to keep it for mine and his dear Aunts Sake." This made a gift the beaux might have loved to receive, but better still was "my fine Cane with the gold head," left to another nephew. Sir Plume would surely covet this, skilled as he was in "the nice Conduct of a *clouded Cane.*" In two codicils signed in 1713 and 1714, the testator bestowed on his legatees many other desirable *objets d'art* and heirlooms, identifying their family associations in touching detail, especially those connected with his dead wife. He leaves a miniature which "at this present 26 Nov: 1713 hangs over my Wifes Picture in my Bedchamber." To his niece Southcott he gives "my little Chagreen case that I always carry about me with the Pictures in it of her Mother and of my Wife." Another bequest to a niece involves "my best Equipage for Tea that is to say my Square Table Six Cupps and Saucers that has feet to them and the sugar dish." Several pictures form part of the legacy, notably a gift to his only surviving daughter Mary of "the fine piece of her Mother done by Sr Godfry Kneller," which she is charged not to dispose of "till She enters into a Monastick Course of Life" (in fact Mary's wedding would ultimately draw her back into the family loops). A second picture of his wife "in a black frame done by Morlands imagining", that is presumably Sir Henry Morland's early copying machine. There is a landscape picture on a fan, and a number of looking glasses. A silver watch goes to Lady Kaye's "waiting woman"- in Pope's poem, the maid Betty must have cast envious eyes on a similar possession of her own mistress: "The press'd Watch return'd a silver Sound." Most telling is the bequest, "Whereas ever since the death of my charming dear Wife I have constantly worne her wedding ring I give and bequeath to my dear Nephew Mr Henry Eyre hoping it may fasten wedding thoughts into him."[18]

Exactly the same features appear in the will of Lady Bedingfield, for which her son Edward served as executor. Property, both large and small, is handed on to her children and grandchildren, but also to the lines of Eyre and Caryll, into which her daughters had married. Among those remembered is a child of John Caryll: "To my Goddaughter Mrs Catherine Caryll a gold Cross." Four generations of the living receive bequests, but the document looks back to the testator's "dear and honoured Husband," her father Edward Paston, and to her grandfather Sir John Sydenham. Friends are affectionately remembered, as are a large group of servants.[19] So it is with the will of Lady Bedingfield's great-granddaughter Mary Paston Southcott. She states that "the Diamonds and other Jewells which I had from the Southcott family which I always looked upon as given to me and to be my Property, I return to the Southcott family."[20] We remember the diamond that Belinda wore in her ear, which would most likely be an heirloom (3: 138). Such items constituted more than personal possessions:

the legatees held them on trust for the wider clan. Equally, the will of Mary's father, proved in 1713, recites a litany of damasks and linen, diapers and holland, as well as the usual snuff-boxes, plate and jewellery, all carefully passed down to appropriate legatees.[21]

What we need understand is that family jewels and religious objects, even holy relics, were closely interfused in Arabella's world. This becomes clear from the example of a Cumbrian gentleman named Sir Henry Fletcher, who went across to Douai to become a priest or monk. In 1712 Fletcher wrote to his lawyer and executor, who happened to be Henry Eyre:

> I also desire that my Little Red Box that has in it my prayer book with the gold cover, my gold Beads, a gold medal, 2 gold crosses, one having a diamond crown and the other a gold crown, gold Holy Water bottle, silver relick case, silver repeating watch, pair of Beads of Blood Stones, with a silver cross with silver medals: a silver cross with a silver crown: my gold cross with a diamond crown has a gold chain to it, all which are in the custody of Mr. Hickins, the goldsmith, and that I desire may be sent to the English Recollets [order of Recollects] at Douay, in Flanders.[22]

As it turned out, the Commissioners for Forfeited Estates had the property seized and intercepted bequests of church and domestic plate that Fletcher intended to make – only the Bishop of Arras got his gold cross. In this passage we come on the sacred and profane in the most intimate conjunction. It is hard to avoid thinking of Belinda's "press'd watch" that "return'd a silver Sound" (1: 18), to take just one instance. When these items were passed on from one generation to another, we may regard them as no more than eighteenth-century bling. Yet some of them might also be objects of piety, used to summon up religious meditation.

Documents like these provide a powerful case against our current understanding of *The Rape of the Lock*. Today almost all critics read the poem in terms of conspicuous consumption among the ruling class. As Pope describes the contents of the boudoir with teasing detail, Belinda stands out as a material girl who fetishizes the rampant commodity culture of her age. The wills reveal that most things with which she surrounds herself would have come down to her as treasured symbols of family identity, and they would have been replete with personal memories. The "sparkling cross" which she wore on her bosom is now treated as an icon of exploitative capitalism round the world. But from a semiological standpoint, the cross bequeathed to the Baron's sister, like the one that Catherine Caryll inherited, had another significance within the recusant community. As with the other "small Remembrances" Lady Bedingfield left to her family, friends and servants, it kept alive an ancestral heritage. The main duty of an heiress was not to flaunt such a bauble, but to preserve it tenderly along with the pious associations it bore. If Arabella really behaved as (the critics allege) Belinda does, then she was acting in flagrant contradiction to the norms of her caste.

IV

Lord Petre made no answer, as we saw, when Caryll wrote to him about the *Rape*. Overall we have little firm evidence about the response of the parties involved to the hidden intricacies of the poem. Pope's later comment, quoted at the start, continues: "Nobody but Sir George Browne was angry, and he was so a good deal and for a long time. He could not bear that Sir Plume should talk *nothing* but nonsense" (*Anecdotes* 1: 45). But something the poet wrote to John Caryll, after the first version came out, belies the opening of this statement. Pope had already revealed to Caryll that he had got Edward Bedingfield to send copies to the Baron and Arabella. As we have just seen, Bedingfield was his friend's maternal uncle. The new letter states, "Sir Plume blusters, I hear; nay, the celebrated lady herself is offended, and, which is stranger, not at herself, but me" (Pope *Corr*, 1: 151).

In truth Arabella had good reason to suspect that Pope acted from mixed motives. His later claim that he originally published because "Copies of the poem got about, and it was like to be printed" (*Anecdotes* 1: 44) echoes an implausible justification put out by every journeyman author. When he revised the poem, he felt it necessary to compose a dedication "To Mrs. Arabella Fermor," which he asserted "the young lady approves" (Pope *Corr,* 1: 207). But the new material reveals more than it conceals, even as it pretends to clear Arabella's name: "As to the following Canto's, all the Passages of them are as Fabulous, as the Vision at the Beginning, or the Transformation at the End; (except the Loss of your Hair, which I always name with Reverence.) The Human Persons are as Fictitious as the Airy ones; and the Character of *Belinda*, as it is now manag'd, resembles You in nothing but in Beauty" (*TE* 2: 143). That dispelled all doubts for anyone still needing to find out whether the heroine represented a real person. In this light we can scarcely put much faith in Pope's claim to Caryll that he had also written "a preface which salved the lady's honour, without affixing her name," that had been "by herself superseded in favour of the dedication" (Pope *Corr*, 1: 207). Of course, the *Rape* did not start the gossip, but it had done nothing at all to stop rumours and innuendos.

Many suppose that Arabella lacked intelligence, but perhaps she was smart enough to make no more waves. Who could wonder if the families felt aggrieved? They had granted access and friendship to one who did not belong to the world of the gentry, and he had taken advantage of the situation to write a poem of high comic bravura, spreading awareness of the story beyond their limited circle. Tales about Arabella unquestionably circulated in her own milieu, as Valerie Rumbold's study of women in Pope's world demonstrates. Henry Moore, whose family seat lay at Fawley on the Lambourn Downs, wrote to Teresa Blount of "Mrs Belinda, whose charms & Gallants desert her so fast that I wonder despair & the spleen have not quite eaten her up." Coming from a major line of local Catholics, Moore knew the participants in the action, and even before the "rape" took place he had shrewdly noted that "the young L^d P that is just entring Cupids Lists" might be susceptible to the feminine charms of the Blount sisters. As for Teresa, she went on speculating about the fortunes of Belle Fermor even when the marriage with Perkins was announced. She hinted that the suitor preferred to visit his intended in the evening because "women and linen look best by candlelight," a proverb Swift had used in *Polite Conversation*. "The writtings [marriage contract] are certainly in hand," Teresa told a relative, "for ye grave face of a Councellor ye Busse on [busy one] of a Trustee and ye gay on of a Bride ever meets one att her hous." The next line is even more suggestive: "Mrs Harret Brown. . .would not believe the Wedding when I saw her; I beg leave to tell her she dose not know my Cosen Bell soe well as I doe."[23] This was probably Henrietta Browne, youngest daughter of the fifth Baron Montagu. If the Blount and Browne clans were talking in this way, what mercy could Arabella expect from her community at large?

As a matter of fact Sir George Browne had more than personal affronts than most to trouble him, for his folks were scattered all over the poem. The Twickenham editor, Geoffrey Tillotson, supplied a useful appendix of "persons concerned" in the *Rape*. However, his family tree linking the Brownes and the Fermors (as well as the Blounts and the Englefields) omits yet one more connection. This was with the Petres: for the seventh Baron, the one immortalized by Pope, had for his grandmother Mary Browne, a daughter of the second Viscount Montagu, and thus first cousin of Sir Plume's father. By this means the Brownes forged another link in the chain uniting Lord Petre and Arabella. Their branch of their family had settled at Great Shefford in the Lambourn valley, where they had sheltered priests in their time.

The open mockery to which the poem subjects Sir Plume raised more potential embarrassments. Just a year after the expanded *Rape* appeared,

1714, the Brownes sold their manor at Great Shefford for £16,000 to Sir William Trumbull of Easthampstead Park, a protestant who was Pope's most important patron throughout his early years.[24] Just at the time Pope was preparing the revised poem, he wrote a letter to Trumbull which shows a most surprisingly detailed knowledge of the Brown family finances.[25] A connection existed even with the lord of the manor of Binfield, John Dancastle, whose ancestor had married into the Browne line almost a century earlier. Dancastle, a Catholic who sold the manor of Easthampstead to Trumbull around 1698, was one of Pope's most trusted friends in the locality, and the young poet spent long periods at his home, where a priest was installed. Moreover, John's brother Thomas helped to transcribe the manuscript of Pope's translation of the *Iliad*, his next major work after the *Rape*. The Dancastles had few social pretensions, but for that reason they may have valued their links with a clan which their friend was now exposing to humiliating and derisive treatment.

Pope makes Sir Plume into a meddling coxcomb, one of Belinda's beaux conveniently on hand to do her service. Along with Browne relatives Arabella had gone as a girl to study at the English convent in Paris, where the elderly sister Winifred Browne had served for almost fifty years (she would also have encountered two nuns who were Petres and three who were Perkins, as well as the mother superior). Arabella stayed at the convent until 1704, when she was about fifteen, at which time her grandmother Lady Browne brought her back to England. However, no personal tie has ever been found between Arabella and Sir George beyond their family connection, and that feels a comparatively distant affair to us. Things look differently when we learn that Browne's will in 1715 named James Fermor, Arabella's older brother, first among his executors. (In the event James would predecease the baronet by several years.) This suggests a much greater intimacy existed than we ever realised. If the head of the Fermor line could be entrusted with the important duty of acting as guardian to the three Browne sons, who were all minors, it does not seem out of place for the real Sir George to defend the honour of James's sister.

By set policy, the poem reduces serious family obligations to a matter of foppish ritual. Browne's will shows that his holdings in stocks and bonds of the South Sea Company, the East India Company and the Bank, as well as his lottery tickets and mortgages, would go to fund generous provision for the boys, unless any of them took to the religious life and had his legacy docked.[26] As it turned out, Sir George was listed in 1718 among the papists whose estates were liable to increased taxation, according to an act passed in the first year of George I. His inheritance would lose some of its value, as happened with most of the families connected to the poem.

As a witness to this testament we find Nathaniel Pigott of the Inner Temple, a non-juror and the most prominent lawyer within the Catholic community. He acted for many of the great Catholic families of the nation and, just months after the signing of the will, mounted what little defence was permitted to the doomed Lord Derwentwater. In this task he was joined by Henry Eyre of Gray's Inn, man of business to John Caryll, but also his first cousin - as we saw, Mary and Frances Bedingfield were the mothers of Eyre and Caryll respectively. Many family wills, such as that of Edward Paston, named Eyre as executor: he also witnessed the will of Thomas Lord Petre, the baron's father. These devout people needed priests to minister to them, but also lawyers to guard them in worldly matters. Pigott happened to be the greatest authority on conveyancing in this era and wrote a treatise on common recoveries, published after his death. In 1698 three manors had been leased to John Caryll, Edward Bedingfield and Pigott. Subsequently Pigott's daughter married Caryll's second son, and as a resident of Whitton the barrister would become a good friend of his neighbour Pope, who wrote his epitaph. It was Piggot's son, a Benedictine father, who administered the last rites to Pope in 1744. Pervasively, the cast of the *Rape* made up an extended clan in which its author moved for the rest of his life.

Beyond all this, some people thought that the character of Thalestris represented George Browne's wife or sister. She utters one of the most famous speeches in the poem, as she reproves Belinda for her conduct:

Gods! Shall the Ravisher display your Hair,
While the Fops envy, and the Ladies stare!
Honour forbid! At whose unrival'd Shrine
Ease, Pleasure, Virtue, All, our Sex resign.
Methinks already I your Tears survey,
Already hear the horrid things they say,
Already see you a degraded Toast,
And all your Honour in a Whisper lost!
How shall I, then, your helpless Fame defend?
'Twill then be Infamy to seem your Friend!

(4: 103-12)

"Friend" in contemporary usage, we recall, often meant "relative." Thalestris places stress, too, on honour, a collective rather than an individual concept in the past. The whispers had certainly gone round the community in which Arabella and the Baron moved. "More men's reputations, I believe, are whispered away, than any other ways destroyed," Pope had written to

Caryll in late 1712, soon after the first version of the *Rape* appeared (Pope *Corr*, 1: 169). That was when some unidentified rumour had begun to circulate about the poet himself. What was sauce for the goose may have ended up as sauce for the gander – to draw on a proverb Swift had used in writing to Stella just a year before (*Journal to Stella*, 1: 174).

Recent scholars, among them Bridget Hill, Olwen Hufton and Amanda Vickery, have illuminated the condition of spinsterhood in the gentry. [27] Women like Frances Fermor experienced the pressures at first hand, and while there are no grounds identifying her with Thalestris she may have viewed Arabella in much the same way that the virago felt about Belinda. Significantly, perhaps, her niece was the only close living relative whom Frances failed to mention in her will: even if she thought that Perkins's wife was amply provided for, she still remembered all her married sisters who were still alive. In reality, the marriage pool for the upper levels of Catholic society covered a very small area of society. Added to this, the financial squeeze imposed by selective taxation rates made it difficult to put up large portions without mortgaging substantial amount of property. As one option girls could become nuns, as did five of John Caryll's six daughters, and five daughters of William Petre of Belhouse at the start of the eighteenth century. Some may have had a genuine calling, but others perhaps chose simply to opt out of a restricted and humiliating marriage market. Henrietta, a younger sister of Arabella, remained single: we do not know how many men she scorned, but the *Rape* could scarcely enhance her prospects. With some malice, the poem portrays bad temper as a shrivelled virgin:

> Here stood *Ill-nature* like an *ancient Maid*,
> Her wrinkled Form in *Black* and *White* array'd;
> With store of Pray'rs, for Mornings, Nights, and Noons,
> Her Hand is fill'd; her Bosom with Lampoons.
>
> (4: 27-30)

The spiteful placing of the hand in propinquity to the bosom reminds us that no one is seeking to explore the ancient maid, least of all her sexual parts; only concealed libels are stored next to her heart. Were there no anxious thoughts at the Fermors' home in case the spinster's bonnet fitted?

Two others who would never marry were Martha and Teresa Blount. The poem certainly had few keener readers than the sisters, especially Martha as John Caryll's goddaughter. Very soon Pope sent her a copy of the collection in which the *Rape* first appeared, writing disingenuously, "yourself and your fair Sister must needs have been surfeited already with this Triffle; and therfore you have no hopes of Entertainment but from the rest of this Booke, wherein (they tell me) are some things that may be dangerous to be lookd upon" (Pope *Corr*, 1: 143). Nothing in the volume was truly as "dangerous" as the *Rape*, and the Blounts cannot have been sated with its contents. For one thing, as Rumbold has shown, the almost Brontëesque circle of fanciful writing in which the sisters took part as young women included Arabella. When a certain "Cosen Belle" turns up in the letters they circulated, Rumbold observes, "the modern reader recognises her with something of a shock as Arabella Fermor, the original of Pope's Belinda."[28] That shock lessens once we discover that a genuine family relationship existed. Indeed, the Blount girls shared a connection with the Fermors on both sides of their ancestry. Through their mother they were third cousins of Arabella, and through their father second cousins once removed. On top of their Caryll and Browne links, this relationship turned the poem into a kind of distorted family history.

We cannot tell whether the Petres and Fermors restored their former close relations. They never engaged in further intermarriage. However, we can be sure that there was no break with the Carylls. Arabella's own sister, Mary Frances Fermor, became abbess of the Benedictine convent at Dunkirk from 1748 to 1764 and maintained correspondence with the Caryll family. As we have seen, the first abbess of this convent had been John Caryll's aunt, and two of his daughters joined the community. One, Sister Mary Romana. served until 1760: the other, who joined in 1714, bore the baptismal name of Arabella, and she too was known in the family as "Bell." Two years later her cousin wrote to John's son that "your sister Bell. . would not change her state to be a queen," a sentiment Pope's Belinda might have struggled to comprehend. The presence of Pastons. Southcotes and Englefields among the nuns will not occasion any surprise. As for Abbess Mary Frances Fermor, she left a very different mark on posterity from her sister Arabella: at her jubilee in 1763 she was celebrated in verses, relating how she left the world's pleasures to spend her days "in charming solitude." In the words of the poet, "Thus fifty years a holy life you've led, / To every vice, to every folly dead." The convent itself survived at Dunkirk until the days of the Terror in 1793, when the nuns were imprisoned and later fled to a new home in England.[29]

V

None of these genealogical involutions would bother anyone today. But they counted for a great deal more in the past, when power and identity inhered in hereditary groups bestowing patronage. We need only think of the table of kindred and affinity attached to the Book of Common Prayer in 1662, setting out the forbidden degrees of marriage, a document which many a bored congregation must have perused in the course of droning sermons. For Catholics, information on this topic held even greater urgency: not only were they a minority population, but the canons of the church narrowed the range of possible partners more strictly than was the case with Anglicans. In fact, it took the Council of Trent to reduce the scope of prohibited affinity from the third to the second degree, meaning that marriage was possible with the second cousin of a deceased spouse. But in the case of direct consanguity, the bar extended as far as second cousins. Such considerations held more than an academic interest for the recusant community. What Pope had done was to unveil bad blood in a circle where blood lines were as jealously hoarded as those in the thoroughbred stud-book.

Of course, the bulk of the audience for *The Rape of the Lock* knew little or nothing about these family secrets. But for those in the know, the poem must have been troubling as well as amusing. More than just exposing a localized scandal, it brought into play many of the stratagems the community used to keep its identity intact. Pope can never have seriously believed that the poem's mock-heroic form took off all the implicit mockery of the families involved. For Caryll, a particularly close friend, the *Rape* would call into question his guardianship of the Baron and his wife. For Lord Petre's widow, it meant constant reminders of a desperately short marriage. For the dowager Lady Petre, the glittering social world evoked in the poem brought up images of a life her recently deceased daughter would never now experience. For Arabella, it gave a public airing to events which had foreclosed the possibilities of a really grand marriage. Even if she herself had no regrets, the Fermors collectively would have deplored the loss of a dynastic connection. As late as 1775, when Samuel Johnson visited an Augustine convent in Paris, he found that "Mrs. Fermor," described as the abbess, "knew Pope, and thought him disagreeable." In the *Lives of the Poets,* Johnson referred to her as "a niece of Mrs. [Arabella] Fermor," and stated that she "mentioned Pope's work with very little gratitude, rather an insult than an honour; and she may be supposed to have inherited the opinion of the family."[30] As usual, Johnson's instincts may provide a reliable guide to the way people felt within the domestic circle. However, Mary Agnes Frances Fermor, actually the sub-prioress, made her profession at the convent in 1740, aged about twenty-one, and so she is unlikely to have had close personal knowledge of Pope.

Some might argue that the poem did no lasting harm. Pope remained on good terms with Caryll as long as the older man lived. Two years after

Lord Petre died, his widow and mother showed some magnanimity in subscribing to the poet's translation of Homer: Catherine wrote to Caryll expressing her readiness to contribute. The two had most likely been recruited by Thomas Southcott, a resourceful Jacobite fund-raiser who could have used the *Iliad* as a blind for his larger task. (One looks in vain for the name Fermor or Perkins in any of Pope's subscription lists, alone among the historic Catholic gentry of the region. They were fairly unbookish people, but that usually didn't enter into it.) In 1718 Caryll was still visiting the Petres at Ingatestone (Pope *Corr,* 1: 518).[31] Sir George Browne may finally have got over his pique, and the Fermors went on their quiet way. But members of the faith must have found it uncomfortable to read a text which so insistently drew attention to the little manoeuvres that sustained the marriage market. The affair sent ripples out over the entire community: after all, the Petres were "the one family of cast iron landed magnates to remain invincibly Catholic from the sixteenth century onwards."[32]

Thanks to the hugely increased publicity that the *Rape* had brought the episode, a small tempest in a domestic teapot had become almost a public event. Within the first few lines Pope sets up a sly hint that Belinda's resistance to the Baron had been part of a calculated strategy:

> Say what strange Motive, Goddess! cou'd compel
> A well-bred *Lord* t'assault a gentle *Belle*?
> Or say what stranger Cause, yet unexplor'd,
> Cou'd make a gentle *Belle* reject a *Lord*?
>
> (1: 7-10)

The tone seems genial enough, with the intimate flash of punning wit on Belle's name. Yet behind the smiling exterior is a cruel accuracy. In his *Letter to Lord Byron* Auden famously says that Jane Austen could describe the "amorous effects of 'brass'," and frankly reveal "the economic basis of society." So too could Pope, or more precisely here the imperatives of a community in danger of losing its battle for survival. Artistically *The Rape of the Lock* needed all of the poet's tact, but in social matters it exhibits a huge and calculated tactlessness.

Notes

[1] Information is drawn from almost a hundred different locations. These include wills, settlements, estate deeds, inventories and correspondence, as well as printed sources such as family and local histories, genealogies (as well as genealogical websites), and newspapers. Here these are not listed individually, except in the case of direct quotation, or those instances where specially important or unique material is utilized. In addition, references to standard sources are normally silent, as follows: *The Complete Baronetage*; *The Complete Peerage*; *Burke's Peerage*; *The Oxford Dictionary of National Biography*; *The History of Parliament*; *The Victoria County History*. The text of the poem is taken from *TE* 2: 144-206.

[2] The best short account is that in *TE* 2: 349-56.

[3] The marriage is recorded in standard guides to the peerage: see for example Sir Egerton Brydges, ed., *Collins's Peerage of England*, 9 vols (London: Rivington and others, 1812), 7: 10.

[4] John Bossy, *The English Catholic Community 1570-1850* (New York: Oxford University Press, 1976), pp. 101-2.

[5] National Archives, PROB 11/470.

[6] National Archives, PROB 11/575.

[7] Centre for Buckinghamshire Studies, D-D/2/23-4, 26: National Archives, PROB 11/588.

[8] *A History of the Benedictine Nuns of Dunkirk. . .edited by the Community* (London: The Catholic Book Club, 1957), p. 57. Earlier sources quoted in the Twickenham edition of the *Rape* give a misleading account: the women named there as Arabella's sisters seem in fact to have been her paternal aunts. Three of them married into the upper echelons of the Catholic gentry: the most notable was Ursula (1662-1748) who married Richard Towneley and became the mother of two prominent Jacobites.

[9] Museum of English Rural Life, Ufton Court Collection, MS 1239/3/30.

[10] National Archives, PROB 11/677.

[11] National Archives, PROB 11/492.

[12] Devon Record Office, Petre MSS, 49/26/7/1.

[13] One of those named is Thomas Clifton, a relative of the Baron on his maternal side (his mother was Mary Clifton of Lytham Hall, Lancaster).

[14] Paul Kléber Monod, *Jacobitism and the English People 1688-1788* (Cambridge: Cambridge University Press, 1989), p. 325.

[15] G.E. Cokayne et al, *The Complete Peerage*, 14 vols (London: St Catherine Press, 1910-2000), 10: 509.

[16] National Archives, PROB 11/532; PROB 11/533. Mary's memorial inscription in Ingatestone parish church states that she died "in the twentith (*sic*) year of her age" on 10 April 1713. For the surrender of a lease by Edward Southcott and Caryll, and dated 2 April 1713, apparently designed to raise her portion, see Devon Record Office, Petre MSS, 123M/L918.

[17] Centre for Buckinghamshire Studies, D-D/2/7.

[18] National Archives, PROB 11/545.

[19] National Archives, PROB 11/471.

[20] National Archives, PROB 11/768.

[21] For a joking confirmation that some of these habits have survived into more modern times, we might think of the mock-will that Auberon Waugh composed at the age of fourteen. He made his father Evelyn the executor, and bequeathed items such as "A blue china statue of Jesus, a rosary from Jerusalem fashioned in dried olives, a jewelled cross from Portofino, a mother-of-pearl cross from Jerusalem, a Pope-blessed rosary from Rome, the Midsomer Norton family bible, a Roman missal and a *Missale Romanum*," and so on. Quoted by Alexander Waugh, *Fathers and Sons: The Autobiography of a Family* (London: Headline, 2004), pp. 308-9.

[22] John Orlebar Payne, *Records of the English Catholics of 1715* (London: Burns & Oates, 1889), p. 131. See National Archives, FEC 1/584-7.

[23] Valerie Rumbold, *Women's Place in Pope's World* (Cambridge: Cambridge University Press, 1989), pp. 48-82, an important discussion of relevant materials partly drawn from the Blount papers.

[24] See Downshire papers, Berkshire Record Office, D/ED/E9. Earlier, in 1706, Browne had executed a form of release of the manor to a group including Nathaniel Piggot (D/EX 476/3).

[25] Pope to Trumbull, 19 December 1713, in George Sherburn, "Letters of Alexander Pope, Chiefly to Sir William Trumbull," *Review of English Studies,* 9 (1958): 388-406.

[26] National Archives, PROB 11/636.

[27] Olwen Hutton, *The Prospect Before Her: A History of Women in Western Europe 1500-1800* (New York; Vintage, 1998), pp. 254-8; Bridget Hill, *Women Alone: Spinsters in England 1660-1850* (New Haven: Yale University Press, 2001); Amanda Vickery, *The Gentleman's Daughter: Women's Lives in Georgian England* (New Haven: Yale University Press, 1998).

[28] Rumbold, *Women's Place*, p. 67.

[29] *History of the Benedictine Nuns*, p. 61, 92-5, 120-7.

[30] *The French Journals of Mrs Thrale and Dr Johnson*, ed. M. Tyson and H. Guppy (Manchester: John Rylands Library, 1932); Samuel Johnson, *Lives of the English Poets*, ed. G.B. Hill, 3 vols (Oxford: Clarendon Press, 1905), 3: 103. The abbess also told Mrs Piozzi that Pope's praise had made Arabella "very troublesome and conceited."

[31] As guardian of the eighth Lord Petre, posthumous son of the Baron, John Caryll is named as a trustee along with Sir Edward Southcott and Catherine, in the son's marriage settlement dated 1732 (Devon Record Office, Petre MSS 49/26/7/2).

[32] Bossy, *Catholic Community*, p. 101.

CHAPTER THREE

SATIRE AS MOCK-SCIENCE:
THE SCRIBLERIANS AND THE SEARCH
FOR THE LONGITUDE

Satire and science have interacted in peculiar ways at times. One such episode took place in 1714 when the British government first offered a prize for the discovery of a successful way to find the longitude at sea. This initiative had as its primary aim that of reducing the heavy toll of shipwrecks caused by the crude navigational method of dead reckoning then in use. Most people today know something of the ensuing events: Dava Sobel gave them new life in her best-selling book *Longitude: The True Story of a Lone Genius who solved the Greatest Scientific Problem of his Time* (1995), which inspired the widely viewed television programme "Lost at Sea" aired on PBS in 1998. After these came a feature film directed by Charles Sturridge in 1999, starring Michael Gambon and Jeremy Irons. All three versions place at their centre the heroic figure of John Harrison and his struggles to perfect a clock which would finally carry off the prize of £20,000. Meanwhile, an early rival who enters the tale has gone down in history as another projector from Yorkshire, named Jeremy Thacker. Unfortunately it looks as if Thacker never existed and his proposal now emerges as a hoax. A strong suspicion arises that the putative scheme came from within the Scriblerus group. Curiously it had its birth at the moment when their brief period of most intense personal contact and collaboration was about to end.

I

The measure to award the government prize was rushed through parliament, passing all stages in the Lords between 5 and 7 July 1714. This haste came from the need to get it on the statute book before parliament was prorogued on the 9th. On that day Queen Anne gave the royal assent, in the last clutch of acts she signed before her death just over three weeks later.[1] The bill concerning the longitude took its place in a group including an act for laying additional duties on soap and paper, one inflicting additional punishments against "Jesuits, priests, and other trafficking papists," one directed against rogues, vagabonds, sturdy beggars, and vagrants, and one to promote "the speedy and effectual preserving the navigation of the River of Thames, by stopping the breach in the levels of Havering and Dagenham."

Before parliament drew up the bill, members had appointed a special committee which taken advice from Isaac Newton and Edmond Halley among others. What emerged was a scheme "for providing a Public Reward for such Person or Persons as shall discover the Longitude at Sea," offering premiums at various levels according to the accuracy achieved by a given method. The new law set up a board of commissioners to act as adjudicators, though this body would hardly ever meet for years to come. The original board included Newton as president of the Royal Society; Halley, as Savilian professor at Oxford; and their enemy John Flamsteed, the astronomer royal. Another ex officio member was the Lucasian professor at Cambridge, a post held by many distinguished mathematicians from Newton to Stephen Hawking. Although the current holder was the blind Newtonian disciple Nicholas Saunderson, one of the important early influences on John Harrison, it was only three years since he had taken over from Newton's successor in the chair, William Whiston, recently expelled from the university for his Arian views.

About a year before the act went through, Whiston had joined with Humphrey Ditton, master of the mathematical school at Christ's Hospital, to publicize what many thought a crack-brained scheme to find the longitude. This involved the use of strategically placed ships which would fire off a number of shells programmed to explode at a set time. Even during foggy weather the explosions would be audible, and just in time for the project a reasonably accurate estimate (very slightly on the high side) had been made for the speed of sound, using gun-shot reports. The findings came from Rev. William Derham, himself a man well versed in clock-making, and they were published by the Royal Society in 1709. The committee had already looked at the Whiston-Ditton proposal, when Newton prevaricated on the feasibility of the idea. Whiston and Ditton optimistically drafted an advertisement to launch a heavy press campaign, announcing the publication of their scheme just four days after the royal assent was given. They claimed that their method had been "so far approved by this present Parliament, that they have passed an Act, ordering a reward of 20000*l.* for such a Discovery." In the event, the flying bombs turned out to be unworkable and did not get into contention for the prize. If Whiston had restrained himself on the subject of the primitive

church and the need for a reformed liturgy, he might have sat in judgment
on his own idea.

Nothing daunted, he arranged a display to prove his theory in July
1715: this involved shooting up rockets at intervals across an area of 36
square miles centred on Hampstead. Two years he announced that he
would be letting off mortars on Hampstead Heath, and asked that "all
curious Persons, within Sixty Miles Distance" would observe the event
and send him information on what they saw or heard. The experiment
satisfied him enough for him to advertise another trial with balls of a
smaller dimension to be launched at Hampstead and Gravesend.[2] Despite
inconclusive results, Whiston never gave up hope on solving the problem.
In 1719 he was back with *The Longitude and Latitude found by the
Inclinatory or Dipping Needle*, a short pamphlet expanded in 1721, with a
dedication to the commissioners. In 1720 he waited upon the king at St
James's, with a new scheme, "which, it is said, is much probable than the
one he presented formerly."[3] As late as 1738 he submitted to the board a
proposal entitled *Longitude Discovered by the Eclipses, Occultations and
Conjunctions of Jupiter's Planets*. It took a lot to deter him.

The prospect of winning the enormous jackpot naturally brought
before the public a rash of methods to ascertain the longitude. Even Sir
Christopher Wren sent the Royal Society a list in cipher of three
mysterious-looking instruments he had devised.[4] Some of the other
proposals rank as absurd, some as well-meant but impracticable. The
means ranged from a universal clock and barometers to the use of tide
tables (a nod at Halley's pioneering work in this area), improved lunar
charts and magnetic compasses. A few came from serious engineers, but
others were the product of back-garden astronomers and deranged
inventors. None of them excited as much popular scorn as the Whiston-
Ditton project, but equally none remotely qualified for the prize.
Subsequently it became possible for scientists to take the lunar route when
Leonhard Euler made a more exact calculation of celestial motions,
enabling Johann Tobias Meyer to provide accurate tables of longitude. But
that opportunity still lay half a century ahead.

Only one of the early proposals has escaped the condescension of
posterity. This came with a pamphlet entitled *The Longitudes Examin'd*,
which appeared early in November. The title-page attributes this short
tract to Jeremy Thacker of Beverley, who signs his opening "epistle to the
Longitudinarians" with the additional phrase "Philomath. Well-wisher to
the Twenty Thousand Pounds." The second half of his work sets out a
method using a clock placed inside a vacuum chamber like a bell jar, and
fitted with an auxiliary spring to supplement the mainspring during

winding. The author then describes some experiments he conducted to test his equipment. Without a single exception historians of science have taken Thacker at his word, and graded his work as a brave near miss among an array of doomed projects. Experts on navigation, horology and cartography have all commended his efforts. Even Rupert Gould (1890-1958), the distinguished naval historian who restored Harrison's clocks, had a good word to say. For the film Jeremy Irons portrayed Gould as an obsessive student of clockmaking techniques, as driven in his own way as John Harrison. When Gould wrote his book on the marine chronometer (this last word, as we shall see, a coinage of Thacker), he credited the projector with having anticipated Harrison by twenty years in devising the auxiliary spring mechanism.[5]

Dava Sobel herself joined in the chorus. She remarked that "one of the most astute, succinct dismissals of fellow hopefuls came from the pen of Jeremy Thacker of Beverly, England," and analysed the account he gave of his experiments. In the light of what he says, the method "fell short of perfection, and Thacker knew it." The equipment could not deal properly with changes in temperature. Moreover, "the plan falls apart," because "Thacker owned that his chronometer occasionally erred by as much as six seconds a day." Consequently, though this proposal was "the best of the lot" reviewed by the board in its first year, it "didn't raise anyone's hopes very high."[6] Since apparently nobody else saw or tested the equipment, this can hardly surprise us.[7]

In fact, the reputation of Thacker as a brave pioneer – the best of the rest – stems from a misreading of a literary joke. The proposal may or may not have come closer to the successful methods Harrison used, but if it did that is no more than a happy coincidence. Abundant evidence exists to show that the real aim of *Longitudes Examin'd* was to parody the other hopeful projects, embedding some apparently plausible scientific discussion.

II

Who, to start with, was Jeremy Thacker? Anyone seeking such a person will draw a blank on the genealogical websites. His name does not appear among the growing number of mathematical teachers up and down the country, and though there was an Anthony Thacker who taught at King Edward's school, Birmingham, this was in the period shortly before his death in 1744 – a generation too late. Jeremy also seems to be absent from local records in Beverley. After 1714 he drops straight back into obscurity. Earlier writers have confidently described him as an inventor and watchmaker; a nautical instrument maker; and even as an experienced navigator. The distinguished scholar, E.G.R. Taylor, included Thacker in her survey of early mathematical practitioners – the bible of this subject. She dubbed him "a Yorkshire gentleman and amateur instrument-maker", but she was unable to cite any external source.[8] Outside the claims of the pamphlet itself, no evidence survives to place him in any of these categories. Even Ruth Wallis and the late Peter Wallis, authors of the most complete "biobibliography" of British mathematicians, did not snuff him out, although they did – almost alone – suggest that Thacker was "perhaps using a pseudonym."[9]

Then we need to inspect the term "philomath." *OED* suggests that the primary meaning was "a student, esp. of mathematics, natural philosophy, and the like." The entry continues, "formerly popularly applied to an astrologer or prognosticator." This is putting the cart before the horse. The once respectable word underwent a precipitous decline around the early eighteenth century, from which it never fully recovered. Commonly it was applied to quacks, often by way of self-description. Writing on fortune-tellers in the *Spectator* no. 505 in October 1712, Joseph Addison referred scornfully to "some prophetick Philomath."[10] A year later, the Tory periodical *The Examiner* spoke of the craze for French prophets in London in the previous decade, and remarked that "not a Philomath or Orthodox Astrologer" could be heard in the din: even the famous almanac-maker John Partridge gave up and resolved to die a second time. (This of course refers to Jonathan Swift's Bickerstaff pamphlets, which had predicted the death of Partridge so convincingly that most people were taken in. *The Tatler* had described Bickerstaff himself as "Philomath.")[11] Leading almanacs like that of John Wing continued to use the label in an unselfconscious way. One or two land-surveyors clung on to the term, and people entering puzzle competitions in magazines used it as a pseudonym. But by 1714 mathematicians and inventors pushing a serious idea found it risky to own up to this profession. The word was left to dodgy projectors and snake-oil salesmen.

We could multiply examples from many sources. It was, however, Swift and his immediate circle who had done most to bring about this linguistic swerve. In 1709 a mock-prophecy appeared under the title of *A Famous Prediction of Merlin,* attributed to "T.N., Philomath," but really from the pen of Swift. In the following years the group of Scriblerian satirists, who also included Alexander Pope, John Gay, Thomas Parnell and John Arbuthnot, wrote a series of pamphlets ridiculing vain and semi-literate projectors who promised the earth and delivered nothing. A favourite mask was that of "E. Parker, Philomath," who produced *A Complete Key to the new Farce, call'd Three Hours after Marriage*

(1717), a solemn pseudo-explication of the Scriblerians' own farce. An exchange in *Three Hours* runs, "Do you deal in longitudes, Sir? – I deal not in impossibilities."[12] In the same year Parker was responsible for *Mr. Joanidion Fielding his true and faithful Account of the Strange and Miraculous Comet which was seen by the Mufti at Constantinople.* The main target is Whiston, who had taken the study of comets into millenarian realms. For the satirists he became the epitome of a learned fool, and either Gay or Parnell joined in with a short and scabrous "Ode for Musick on the Longitude."[13] Arbuthnot himself returned to the bomb vessels project in a broadsheet, *The Humble Petition of the Colliers* (1716).[14] Many of these riffs on deluded quasi-science are reorchestrated in the *Memoirs of Martinus Scriblerus,* assembled by Pope after his collaborators had died or in Swift's case descended into senility. Among other touches, the *Memoirs* have a reference to the hero's "Method of discovering the *Longitude* by *Bomb-Vessels.*"[15]

One of these pamphlets stands out for a particular reason: *Annus Mirabilis* (1722), also probably written by Pope and Arbuthnot in collaboration. This predicts a universal sex-change, induced by a conjunction of the planets. The title-page names its author as "Abraham Gunter, Philomath. A Well-wisher to the Mathematicks." This exactly matches the formula used by Jeremy Thacker – whose name follows the very same cadence as that of Gunter, another ghost. *Annus Mirabilis* mocks both the wild fantasies of the astrologers and the crazed certainties that Whiston displayed of the links between celestial activity and life on earth. Similarly, in Pope's *Key to the Lock* (1715), the author is named as Esdras Barnivelt, Apoth. At the start of this pamphlet, which offers a preposterous reading of the poet's great mock-heroic, Barnivelt receives a set of complimentary verses from "a Well-willer to the Coalition of Parties."[16] While it is possible in theory that Gunter and Barnivelt were simply copying the formula used independently by Thacker, such a reconstruction of events defies commonsense.[17]

But what of the experiments that Thacker described in careful detail? They follow the accustomed pattern of Royal Society transactions, with painstaking mathematical logic:

> As for Example, if the Semicircle FPB be of about nine Inches Radius, and the Pendulum describes nearly a Quadrate of it each Vibration, as it will do in going from *a* to *b*, then the Arc describ'd, will run pretty much out of the Cycloid; but if the Radius of FPD, or what is the same, the Rod of the Pendulum, be four times as long as that which is made use of to swing Seconds, and the Pendulum itself pretty heavy, it will swing in the Arc DPπ, where the Circle and the Cycloid are sensibly the same Line; and

therefore if no Force makes the Pendulum fly out farther than ordinary in
its Vibrations, they will be all perform'd in the same Time, because then
the Cycloidal Arcs are describ'd.[18]

Along with the accompanying diagrams, this looks convincing enough to
an inexpert eye. But so does this:

> To explain the manner of its progress, let *A B* represent a line drawn across
> the dominions of Balnibarbi, let the line *c d* represent the loadstone, of
> which let *d* be the repelling end, and *c* the attracting end, the island being
> over *C*: let the stone be placed in position *c d,* with its repelling end
> downwards; then the island will be driven upwards obliquely towards *D*.
> When it is arrived at *D*, let the stone be turned upon its axle, till its
> attracting end points towards *E*, and then the island will be carried
> obliquely towards *E*; where, if the stone be again turned upon its axle till it
> stands in the position *E F,* with its repelling point downwards, the island
> will rise obliquely towards *F*, where, by directing the attracting end
> towards *G*, the island may be carried to *G*, and from *G* to *H*, by turning the
> stone, so as to make its repelling extremity to point directly downward.[19]

That is Gulliver on his third voyage, as he describes the workings of the
flying island of Laputa – and he too has his helpful diagram in the text.
What the historians of longitude seem to have missed is that satires had to
make their pseudo-science *look* as though they were the real thing.

The longitude pamphlet ends with a sneer at the Heath Robinson
engines that inventors had dreamt up to boost their proposals: "In a word, I
am satisfy'd that my reader begins to think that the Phonometers,
Pyrometers, Selenometers, Heliometers, Barometers, and all the Meters
are not worthy to be compar'd with my Chronometer."[20] Thacker may
have come up with a term of lasting scientific currency, but that does not
mean that he really constructed or tested such an instrument. Unlike
Harrison, he had no need to produce anything that would work. He merely
had to mimic viable procedures, and use the right descriptive language.
Unlike the serious projectors, he could afford to point out the ways in
which his system went wrong – thus transparently undercutting his boast
that it easily outdid all the methods previously published. That claim just
echoes the sales talk of an immodest proposer.

III

Everything about this pamphlet should have raised a warning flag. We
have not gone past the title-page when we read of the author's
"Description of a smart, pretty Machine Of my Own, Which I am (almost)

sure will do for the Longitude, and procure me the Twenty Thousand Pounds." Several features alert the reader: the waggish parenthesis, the casual expression "will do for the Longitude," and the accents of a *petit maître* in "a smart, pretty Machine Of my Own." Earnest projectors never went about their business in this way. Thacker's absurdly grandiose style moves beyond the wishful language of the usual dotty aspirants for the prize. His unblushing admission that he only cares about the twenty thousand pounds, with no figleaf claims of benefit to mankind, marks his proposal as equally untypical, and even less likely to have won over the commissioners. He shows the same unblushing evasiveness as the authors of the most threadbare schemes put before the public: "As for my Method of knowing what a-Clock it is at the Place where the Ship is, I shan't trouble my Reader with it, 'till I come back and mention it in the Memorial which I shall present to the Commissioners, and prove by Witnesses."[21]

Assuming that the *Longitudes Examin'd* had a satiric intent, we might wonder if the Scriblerians had anything to do with the elusive suspect, Jeremy Thacker. Since 1709, as we just saw, they had displayed a strong inclination towards hoax proposals on topics of this kind. Of course, they were not alone in keeping a close eye on the longitude story, and plenty of other people found most proposals risible. However, thanks to the work of Marjorie Hope Nicolson and G.S. Rousseau we know that Pope attended Whiston's coffee-house lectures in 1713, and that the self-publicizing mathematician became a recurrent object of the group's satiric work for several years.[22] In August 1714, immediately prior to the appearance of Thacker's pamphlet, these lectures were extended to cover "the Discovery of the Longitude."[23] Moreover, Whiston had actually sought Swift's help in 1712 when he first devised his scheme with Ditton. As Swift explained the matter to Stella, "Do you know what the Longitude is? a Projector has been applying himself to me, to recommend him to the Ministry, because he pretends to have found out the Longitude. I believe He has no more found it out than he has found out mine [arse]. However I will gravely hear what he says, and discover him a Knave or Fool " (*Journal to Stella*, 2: 527). Soon after he took up the matter with Archbishop William King:

A Projector has lately applied to me to recommend him to the Ministry, about an invention for finding out the Longitude. He has given in a Petition to the Queen by Mr. Sec. St. John. I understand nothing of the Mathematicks, but I am told it is a Thing as improbable as the Philosopher's stone, or perpetual Motion.

(Swift *Corr*, 1: 421)

As Dava Sobel noted, when Gulliver envisaged the sights he would witness if he had the lifespan of a Struldbrugg, he went into his salivating mode: "I should then see the discovery of the longitude, the perpetual motion, the universal medicine, and many other great inventions, brought to the utmost perfection."[24] That shows what Swift thought of the chances. Much more to the point, *The Longitudes Examin'd* contains a sneer at the author of one hapless scheme: "If he would have this Instrument go, let him consult about it with the Inventors of a perpetual Motion."[25]

Long afterwards this story had a curious epilogue. In 1727 a certain John Wheldon wrote to Swift, concerning his own method for finding the longitude. He had been told that Swift was 'a Lover of the Mathematicks.' Swift replied from Holyhead, on his way back to Dublin from England with seeming indignation:

> I understand not Mathematicks, but have been formerly troubled too much with Projectors of the Longitude to my great Mortification and some Charges by encouraging them. It is only to Mathematicians you must apply. Newton, Halley and Keil have all told me they doubted the Thing was impossible. . . One of my Projectors cut his Throat, and the other was found an Imposter. That is all I can say; but am confident you would deceive others, or are deceived yourself.
>
> (Swift *Corr*, 3: 128-9)

One more circumstance needs attention. The pamphlet by Thacker was actually reprinted, with slight cuts, in a two-volume collection called *The Miscellaneous Works of the Late Dr. Arbuthnot* (Glasgow, 1751). The *Works* contained some irresponsible attributions, which have been quietly dropped by subsequent scholarship. But they do include a few authentic items, and we ought to reserve the possibility that *The Longitudes Examin'd* might also be genuine. John Arbuthnot (1667-1735) was a true polymath: a Scottish physician to the queen, mathematician, student of probability and coinage, classical scholar, a lover of music who belonged to the Handel circle, and a witty polemicist who had enshrined John Bull as the stereotypical Englishman in a series of pamphlets published in 1712. But need to recall that before Arbuthnot came to know his fellow satirists in the Scriblerian group he was already well known in the scientific community. As early as 1698, a leading naturalist and Celtic scholar, Edward Lhwyd, termed him an "excellent Mathematician; and one very well skilled in experimental philosophy."[26] Clearly *The Longitudes Examin'd* must have been written by a competent scientist, a well connected observer, and a skilled author of caustic satire. Not many candidates present themselves, and none who had been – like Arbuthnot as a young man – a teacher of mathematics.

In fact, we can fit the pamphlet into the established narrative of the Scriblerian project with a surprising degree of precision. We know that Arbuthnot took a close interest in the developing longitude story, and that he had actually been waiting for the Whiston-Ditton scheme to come out. On 17 July 1714, just days after the longitude bill passed into law, he wrote to Swift:

> Whetstone has at last publish'd his project of the longitude the most ridiculous thing that ever was thought on, but a pox on him he has spoild one of my papers of scriblerus, which was a proposal for the longitude not very unlike his to this purpose, that since ther was no pole for East & west that all the princes of Europe should joyn & build two prodigious poles upon high mountains with a vast light house to serve for a pole Star. . . . Now you must understand, his project is by light houses & explosion of bombs, at a certain hour. [27]

This clue has been missed because Thacker's proposal took a different form, with no mention of erecting new "poles". But the letter shows that Arbuthnot had planned a Scriblerian pamphlet on this very topic. It was at this juncture that the doctor, despite all the political struggles at court, was most assiduously pressing on with his work on the incipient *Memoirs of Scriblerus*, as he reported to Swift in his preceding letter of 26 June. He did this with the encouragement of his friends in the club of satirists: on 18 June Pope jokingly wrote that Arbuthnot could only suppose the only reason Swift has suddenly disappeared from town to rusticate in a remote village on the Berkshire downs was "to attend at full leisure to the life and adventures of Scriblerus" (Swift *Corr*, 1: 620, 625).[28] Of course, the rationale of the entire Scriblerian project lay in the desire to ridicule inept and pretentious efforts within the world of learning. The enterprise had come to its most active and (for many years) its most productive life during this summer of 1714.

Meanwhile, on 27 July the political crisis which had been looming over the nation for months finally came to a head with the dismissal of Oxford (the honorary sixth member of the Club) from his post as lord treasurer. Within five days the queen herself was dead. Swift and Parnell soon left for Ireland, just as Gay prepared to follow the new king from Hanover to London. The Scriblerus Club was fragmented and dispersed, and would never again meet as a full collective unit. In a joint letter he wrote with Pope to Arbuthnot on 2 September, Parnell looked back fondly on the happy collaboration of recent days, when "the Immortal Scriblerus

Smild upon our endeavors. . .Yet art thou still if thou art alive O Scriblerus as deserving of our Lucubrations." In his portion of the letter, Pope referred back to these comments by Parnell:

> Tho' he mentions the name of Scriblerus to avoid my Reproaching him, yet is he conscious to himself how much the Memory of that Learned Phantome which is to be Immortal, is neglected by him at present. But I hope the Revolutions of State will not affect Learning so much as to deprive mankind of the Lucubrations of Martin, to the Encrease of which I will watch all next winter, and grow pale over the midnight Candle.
>
> (Pope *Corr*, 1: 250)

The "Revolutions of State" had indeed put a brake on the progress of the *Memoirs of Scriblerus,* but they had not daunted Arbuthnot. On 7 September the doctor replied:

> This blow has so rous'd Scriblerus that he has recover'd his senses, and thinks and talks like other men. From being frolicksome and gay he is turn'd grave and morose. His lucubrations lye neglected amongst old newspapers, cases, petitions, and abundance of unanswerable letters. I wish to God they had been amongst the papers of a noble Lord [Bolingbroke] sealed up. Then might Scriblerus have pass'd for the Pretender, and it would have been a most excellent and laborious work for the Flying Post or some such author, to have allegoriz'd all his adventures into a plot, and found out mysteries somewhat like the Key to the Lock. Martin's office is now the second door on the left hand in Dover-street [Arbuthnot's new home], where he will be glad to see Dr. Parnell, Mr. Pope, and his old friends, to whom he can still afford a half pint of claret. It is with some pleasure that he contemplates the world still busy, and all mankind at work for him.
>
> (Pope *Corr*, 1: 251)

In the event it was Arbuthnot who showed the most resilience and the greatest readiness to get on with business as usual. If anyone in the group would be capable of picking up the satiric pieces after the tumultuous events in July and August, it was he.

IV

Those wanting to take Thacker at face value have neglected to explore his intricate set of allusions. The writer evidently had a close familiarity with the published projects: he refers to their authors by initials or abbreviated forms, but each can be identified. Among the hopefuls we find Robert Browne, "the Corrector of the Moon's Motion"; Isaac Hawkins, promoter of a barometric scheme; and Francis Haldanby, who drafted an abject appeal to the rising politician James Stanhope. One individual who promised to make the secret of the longitude "known to the meanest capacity" turns out to be Samuel Watson, a clock-maker in Long Acre. (He also claimed to have sold a moving ephemeris to Charles II and a chronological automaton to Mary II.) We can also spot Sebastiano Ricci, who had acted as publicist for a new method devised by the Venetian mathematician Dorotheo Alimari with an unsubtle dedication to the commissioners, dated 31 August 1714. Alimari's proposal used an instrument outwardly resembling both an astrolabe and a sun-dial. The most interesting of those named is Case Billingsley, an archetypal projector later involved in South Sea scams and the fraudulent York Buildings Company. His presence indicates that the chase for the prize attracted not just scientific charlatans but also a sprinkling of routine con-men. [29]

Whiston may have offered a soft target, but the pamphlet extracts some equally effective comedy from lesser known participants in the quest for the longitude. Among these is one writer who prefaced his effort with fulsome dedications to the King, the Prince of Wales, the Royal Society and his ingenious reader. Thacker obviously meant Benjamin Habakkuk Jackson, later patentee of a swimming engine, and author of a miscellaneous tract entitled *Some new Thoughts Founded upon New Principles, concerning a Threefold Motion of the Earth,* intended as the prelude to a great new scientific excursion. The title-page lists a series of topics ranging from the rectification of the calendar to "the finding out the true place of the moon." They all receive skimpy treatment, and only in the final paragraph does the writer address the last named of his topics, "facilitating the discovery of the longitude." In the manner of Swift's narrator in *A Tale of a Tub,* Jackson merely promises that he has something on the subject "to offer to the Publick hereafter."[30] So feeble an effort might almost be a hoax; but Thacker has fun in showing up the absurdities of the confused *Thoughts.* "The Body of the Book was wrote in a Language that I could not understand," he writes, "and so I must suspend my Judgment, till I have sent it to be perus'd by my learned Friend Mr. *Gr--n,* of *Cambridge*; for this Book may contain some of the Conclusions which follow from the Principles of his new Philosophy." [31] This is a feline sideswipe at *The Principles of Natural Philosophy, in which is shewn the Insufficiency of the Present Systems, to give us any just Account of that Science* (1712), by the eccentric natural philosopher Robert Greene.

These references hold another level of importance: they can be dated from newspaper advertisements. Thus we can tell that the ever–ready Case Billingsley had his scheme in place to put before the public by 23 August, while Jackson issued his proposal soon after 7 September and Isaac Hawkins his own on 14 September. Samuel Watson announced his machine in the press on 7 October; John Coster (mentioned in the Thacker's postscript) followed on 12 October; and Haldanby (also in the postscript) brought out his pamphlet on 16 October, the same day as Sebastiano Ricci. These provide a terminus a quo for Thacker's publication. Their appearance, and that of other longitude proposals not mentioned in the text, indicates that *Longitudes Examin'd* must have been written very shortly before it went into print. The dates fit precisely with the burst of renewed satiric energy Arbuthnot described in his letter to Pope on 7 September, when Scriblerus observed "all mankind at work for him."

At the start of his work Thacker unconvincingly claimed that most of the longitude pamphlets were sold off before they reached "our *Northern* Booksellers."[32] In reality an efficient book distribution system ensured that advertisements for hot items appeared in the provincial press within days of their launch in London. The author's pose as an isolated yokel is belied by a wide range of references to the scientific community, from Leibniz down. We can identify one of the commissioners, John Keill, a fellow-Scot whose work Arbuthnot had long supported. In 1708 Keill sought the Savilian chair, with the backing of both Halley and Arbuthnot, though opposed by Flamsteed. Another acquaintance was John's brother Dr James Keill, whose "iatro-mathematical" works Arbuthnot cited in his own publications.[33]

A less kindly reference to "my Friend K-th" points to James Keith (1685-1726), one more London physician from Scotland, and an early advocate of inoculation for smallpox. He was a product of Aberdeen university, like Arbuthnot. The two men came into contact in 1712, when they were rival candidates for the post of physician to Chelsea Hospital. Keith had presented a paper on the longitude to the Royal Society in 1710.[34] A provincial philomath, however able, would scarcely have had information of this kind at his finger tips. The presence of these Scotsmen may or may not provide a reliable clue. "Thacker", an obsolete and dialect variant for "thatcher", survived longer in the Scots language: Allan Ramsay, who completed his apprenticeship to a wig-maker in Edinburgh about 1709, later spoke of himself as a "skull-thacker," and he used the expression "Thack House" in *The Gentle Shepherd*, his most popular work. *Thacker* appears in the attached glossary of Scots words "which are rarely or never found in the modern English language."[35] Was Jeremy stitching up the credulous public with a hidden Scottish pun?

Only one close to events could have picked off so many targets. Arbuthnot's friends included Halley and Newton, with both of whom he currently served on boards such as the commissioners for building the fifty new "Queen Anne" churches in London. As far back as 1701, in his *Essay on the Usefulness of Mathematical Learning* Arbuthnot had stressed the need to find a practicable means of finding the longitude at sea, and commended Halley's expertise in this branch of study.[36] The praise represented more than an empty compliment: in this very year, 1714, Halley published a brief article in the *Philosophical Transactions* in which he tried to fix the longitude of the Straits of Magellan more accurately.[37] Moreover, in 1712 Arbuthnot had been appointed along with Halley to a committee of the Royal Society, charged with the task of determining the priority of Newton and Leibniz in developing calculus. It was Keill who had mainly fomented this acrimonious debate.

One pointer towards the author's background may lie in a self-debunking Latin quotation that Thacker placed on his title-page: "quid non mortalia pectora cogis, auri sacri fames!" (to what lengths does this damned lust for gold drive the human spirit). This was a familiar tag from the third book of the *Aeneid*, subsequently quoted by Seneca, and paraphrased by Dante in the *Purgatorio*. Just three years before, Pope had played on the phrase in *An Essay on Criticism*: "To what base Ends, and by what abject ways, / Are Mortals urg'd thro' *Sacred Lust of Praise!*" (*TE* 1: 296). Anyone close to the Scriblerian group would hardly have missed the allusion. But it was not the sort of thing that rolled off the tongue of other projectors. In any case, this maxim could serve only to undercut the pseudo-projector's motives.[38]

A further piece of evidence bears on the issue. *The Longitudes Examin'd* carries the name of James Roberts in its imprint, but he worked as a distributor who seldom owned copyrights. The real instigator, it now emerges, was the notorious Edmund Curll. His name figures at the head of four booksellers in a press advertisement on 9 November 1714; and the last leaf of the pamphlet displays announcements for two of his characteristic works on impotence.[39] Whereas Roberts's name appears on further items, including a second edition of the Whiston-Ditton proposal in 1715, Curll did not publish any other tract on longitude.[40] It was not like him to miss out on such a hot topic. Of course, Dr Arbuthnot would coin the most famous one-line appraisal of Curll, whose biographies he described as a new terror of death. But the Scriblerian group never showed any reluctance to use Curll's services when it suited them. The most famous case involves the trick by which Pope enlisted the aid of Curll in publishing his correspondence. But as early as 1716, at the latest, the Scriblerians were conniving in supposed "piracies" by the master poacher.

Since historians took the linguistic turn some two decades back, they have been more scrupulous in looking at rhetorical features of a text. But the case of Jeremy Thacker shows the need to inspect the full array of evidence, decipher embedded cultural allusions, and consider the publishing history. If *The Longitudes Examin'd* can no longer be regarded as a serious attempt to win the prize, it deserves notice as an amusing response by a privileged insider – most likely Dr John Arbuthnot - to the mania set off by the act of 1714. While no absolute proof exists that the pamphlet proceeded from the Scriblerus circle, the evidence assembled here shows, at the least, that that it uses the precise range of satiric techniques employed at this juncture by Swift, Pope and Arbuthnot.[24]

Notes

[1] For the course of the bill through the House, see *Journal of the House of Lords* (London, n.d.), 20: 745, 750, 758.

[2] *Post Man*, 14 July 1715, 14 May 1717; *Daily Courant*, 5 June 1717.

[3] Applebee's *Weekly Journal,* 19 November 1720.

[4] *The Correspondence of Isaac Newton,* ed. H.W. Turnbull, J.F. Scott, A.R. Hall, and Laura Tilling, 7 vols (Cambridge: Cambridge University Press, 1959-1977), 6: 193. For the committee's examination of the proposed bill, and Newton's reaction, see 6: 161-3.

[5] R.T. Gould, *The Marine Chronometer: Its History and Development* (London: Potter, 1923), p. 34. For Gould's remarkable career, see Jonathan Betts, *Time Restored: The Harrison Timekeepers and R.T. Gould, the Man Who Knew (Almost) Everything* (Oxford: Oxford University Press, 2006).

[6] Dava Sobel, *Longitude: The True Story of a Lone Genius who solved the Greatest Scientific Problem of his Time* (New York: Penguin, 1996), pp. 56-9.

[7] In response to an earlier version of this essay, which was published in the *Times Literary Supplement* on 14 November 2008, the distinguished horologists Jonathan Betts and Andrew King pointed out that we cannot be sure that no tests of the supposed device were carried out (see *TLS*, 20 March 2009). They consider it "highly likely that such a machine was actually made." In addition they contend that Thacker could well have been a real figure, even though evidence for his existence has not emerged. A finite possibility exists, of course, that the real Jeremy Thacker may some day stand up. But this seems likely to be a vain hope, since we have good sources for Beverley, for mathematical schools, and for the Thacker family genealogy. Moreover, there is no obvious reason why a serious projector would cloak his bid for the prize in this satiric form. For a fuller argument, see my reply to Betts and King in *TLS,* 4 April 2009.

[8] E.G.R. Taylor, *The Mathematical Practitioners of Tudor & Stuart England* (Cambridge: Cambridge University Press, 1954), p. 306.

[9] R.V. and P.J. Wallis, *Biobibliography of British Mathematics and its Applications*, Part II, 1701-1760 [all published] (Newcastle upon Tyne: Project for Historical Bibibliography, Epsilon Press, *c.*1985), p. 67.

[10] *The Spectator*, 8 vols (London: Buckley and Tonson, 1713), 7: 170.

[11] *The Lucubrations of Isaac Bickerstaff Esq*; 4 vols (London: Lillie and Morphew, 1711), 4: 249.

[12] *Three Hours after Marriage. A Comedy* (London: Lintot, 1717), p. 41.

[13] See Gay, *Letters*, p. 23; R.L. Hayley, "The Scriblerians and the South Sea Bubble: A Hit by Cibber," *Review of English Studies*, 24 (1973), 452-57. One of the Scriblerians, perhaps Gay, wrote *A True and Faithful Narrative of What Passed in London*, later reprinted in the group's *Miscellanies*. It pours scorn on Whiston, who is made to offer a confident announcement of the end of the world, owing to an approaching comet. The item has been dated 1714, but it refers at the start to "Tuesday 13 October," which would fit 1713 or 1719 rather.

[14] *To the Right Honourable the Mayor and Aldermen of the City of London: The Humble Petition of the Colliers, Cooks, Cook-Maids, Black-smiths, Jack-makers, Brasiers, and Others* (London: J. Roberts, 1716), p. 2.

[15] *Memoirs of Martinus Scriblerus*, p. 167. The method devised by Scriblerus, involving a plan to "make the Longitude as easy to be calculated as the Latitude," with the construction of *"Two Poles* to the *Meridian"* (168), is essentially the one mentioned in Arbuthnot's letter to Swift, cited on p. 54.

[16] "Abraham Gunter", *Annus Mirabilis: or, The Wonderful Effects of the Approaching Conjunction of the Planets Jupiter, Mars, and Saturn* [1722], p. 1; "Esdras Barnivelt, Apoth.", *A Key to the Lock* (London: J. Roberts, 1715), p. 5. As well as Gunter and Parker, the Scriblerians used the name of "Sir James Baker." He was the supposed author of *God's Revenge against Punning* (1716), yet another squib that refers to the triumph of *"Whistonism."* See Pope *Prose*, 1: 270.

[17] Among others who recalled the controversy over the prize was Matthew Prior, a friend of Swift, Pope, and the other Scriblerians. In *Alma* (c.1716) he wrote of illusory schemes such as squaring the circle, and added, "The Longitude uncertain roams, / In spight of WH---N and his Bombs." See *The Literary Works of Matthew Prior*, ed. H.B. Wright and M.K. Spears (Oxford: Clarendon Press, 2nd edn, 1971), 1: 510.

[18] *Longitudes Examin'd*, pp. 10-11.

[19] *Gulliver's Travels*, 3: 3 (Swift *Prose*, 11: 168-9).

[20] *Longitudes Examin'd*, p. 23.

[21] *Longitudes Examin'd*, pp. 19-20.

[22] Marjorie Hope Nicolson and G. S. Rousseau. *"This Long Disease, My Life": Alexander Pope and the Sciences* (Princeton: Princeton University Press, 1968), pp. 137-87, contains by far the best account of this aspect of Scriblerian activity.

[23] *Daily Courant*, 10 August 1714.

[24] *Gulliver's Travels*, 3: 10; Sobel, *Longitude*, p. 56.

[25] *Longitudes Examin'd*, pp. 6-7. Compare the schemes of the deluded Martin, which included along with the longitude "Projects of *Perpetuum Mobiles*": see

Memoirs of Martinus Scriblerus, p. 167. More generally, we learn that Martin occupied himself with "whole Treatises, Advices to Friends, Projects to First Ministers, Letters to Members of Parliament, Accounts to the Royal Society, and innumerable others," (169), a list that embraces the full gamut of longitude proposals - Thacker's, of course, included.

[26] Lhwyd to John Morton, 23 February 1698, quoted by Joseph M. Levine, *Dr. Woodward's Shield: History, Science, and Satire in Augustan England* (Berkeley: University of California Press, 1977), p. 40. The fullest account of Arbuthnot's varied intellectual work remains Lester M. Beattie, *John Arbuthnot: Mathematician and Satirist* (Cambridge, MA: Harvard University Press, 1935); a new study is badly needed.

[27] Swift *Corr*, 2: 11-12. In a sentence elided from this quotation, Arbuthnot states, "I was thinking of a calculation of the time charges & dimensions." Obviously Thacker's proposal has been drawn up with a similar attention to the exact numerical data. The government prize was of course a matter of general discussion: Swift himself had referred to it jokingly in a letter to Arbuthnot of 3 July (1: 630).

[28] On 3 July Swift wrote to Arbuthnot with reference to his friend's work on the *Memoirs*, "I wonder how You can have a Mind so degagè in a Court where there is so many Millions of things to vex you" (Swift *Corr*, 1: 630). On 11 July Pope told Swift that the Scriblerian project would have to lie fallow for a time owing to the pressure of public events (1: 645); nevertheless, as we have seen, Arbuthnot was still contemplating a satire on Whiston almost a week later. Swift responded to his letter on 25 July with the comment, "It was a malicious Satyr of yours upon Whiston, that what you intended a Ridicule, should be any way struck upon by him for a Reality. - Go on for the sake of Witt and Humor, and cultivate that Vein which no Man alive possesses but your self" (2: 26). Perhaps *The Longitudes Examin'd* could be the work Arbuthnot composed in order to meet his friend's request.

[29] *Longitudes Examin'd*, pp. 2-8.

[30] B[enjamin] H[abakkuk] J[ackson], *Some New Thoughts founded upon New Principles, concerning a Threefold Motion of the Earth* (London, printed for the author, 1714), p. 12.

[31] *Longitudes Examin'd*, p. 8.

[32] *Longitudes Examin'd*, p. 1.

[33] See for example John Arbuthnot, *An Essay concerning the Effects of Air on Human Bodies* (London: Tonson, 1735), p. 65. James Keill was a fellow member of the Royal Society, and he obtained one of the "dubious" degrees awarded by Aberdeen University. Arbuthnot had obtained an MA there by the orthodox route. See F.M. Valadez and C.D. O'Malley, "James Keill of Northampton, Physician, Anatomist and Physiologist," *Medical History*, 15 (1971): 317–35. For the friendship with John Keill, see *The Correspondence of Dr John Arbuthnot*, ed. A. Ross (München: Wilhelm Fink Verlag, 2006), p. 125. The most up to date account of Arbuthnot's career can now be found in *Correspondence,* ed. Ross, pp. 29-93.

[34] Keith (d. 1726) was a member of the circle of Dr George Cheyne, and also at the heart of a mystical group chiefly based in Aberdeen (though he himself practised in London). Neither connection would have protected him from Arbuthnot's satire.

[35] Allan Ramsay, *The Gentle Shepherd: A Scots Pastoral-Comedy* (London: Watson, 1730), pp. 14, 81.

[36] John Arbuthnot, *An Essay on the Usefulness of Mathematical Learning* (Oxford, 1701), p. 49.

[37] *Philosophical Transactions,* 29 (1714), 165-8.

[38] At the end of the main text Thacker cites another double-edged line, "lenta salix quantum pallenti cedit olivae" (p. 20). The verse comes from Virgil's *Eclogues,* 5: 16: "as much as the bending willow gives way to the pale olive."

[39] Advertised as published "this day", printed for Curll, J. Pemberton, J. Taylor and J. Roberts, "for so small a Price as 6d., with a large Plate into the Bargain", *Post Man,* 9 November 1714. The third name is almost certainly a misprint for William Taylor, later publisher of *Robinson Crusoe.* He often collaborated with Curll in books issued between 1710 and his death in 1724. For example, the *Works of Archibald Pitcairn,* ed. George Sewell, were advertised by Curll, Pemberton and Taylor in the same newspaper on 23 November 1714. Thacker's pamphlet is listed in the *Monthly Catalogue* for November 1714, printed for Roberts (again, an unreliable statement as regards the true instigator).

[40] It is equally characteristic of Whiston, that in advertising the new edition he stated that he was "desirous to call in" the first edition, and offered buyers who brought in the earlier version the new one at a price of 6d. rather than 1s.6d. – a sales ploy of Curllian ingenuity. See *Daily Courant,* 29 March 1716.

CHAPTER FOUR

"WHOLESOME COUNTRY AIR": RUSTIC EXILE IN POPE AND PUSHKIN

A poem by Pope which has lately risen in critical esteem is the *Epistle to Miss Blount, on her leaving the Town after the Coronation.* Written presumably in 1714, and first published in the *Works* of 1717, this was a comparatively neglected item in the canon until a generation ago. Recent commentators have remedied that situation, and now it ranks as one of the most exemplary cases among the shorter poems. However, we have missed the fact that the epistle stands at the head of a notable series of literary essays on the theme of the bored young person (generally a lady), condemned to frustration in a remote rural setting. On one level this is simply an inversion of traditional retirement poems, which celebrated the virtues of plain country living. The metropolis, commonly imaged as a scene of dissipation, here becomes an exciting alternative to the tedious routine of some provincial back-water. Here I shall attempt to set Pope's epistle in the context provided by a handful of later instances of what may be called the rustication topos. Brief parallels are provided by Johnson and (a real-life, rather than fictional, case) Mary Wollstonecraft. A much deeper mode of convergence can be seen in a poem by Pushkin, Зима ("Winter"), written in 1829. Despite the gap of a century, and the different national and cultural background of the two writers, an astonishing degree of similarity in theme, tone and poetic treatment should become apparent.[1]

I

Pope's epistle has now become sufficiently well known for an elaborate description to be unnecessary. In what follows, I shall draw attention directly to features of the poem that represent its mode of operation as a treatment of the rustication theme. But this does not mean that questions of artistic merit are entirely supplanted: for the characteristic slant which Pope gives the material is naturally defined by those qualities of tone, diction and metrics which figure so largely in his poetic workmanship.[2]

One of the most significant aspects of the epistle lies in its construction by means of five verse paragraphs, fairly even in length and almost stanza-like in form. In his familiar manner, Pope traverses large tracts of emotional space in these five sections, modulating from whimsy to tenderness, from bluff humour meditative introspection. Usually the rustication topos includes some element of comedy, but Pope is driven to portray the girl at the centre of the poem with some sympathy, and his delicate shift from satire to inward self-communion mirrors a process clearly visible in *The Rape of the Lock,* whose five-canto version is nearly contemporaneous. In the opening paragraph we approach the world of Restoration comedy, and though the heroine is designated "Zephalinda" (a word obviously suggestive of high romance on the seventeenth-century model), the initial impression we are given is closer to that of an *ingénue* in Congreve, perhaps some town-girl reversing Miss Prue's journey to London.

The very first couplet suggests the dependence and obligation bound up in the young lady's situation:

As some fond virgin, whom her mother's care
Drags from the town, to wholsom country air. . .   (1-2)

As a leading strategy of the poem, Pope subverts the Augustan manuals of health-care, and jokingly associates their positives (avoidance of stress, spartan diet, regular hours, and so on) with all that is most tedious to a lively young girl. For Zephalinda, the art of preserving health means banishment to a rural backwater, with a total absence of worthwhile social contact — and above all sexual contact. Zephalinda's newly learnt attributes of "roll[ing] a melting eye" and attracting a "spark" will go to waste in the all too "wholsom" atmosphere of the country retreat. The play on "wholsom" makes this point without delay; the young lady is dispatched to the country for reasons that are putatively medicinal, but the real effect is to consign her to a safer environment where the dangers of an amorous contagion are removed.

Pope draws this contrast between the tedium of the countryside and the exciting urban world she has lost most explicitly in the second paragraph. Instead of opera, assembly, playhouse and park, Zephalinda finds herself confined to insipid round of predictable activities:

She went, to plain-work, and to purling brooks,
Old-fashion'd halls, dull aunts, and croaking rooks...
                                                        (11-12)

The epithets in the second line here are more or less transferrable. A middle-aged, spinsterly routine is imposed by tiresome relatives — one can imagine the fine young lady of Swift's *Polite Conversation* mouthing clichés to point up the futility of such an existence. The new regime consists of walks, prayers, reading, and tea-drinking (expressed in a characteristic zeugma in line 15). Zephalinda is reduced to unstimulating beverages like tea and coffee. Not surprisingly, as Pope expresses it in a wonderfully drawn out and tongue-twisting line, she is brought in her disappointment and distraction to a trance-like state — "Or o'er cold coffee trifle with a spoon" (17). She watches the interminable progress of the clock hand as it arrives at the biggest event of the day so far, dinner at twelve noon precisely. Then the long afternoon, until final release in the evening — "Up to her godly garret after sev'n" (21), where godliness is next to incarceration.

In the third paragraph Pope introduces a more robust note with the entry of a booby squire, as a pathetic substitute for the sophisticated men about town who have "squired" the girl in more interesting ways. This hearty bumpkin "visits with a gun", and thinks the most endearing gesture he can perform for a young lady is to present her with dead birds that he has shot. His coarseness emerges when he chooses to bring his hounds into the drawing room (they are easier for him to view with affection than a girl, perhaps), as well as his clumsy love-making with "nods, and knees beneath a table". In his archetypal English way, he thinks that fine words are too fancy for a sturdy young fellow like himself, not suspecting that pretty speeches are exactly what poor Zephalinda would most like. Horsey, insensitive, smelling of the field, he represents in his own person many of the unattractive features of country living which she has come to dread. A few touches recall the rumbustious young fools in Jane Austen, such as Tom Bertram, or even some older (and nicer) buffoon such as Sir John Middleton. Here, the squire's very lack of sexual danger forms part of his unacceptability. Boorish manners of this kind are simply an expression of the loss of civility which Zephalinda must endure on her translation from urban society. Pope himself obviously did not locate virtue in metropolitan surroundings in so callow a fashion, but at some level he certainly understood the sense of deprivation which total immersion in plain-living country society could bring to a sophisticated young lady from the world of the court and the city.

The fourth paragraph takes us away from the rural scene, at least in the imagination of the heroine (now addressed directly in the second person, but still recognizably the same figure as Zephalinda). Picturing in her mind "Coronations. . . on ev'ry green", she transforms her hated surroundings into a backcloth for courtly doings, with a variety of grandees (all, once more, male) passing before her eyes as in some splendid ceremony. But the vision is soon dispelled: the coronets and sceptres vanish, and "leave you in lone woods, or empty walls" (40). Again the epithets could be transferred without loss of meaning. It requires no advanced semiological exercise to discover that the life of the town signifies sexuality and fulfilment, as well as just pleasure; the language applied to the rural world is drawn from the discourse of duty, self-abnegation, moral improvement and (comically viewed, but as in the case of Belinda seen by Pope as a truly fraught concept) chastity.

The poet employs another favourite strategy in the last paragraph, where he shifts to a more personal mode. Back in the town, he acts in a directly contrary fashion to Zephalinda, musing on his mistress in the country, with her "sprightly eyes", whilst surrounded by the bric-à-brac of city life – "Streets, chairs, and coxcombs rush upon my sight." In one way this mirror-image effect works to support Zephalinda's dreams, confirming the potency of the imagination and the irrelevance of one's surroundings. Yet, in a different way, the contrast also serves to point up the absurdity of her visions, since it inescapably suggests that her fine ideas of town-life are all ultimately based on illusion. London is not just coronations; there is noise and bustle, and the attractive "sparks" are perhaps really unappealing coxcombs after all. Even in the midst of all the ceaseless activity of the urban streets, the poet finds himself abstracted and uneasy: _ to this extent, Zephalinda's vision of high urban living is falsified by the closing lines of the epistle. The poem simultaneously underwrites her fantasies and controverts their validity. For Pope, the fears of all too blameless country existence are understandable, and yet at the same time preposterous or risible.

Not many dispute the fact that Pope had great sensitivity towards the interests of women, though the depth of his insight is highly controversial. A number of letters reflect his characteristic concerns in this area, most obviously those written in the early years of the Hanoverian regime, when Pope along with the Blount sisters moved in a circle of bright young things in and around the royal household. A letter that he wrote to the sisters in September 1717 comically reduces George I's court to the level of "a lone House in Wales." Suggestively the passage deals with boredom, social deprivation and isolation, all viewed from the perspective of a young woman.

> We all agreed that the life of a Maid of Honor was of all things the most miserable: & wished that every Woman who envy'd it had a Specimen of it. To eat Westphalia Ham in a morning, ride over Hedges &

ditches on borrowed Hacks, come home in the heat of the day with a
Feavor, & what is worse a hundred times, a red Mark in the forehead with
a Beaver hatt; all this may qualify them to make excellent Wives for Fox-
hunters, and bear abundance of ruddy-complexion'd Children. As soon as
they can wipe off the Sweat of the day, they must simper an hour, & catch
cold, in the Princesses apartment; from thence *To Dinner, with what
appetite they may* - And after that, till midnight, walk work, or think,
which they please? I can easily believe, no lone House in Wales, with a
Mountain and a Rookery, is more contemplative than this Court; and as a
proof of it I need only tell you Mrs Lepell walk'd all alone with me three
or four hours, by moonlight; and we mett no Creature of any quality, but
the King, who gave audience all alone to the Vice-chamberlen, under the
Garden-wall.

In short, I heard of no Ball, Assembly, Basset-Table, or any place
where two or three were gather'd together, except Mad. Kilmanzech's, to
which I had the honour to be invited, and the grace to stay away.

(Pope *Corr*, 1: 427)

Here feelings of affection, pity, and perhaps envy, mingle; but there are
also the comic reversals or correlatives of such feelings. As with the
epistle, we find Pope bantering on a subject which yet calls out some of
his deepest sympathies. It is hardly a proof of social ostracism to meet
with only one person on an evening walk, if that person happens to be the
sovereign of the realm, giving audience to a high official at court.
Nevertheless, Pope's capacity to imagine is what is at issue here; and to be
able to take on the imaginary sufferings of the spoilt and under-employed
maid of honour is itself a clue to his own psychological make-up. The
ennui of physically healthy and active people is tantalizing to a crippled
invalid; just as the equivocal "maiden" status of these young ladies could
not fail to preoccupy a man who was debarred from normal sexual
expression. In the situation of women, as in those of Belinda or
Zephalinda, Pope evidently found much that reflected on his own
condition.

II

One of the bright young ladies whom Pope came to know best as he
approached thirty was Lady Mary Wortley Montagu. She herself revised
an older poem on the very subject under consideration here. "The Bride in
the Country" deals with a girl dispatched to a secluded rural home with a
bumpkin tor a husband. Lady Mary had known isolation in her youth at
Thoresby, and had experienced marriage to a tedious and limited husband.
But autobiography is not particularly relevant: the rustication motif had

developed its own impetus, and poems with titles like "On Miss ——'s Retirement into the Country" often appear in the magazines. Charlotte Lennox's quixotic heroine ponders the restrictions that are (but maybe should not be) imposed by secluded living in a remote spot: "The perfect Retirement she lived in, afforded indeed no Opportunities of making the Conquests she desired; but she could not comprehend, how any Solitude could be obscure enough to conceal a Beauty like hers." Arabella is a descendant of Zephalinda, and differs chiefly in that her addiction to books has caused her to pine for the knights errant of romance, rather than the gartered earls of court pageantry.[3]

Another notable woman of letters, Elizabeth Montagu, provides different evidence. Her father was in the habit of breaking out in exclamations against the country, and declared that living there was tantamount to sleeping with one's eyes open. Elizabeth herself encountered a real-life version of Zephalinda's "old-fashion'd halls". As an eligible young woman she spent some time in Kent, where she found the available suitors to be no better than dull and boorish clods. As her biographer comments, "their scarlet waistcoats did not impress her like Mr Lyttelton's birthday suit" (i.e. court dress). She was not to be won by some foxhunting clown. In fact, she married a man who was many ".ears her senior, and who led a sedentary life, his prime addiction being the study of mathematics. A person who was later to cross swords with Mrs Montagu, that is James Boswell, devoted three numbers of his periodical *The Hypochondriack* (September to November 1780) to the limited pleasures, as he saw it, afforded by country life, though Boswell is thinking about the lack of stimulation he himself experienced, rather than the deprivations peculiar to a young lady.[4]

The case is different with Boswell's own lodestar, Samuel Johnson. Three *Rambler* papers from the late summer of 1750 bear directly on our theme here. Two letters from Euphelia and one from Cornelia variously approach the rustication motif. The fullest presentation of the issues comes in the earliest of the three, that is *Rambler* no. 42, whilst Euphelia continues her narrative in no. 46 ("While I am thus employed, some tedious hours will slip away, and when I return to watch the clock, I shall find that I have disburdened myself of part of the day"). Finally, in no. 51 Cornelia gives a slightly different view of the retired life.[5]

In the first of these papers, Johnson writes in the person of a young lady "bred . . . in a perpetual tumult of pleasure", who has grown accustomed to a round of visits, play-houses, balls, masquerades and the like. She is well educated in fashionable dress and in the decorum of the card table. Finally, at the age of twenty-two, she is sent off to pass the summer with "a rich aunt in a remote country" (aunts, in this tradition, are synonomous with a backwater existence). Euphelia's hopes are initially high, since she has imbibed unrealistic ideas from literature— but disillusion is soon to overcome these expectations:

> I will confess to you, without restraint, that I had suffered my head to be filled with expectations of some nameless pleasure in a rural life, and that I hoped for the happy hour that should set me free from noise, and flutter, and ceremony, dismiss me to the peaceful shade, and lull me in content and tranquillity. To solace myself under the misery of delay, I sometimes heard a studious lady of my acquaintance read pastorals, I was delighted with scarce any talk but of leaving the town, and never went to bed without dreaming of groves, and meadows, and frisking lambs.
>
> At length I had all my cloaths in a trunk, and saw the coach at the door; I sprung in with ecstasy, quarrelled with my maid for being too long in taking leave of the other servants, and rejoiced as the ground grew less which lay between me and the completion of my wishes. A few days brought me to a large old house, encompassed on three sides with woody hills, and looking from the front on a gentle river, the sight of which renewed all my expectations of pleasure, and gave me some regret for having lived so long without the enjoyment which these delightful scenes were now to afford me. My aunt came out to receive me, but in a dress so far removed from the present fashion, that 1 could scarcely look upon her without laughter, which would have been no kind requital for the trouble which she had take to make herself fine against my arrival. The night and the next morning were driven along with enquiries about our family; my aunt then explained our pedigree, and told me stories of my great grandfather's bravery in the civil wars, nor was it less than three days before I could persuade her to leave me to myself.

As time passes, things get worse rather than better:

> At last oeconomy prevailed, she went in the usual manner about her own affairs, and I was at liberty to range in the wilderness, and sit by the cascade. The novelty of the objects about me pleased me for a while, but after a few days they were new no longer, and I soon began to perceive that the country was not my element; that shades, and flowers, and lawns, and waters, had very soon exhausted all their power of pleasing, and that I had not in myself any fund of satisfaction with which I could supply the loss of my customary amusements.
>
> I unhappily told my aunt, in the first warmth of our embraces, that I had leave to stay with her ten weeks. Six only are yet gone, and how shall I live through the remaining four? I go out and return; I pluck a flower, and throw it away; I catch an insect, and when I have examined its colours, set it at liberty; I fling a pebble into the water, and see one circle spread after

another. When it chances to rain, I walk in the great hail, and watch the
minute-hand upon the dial, or play with a litter of kittens, which the cat
happens to have brought in a lucky time.

My aunt is afraid I shall grow melancholy, and therefore encourages
the neighbouring gentry to visit us. They came at first with great eagerness
to see the fine lady from London, but when we met, we had no common
topick on which we could converse; they had no curiosity after plays,
operas, or musick: and I find as little satisfaction from their accounts of the
quarrels, or alliances of families, whose names, when once I can escape, I
shall never hear. The women have now seen me, know how my gown is
made, and are satisfied; the men are generally afraid of me and say little
because they think themselves not at liberty to talk rudely.

Thus am I condemned to solitude; the day moves slowly forward, and I
see the dawn with uneasiness, because I consider that night is at a great
distance. I have tried to sleep by a brook, but find its murmurs ineffectual;
so that I am forced to be awake at least twelve hours, without visits,
without cards, without laughter, and without flattery. I walk because I am
disgusted with sitting still, and sit down because I am weary with walking.
I have no motive to action, nor any object of love, or hate, or fear, or
inclination. I cannot dress with spirit, for I have neither rival nor admirer. I
cannot dance without a partner, nor be kind, or cruel, without a lover.

"Such is the life of Euphelia", we are told, and the letter ends with a plea
for sympathy and guidance:

> I shall therefore think you a benefactor to our sex, if you will teach me the
> art of living alone; for I am confident that a thousand and a thousand and a
> thousand ladies, who affect to talk with ecstacies of the pleasures of the
> country, are in reality, like me, longing for the winter, and wishing to be
> delivered from themselves by company and diversion.

Euphelia is cousin to Charlotte Lennox's heroine, Arabella, in *The Female
Quixote,* and of course we are reminded of the "glimpse of pastoral life" in
chapter 19 of *Rasselas,* where the false expectations induced by literary
pastoralism are exposed to merciless gaze. However, the closest analogue
is with Zephalinda, and in this instance we may reasonably suspect a line
of direct influence. Johnson would certainly have known the epistle, and
his *Rambler* paper may be seen as an extended paraphrase of the earlier
work, with terse Popean phrases such as "dull aunts" or "purling brooks"
subjected to comic amplification. It is one of the most brilliant literary
renditions of the topos, even though its tone is more distant than that of
Pope —Johnson assuredly shared in some of Euphelia's distaste for a
vacant life, but he does not allow his own feelings to enter the text as
Pope's do in the epistle.

A final English example takes us back to real life, rather than fictional expressions of the theme, The passage in question occurs in a letter from Mary Wollstonecraft in November 1786, written when she was serving unhappily as a governess in deepest County Cork. She reported gloomily to her sister Everina on her nervous irritability, caused by the uncongenial way of life in a remote district, where her employer Lady Kingsborough oppressed her with pet-dogs and empty talk. But the real Mary secretly rebels as she pretends to comply:

> I am almost tormented to death by dogs — But you will perceive I am not under the influence of my darling passion pity; it is not always so, I make allowance - and *adapt* myself— talk of getting husbands for the *Ladies* — and the *dogs* — and am wonderfully entertaining and then I retire to my room, form figures in the fire, listen to the wind or view the Galties a fine range of mountains near us — and so does time *waste* away in apathy or misery — I would not write thus to Eliza — she cannot discriminate; but to you I *cannot* be reserved — and I hope the dreadful contagion will not infect you — I am thought to have an angelick temper.

This is the first fully serious passage on the theme which we have encountered, and we might feel some embarrassment about permitting its inclusion in the tradition at all. But the phrasing approaches Pope's so closely when Mary speaks of "form[ing] figures in the fire" that we are led to observe the parallels with the literary topos, however they may be transmuted by the anguish Wollstonecraft felt. Taken as a whole, her letter provides a nonfictional control by which we may gauge the development of the rustication motif in fictional contexts. The "boisterous spirits and unmeaning laughter" of Mary's companions represent what was possibly a more actual threat than the hallooing and nudging of a clumsy squire. The comparative refinement of Lady Kingsborough's family embodies a shift in social history; the new boors, at the end of the eighteenth century, are as likely to have read a few books as to have learned plain-work, even though their chief topics of conversation remain "matrimony and dress".[6]

III

Pushkin's poem dates from November 1829, when he paid a visit to friends in the country. It is not among his best-known works, either in Russia or in this country, but A.D.P. Briggs has made an excellent case for seeing the work as a highly representative item in the canon:

If the formal characteristics of this poem may be taken as typical of Pushkin's method, it is no less true that the content reflects a number of familiar Pushkinian preoccupations and attitudes. The naturalistic, detailed description of country life, thoughts about the distractions available for bored people, the consolation provided by literature, the processes of poetic inspiration, the transcendent excitement of erotic adventures, the deep integration of the poem into actual events of the poet's life and its lightly mocking general tone — all of these salient characteristics of "Zima. . .", here presented in encapsulated form, are to be found widely dispersed and embellished throughout the whole body of Pushkin's lyric and other poetry. It may safely be said, in fact, that few other poems encompass such a broad range of the poet's main ideas.[7]

It is astonishing how much of this applies directly to Pope's epistle. We do not find much in the way of detailed or naturalistic description in Pope; literary consolations are only very obliquely contemplated, whilst any reference to Pope's own life at the close of the epistle is playful and teasing. Nevertheless, as Briggs shows in his close analysis of *Zima*, the central concern of Pushkin's composition is very nearly allied, the tone is instantly recognizable, and the local strategies again and again are reminiscent of Pope. The most obvious distinction lies in the narrative stance, for Pushkin writes in the first person, and experiences boredom rather than observing it. In practice this is not so important a difference as we might expect.

Pushkin begins with a one-word sentence, followed by a mock-petulant question.— "Зима. Что делать нам в деревне?", that is "Winter. What is there for us to do in the country?" The narrator is brought an early-morning cup of tea by a servant, and bombards him with questions. Is it worth getting up to ride, or would it be better to pass the time until lunch dragging one's way through old magazines left by a neighbour? (As with Zephalinda, mealtimes are an oasis in the desert of tedium.) The members of the house-party decide to go hunting, but without success. There follows a cacophonous, spluttering line, "Kuda kak veselo! Vot vecher: v'yuga voyet" (What fun! Now it is evening; the blizzard howls). As Briggs puts it, the line "possesses an abecedarian clumsiness that seems unbelievable in such an accomplished versifier". This "over-emphatic alliteration" is used, the critic argues, to bring out "the deadening dullness of empty country life [which] is about to descend once more". Such techniques are the more attainable because of Pushkin's choice of the dignified iambic hexameter as his verse-form: the potential tedium of the long line is apt to his purposes. Other verses (lines 15, 22, 29) exploit this potential. The second of these actually expresses an idea very close to Pope's "needless Alexandrine" (a point Briggs does not overlook): "The verse crawls lamely along, foggy and frigid". "It is another distinguishing feature of Pushkin's work", remarks Briggs, "that he is attracted to the depiction of different moods in quick succession and has a particular facility for easy modulation from one to the next", as at line 83 (pp. 35-6). It needs no emphasis that such transitions in mood are central to Pope's purposes in his epistle.

The narrator tries to read in order to allay his boredom, but he is unable to concentrate; he closes the book, seeks to write with no more success, and goes into the adjoining room. There he finds a conversation in progress on banal local topics. His hostess is knitting away with sour attention, or turns to the cards for a little fortune-telling (not much more promising than the squire's "Whisk"). The poet's feelings burst forth at line 29: "Toska! Tak den' za dnem idet v uyedinenii" (What sheer pain! So it goes day after day, out in this total isolation). The Russian word *uyedinenii,* literally solitude or seclusion, can have a more favourable overtone of "retirement": but that is of course an irony inherent in Pope's epistle too, for to withdraw as Zephalinda does from the bustle of the city was the gesture of many an Horatian versifier in the eighteenth century. Both poets achieve part of their effect by silent refutation of conventional wisdom concerning the benefits of retirement.

There is a major shift in *Zima* at this point. Indicatively the new scene is incorporated in an "if" clause, much as Pope wraps up his message within a putative simile: "But if in the sad village as evening comes on and I sit in a corner over the draughts board, a coach or a sleigh should unexpectedly arrive with a family from far off. . ." Then a new burst of social activity will begin, all the more vivid by contrast — again the dialectic is parallel with the court/ country opposition of Pope's epistle. Above all, there is a promise of sexual intrigue: at first lingering but oblique glances, then a few hesitant words, developing into freer conversation, laughter and songs; ultimately lively waltzes, a whisper at the table, languorous gazes, light-hearted badinage, a chance to prolong encounters on the narrow staircase. This is the kind of social and sexual round which Zephalinda dreams of when she is deprived of city life; put otherwise, it is the sort of courtship which the squire's behaviour crudely parodies. Pushkin has brought this world of amenity brought into his rural retreat at the climax of his poem; a reversal, as Pope's ending had been, but executed in a different direction. *Zima* ends in a mysterious way, its last line unrhymed as the couplet is left suspended halfway through its course; where Pope brings us a tantalizing hint of sexual desire, apparently unfulfilled, in his concluding paragraph, Pushkin suggests consummation without any explicit reference: "How cool and crisp is the Russian girl, dusted with the snows [of her country]."

There is much in Briggs's thoughtful reading of the poem which helps to explain Pushkin's, as it were unconscious, absorption of an English topos. The critic sees Pushkin's treatment of the "patrician" form of the alexandrine as exemplifying the writer's "attitude to inherited literary canons, an attitude nicely summed up by [A. Tertz (Sinyavsky)] as follows: "Pushkin did not develop and extend tradition, he teased it, lapsing at every end and turn into parody" (p. 31). Literary parody generally involves playful treatment of conventional postures, more widely defined, and the congruities between two poets at either end of Europe, a century apart, reflect their similar response towards conventionality in behaviour and in poetic idiom. The most immediately striking resemblances concern small details of observation, closely allied minutiae of country life: the obligatory teacup, the somnolent pose, the silent lovemaking, the waiting for an appointed mealtime. However, a deeper level of imaginative convergence is apparent in the way that each writer exploits poetic form (locally, rhythm and syntax, deliberate cacophony; more broadly, verse- paragraphs which are typographically visible in Pope but not in Pushkin). Briggs speaks of the Russian poet's "unique capacity in versification for the exact attunement of ends and means" (p. 33). Perhaps "unique" is too strong, even if we grant Pushkin greater eminence overall: for the epistle shows Pope in his most virtuosic manner, notably in the second paragraph. His elision of strong active verbs in lines 15-22, with its emphasis on directionless and almost somnambulistic infinitives, until even these disappear and are replaced by prepositions as the only agent of motion — this is all in the vein of Pushkin. Both poets use clear and almost conversational language, interspersed with recollections of higher literary pretension: romance, epic, noble Horatian acts of renunciation. Both dramatize contrasts through stylistic means; both convey the *frisson* of sexual excitement through hints and gestures rather than explicit narrative. Above all, each poem conveys a sense of expectancy amid the boredom, and manages to make the subject of dullness an object of intense imaginative vitality.

The topos which we traced first in Pope finds echoes and transpositions in Johnson and Mary Wollstonecraft among others; but its more richly suggestive implications lie dormant until we reach Pushkin, an even greater poet but one who could not have read Pope's original. Finally, it is the most surprising testimony to the enduring centrality of Pope in European literature that his little drama of rustication should have been replayed, with so many nuances still precisely in place, at such another time, in such another place by such another author.

Notes

[1] I am grateful to Professor Tony Briggs for his advice not only on Pushkin but also on the convergences with, and divergences from, Pope's epistle.

[2] The text follows *TE* 6: 124-7.

[3] Jonathan Curling, *Edward Wortley Montague 1713-1776* (London: Andrew Melrose, 1954), p. 15; Charlotte Lennox, *The Female Quixote,* ed. Margaret Dalziel (London: Oxford University Press, 1970), p. 7.

[4] Dr [John] Doran, *A Lady of the Last Century* (London: Richard Bentley, 1873), p. 15; James Boswell, *The Hypochondriack,*ed. Margery Bailey (Palo Alto, CA: Stanford University Press, 1928), 2: 15-28.

[5] Samuel Johnson, *The Rambler,* ed. W.J. Bate and A. B. Strauss, in *The Yale Edition of the Works of Samuel Johnson* (New Haven: Yale University Press, 1969) 3: 229-31, 247-52, 273-9.

[6] *The Collected Letters of Mary Wollstonecraft,* ed. Janet Todd (New York: Columbia University Press, 2003), p. 91.

[7] A.D.P. Briggs, "An Approach to Pushkin through One Poem" in *Alexander Pushkin: A Critical Study* (London: Croom Helm, 1983), pp. 27-43; quotation from p. 37.

CHAPTER FIVE

WHY *TRIVIA*?
MYTH, ETYMOLOGY, AND TOPOGRAPHY

John Gay's *Trivia* is generally regarded as the outstanding English poem in its genre, that is the mock-classical vein of urban pastoral or "town eclogue." This mode had been recently developed in some short pieces in verse by Jonathan Swift, most famously the *Description of a City Shower.* At the start of 1716, *Trivia* came out in three books with the sub-title "The Art of Walking the Streets of London." As that formula suggests, the work extends this new form by drawing on other models notably the didactic element in the *Georgics* of Virgil, which coalesced with the ancient "Ars" or how-to-do-it poem. The opening lines of the first book, moreover, supply something not far short of an epic proposition and invocation:

> Through Winter Streets to steer your Course aright,
> How to walk clean by Day, and safe by Night,
> How jostling Crouds, with Prudence to decline,
> When to assert the Wall, and when resign,
> I sing: Thou, *Trivia*, Goddess, aid my Song,
> Thro' spacious Streets conduct thy Bard along;
> By thee transported, I securely stray
> Where winding Alleys lead the doubtful way,
> The silent Court, and op'ning Square explore,
> And long perplexing Lanes untrod before.
>
> (1: 1-10)

These lines suggest that Gay's parody of the stylistic gestures of classical verse is overt and uncomplicated. Very much the same technique can be seen in later passages, too, such as this:

> Yet let me not descend to trivial Song,
> Nor vulgar Circumstance my Verse prolong;
> Why should I teach the Maid when Torrents pour,
> Her Head to shelter from the sudden Show'r?

Nature will best her ready Hand inform,
With her spread Petticoat to fence the Storm.
Does not each Walker know the warning Sign,
When wisps of straw depend upon the twine
Cross the close Street; that then the Paver's Art
Renews the ways, deny'd to Coach and Cart?

(2: 301-10)

At the same time Gay enlists other motifs of ancient poetry, for example an aetiological digression in Book 1. This explains how pattens (clogs or over-shoes) came into use, by means of an extended narrative of the apparition of Vulcan to a maiden called Patty: "Say from what Art Divine th' Invention came, / And from its Origine deduce the Name" (1: 221-2).

Trivia has attracted a respectable amount of commentary, appropriate perhaps to its status as a minor classic. Much of this work has addressed the relation of the poem to its ostensible model, the *Georgics*.[1] However, virtually nothing seems to have been said about the choice of a title, or the implications of this for the work as a whole. The fullest explanation was given by the editors of Gay's *Poetry and Prose*:

> *Trivia* means streets and was probably chosen over the other Latin words with the same meaning because there was a Roman goddess Trivia who could be invoked as patroness of the poem. In fact Trivia was not the goddess of streets and highways as Gay pretends (see his Index s.v. *Trivia*), but a name for the three-bodied or three-headed goddess Hecate. Gay makes nothing of the sinister associations of Hecate, who was seen at road junctions at night accompanied by demons, or of the road junction (the root meaning of *trivia*) where Oedipus killed his father, though he uses Oedipus as a hyperbolic example of the dangers of quarreling for the wall on rainy nights (III. 213-24).[2]

This certainly marks an advance on what W.H. Williams had written in his edition of the poem: "The title *Trivia* is probably not intended to be the name of the goddess, but the plural of *Trivium,* 'a place where three roads meet,' commonly used in Latin in the plural, with the meaning 'public streets,' as in Horace, *Ars Poetica*, 245, *innati triviis ac paene forenses.*"[3] To this we might add a single sentence in an essay by Martin C. Battestin, which states that the poem takes its title from "the Roman name for Diana or Hecate," and that it is Trivia, "goddess both of virgin forests and of the underworld" whom Gay invites to conduct us in Virgilian fashion "through the regions of Dis."[4]

All these commentaries seem to me to mention some relevant facts, but to miss much of the point. The editors, Dearing and Beckwith, omit all reference to Diana; while Williams is surely wrong to dismiss the presence of the goddess entirely. After all, Gay placed two entries for Trivia in the index to his poem: the first refers to Book 1 and reads, "the Goddess of Street and High-Ways, invok'd," while the second relates to Book 3, and reads, "*Trivia* invok'd as *Cynthia.*" Battestin labours to be brief and confuses some of the issues, even though his invocation of the underworld is suggestive. To get at the overtones of the name, we need to consider aspects of myth and etymology. It is logical to start with the mythical roots.

I

The name Trivia did indeed serve as an epithet for the Greek deity Hecate, perhaps an earth-goddess in origin, who was mentioned by Hesiod among others.[5] She became associated with the world of the dead, and one incarnation identified her with Persephone/Proserpina in the infernal regions. But her threefold nature, adumbrated in the name, allowed her to be seen also as Selene/Luna in the heavens, and Artemis/Diana on earth. This identification would be most familiar to classically trained readers of Gay's time through a line in the fourth book of the *Aeneid*, where the abandoned Dido lights her funeral pyre. The attendant priestess invokes three hundred deities of night, including "tergeminam Hecaten, tria virginis ora Dianae" (threefold Hecate, the triple faces of the virgin Diana).[6] Such obsessive use of triads is common in rites of conjuration, which is much what Dido performs. As *The Magic Flute* reminds us, it is also central to masonic ritual: indeed handbooks of freemasonry made much of the threefold goddess.[7] At the start of Gay's poem then, the muse (herself one of a group of three times three) is stationed at the head of a three-part structure. Book 1 leads us into the city, as a visitor would approach it, a movement confirmed by the title-page epigraph.[8] Books 2 and 3 then branch out in alternative directions, that is "walking the streets" either by day or by night.

Hecate was known sometimes as the Artemis of the cross-roads, since her cult flourished at such junctions. Here sacrifices were made to the goddess, and propitiatory gifts left. (Ovid touches on this in the *Fasti*, 1: 389). She was portrayed with three faces, and statues with a triangular aspect were set up at the ritual sites. Both Greeks and Romans regarded her with fear, and declined to confront her face to face. At night she haunted graveyards and the scenes of crimes, particularly murders - some believed that she might drink the blood of the victim. The adjectives describing her attributes in Latin, *Diva triformis/ tergenia/ triplex/ triceps,* explain how Trivia might have been assimilated into her cult. In the case of the last epithet, the three heads would be those of Proserpina, Luna and Diana: see Ovid, *Metamorphoses* 7: 194, as well as Horace, *Odes*, 3. xxii: 4, a short poem addressed to Diana.

When the name Trivia began to be used of Diana, it was clearly with a recollection of her kinship with Hecate under one aspect. Virgil employs this form several more times in the *Aeneid*, including three places in Book 6: this was a section of the poem always strongly present in the mind of the Scriblerian satirists, and universally familiar to an educated audience. Equally, Ovid alludes to Diana as Trivia at the start of the Callisto episode in the *Metamorphoses* (2: 416). Thus Diana as goddess of the forests would be available to Gay when he used the name, but Battestin does not explain why this might be an apt mythological association.

Let us now turn to the lexical issues. The common noun *trivium* in classical Latin meant originally a crossroads, and then the public highway, and was most often used in the plural: thus Horace employs it in a passage on a cheating beggar (*Epistles* 1.xvii: 58), which is recalled in *Trivia* 2: 137-8. Virgil uses the noun in a literal, but also punning, sense in *Aeneid,* 4: 609: "nocturnisque Hecate triviis ululata per urbes," that is "(the name of) Hecate, screeched out in the city streets by night." This has obvious connections with the "motto" which Gay places at the end of his Advertisement, taken from Virgil's *Eclogues* 3: 26-7: "Non tu in triviis, indocte, solebas / stridenti miserum stipula disperdere carmen?" (Was it not your inept way to ruin some pathetic song at the cross-roads with a grating pipe?) This is part of the verbal battle prior to a song contest. Gay applies the allusion to potential critics, who "will so far continue [their] Favour" as to write against the poem. By doing so he casts his detractors as incompetent balladeers or buskers, who produce a debased street music. What this indicates is that a sense "some insignificant items" for the plural would not be possible. The only cognate form in Latin with the required overtones was an adjective *trivialis*, meaning "of the streets" and hence vulgar or ordinary. In English, the usage "trivia" to indicate unimportant facts did not evolve until the twentieth century: and it was not until the late 1960s that a quiz game emerged which helped to inspire expressions such as "football trivia," as well as the allied form "trivial pursuit." It is true that the modern adjectival sense of "trivial" had entered English centuries earlier, and was employed by Thomas Nashe among others. That it existed in 1716 and was familiar to readers in Gay's audience is of course established by a single line in a recent poem by his friend Alexander Pope: "What mighty contests spring from trivial things" (*The Rape of the Lock* 1:

2). In fact Gay uses it himself: "Yet let me not descend to trivial Song, /Nor vulgar Circumstance my Verse prolong" (2: 301-02).[9]

This analysis shows that there was no common noun *trivia* in either Latin or English which could precisely mean what we have in mind when we employ the word today. Naturally, the proximity of the adjective derived from the root noun would allow Gay to introduce a pleasing equivocation; but he selected his title as a more than a simple denotative label. Pursuing the etymological, rather than mythical, side of the issue, we can observe that crossroads are indeed an apt emblem of the poem's action, or much of it: junctions which the pedestrian has to negotiate, and choices which have to be made between courses to follow and those to avoid. The more literal sense is supported by a reference in Gay's work to Seven Dials, in the neighborhood of St Martin's Lane and Long Acre:

> Where fam'd Saint *Giles*'s ancient limits spread
> An inrail'd Column rears its lofty Head,
> Here to sev'n Streets, sev'n Dials count the Day,
> And from each other catch the circling Ray.
>
> (2: 73-6)

This reads almost like an onomastic riddle, or one of Wordsworth's "Poems on the Naming of Places." The underlying fact is that a Doric column was erected at this spot with a sun-dial on each of its seven faces, pointing towards the seven streets which met here in a star formation. A third element, that is topography, now enters the picture.[10]

II

In ancient times, as we have seen, Trivia was worshipped at such a junction, with a three-faced statue to mark the locality. Gay's contemporaries in London could readily have imagined this kind of tripartite construction, which might have been placed for example where the statue of Charles I commanded views down the Strand, along Cockspur Street and into Whitehall, as this was one of the "focal centres of London."[11] A contemporary description stated that "the open place usually called Charing Cross. . .is of a triangular form, having Pall Mall and the Haymarket on the north-west, the Strand on the east, and the street before Whitehall on the south."[12] It is at precisely this spot that the bootblack boy takes up his position in the long episode of Cloacina, which Gay added to the second edition in 1720. (Amusingly, he stands at the "frequented Corner" with a *tripod* as his stock in trade.)

> The Youth strait chose his Post: the Labour ply'd
> Where branching Streets from *Charing-cross* divide:
> His treble Voice resounds along the *Meuse*,
> And *White-hall* echoes - *Clean your Honour's shoes.*
>
> (2: 213-16)

Here, it could be argued, lay the crossroads of the capital.

That may appear simply a bad pun: but the connection looks rather less fortuitous if we remind ourselves of the buried history of the name. "Charing" comes from an Old English word meaning a turn or bend, and probably refers to "the well marked bend in the old main road from London to the west." The village grew up where the road to Westminster branched southward. As for the second element in the name, it "refers to an 'Eleanor Cross' (the last of twelve crosses set up in 1290 by Edward I at the places where his Queen's coffin rested on its journey from Harby in Nottinghamshire to Westminster Abbey.)"[13] The cross stood here until it was torn down by the populace during the Civil War as a relic of superstition. After the Restoration the statue of Charles I went up exactly where the cross had been, in an attempt to resacralize the spot. If any heathen deity could be thought a suitable guardian of these hallowed sites, it must surely be Hecate/Trivia, whose special terrain included roadside graves.

There is a deep poetic truth in Samuel Johnson's celebrated remark, "Why, Sir, Fleet-street has a very animated appearance; but I think the full tide of human existence is at Charing Cross."[14] The contrast lies between the single axis of Fleet Street, busy as it may be, with the more complex and varied locus which is Charing Cross. We must picture central London as it existed at the time. As yet there was no Trafalgar Square nearby, just as there was no Piccadilly Circus, Leicester Square or Oxford Circus. The nearest thing to a communal space, an agora or forum on the ancient model, was the crossroads, where various routes of the city - whether those of trade, entertainment, government or church - came together. Notably, the word *tide/s* occurs no less than nine times in Gay's poem. It is applied to crowds of people, and to the River Hebrus down which the head of Orpheus floated: but mostly it is used more literally of the currents of mud and sewage that coursed through London streets. All but one of the occurrences are found in Book 2, and the heaviest concentration appears in this same episode of Cloacina.[15] As the heroine of the most extended digression, she is termed the "Goddess of the Tide" (2: 115), and she serves as an apt deity for a poem in which the movement of dirt supplies an underlying energy system for the town, like some superhighway of liquid power. Much as in Swift's *Description of a City Shower* (one of the models from which Gay admitted taking "several Hints"), we see "Torrents rush from *Holborn*'s fatal Steep" (2: 174), with the refuse carried down a black canal of mud. Cloacina glides into the Fleet Ditch, and "shoots beneath the Tides" (2: 168). The tide of human existence flows here in some hidden and disconcerting channels.

In any case, *Trivia* often concerns itself with "branching streets," liminal areas where the topographic and social boundaries merge. One extensive passage directs a pedestrian who is confronted by the "Pass of St Clement," in more banal terms the place where St Clement Danes made an island within the paved way of the Strand. The wording might suggest historic sites such as the narrow defile of Thermopylae. Many passages focus on *crossings*, that is transitions from one setting to another, especially where it is potentially a movement from a secure to an insecure location: "Yet never stray / Where no rang'd Posts defend the rugged Way" (2: 227-8).[16] Moreover, Gay devotes paragraphs to "The danger of crossing a square by night" and to "crossing the street". These contain some early warnings on jaywalking, as well as a demonstration that the traffic gridlock already existed: "If Wheels bar up the Road, where Streets are crost, / With gentle Words the Coachman's ear accost" (2: 165-6).[17] At the same time these sections of the poem make it clear that to "cross" into some privileged areas like Lincoln's Inn Fields was to transgress the prudent limits of travel in London.[18] (We shall come back to this issue a little later.) For the unwary, sudden glimpses open up into an underworld, like the cave of Avernus sacred to Hecate: "Let not thy vent'rous Steps approach too nigh, /Where gaping wide, low steepy Cellars lie "(3: 121-1). Trivia alone can ensure safe passage:

> By thee transported, I securely stray
> Where winding Alleys lead the doubtful way.
> The silent Court, and op'ning Square explore,
> And long perplexing Lanes untrod before.

> (1: 7-10)

In addressing the goddess, Gay characterizes the streets, this early, as "thy Realm" (1: 11). Beyond this, Gay creates a reflexive play on his own desire "To tread in Paths to ancient Bards unknown" (1: 19), a verse which identifies the daring moves of the innovative author with the bold peregrinations of the walker.

Seven Dials remained notorious into Victorian times as the heart of a jumbled, rackety, crime-ridden district. Charles Dickens allots it a chapter in *Sketches by Boz*: "But what involutions can compare with those of Seven Dials? Where is there such another maze of streets, courts, lanes,

and alleys?" None of the seven roads converging here was a major
thoroughfare: six were distinguished by the word "Great" or "Little," but
the great were only relatively so. This made it a Spaghetti Junction of side-
streets, near the top of a three-sided area bordered by the Strand on the
south, St Martin's Lane on the west, and Drury Lane on the east. The apex
of this triangle lay near St Giles in the Fields church, while the base joined
Charing Cross and St Clement Danes. This area enclosed the main red-
light district of the city, with Covent Garden in the center. Here was a
diverse region of sex, commerce, markets, gambling, theatrical life, and
booksellers amongst much else, and this is the heart of the world described
in *Trivia*.[19] We have only to glance at a contemporary map of London to
see the acute angles formed by the courts, passages and alleys as they
abutted on one another in strange rhomboidal patterns.[20]

Aptly to the purpose, Gay's most famous work, *The Beggar's Opera*, a
decade later, made conspicuous reference to this part of the city. The play
opens with a prologue scene, and in its first very first speech the putative
author declares his local allegiance: "I own myself of the Company of
Beggars; and I make one at their weekly festivals at St Giles's." The joke
(not usually explained by editors) lies in the fact that St Giles was the
patron saint of outcasts, cripples and beggars. There had been a medieval
leper hospital here, dedicated to the saint, and founded by Queen Matilda
in the twelfth century, as "a sanctuary for the accommodation and
maintenance of forty of the stricken wretches." It was the queen who
started the custom of presenting "a cup of charity" to condemned prisoners
as they came up to St Giles: at one time the gallows were set up here, next
to the hospital wall, before they were moved to Tyburn. Then, in the
second act of the *Opera*, when the prostitutes need to assemble at the their
traditional home in the "hundreds of Drury," a messenger is sent "for one
in *Vinegar Yard* [at the back of the Theatre Royal] and for the rest of them
somewhere about *Lewkner's Lane*" - a notorious passage-way near the tip
of the triangle at Broad St Giles's. In Lewkenor's Lane, too, the model for
the thief-taker Peachum in Gay's *Opera*, Jonathan Wild, first set himself
up in London as a receiver and pimp, amid "gimcrack dram-shops,
brothels and night cellars that packed the Lane from end to end."[21] The
escape-artist Jack Sheppard, whose career is ironically echoed in
Macbeth's "breaks" from gaol, frequented a tavern in Lewkenor's Lane:
here he met his doxy Edgeworth Bess, and together they set up a brandy-
shop there. It was in the "receptacle of sharpers, pickpockets, and
strumpets" around Drury Lane that he led his pursuers a dance through a
tangle of narrow byways while on the run from Newgate.[22] After his
execution, Sheppard's body was taken to a tavern in Long Acre, and a

familiar Covent Garden riot started when locals heard a rumor that the surgeons had taken his cadaver. It was in St Giles's, too, that Mary Young, who became known as "Jenny Diver" (the name Gay uses for one of the women of the town), was initiated into the art of pickpocketing.

By the time of *The Beggar's Opera*, the quarter had lost further repute, and in the middle of the century came William Hogarth's *Gin Lane*, which most commentators situate here. "The scene is set in St. Giles where in 1750 every fourth house at least was a gin-shop. Its eighty-two 'two-penny houses' were also brothels of the lowest class and places for receiving goods."[23] If Hogarth were maintaining strict topographic accuracy (which is by no means always his habit), then the vista towards St George's Church, Bloomsbury would indicate that the setting must be placed near the apex of the triangle just described, and very close to Seven Dials. The way to the church is blocked off by a rough palisade of crossed timbers, recalling the obstructions which impede movement in *Trivia*. A likely site for the vantage-point is at the very top of Monmouth Street, which led up to St Giles's churchyard, skirting Seven Dials by a few yards. It was a center of the second-hand clothing trade, as *Trivia* reminds us: "*Moor-field* [yields] old Books; and *Monmouth-street* old Suits" (2: 548). One bizarre fact about Hogarth's portrayal of *Gin Lane* is that the most prominent symbol in the design is a pawnbroker's sign, appearing to crown the spire of St George's in the position where a cross should stand. This has been read by Ronald Paulson as representing a false Trinity; but the three brass balls make up one more grim triptych of urban semiology.[24]

Many of the problems in this quarter of the city arose from the fact that St Giles's was an out-parish, which belonged neither to the liberties of the City of London, nor to Westminster. "The poorest parts of eighteenth-century London - the dilapidated courts and alleys, the crumbling tenements and the dangerous districts - were chiefly in the belt which had grown up round the City between the reign of Elizabeth and the end of the seventeenth century." Here building codes were less stringently applied, and side-streets were no longer constructed at right angles to the thoroughfare, as in the old city. In this way evolved the characteristic cityscape described in *Trivia*:

> There were, . . .in densely populated districts, courts within courts, and alleys behind alleys forming perfect labyrinths and suggesting by their ground plan that closes and yards had been progressively and in a haphazard way covered with buildings. Such buildings were often mere encroachments. Even the thoroughfares were encroached upon. A temporary stall or shed would imperceptibly grow into a permanent building.

Gay actually refers to the manner in which "encroachments" occur, though his first example relates to the construction of St Clement's Danes church,

> Whose straiten'd Bounds encroach upon the *Strand*;
> Where the low Penthouse bows the Walker's Head.

(3: 18-19)

Another aspect of the problem related to the overcrowding that came with heavy migration, both internal and external, and thence to ever-present sanitary difficulties. When the plague threatened to return to London in 1720, the graveyard of St Andrew's, at the other end of Holborn, was closed by order of the privy council, so offensive had it become. One year later a report drew attention to the filthy pits, called the poor's holes, into which corpses of the indigent were thrown, in parishes such as St Martin's and St Giles's, and then left to rot in the open. A "noisome stench" given off by these pits "stow'd with dead bodies" made the health risk all too apparent. Such pits were dug by the parish "in their graveyards or other annexed burial grounds," which here points to places such as the angle of St Martin's Lane and the Strand, as well as the land on the south side of Broad St Giles in the direction of Monmouth Street, a stone's throw from Seven Dials.[25]

It is natural to suppose that a crossroads such as Seven Dials existed not as a part of a grand urban design, but as the remnant of a higgledy-piggledy process of unplanned growth. After all, the Great Fire of 1666 had not reached this far, and some medieval building lines were intact as far as the city extended. In fact Thomas Neale had laid out this part of St Giles's in the early 1690s as a deliberate experiment in land use. However, he quickly disposed of his interest in the site, and a number of speculative builders carried out the development of the triangular plots, which were sold off in small parcels. As a result, when Gay's hapless countryman stumbles on St Giles's, in the immediate vicinity of Seven Dials, he is completely at a loss. "Bewildered," he attempts to find his way and follow confusing signs:

> Enters the narrow Alley's doubtful Maze,
> Tries ev'ry winding Court and Street in vain.

(2: 80-1)

A parallel anecdote is told in Book 3, about a Devon yeoman who encounters a "fraudful Nymph," one of those trudging "the Rounds of *Drury-Lane*." She leads him "through winding Alleys to her Cobweb

Room" (3: 285-92). As he leaves in his drunken stupor, reeling "from Post to Post," the rustic unwisely challenges authority:

> The vagrant Wretch th' assembled Watchmen spies,
> He waves his Hanger, and their Poles defies.
>
> (3: 295-6)

As a result he ends up the night confined, "deep in the *Round-House* pent" (3: 297). One such parish round-house would enter the national consciousness just eight years later, when Jack Sheppard brought off the first of his famous escape routines. (He had previously sprung Edgeworth Moll from the same location.) Sheppard had been betrayed while playing skittles at a victualling-house near Seven Dials: he was taken to the lock-up just round the corner, but easily regained his freedom from the third story, dropping down on a knotted sheet into the adjoining churchyard. Needless to say, the round-house - and the graveyard - were those of St Giles's.[26]

III

In the earlier passage quoted, a comically inflated simile draws in Theseus as he "travers'd the dang'rous Labyrinth of *Crete*" (2: 84), and this may serve to bring us back to the mythical dimension. Under the relevant aspect of her divinity, Trivia symbolized the multifaceted and delusive reality of the urban environment. The goddess herself represented a kind of deified version of the Duke in *Measure for Measure*, described by Lucio as "the old fantastical Duke of dark corners." Her province was of course night, and we recall from the first two lines of the poem that the "art" of walking the streets of London involves negotiating a passage through hostile territory:

> Through Winter Streets to steer your Course aright,
> How to walk clean by Day, and safe by Night.
>
> (1: 1-2)

Trivia is specifically entrusted with the task of shepherding the walker in situations "where winding Alleys lead the doubtful Way," amid "long perplexing Lanes" (1: 8, 10). Again, at the start of Book 2, the goddess is asked to act as a protector in the face of these dangers: "Now venture, Muse, from Home to range the Town, / And for the publick Safety risque thy own" (2: 5-6).

As its title indicates, Book 3, "Of walking the Streets by Night," enforces this connection most explicitly. At the outset, a second apostrophe is directed to Trivia, in her incarnation as Diana/Luna:

> O *TRIVIA*, Goddess, leave these low Abodes,
> And traverse o'er the wide Ethereal Roads,
> Celestial Queen, put on thy Robes of Light,
> Now *Cynthia* nam'd, fair Regent of the Night. . .
> O may thy Silver Lamp from Heav'n's high Bow'r
> Direct my Footsteps in the Midnight Hour!
>
> (3: 1-4, 7-8)

The drift is clear. Up till now Trivia has been operating as the earthly Diana: perhaps, in the mythical inset of a descent under the Fleet Ditch in Book 2, as Proserpina.[27] Now she is invoked with the aim of engaging her help in withstanding the perils of nocturnal London. Perhaps Gay is referring back to his principal model, and recalling the opening of the first *Georgic*. There Virgil mentions a succession of deities, ranging from Ceres to Silvanus, prefaced by the heavenly bodies: *vos, o clarissima mund/ lumina, labentem caelo quae ducitis annum. . .* (1: 5-6). As suggested in the headnote by Gay's editors, already quoted, the only direct reference to a three-way crossing in this book occurs when a short apologue concerning Oedipus is introduced: "Where three Roads join'd, he met his Sire unknown" (3: 217). For the rest, Gay's emphasis is on matters such as "the frequent Dangers of the Night" (3: 244), along with the haunts of prostitutes. Significantly perhaps, the ladies of the night gather at a *crossing*, that is the point where a road leading from Drury Lane made a T-junction with the Strand.[28]

> O! may thy Virtue guard thee through the Roads
> Of *Drury*'s mazy Courts, and dark Abodes,
> The Harlots' guileful Paths, who nightly stand,
> Where *Katherine-street* descends into the *Strand*.
>
> (3: 259-62)[29]

This must belong to the world of the threefold goddess in her role as Hecate, lurking in the dark alleys by night. Only in a plainly ironic or burlesque sense could the guardian of such polluted places be identified with Diana, the virgin queen whose realm lay in Arcadian forests.

At this exact spot, too, Londoners would recognise one of the sites for erecting the pillory, a punishment to which Gay alludes briefly at 2: 221-6. (Just down the road lay the best known of these sites - Charing Cross.) In 1727 the City Under-Marshal, Charles Hitchen was sentenced to stand in the pillory here after his conviction for attempted sodomy at a Charing Cross tavern. Hitchen had once employed the arch-criminal Jonathan Wild, but he later turned against his former associate, and rode in the procession to Tyburn when Wild was hanged in 1725.[30] The outcome of this sentence was as brutal a piece of street theatre as the city could provide:

> Last Tuesday Mr. Hitchen was erected on the Pillory over-against Catherine-street in the Strand. His friends had so barricadoed the Avenues leading to him with Coaches and Carts, as almost render'd the Approaches of the Mob inaccessible: However, the Artillery used in these Occasions, play'd incessantly from all Corners, and a Battery in Catherine-street, conducted by a great Number of Drury-lane Ladies play'd with good Success for Half an Hour. Mr. Curll's Windows suffer'd pretty much by it; and the Constables, endeavouring by a Sally to level that Work, were drove back to the Pillory by a strong Body of the Mob, tho' not without some Blood spilt on both Sides. All Means used by the Peace Officers and Mr. Hitchen's Friends and Brethren (sic) to repel the Fury of the Populace proving ineffectual, the Criminal met with the Reward due to his Demerits. He was taken down at the usual Time, and carried back to Newgate, almost ready to expire, with the Fatigue he had undergone in the Rostrum, his Night-Gown and Breeches being torn in Pieces from his Body.[31]

Sometimes things went even further. In 1723 a criminal who had been found guilty of making false accusations of treasonable practices did not survive the hour he stood in the pillory at Charing Cross. He was pelted unmercifully, and choked by the mud heaped upon him.[32] Nine years later another would-be informer was killed when the pillory was pulled down by the mob, who trampled him underfoot and dismembered him. This time the location was Seven Dials.[33] If Hecate had any favorite haunts in contemporary London, they must surely have lain where crime and punishment left their mark in blood, above all at ominous crossroads like Seven Dials, the Catherine Street junction - where executions sometimes took place - and Charing Cross.

Of course, those deemed to have committed a more serious offense against the state would end up not on the pillory, but at "the triple tree" or triangular gallows set up "where three Roads join'd." This marked the intersection of the Oxford turnpike route, otherwise Tyburn Road, running west and Marybone Lane running north, in another T-junction: we might think of Hogarth again, as the last scene of the idle apprentice's life in *Industry and Idleness* (1747) shows the tripod in stark relief. Gay never once mentions the existence of capital punishment, if we except a passing reference to the fact that butchers were "always foremost in the Hangman's

Train" (2: 43-4). It is tempting to see this as a way in which the poet averts his eyes from the worst fate which might befall a Londoner, just as the Romans turned their face away from Hecate, fearing to meet her gaze. But there is a simple and decisive explanation for this absence.

Gay had completed his main draft of the poem in the summer of 1715. Soon after, the Jacobite rising broke out: London was awash with speculation and hasty preparations to combat the rebellion began in July, prior to the raising of the Stuart flag at Braemar on 6 September. Gay had plenty of time to review his text before *Trivia* came out on 27 January 1716. In the aftermath of the recent rebellion, three of those captured had been hanged at Tyburn in December. The Jacobite lords who had been taken prisoner at Preston were brought to London on 10 December: the fate in store for them was heralded on 9 January in the King's speech at the opening of parliament. A day later, Pope wrote to a friend that Gay's poem was "just on the brink of the press."[34] By 19 January articles of impeachment had been drawn up, and the peers examined by the House of Lords. On 9 February six of the seven pleaded guilty and received a sentence of death, and two of the condemned lords were beheaded at Tower Hill on 24 February.[35] The block was placed on the crest of the hill, in a position now occupied by Trinity Square: from here roads radiated out in several directions, among them Thames Street, mentioned in *Trivia* (see p. 94), Tower Street, Woodroff Lane, the Minories, Rosemary Lane - better known as Rag Fair - and East Smithfield. Meanwhile the Pretender himself, who had arrived in Scotland as late as 22 December, had now slipped away from the coast. Many of the lesser fry among the rebels were tried at Liverpool, Chester or Liverpool, and a long line of them went to the scaffold in the same time-period. It would have been unbelievably tactless for Gay to make any reference to executions at this juncture. In *The Beggar's Opera* Gay does not scruple to mention Tyburn, which hangs over the entire action right through to Macheath's absurd reprieve at the end: but that was in 1728, when people might have thought of Jack Sheppard and Jonathan Wild when they heard talk about gaols and death sentences. In 1716 this evoked rather thoughts of state trials and political upheavals.

This silence raises a wider question. It must be admitted that some of the attributes of Trivia, as well as some qualities of her cult, are ignored: Gay makes virtually nothing of her association through Hecate with sorcery, except in so far as this has been perverted into the tricks of the town:

> Who can the various City Frauds recite,
> With all the petty Rapines of the Night?

> Who now the *Guinea-Dropper*'s bait regards,
> Trick'd by the Sharper's Dice, or Juggler's Cards?
>
> (3: 247-50)

Equally, the persistent concern of the poem with crime mostly concerns attacks on the person related to theft or mugging (for example, "That Crutch which late Compassion mov'd, shall wound / Thy bleeding Head, and fell thee to the Ground," 3: 137-8).[36] Crossing "dark Paths by Night" (3: 128) is likely to incur for the walker just bumps and bruises. At worst, there are depredations by the notorious - but possibly mythical - Scowrers and Mohocks, whose "desp'rate Deeds" (3: 329), alleged to include savage mutilation of their victims, the poet primly refuses to describe. Gay recommends that the pedestrian should not risk his blood in a street brawl: it is at this point that the case of Oedipus is brought up. There is a single verse paragraph on "funeral Pomp" (3: 225-36). However, the particular association of Hecate with the corpses of murdered individuals is absent.[37] Once again, this is easily explained by the extreme political tension of the moment. It also conforms with Gay's tongue-in-cheek assurance that, in "Happy *Augusta*! Law-defended town," the populace is free from the vendettas, stabbings and political assassinations of Catholic Europe: "No *Bravos* here profess the bloody Trade" (3: 145-52).

A curious sidelight on Gay's intentions emerges in a poem he wrote two or three years later, the *Epistle to the Right Honourable William Pulteney, Esq*. This contains a passage harking back to *Trivia*:

> Shall he (who late *Britannia*'s city trod,
> And led the draggled Muse, with pattens shod,
> Through dirty lanes, and alleys doubtful ways)
> Refuse to write, when *Paris* asks his lays!
>
> (11-14)[38]

In Book 1, we recall, the poet had included a short Ovidian fable, describing Vulcan's contrivance of pattens for the use of a country girl named Martha, known as Patty. It is tempting to see this as a fanciful compliment to Pope's friend Martha ("Patty") Blount, whom Gay certainly knew by this date.[39] The episode was introduced with the lines, "But O! forget not, Muse, the *Patten*'s Praise, / That female Implement shall grace thy Lays" (1: 219-20). As Gay described the poem in retrospect, it was the author who had "led" the bedraggled muse around the lanes and alleys of London, so that she needed to be equipped with her own protective footwear. This is not how the rhetoric had originally worked: Trivia is obviously familiar with all the darkest and dirtiest corners of the town, and it is she who conducts the poet on his "Course" through the winter streets.

One more feature of the publishing history remains. In the poem Gay has a short section on booksellers' wares (2: 551-68), but the only member of the trade he mentions by name is Bernard Lintot. It was Lintot who published *Trivia* and the title page reveals his trade sign: "*LONDON:* at the *Cross-Keys* between the *Temple* Gates in *Fleetstreet.*" Above this legend comes the first emblem that the reader encounters: the bookseller's emblem, two keys in a saltire (X) shape, amid scrollwork. We reach London, then, by way of a device which expresses branching or intersection.

IV

Earlier, we touched on the element of transgression in the walker's passage through the streets. This is perhaps an over-employed concept these days, but it applies in the most literal way to *Trivia*, as a return to etymological considerations will show. The Latin deponent verb *gradior* (I walk) gave rise to numerous cognate forms with the help of prefixes. Among others there were *aggredior, circumgredior, congredior, egredior, ingredior, praegredior regredior, retrogradior, suggredior,* and *supergredior*. Obviously many English derivatives can be traced back to these verbs in the participle form: aggression, congress, egress, ingress, regress, retrogression, and so on. The most relevant cases here are *digredior* (I depart or deviate); *progredior* (I proceed); and *transgredior* (I pass over). In the first of these instances, it is plain that Gay deliberately parodies the digressions of epic form, as shown by the introduction to his narrative of Cloacina:

> Here let the Muse, fatigu'd amid the Throng,
> Adorn her Precepts with Digressive Song.
>
> (2: 103-04)

Elsewhere the poem contains short inset episodes such as the story of Patty, mentioned previously, or that of the fruit-girl Doll, killed as she tried to cross the frozen Thames in the harsh winter of 1709-10 (2: 381-98).

This brings us to *progredior*. The word "progress" was still used in the literal sense of a journey: thus, there are books in this period describing Queen Anne's progress to Bath, a certain Taffy's progress from Wales to London, and Dr Henry Sacheverell's triumphant progress form London to Shropshire. More specifically, in official guides to the history and topography of the capital, it was usual to make an orderly progression through the parishes and wards of the City of London and Westminster. This is what we find in John Strype's revision (1720) of the great Elizabethan *Survey of London* by John Stow. As we should expect, it is the method employed by the Company of Parish Clerks when they compiled their *New Remarks on London, or A Survey of The Cities of London and Westminster, of Southwark and Part of Middlesex and Surrey Within the Circumference of the Bills of Mortality Collected by the Company of Parish-Clerks* (1732). Even an informal treatment like that of Daniel Defoe, in his *Tour thro' the Whole Island of Great Britain* (1724-26) begins by "taking a measure" of the dimensions of the extended city. Across a span of some five pages Defoe defines the outer limits of London, as he conceives them. His treatment in the ensuing description does not follow this imaginary peregrination, since the organization is by topics (churches, markets, docks, and so on), but it is divided into separate sections on London and Westminster.[40]

Things could not be more different in *Trivia*. Gay carries out no such beating of the bounds, and never attempts to measure the scale of his journey. The walker does little more than wander the streets in a capricious fashion: the order in which landmarks occur is almost entirely arbitrary. The narrative moves from the fashionable Mall at the Court section of town, what later became the "West End," to the commercial districts of the old City, such as the market for fish at Billingsgate, that at Thames Street for cheese, and for meat at Leadenhall Street and Newgate. There is brief mention of the Tower, of the bear-garden out north at Hockley in the Hole, of bustling Watling Street, and of the New Exchange in the Strand. At various points we reach the "Paths of fair *Pell-mell*" (modern Pall Mall) (2: 257), we catch a glimpse of deer in nearby St James's Park, and we enter the great mansions such as Burlington House. At others we turn inside "the *Temple*'s silent Walls" (2: 477) or retrace the road to Tyburn at Holborn. As already described, much of the poem concerns itself with the squalid purlieus of St Giles's and surrounding areas. Once we venture on the dangerous currents of the river in a leaky boat. It would make little sense to try to plot the course along which these various locations are called up in the text of the poem. The result could only be a bewildering vortex of lines crossing and recrossing one another. London is a city where the heedless traveler, like the countryman lost in St Giles's, "doubles o'er his weary Steps again" (2: 82).

Progress is constantly resisted, especially in "the dang'rous Night" (3: 113), in this crinkum-crankum world of sly corners:

Though you through cleanlier Alleys wind by Day,
To shun the Hurries of the publick Way,

> Yet n'er to those dark Paths by Night retire;
> Mind only safety, and contemn the Mire.
> Then no impervious Courts thy haste detain,
> Nor sneering Ale-Wives bid thee turn again.
>
> (3: 127-30)

Once more, toponyms underline the point. There was even a Turnagain Lane, a short street in the notoriously crowded area round the ominously sited church of St Sepulchre's, where every death-cart paused on its journey to Tyburn.[41] This lane led down to the Fleet Ditch from Snow Hill, a narrow and crooked street which Gay mentions in connection with the Scourers and Mohocks, referring to a story that an old woman had been rolled in a wine-barrel down the slope: "I pass their desp'rate Deeds, and Mischiefs done, /Where from *Snow-hill* black steepy Torrents run" (3: 329-30). (*Transgredior* could also mean pass over, or omit.) This is another of the places in the text where Gay obviously recalls the *City Shower* of his friend and model Swift:

> They, as each Torrent drives, with rapid Force
> From *Smithfield*, or *St Pulchre*'s shape their Course;
> And in huge Confluent join at *Snow-Hill* Ridge,
> From the huge Confluent prone to *Holborn-Bridge*.
>
> (57-60)

As Gay's editors remind us, "the streets in question have roughly the shape of a wishbone: that from St Sepulchre's church past Lamb's Conduit to Holborn Bridge is Snow Hill, that of Smithfield to the Conduit is Cow Lane."[42] In Swift's poem the tides of filth sweep down from Smithfield and Newgate into the ditch; Gay's lines connect with his earlier reference to "*Holborn*'s fatal Steep" (2: 174) and thus recall the criminal history of the area.[43] Again we encounter a baleful three-way fork in the road. The passage also serves to show that central London had more sharp declivities to negotiate than we might realize today: engineering projects such as the creation of Holborn Viaduct here in the nineteenth century have flattened out the landscape to promote comfortable transit of the city.[44]

Typically, the itinerary of *Trivia* avoids movement in long straight lines, because of the numerous impediments encountered.[45] Even a major crosstown route, Thames Street, should be avoided:

> Or who that rugged Street would traverse o'er
> That stretches, O *Fleet-ditch*, from thy black Shore
> To the *Tow'rs* moated Walls?
>
> (2: 245-7)

"Traversing" such a landscape becomes a matter of constantly looking out for ways of escape:

> There may'st thou pass, with safe unmiry Feet,
> Where the rais'd Pavement leads athwart the Street.
> If where *Fleet-Ditch* with muddy Current flows,
> You chance to roam; where Oyster-tubs in Rows
> Are rang'd beside the Posts; there stay thy Haste. . .
>
> (3: 187-91)

These complex moves are caused, again, partly by the unplanned growth of the city. But they also reflect distinct rhetorical choices on Gay's part. His walker crosses the boundaries of the city, just as the poem switches from the terrestrial to the subterranean, and veers between topographic realities and mythical divagations. Safe, untroubled "progress" is not an option, and so the work advances through a series of transgressive acts, leading us through the labyrinth of streets and crossings which make up the network of London life.

V

From all this evidence it is possible to work out a fuller rationale for Gay's choice of a title. Starting from the goddess who is invoked as the muse, we can easily see that Trivia is an apt choice for a poem in three parts, branching out in a Y-shaped design to display three faces of city life. Secondly, she is, *pace* Dearing and Beckwith, an appropriate deity to preside over the life of "streets and highways." The association of her cult with crossings aids the rhetoric of the poem, with its recurrent emphasis on dangerous swerves and slippages which are incident to moving about London, as "tides" flow above and beneath ground across town. Thirdly, Trivia properly takes an overseeing role in the third book, devoted to night. Fourthly, she is present ironically as Diana/Luna, as part of the wider poetic mechanism which projects pastoral or georgic elements on to an urban screen.

We have also the literal sense of "trivia," in its usage as a common rather than a proper noun. In Latin it referred to the public highway, a key consideration in view of the fact that the term *street(s)* occurs some forty-four times in the poem, along with expressions like *alley, way, court, corner* and *lane.* In English, as we have seen, there was no current application for the word, and a link with the adjective *trivial* could be effected only by a daring and original macaronic pun. There is possibly one other hidden association: in a poem which systematically breaks the boundaries of genre, as an urban georgic, there may be an echo of *Tristia*, the work Ovid wrote in his exile from Rome at the bleak retreat at Tomis. Ovid's situation is reversed in *Trivia*, where the poet, born and raised in far-off Devon, rejoices in his mastery of metropolitan lore. In fact he makes fun of a clodhopping peasant from his home county, who visits the capital and is trapped by the lure of prostitutes (3: 285-306). Such a perfect inversion suggests that Gay was playing on the form of the word, merely substituting for "sad things" a coinage of his own, with the meaning "slight things." The device belongs in a literary act of crossways movement - translation and generic transformation.

Tom Woodman has argued that, despite its range of allusion to "all the rich traditional complexes about art and nature," *Trivia* is ultimately "secular and largely demystified."[46] If this is true, then it surely has intimate connections with Gay's choice of a tutelary goddess in Trivia - a figure who could bridge the gap between ancient myth and down-to-earth contemporary reality, and could serve as a proper guardian for the street-folk of London as they negotiated the hazards of crossing the town.

Notes

[1] The most informative is Dianne S. Ames, "Gay's *Trivia* and the Art of Allusion," *Studies in Philology*, 75 (1978): 199-222. Some useful local parallels are explored by Arthur Sherbo, "Virgil, Dryden, Gay, and Matters Trivial," *PMLA*, 85 (1970): 1063-71. However, none of these articles deals with the title directly. On the poem generally, the most important study is now *Walking the Streets of Eighteenth-Century London: John Gay's Trivia (1716)*, ed. Clare Brant and Susan E. Whyman (Oxford: Oxford University Press, 2007), a valuable collection of essays on almost every aspect of the work.
[2] Gay, *Poetry and Prose*, 2: 548-9. This is the text cited throughout.
[3] *Trivia: or, The Art of Walking the Streets of London*, ed. W.H. Williams (London: Daniel O'Connor, 1922), p. 59.
[4] M.C. Battestin, "Menalcas' Song: The Meaning of Art and Artifice in Gay's Poetry," *Journal of English and Germanic Philology*, 65 (1966): 662-79.
[5] For the roots of the cult, see *Der Neue Pauly* (Stuttgart: J.B. Metzler, 1996-), 5: 267-8, s.v. "Hekate." A convenient summary can be found in *Lemprière's Classical Dictionary* (London: Bracken Books, 1994), p. 294.
[6] *Aeneid* 4: 511. Williams, p. 80, quotes this line, but refers to it as "IV, 54."
[7] Diana "is called *Triformis* and *Tregemina*, I. Because, she is One, yet she has a theefold Office; for she is *Luna* in the Heavens, *Diana* upon Earth, and *Hecate* in Hell". See Andrew Tooke, *The Pantheon* (1713), p. 241, cited by Paulson, *Hogarth*, 2: 412. There is no evidence that Gay was a freemason, although a few years later Pope and Arburthnot were, along with many other friends.
[8] From Virgil. *Eclogues*, 9:1: "Quo te Mœri pedes? An, quo via ducit, in Urbem?"

[9] Dearing and Beckwith point out (*Poetry and Prose,* 2: 561) that Gay may have recalled *Georgics* 1: 176-7. The corresponding adjective in the Latin is *tenuis.*

[10] The dial was sculpted by Edward Pierce, as part of the development by Thomas Neale *c.*1694. It was taken down in 1773; a modern replica was erected in 1989. For a time there were only six streets meeting here.

[11] Gay, *Poetry and Prose,* 2: 558.

[12] "Don Manoel Gonzales", *London in 1731,* ed. Henry Morley (London: Cassell, 1881), pp. 132-3. This is an imaginary voyage first published in 1745, but clearly dating from some years earlier.

[13] A.D. Mills, *A Dictionary of London Place Names* (Oxford: Oxford University Press, 2001), p. 44.

[14] James Boswell, *Life of Johnson,* ed. R.W. Chapman (Oxford: Oxford University Press, 1980), p. 608, under 2 April 1775.

[15] Gay adds a learned note citing authorities such as Lactantius. The purpose is to remind us that there was a genuine Roman goddess named Cloacina, whose role was to preside over the Cloaca which ran beneath the city.

[16] The posts (large blocks of stone, dividing the roadway from the pavement) are clearly visible in the headpiece to *Trivia,* a small vignette which shows a junction. Paviers are at work (see 1: 13-14); and a carriage with two horses almost blocks the way.

[17] Later comes more advice: "Thou never wilt attempt to cross the Road, / Where Alehouse Benches rest the Porter's Load" (3: 115-16).

[18] Gay contrasts the relative safety of the public streets with the perils to be faced in the side-walks: "Where *Lincoln's-Inn,* wide Space, is rail'd around, / Cross not with vent'rous Step" (3: 133-4), for fear of the lurking thief and the deceptive linkman. Although the Fields formed a fashionable residential area, the character of the locality was affected by the presence of the theatre (where *The Beggar's Opera* enjoyed its huge success) and the network of narrow lanes between the square and Holborn. These included Whetstone Park, once among the most notorious streets in all London for prostitution; and the "*Lincoln's Inn Bog-Houses,*" where homosexuals had one of their "markets" or trysting-places. See *Hell upon Earth* (London, 1729), p. 43.

[19] It was already the artists' quarter, a position confirmed when St Martin's Academy opened in October 1720 at Russell's meeting-house, Peter's Court, on the west side of St Martin's Lane.

[20] The left-hand corner at the base was formed by St Martin's Lane and the Strand. Behind this angle lay another of the notorious rookeries of London, known as "the Bermudas," which included a colony of cooks' shops catering to the poor known as Porridge Island and the tangle of narrow alleys around Round Court. For an illustration, see Hugh Phillips, *Mid-Georgian London: A Topographical and Social Survey of Central and Western London about 1750* (London: Collins, 1964), p. 126.

[21] Howson, *Thief-Taker,* 45-6. Wild lived in Lewkenor's Lane in 1713, and then opened a "lost property" office there in 1720 - dates neatly straddling the appearance of *Trivia.*

[22] In *Trivia*, Gay slyly observes how "Soft at low Doors, old Letchers tap their Cane, / For fair Recluse, that travels *Drury-lane*" (2: 281-2). For details of Sheppard's career, see [Daniel Defoe], *The History of the Remarkable Life of John Sheppard* (1724), reprinted in *Selected Poetry and Prose of Daniel Defoe*, ed. Michael F. Shugrue (New York: Holt, Rinehart and Winston, 1968), pp. pp. 232-68. The most searching attempt to locate Sheppard within the subculture of criminal London is that of Peter Linebaugh, *The London Hanged: Crime and Civil Society in the Eighteenth Century* (Cambridge: Cambridge University Press, 1992), pp. 7-41.

[23] M. Dorothy George, *London Life in the Eighteenth Century* (London, 1925: rptd New York: Capricorn, 1965), p. 42.

[24] See Paulson, *Hogarth*, 3: 21. Gay, too, recalls "the griping Broker" (1: 117). Paulson has acutely observed that *Trivia* seems to have served as a source book for Hogarth" in the *Four Times of Day* (see *Hogarth*, 2: 141-8). Much of the evidence collected in this essay could be used to confirm Paulson's argument. "Noon" is set in Hog Lane, on the western parochial boundary of St Giles's: the parish church can be seen in the background.

[25] George, *London Life*, pp. 68, 73, 355. St Giles in the Fields was one of the largest London parishes, after St Martin's and St Giles Without, Cripplegate (George, *London Life*, pp. 411-17). It naturally figured heavily in the crime statistics: Linebaugh, *London Hanged*, pp. 107-10, disputes George Rudé's distinction between the wage-earning settlements of Shoreditch and Spitalfields, as against the "criminal elements" prominent in St Giles's and St Martin's. But whatever the *origin* of the criminals, tabulated by Linebaugh, there is no doubt that the *site* of crimes and the residence of *victims* were disproportionately high in St Giles's.

[26] A generation later, Henry Fielding described the appearance of the prostitute Blear-Eyed Moll in *Amelia* (1: iii): "nothing more ragged, or more dirty, was ever emptied out of the Roundhouse at St. *Giles's*."

[27] Gay would have been aware that antiquarians were currently debating the well-entrenched myth that a temple of Diana once lay under St Paul's Cathedral in London. The story went back to Camden's *Britannia*, but had been revived in a pamphlet issued in 1713 by Dr John Woodward. He was one of the prime targets of the Scriblerian group and the butt of a play, *Three Hours after Marriage*, written by Gay with the help of Pope and Dr John Arbuthnot. This came out in January 1717, just a year after *Trivia*. See Joseph M. Levine, *Dr. Woodward's Shield: History, Science, and Satire in Augustan England* (Berkeley: University of California Press, 1977), pp. 138, 148-50.

[28] Fifty yards to the east, in the middle of the thoroughfare, stood a watchhouse, where the harlots would be locked up for the night (cf. *Trivia*, 2: 490). Another thirty yards further on, the new church of St Mary le Strand was being built on an island site by James Gibbs (1714-24) at the time *Trivia* came out - another street "obstruction" in its way, like St Clement's, which meant that pedestrians found their way "encumbered by huge blocks of stone" during the building process: see E. Beresford Chancellor, *The XVIIIth Century in London: An Account of its Social Life and Arts* (London: Batsford, n.d.), p. 192. For the sequence of events during

construction, see Terry Friedman, *James Gibbs* (New Haven: Yale University Press, 1984), pp. 42-53. Gay would have known of events here, because his close friend Dr John Arbuthnot had served as one of the commissioners from the new churches from 1713 to 1715, and had been personally involved in the development of the site. Here, too, Pope had his dunces foregather, at a point where "A Church collects the Saints of Drury-lane" (*Dunciad* 2: 30). See Chapter 11 below for fuller details.

[29] In 1730 tradesmen living in "Bridges-street, Catherine-street, and Places contiguous to Drury Lane" laid an official complaint concerning the thieves, pickpockets and other lewd persons who were "harbour'd and entertain'd in several night-houses and other houses of ill fame in that neighbourhood." The Westminster justices met at the Covent Garden vestry and issued warrants against ten such houses, ordering the arrest of their keepers (*London Journal*, 18 July, 19 September; *British Journal*, 28 July 1730).

[30] See *The Proceedings of the Sessions of the Peace* [Old Bailey records], 12 April 1727, p. 8. For Hitchen's career, see Howson, *Thief-Taker*, passim, and J.M. Beattie, *Policing and Punishment in London 1660-1750: Urban Crime and the Limits of Terror* (Oxford: Oxford University Press, 2001), pp. 252-6.

[31] Read's *Weekly Journal*, 6 May 1727. The reference in the text is to Edmund Curll, the notorious bookseller, who would himself stand in the pillory at Charing Cross a few months later. Curll's shop was situated at this same junction, "over against *Catherine-Street*, in the *Strand*." For the publisher's migrations, see Paul Baines and Pat Rogers, *Edmund Curll, Bookseller* (Oxford: Clarendon Press, 2007).

[32] See J.M. Beattie, *Crime and the Courts in England 1660-1800* (Princeton: Princeton University Press, 1986), pp. 467-8.

[33] For the pillory and other criminal associations of Seven Dials, see also Phillips, *Mid-Georgian London*, p. 219.

[34] Pope *Corr*, 1: 326.

[35] One was the Earl of Derwentwater, whose family connections included several people well known to Pope, and who had subscribed to the first volume of the *Iliad* in 1715. Through a sequence of marriages within this generation, he was actually a brother-in-law of Martha Blount, as the term then extended.

[36] In one passage, turnips and eggs rain down "thick as hailstones" on a criminal in the pillory (2: 221-6), but the tone is purely comical.

[37] There is one joking reference to the undertaking profession, where "Th' upholder, rueful harbinger of death, / Waits with impatience for the dying breath", followed by a comparison with vultures hovering over the carnage of a battle-field (2: 469-70).

[38] *Poetry and Prose*, 1: 208. The poem was first published in 1720, but may have been written as early as 1717.

[39] Later they were close friends: it was apparently Martha who had to inform Pope of Gay's death. See Pope *Corr*, 3: 335-6.

[40] Letter II in *A Tour*, Vol. 2 (1725): see Defoe, *Tour*, 2: 66-73. At the start Defoe carefully sets out the ten parts of the city he intends to cover, that is the city and

liberties of London and of Westminster, the Tower Hamlet, the Middlesex suburbs, the borough of Southwark, and so on (p. 73).

[41] "Turn-again lane" was an expression, now obsolete, to mean "a blind alley, a cul-de-sac; also a winding or crooked lane" (*OED*).

[42] *Poetry and Prose*, 2: 570.

[43] See *Poetry and Prose*, 2: 558.

[44] Similarly the building of the Thames Embankment has made Gay's line about Arundel Street, "Behold that narrow street which steep descends" (2: 481) less applicable to the lie of the land today.

[45] There is even a brief reference to road works, causing the street to be closed to vehicular traffic while repairs are carried out (2: 307-10).

[46] Tom Woodman, "'Vulgar Circumstance' and 'Due Civilities': Gay's Art of Polite Living in Town," in *John Gay and the Scriblerians*, ed. Peter Lewis and Nigel Wood (London: Vision, 1988), pp. 83-93, quotation from p. 90.

CHAPTER SIX

LOOKING FOR MR CURLL'S AUTHORS: POPE'S *FURTHER ACCOUNT*

In 1716 Alexander Pope wrote two of his most characteristic satires in prose on the subject of the publisher Edmund Curll. The first pamphlet, *A Full and True Account of a Horrid and Barbarous Revenge by Poison, on the body of Mr. Edmund Curll, Bookseller,* appeared around 31 March. It is a parody in miniature of Curll's own instant lives of those who had recently died, ending with the accustomed formula, "With a Faithful Copy of his Last Will and Testament." The second item, *A Further Account of the most Deplorable Condition of Mr. Edmund Curll, Bookseller,* which came out at some date between May and December of the same year, affects to continue the narrative provided in *A Full Account* by "a faithful, tho' unpolite Historian of *Grub-street.*" Both works contain some of Pope's most mischievous writing concerning the London book trade, and they provide a working base for his later deployment of material concerning the world of Grub Street in *Peri Bathous* and *The Dunciad.* In particular, the *Further Account* demonstrates that, long before Pope is known to have recruited Richard Savage as his informant, he had an astonishingly close knowledge of this milieu. We can gauge the degree of interest he took in such matters from a letter he wrote to Lord Burlington around November 1716, describing a conversation he had with the publisher Bernard Lintot, as together they made the long ride from Windsor Forest to Oxford. This plays around Lintot's dealings with his authors, particularly translators. Such an exchange would certainly have given Pope a clear sense of what was going on in the literary market place.[1]

However, neither pamphlet has ever been fully edited or explicated, which is particularly regrettable in the case of the second item. One attempt has been made to survey a single key passage, seen as "what is practically a working gazetteer of the subculture formed by professional writers at this time," and perhaps rashly a separate account was promised, with the aim of establishing the identity of the persons and places mentioned.[2] While quite a lot remains uncertain, it is now possible to draw on a wider range of information and to explain some references which previously eluded enquiry. Much more precise detail can now be given concerning several of the places to which Pope refers as the haunt of men and women of letters.[3] Although the identity of those individual writers as they appear in the text can be specified with certainty only in a few cases, this is a task which would have defeated most contemporary readers, outside a very narrow circle of the literary world. Apart from that, some additional information has come to light, which makes educated guessing a feasible proposition and rules out some earlier conjectures. As a result we can assemble a more comprehensive picture of the London book trade, as Pope etches the scene for his satiric purposes.

I

One section of *A Further Account* concerns Curll's efforts to call together his flock of hack authors in order to launch a retaliatory campaign against Pope, who had lately been responsible for administering an emetic to the bookseller. A "general Summons" goes out to the key writers who worked most regularly for Curll.[4] In all fifteen individuals are to be sought by a porter, and they are spread around thirteen addresses in the capital. The "instructions" to the messenger are extraordinarily specific, and while some may be blurred or deliberately misleading, they do enable us to fix a number of those involved and, more frequently, their abodes. At this point in the text, we have already had mention of one of Curll's fellow-booksellers, John Pemberton, and one of his authors, John Oldmixon. When the group is assembled, other writers are named: John Dennis, Charles Gildon, Susanna Centlivre and Sir Richard Blackmore. Not all those named in the text need automatically have been among those summoned to Curll's shop in Fleet Street: indeed, it is unlikely that Blackmore as a busy and fashionable physician was at the beck and call of any bookseller. However, further clues are provided by the descriptions and addresses found in the directions Curll gives to his porter.

The first instruction reads: "At a Tallow-chandlers in *Petty France*, half way under the blind Arch: Ask for the Historian." Quite possibly this means not Petty France in Westminster, but a street on the eastern edge of Moorfields in Bishopsgate Ward Without, on a site developed later in the century as "New Broad Street." The original Bedlam hospital had stood here before it moved a short distance west in 1676. In Defoe's *Journal of the Plague Year* (1722), the narrator H.F. makes his way "thro' a narrow Passage from *Petty-France* into *Bishopsgate* Church-Yard, by a Row of

Alms-Houses." He encounters "a Dwarf-Wall with a Palisadoe on it, on the right Hand; and the City Wall on the other Side, more to the right." This suggests that a "blind," that is partially or wholly blocked, archway might have been positioned here. It was described in 1742 as "as a street of mean Buildings, denominated *Petty France*, from its being at first inhabited by People of that Nation.'[y] The adjoining land was taken up by St Botolph's burial ground. This would put the historian at the less fashionable City end of the town. His identity cannot be firmly established: among those who had written works described, more or less aptly, as "histories" for Curll were John Asgill, Oldmixon and John Henley, but none seems clearly indicated here. Asgill spent time in the Fleet prison, but otherwise his movements in London are hard to trace. Henley seems never to have lived in the City proper. Although a new passage to Bishopsgate was constructed in 1730, Petty France remained an alternative name for New Broad Street at late as 1744. Nevertheless, it might be that Petty France, Westminster, is indicated, and if so, then we might think of Aaron Hill, who moved to this street in 1715. However, his was a substantial house with a large garden, in what John Stow termed "a good handsome Street," wholly residential in character: a description which clashes in every respect with Pope's wording.[4] Moreover, Hill's one vaguely historical work at this date, *A Full and Just Account of the Present State of the Ottoman Empire in all its Branches* (1709), was not issued by Curll, who never established any close links with Hill. In my view this latter possibility can be ruled out.

Second comes the following: "At the Bedsted and Bolster, a Musick House in *Morefields*, two Translators in a Bed together." An obvious candidate here would appear to be Ned Ward, but it was not until 1717 that he took over the Bacchus Tavern in Moorfields: he stayed there for another thirteen years. Since 1712 he had been operating an alehouse in Red Bull Yard, on the west side of St John's Street near Clerkenwell Green.[5] If it seems implausible that Pope would have a detailed acquaintance with a hack's wanderings around London, we should recall the note he appended to a brief reference to Ward in *The Dunciad Variorum* in 1729: "He has of late Years kept a publick house in the City (but in a genteel way) and with his wit, humour, and good liquor (Ale) afforded his guests a pleasurable entertainment, especially those of the High-Church party. JACOB *Lives of the Poets*." In 1735 Pope updated the note: "Ward in a Book call'd Apollo's Maggot, declar'd this account to be a great Falsity, protesting that his publick House was not in the City, but in Moorfields."[6] Interestingly, Ward claimed that he had never lived in the city in his life, and that Pope was "reporting things contrary to his own

Knowledge and Conscience, for [he] has drank Wine at Ward's House, and knows it to be a Tavern."[7] Ward's biographer points out that in his role as master of the Bacchus Tavern, "against the middle of Middle-Moorfields," his property lay in the parish of St Botolph's - just as the previous address, in Petty France, did. As Ward himself noted, it was a densely populated area, "Which has more Courts and Allies in it, / Than I could name by this day sennit."[8]

In any case, Ward can be eliminated, first because he was not primarily a translator, and Pope would certainly have named him in another role. Second, the context suggests that the individuals were guests rather than fulltime occupants of the music house. All this being so, we must look elsewhere. Curll's leading translators at this date included Robert Samber, John Ozell and such versatile authors as Oldmixon, Gildon, and George Sewell. None has a known connection with this district of London. In fact Oldmixon was on the point of moving to Bridgwater in Somerset, leaving his wife and family behind in Howard Street, off the Strand. Pope's deliberate innuendo regarding the coupling of the two persons could point to an established team of translators: however, Ozell's most frequent collaborator had been Samuel Cobb, a former master at Christ's Hospital, who died in 1713. More than once Pope singled out Ozell's "poor Version" of Boileau, co-published by Curll, and he resented the way in which Ozell had referred to his old friend Wycherley.[9] In the *Full Account* Pope had mentioned "The *French Cato*" as "damnably translated": this was a version by Ozell of *Caton d'Utique*, a tragedy by the diplomat François-Michel-Chrétien Deschamps, issued by Curll on 22 May. As a result, Ozell would surely have been the first name which came to mind when Pope was seeking a translator used by Curll.

The identity of the other writer remains unclear. What is certain is that Pope knew of the many associations of homosexuals with Moorfields, which was a favourite place of assignation for gay men at this time. More directly still, some of the taverns around this district were frequented by sodomites: in 1712, Constable Wise of Shoreditch reported that Charles Hitchen, the corrupt Under-Marshal of the City of London, was regularly to be found in such houses as the Three Tuns and the Black Horse in Moorfields.[10] These taverns adjoined the open spaces, where a path dividing the Upper Fields from the Middle Fields had become known as "Sodomites' Walk." Wise's concern related to the fact that Hitchen may have been associating too freely with burglars and other criminals, and had established Fagin-like relations with a gang of boy pickpockets. Years later Hitchen was exposed as an active sodomite, who was caught *in flagrante* at a tavern in Charing Cross: he was subsequently committed to

Newgate and sentenced to stand in the pillory. Trial reports often mention the fact that homosexual contacts were made at inns and alehouses in Moorfields.[11] We should have to impute to Pope an innocence he rarely displayed in worldly matters to suppose that his reference to the two men in bed together in Moorfields occurred by chance.

Next is the instruction: "At the *Hercules* and *Still* in *Vinegar-Yard*, a School-Master with Carbuncles on his Nose." The location presents no problem. Vinegar Yard lay on the west side of Drury Lane, at the very back of the Theatre Royal, and adjoining what was sometimes called "the Playhouse Passage." According to the revision of Stow's *Survey of London* by Rev. John Strype, published in 1720, this court was "indifferent broad, but ordinarily built and inhabited."[12] The proceedings of Old Bailey trials in this period show that the short street had close connections with crime and prostitution: its businesses included pawnbrokers and second-hand clothing establishments (often used as a cover for disposal of stolen goods). It was an area rife with brandy-shops and ale-houses which was the setting for murders, assaults and even highway robbery. In 1742 a witness refers to the gaming table in Vinegar Yard. One relevant case is that of Margaret Roberts and Sarah Alexander, of the parish of St Giles in the Fields, who were charged in December 1724 on two counts of stealing articles of clothing. On the second charge they were both acquitted, it may be in part because they accused a chief prosecution witness, resident in nearby Colson's Court of being a "common whore." On the first Roberts was convicted, and sentenced to transportation, but Alexander was acquitted, after a story involving the claim that she went with Roberts to a gin-shop in Vinegar Yard, and later left garments the other woman had stolen in pawn.[13] This might well be the very site of the Hercules and Still, though it is not possible to find a business so named in the records. That writers might be linked with the yard, around the time Pope was writing, we can deduce from Thomas Gordon's essay in *The Humourist* (1720), which describes the meeting of a fictional club of authors in this precise locality.[14]

As for the schoolmaster, one more clue is provided by a later resolution taken by the assembled group of writers: "*Resolv'd*, That no Member of this Society for the future mix *Stout* in his *Ale* in a Morning, and that Mr. *B.* remove from the *Hercules* and *Still.*"[15] This narrows the field, eliminating such bibulous persons as Laurence Eusden, but does not permit any certain identification. A possible lead might be afforded by a line in Book 2 of *The Dunciad*, referring to the sports of the hack authors, "Breval, Besaleel, Bond, the Varlets caught."[16] One name here is that of William Bond, although his known links with Curll do not begin until

1719 (much of his work for the publisher was signed "Henry Stanhope"), and he is not known to have worked as a schoolteacher. The address in Vinegar Yard would suit someone with Bond's dramatic interests, since he was both playwright and occasional actor. Bond enjoyed the friendship of Aaron Hill, and he was active in a literary circle including Curll's authors Martha Fowke, Philip Horneck, Susanna Centlivre, Ambrose Philips, George Sewell and others.[17] Another figure with theatrical connections who was writing regularly for Curll by 1717, if not earlier, was John Durant Breval, a product of Westminster School and Trinity College, Cambridge. He had become a fellow of the college but was expelled for misconduct in 1708. He later served in the army, and in 1720 acted as bear-leader for the grand tour of the future Earl of Cholmondley. Breval was at least qualified to be a teacher. The poet Bezaleel Morrice seems a less plausible identification, partly because it seems unlikely that Pope would use the form "Mr. *B*.": as the note by "Scriblerus" remarks, "As for *Besaleel*, it carries Forgery in the very name, nor is it, as the others are, a surname." Another dunce who fits one part of the specification was Abel Boyer, the Huguenot compiler who had acted as French tutor to the young Duke of Gloucester (son of the future Queen Anne) and produced an Anglo-French dictionary (1699), supposedly for his pupil's use. He also wrote *A Compleat French Master, for Ladies and Gentlemen* (1694). A more decisive consideration is that Boyer seems never to have worked for Curll, despite his prolific career as writer, translator and journalist.[18]

The following line runs, "At a Blacksmiths Shop in the *Friars*, a Pindarick Writer in red Stockings." Commentators have seen this as pointing to Ambrose Philips, chiefly on the basis that Pope referred to red stockings in a poem, "Macer" (*c*.1715), now confidently believed to relate to Philips.[19] As is well known, Pope and Philips had already clashed over their respective pastorals, and political divisions had further soured their relations at the time that rival versions of Homer were projected by Pope and Tickell in 1714. The description must refer to the translations of Pindar's first two Olympian odes, since Philips's own original odes had not yet appeared. The location must be Whitefriars, the precinct called "Alsatia" which had long been a refuge for fugitives, and where debtors in particular claimed sanctuary. As Macaulay put it in colourful style, " Insolvents consequently were to be found in every dwelling, from cellar to garret."[20] That Philips lodged with a blacksmith may have been a real fact, but more likely it is a comically inapt conjunction for the "nambypamby" poet.

The fifth instruction takes the form, "In the Calendar Mill Room at *Exeter* Change, a Composer of Meditations." The only work issued under

Curll's name by this date which included this term was a translation of the *Meditationes sacrae* of the protestant theologian Johann Gerhard, published under the title *The Christian's Support under all Afflictions: being the Divine Meditations of John Gerhard* (1709; second edition 1715). The book was englished by Thomas Rowell, an obscure clergyman.[21] A more promising candidate may be Francis Bragge, D.D. (1664-1728), who compiled *Prayers and Meditations upon Several Uncommon Subjects and Occasions*, published by one S. Ballard (*c.*1715). Bragge had written a fair amount for Curll, notably books on the trial of Jane Wenham for witchcraft - he actually gave evidence against the defendant in court.[22] However, his living was in Hitchin, Hertfordshire, and he does not appear to have held lectureships in London, although an earlier work *A Minister's Counsel to the Youth of his Parish when Arriv'd to Years of Discretion* (1699) was addressed to "the societies in and about London." The Exeter Exchange was located on the north side of the Strand, a short distance to the west of the shops of several leading booksellers - including those of Jacob Tonson (since 1710) and Curll himself (from 1723), whose shop on the corner of Burleigh Street was said to adjoin the Exchange. *The Dunciad* would cause members of the publishing industry ("Authors, Stationers") to foregather very close to this spot for their own grotesque Olympiad, in which Curll wins the first prize. In 1730, as it happened, his shop moved to Burleigh Street, on the angle of which stood the Exchange. A variety of activities were carried out on the premises, here involving a machine "in which cloth, paper, etc. is pressed under rollers for the purpose of smoothing or glazing" (*OED*, "calender," *sb.*, 2).[23] Curll himself sometimes held book auctions at the Exchange, possibly in the warehouse of his master Richard Smith. However, the best known role of the exchange was as a site of the undertaking business, which may indicate a grisly joke on Pope's part about the author quartered here.

II

For the next port of call, we move about two hundred yards to the north. The text reads, "At the Three *Tobacco Pipes* in *Dog* and *Bitch* Yard, one that has been a Parson, he wears a blue Camblet Coat trim'd with black: my best Writer against *revealed Religion*." The only inn recorded with this exact name was one located near St Martin's in the Field's church, at the west end of the Strand, in the vicinity of Lancaster Court. On an earlier occasion I surmised that Dog and Bitch Yard was more likely to have been situated in the adjoining parish of St Giles's. This was partly on the basis of a reference in a comedy by John Dryden, *The Wild Gallant* (1663), where the bawd Lady du Lake acknowledges that she lives "in St. *Luknors* Lane at the Cat and Fiddle." Two of her whores lodge respectively in Dog and Bitch Yard and "Sodom." Loveby, the gallant of the title, expostulates with her: "Plague had you no other places in the Town to name but *Sodom*, and *Luknors-Lane* for Lodgings."[24] This would indicate that we need to seek an address closer to Drury Lane than Charing Cross. Although contemporary maps and directories give no direct help, a careful application to *Remarks on London* by William Stow (1722) will supply the necessary clue. This occurs in Stow's entry: *"Turnstile Alley*, in Drury lane, L[ondon]. It was formerly (when a most notorious Nest of Strumpets) called *Dog and Bitch Yard*." Turnstile Alley in turn can be found on maps of the city: it formed the narrow eastern portion of Castle Street, the road running parallel to Long Acre, and entered Drury Lane almost opposite the entry to Lewkners Lane on the other side of the street. The alley was known as a site of prostitution, as emerges from a work which identified the main resorts of women of the town: "They were dispersed through every quarter of the town; but Moor-Fields, Whetstone's Park, Lukeners's Lane, and Dog and Bitch Yard, were their capital seraglios."[26]

It is now possible to extend the surmise and propose that the establishment in question was one mentioned in a court case at the Old Bailey in July 1726. The trial was that of Martin Mackintosh, who had been indicted for assaulting Joseph Sellers with intent to commit with him "the detestable Sin of Sodomy." The alleged victim, evidently an under-cover informant, deposed that he was conducted "to several Sodomitical Houses in order to detect some Persons who frequented them." Among these was the house of Mr Jones, "a Tallow-Chandler, at the Tobacco Roll and Crown or 3 Tobacco-Rolls know not which in Drury-Lane."[25] This places the address in the exact topographic and moral context for which Pope's satire calls.

Once more, the location does not enable us to fix which of Curll's authors is meant, and no one obviously fills the bill in this case. The "best Writer" available for the purpose among the staff of house authors might appear to be Charles Gildon, although his works on deism to which Pope refers in a note to *The Dunciad* were produced before Curll started up in business.[26] In any case, Gildon is a stronger candidate in another category - and he had never been in holy orders. Others who do meet this requirement seem not to have worked for Curll. The most likely name is that of John Toland, although he would appear to be a long shot at first sight. Toland, not previously regarded as one of Curll's stable, was thought by many to have been taken orders in early life: in *An Argument against Abolishing Christianity,* Swift calls him "An *Irish* priest, the Son of an *Irish* Priest."[27] This was quite wrong, but it is possible that Toland was once destined for the Presbyterian ministry. According to his editor, the Huguenot and Baylian author Pierre Des Maizeaux, some "eminent dissenters" supported his studies at Leiden, in the hope that he "in time, he wou'd be serviceable to them in the quality of a Minister."[28] In the event the young man did not become a clergyman, but Pope may have been unaware of that fact, or have chosen to ignore it. However, Toland certainly operated within Curll's circle of authorship. He had written for the bookseller's early partner Egbert Sanger, while several of his books at the start of the Hanoverian dynasty were brought out by publishers like Ferdinand Burleigh and William Mears who often acted as a cloak for Curll.[29] We know that Curll charged Toland for printing expenses in 1714 in connection with an unidentified work entitled "New Gospel Discovered". This may be part of *Nazarenus,* published by Roberts and others in 1718. At the same time, Curll lent the needy author two guineas. Moreover, in 1718 Toland drafted a letter to the publisher, on the subject of his proposed *History of the Druids* (posthumously published as *A Critical History of the Celtic Religion*).[30]

By this time Toland's worldly affairs were in decline; he is said to have been meanly housed in a carpenter's house in Putney, where he spent his days in poverty, made all the worse by losses in the South Sea Bubble, prior to his death in 1722. His correspondence with Viscount Molesworth reveals his declining health and morale: Molesworth even alludes to the "poverty" of his landlady.[31] But there had been one more burst of the old energy when Toland helped to set up the first Order of Druids in 1717. Following a meeting at the Apple Tree Tavern in Charles Street, Covent Garden, he was allegedly inaugurated as arch-druid of the "Mother Grove" at a ceremony on Primrose Hill during the autumnal equinox.[32] The intriguing fact here is that Charles Street lies not quite a hundred yards south of Dog and Bitch Yard, just across Covent Garden market. Toland appears in *The Dunciad,* in the company of Matthew Tindal, where the two men figure as those "not so happy as to be obscure, who writ against the Religion of their Country."[33] The close similarity in wording with the *Further Account* (writing against religion) may just be a coincidence, but it may not. One reason for placing credence in this connection is that in 1722 there appeared one of the famous instant biographies, entitled *An Historical Account of the Life and Writings of the late Eminently Famous Mr. John Toland. By one of his most Intimate Friends. In a Letter to the Lord ****.* This book carries on its title-page the names of the usual suspects (Roberts, Mears, Brotherton, Graves and Chetwood), but Curll almost certainly had a hand in the publication, and may well have been the author.

The next stage would involve only a short step for the porter. His instructions here run, "At Mr. *Summers* a Thief-Catchers, in *Lewkners* Lane, the man that wrote against the Impiety of Mr. *Rowe*'s Plays." This time there can be little doubt that Gildon is the man. He had been responsible for *A New Rehearsal, or Bays the Younger*, published in April 1714, with a second edition in May 1715.[34] This, a mock-drama, did more than assail Rowe, a close friend of Pope at this juncture. It was also the first substantial attack which Curll launched against Pope, for its second part contains sarcastic comments on "Sawney Dapper" and many of the early poems. The *Full Account* makes it plain that Pope knew his man, since it includes a statement given to Curll, "Mr. *Gildon's Rehearsal*: or *Bays the Younger*, did more harm to me than to Mr. *Rowe*."[35] Pope did not forget about this satire, and mentions it in a *Dunciad* note. Curll asserted in his *Key* to the poem (1728) that Gildon had written another abusive pamphlet, entitled *A True Character of Mr. Pope and his Writings*, which appeared under the imprint of Sarah Popping (a cover for Curll, as often) in May 1716. This was just in time to have caught Pope's attention for the *Further Account*. However, Curll later corrected himself and gave the work to Dennis, a shift Pope naturally observed.

Lewkners Lane turns up with almost ubiquitous monotony in the literature of the Restoration and early eighteenth century. Situated at the top end of Drury Lane, not far short of its junction with St Giles's High Street, it ran barely a hundred yards north-eastwards- yet its associations with vice and squalor gave it a disproportionate prominence. As we have already seen, Dryden names it as the residence of a bawd, while Samuel Butler wrote in *Hudibras* of "The nymphs of chaste Diana's train, / The same with those of Lewkner's Lane." A link to one of the other addresses on the list is provided by a closely parallel scene in *The Beggar's Opera* (II.iii) a few years later, when Macheath likewise sends a porter to seek out the "ladies" he would like to entertain. One of the street-girls is to be found in Vinegar Yard, and one in Lewkners Lane. But Pope's reference has even more edge and particularity. At this very moment there was a real-life "Somers a Thief-taker in Newtner's Lane," who would figure in Applebee's *Weekly Journal* on 8 September 1716. A few years earlier a more resonant connection had been forged, when the most famous of all thief-takers, Jonathan Wild, set up shop with a brothel in the street in late 1712 after gaining discharge from a debtors' gaol. Wild did not stay very long there with his mistress Mary Milliner (or Molyneux), but his brother Andrew later kept a "case" at the Black Boy in Newtonhouse Lane, another form of the name.[36] As a further indication of the character of this street, the escape-artist Jack Sheppard, whose career is ironically echoed in Macbeth's "breaks" from gaol in *The Beggar's Opera*, frequented a tavern in Lewkners Lane: it was known as the Black Lion, and operated also as a brothel. Here Sheppard met his doxy Edgeworth Bess, and together they set up a brandy-shop, which equally seems to have provided sexual services and to receive stolen goods. That was about six years ahead when *A Further Account* came out; but as often Pope seems to have had an acute sense of the way things were going.

III

The eighth item on the list reads: "At the Farthing Pye House in *Tooting Fields*, the young Man who is writing my new *Pastorals*." This, as has been pointed out more than once, must refer to Thomas Purney, whose *Pastorals. After the Simple Manner of Theocritus* were published by Curll and Rebecca Burleigh (a longtime coadjutor of his), together with J. Brown, on 16 November 1716. Purney was a recent Cambridge graduate aged only twenty-one. Three years later on the death of Paul Lorrain, who had held the post since 1700, he succeeded as the official "Ordinary" (chaplain) of Newgate prison, and took over the preparation of the "Accounts" which described the "behaviour, confessions and last speeches" of prisoners who had gone to the gallows. A contemporary referred to him as "a Young Suckling Divine of 24 Years of Age," unripe for the task.[37] Nevertheless, in this capacity he became better known than as a poet. Ault suggests that Pope must have had a sight of Purney's book, with its naïve endorsement of "simple" pastoral, since otherwise "it is difficult to understand why [he] should have alluded to Purney at all."[38] In fact Pope had no particular quarrel with some of Curll's writers: it was their association with the bookseller which earned them a reference. This circumstance weakens Ault's argument that the *Further Account* must have been written after the appearance of the *Pastorals* in November.

As the century wore on, the "Farthing Pye House" which gained most celebrity was the one situated on the road from Marylebone to Tottenham Court Road. However, Pope certainly means an older one, on Windmill Hill between Moorfields and Hoxton. This location, mentioned in Defoe's *Colonel Jacque*, is properly termed Tenter Fields. It is something of a misnomer, since alcoholic drinks could certainly be obtained here: we can tell this from a number of transcripts of trials, which also reveal that it was common for criminals to meet another there. In 1739 it was described by a witness, a drawer or waiter there, as "the Farthing Pye House, the Sign of

the Maiden Head, a Publick House on Windmill Hill."[39] Purney may well
have been getting to know some of his future customers on the road to
Tyburn if he really spent time at this spot.

Next comes the longest set of instructions: "At the Laundresses, at the
Hole in the Wall in *Cursitors* Alley, up three Pair of Stairs, the Author of
my *Church History*- if his Flux be over - you may also speak to the
Gentleman who lyes by him in the Flock Bed, my *Index-maker*." Both
these individuals present difficulties. Curll had no church historian in the
obvious sense: the nearest to such a thing in recent years came in the work
of George Sewell, who had devoted a number of tracts to the Bishop of
Salisbury, Gilbert Burnet, targetting in particular *The History of the
Reformation in England*, whose third and last volume appeared in the year
of his death, 1715. The most suitable candidate for the role of index-maker
is likewise a figure who might fit in several categories. This is John
Oldmixon, who had lately compiled an index for Abraham van
Wicquefort's *Ambassador*, published by Lintot in April 1716. In his first
attack on Curll, the *Full Account*, which came out around 31 March, Pope
had Lintot conferring with Curll in order to "settle" the title-page of this
work.[40] That might suggest that the two booksellers had a share in the
volume, although Curll never seems to have advertised it. Later in the year
Oldmixon compiled the key to *Court Tales*, issued as a product of Roberts,
but really Curll's handiwork. In 1718 he was responsible for indexes both
to *The Old and New Testament Connected*, by Humphrey Prideaux, and to
volumes 2 and 3 of *The History of England,* by Laurence Echard (both
works published by Jacob Tonson). As a result of this last undertaking, he
was attacked in a pamphlet called *The Index-Writer* (1729), a detailed
analysis of his Whiggish entries for a largely Tory history. In a note to *The
Dunciad*, it is worth stressing, Pope pays special attention to Oldmixon's
alleged perversions of historical texts. All these facts prompt the view that
Oldmixon is the strongest candidate for this role.[41]

Cursitors Alley ran a dog-leg course at the upper end of Chancery
Lane, first east and then north, through Castle Yard to Holborn. Later in
the century, the Hole in the Wall was a well known public house: it is
mentioned in Old Bailey trials in 1763 and 1781, and appears briefly in
William Hazlitt's famous essay "The Fight." As mentioned earlier,
Oldmixon was just about to leave London to take up a post as customs
collector in Somerset. When he came back to the capital about fifteen
years ago, he was living in Southampton Buildings, the next court at the
top of Chancery Lane to Cursitors Alley. It seems possible that he would
return to a site close to a former home. In any event, Pope's reference
carries with it the usual air of verisimilitude: it is amusing to note that in

1751 a witness at the Old Bailey mentioned a laundress who had lodgings in White's Alley, Chancery Lane. This was a court running back-to-back with Cursitors Alley for the length of its east-west section. Almost opposite on the west side of Chancery Lane could be found Chichester Rents, where Gildon was living in 1719.

The tenth direction to the porter takes this form: "The *Cook's Wife* in *Buckingham* Court; bid her bring along with her the *Similes* that were lent her for her next new Play." This is the easiest of all to unravel. Pope refers to Susanna Centlivre, who had been living since late 1712 or early 1713 in Buckingham Court, Charing Cross. This was a short and narrow street off the west side of Whitehall, running into Spring Garden: it was here that she died in 1723. Her husband was Joseph Centlivre, employed in the Privy Kitchen as "yeoman of the mouth" successively under Queen Anne and George I. The couple had married in 1707. Curll had published recent plays by Centlivre, and Pope suggests in the *Further Account* that she was involved in a satire directed against him on 31 May: "*Resolv'd*, That a *Ballad* be made against Mr. *Pope*, and that Mr. *Oldmixon*, Mr. *Gildon* and Mrs.*Centlivre* do prepare and bring in the same." This was a charge he repeated in the notes to *The Dunciad*, but Curll denied her responsibility, stating that this work, *The Catholick Poet*, was written by Oldmixon alone, with "not one Word by Mrs. *Centlivre*."[42] As for the new play, this is assuredly *The Cruel Gift*, a tragedy which would be performed at Drury Lane on 17 December and then published by Curll in January 1717. According to Sewell, who provided a prologue, the play had been written two years before, having presumably been held over because of political sensitivities at the time of the Jacobite rising. Rowe supplied the epilogue, and according to one early source he gave some "slight touches" to the author, whom he greatly admired, "particularly a Simile of an *Halcyon* building her Nest in fine Weather. . .was his." It has been speculated by Centlivre's biographer that it was through his friendship with the poet laureate, Rowe, that Pope came to know of this aid.[43] In general this makes a plausible case: Pope's informants cannot all be identified, but his surprisingly close knowledge of doings in the bookseller's workshop seems to derive at least in part from Lintot and Rowe, who was himself regularly published by Curll.[44]

Following this, the porter must scoot across London: "Call at *Budge Row* for the Gentleman you use to go to in the Cock-loft; I have taken away the Ladder, but his Landlady has it in keeping." This is the only instruction which bears out the canard, retailed in contemporary and later sources, that Curll kept his authors virtually under house arrest while they completed his commissions. That landladies took care to secure the "moveables" of struggling authors is a comic motif used in the first scene of Henry Fielding's play *The Author's Farce* (1730), a work featuring an obvious caricature of Curll in the guise of the grasping "Bookweight." It is clearly impossible to fill out such a vague reference to an unnamed gentleman, but Budge Row can be precisely plotted. It ran from Wallbrook to New Queen Street, in the heart of the City - the only address on the list which belongs within the ancient walled capital, now the commercial centre of town.

Last comes a casual instruction in throwaway style: "I don't much care if you ask at the *Mint* for the old Beetle-brow'd Critick, and the purblind Poet at the Alley over against St. *Andrew Holbourn*. But this as you have time." As is well known, the Mint was a refuge for debtors, south of the river in Southwark. As recently as 12 August 1715, the former laureate, Nahum Tate, had died within the precincts of the Mint.[45] A Tory poem which has sometimes been attributed to Swift, *John Dennis, the Sheltring Poet's Invitation to Richard Steele, the Secluded Party-writer, and Member; to come and live with him in the Mint* (1714), places the famous critic in this locality. It is known that between 1711 and 1715 Dennis lived for much of the time "within the verges of the royal court," in order to escape arrest for debt. He sold a sinecure government post at the end in January 1715, and should have been free to move about as he wished: in 1716, we are told, "he left London in June, was in Hanworth on the 20th of September, and back in Whitehall on October 3." The following year he made a short tour of "the wilds of Surrey."[46] Pope is not on his oath in his satire, but we can be sure that Dennis, a native Londoner, would not have been far from the action. He had produced *A True Character of Mr. Pope* for Curll on 31 May: while it is not clear that Pope knew the identity of the author at first, the two men had been at odds since the time of *An Essay in Criticism* in 1711, Furthermore, Dennis was the only well-known critic who could reasonably be described as "old," even by the elastic standards of the age: he was fifty-nine, as against Gildon's fifty-one years and Oldmixon's forty-three. In an passage from Book 2 of *The Dunciad* in which Dennis reflects "Milo-like" on his age: "Am I now threescore?" A note refers us to the *Metamorphoses*, Book 15, where the athlete Milo deplores the loss of his former Herculean strength in his senility.[47] Dennis is frequently described with a scowl on his face, perhaps a comment on his attitudes more than on his physiognomy. But Dennis was the first of Pope's opponents to make explicit reference to the poet's bodily deformities, and this might explain why the only physical description of any of the authors occurs at this point. In an earlier prose satire, *The Narrative of Dr. Robert Norris* (1713), Pope had portrayed Dennis in similar words: "His Eye-brows were grey, long, and grown together, which he knit with Indignation when any thing was spoken."[48]

The other part of this instruction is less straightforward to interpret. A forest of small streets had grown up in the vicinity of St Andrew's church, which stood on the rise of Holborn Hill, just above the bridge spanning the Fleet Ditch. As John Strype would record in 1720, the area around here was "a Place of little Account, both to Buildings and Inhabitants; and pestered with small and ordinary Alleys and Courts, taken up by the meaner Sort of People." Almost directly opposite the church, running northwards, was Field Lane, notorious as part of "a separate town or district calculated for the reception of the darkest and most dangerous enemies to society."[49] In this very street was found Mother Clap's molly house, "next to the *Bunch of Grapes*."[50] We need not suppose that the author in question lodged in this particular alley (Field Lane was little more), but Pope has phrased the directions in a way that might remind knowing readers that this address lay close to the road to Tyburn. As for the purblind poet, the only suggestion offered so far is yet again that of Gildon, who did suffer from failing eyesight in his last years.[51] But that he was far from unique in the group in that respect; and the works which had brought him to Pope's attention were not poems for the most part: the brief biography appended to *The Dunciad* concentrates on Gildon's prose, as "a writer of criticisms and libels of the last age."[52] On the other hand, it is true that in *An Epistle to Arbuthnot* Pope linked the two men under consideration here: the earliest version, drafted around 1715, reads:

> If meagre Gildon draws his venal Quill.
> I wish the Man a Dinner, and sit still;
> If D-- rhymes, and raves in furious Fret,
> I'll answer D---s, when I am in debt:
> Hunger, not Malice, make such Authors print,
> And who'll wage War with Bedlam or the Mint?[53]

All this really establishes is Pope may have associated Dennis with the Mint, and very likely thought Gildon a serious irritant, who deserved a prominent place among the hacks of the day. Curll had numerous poets on his books, and some of them made it into *Peri Bathous* and/or *The Dunciad*. Finally, as we have seen, Gildon fits the context exactly in the case of the man who wrote against Rowe's plays. The poet must be sought elsewhere, but the field is too open to permit any kind of certainty: it includes minnows such as Thomas Foxton and Francis Chute, active for Curll at this time.

One more paragraph in the *Further Account* relates to the summons. In this the narrator reports that all those whom the porter called on appeared at Curll's shop on time, except two: "one of whom was the Gentleman in the Cock-loft, his Landlady being out of the way, and the *Gradus ad Parnassum* taken down; the other happened to be too closely watch'd by the Bailiffs." This latter figure could be anyone, apart from those known to attend, such as Gildon and Oldmixon. In addition, the resident of Budge Row can be effectively taken out of contention.[54]

Considerable room for guesswork remains. No firm niche has been found for Lewis Theobald, who by 1716 had acquired a healthy back-list of publications, had started to offend Pope, and had written items for Curll. In the 1720s and 1730s Theobald was living at Wyan's Court, near Bloomsbury Square. Another obvious absentee is William Pittis, one of Curll's most prolific authors, and noted for his speed in producing lives of the recently departed. Since Pittis is not known to have attacked Pope, he might have escaped mention on that ground alone, but this seems unlikely. We have not managed to assign a clearcut role to Dr George Sewell, one of the most likely targets of the satire: Pope certainly knew all about him, since he crops up as "sanguine Sew-" in an early draft of the same episode of the *Epistle to Arbuthnot* just discussed.[55] He is clearly the best candidate for the role of church historian.

All the locations in the pamphlet may now be defined with a high degree of confidence. Among the authors, Philips, Gildon, Purney, Centlivre and Dennis may be considered virtual certainties. Ozell as one of the translators and Oldmixon as index-writer rank as high probabilities, while as just noted Sewell offers a strong possibility. Other identifications can only be highly conjectural in the present state of our knowledge, with Toland the most arresting among outside chances.[56]

IV

Some general conclusions follow from the evidence cited here, even though the identity of many of the authors cannot be definitively established. We have seen that Pope maintains an exceptionally tight hold on topographic detail. Even for those who could not pick up all the local thrusts (surely a majority of the audience even in the eighteenth century), enough clues are left to allow readers to gain a clear picture of the milieu in which Curll's writers operated. The dwellings of these men are impermanent, often simply rooms in taverns, and they are mostly found in cheap letting areas where substantial citizens would never have chosen to live. We need to remember that this is a slanted version of reality, produced for satiric purposes. Somewhat unfairly, Pope contrives to associate professional authorship with unsalubrious parts of London, linked to crime, destitution or sexual transgression: for example, the Mint, Whitefriars, Moorfields, Vinegar Yard, and Lewkners Lane. He even uses the seemingly obsolete, or at most popular, name of Dog and Bitch Yard. To create the effect he wants, he leaves out writers like Blackmore and Leonard Welsted who did not depend on Curll for the major part of their livelihood, and who could afford to reside in more affluent districts.[57]

Rhetorically this works to insinuate the idea that Curll has a corps of starveling writers at his disposal. We can easily forget that few of these authors were wholly dependent on Curll for their livelihood: they wrote for newspapers and the stage, as well as for a variety of other booksellers. It is also easy to overlook the fact that a good part of Curll's list was provided by scholars and gentlemen, especially where his extensive library of serious books on antiquarian subjects was concerned. Since Pope's aim was to portray Curll as a purveyor of gutter-press productions, he needed to keep these other considerations out of the reader's awareness. Whatever the merits of the pamphlet may be, these obviously cannot be equated with the historical accuracy, or otherwise, of references to persons or places named in the text. Nevertheless, Pope's victims had learnt to dread the precision of his onslaughts, and the *Further Account* surely gains cogency from the level of specific detail it commands.

Notes

[1] Pope *Corr*, 1: 371-5.

[2] Pat Rogers, *Grub Street: Studies in a Subculture* (London: Methuen, 1972), pp. 76-83.

[3] Several contemporary maps of London have proved useful, notably John Rocque's "Plan of the Cities of London and Westminster and Borough of Southwark" (1727), now available together with an index as *The A to Z of Georgian London* (Lympne, Kent: Harry Margary, 1981). Among various contemporary guidebooks the most detailed topographically is *New Remarks of London* (1732), compiled by the Company of Parish Clerks.

[4] Pope *Prose,* 1: 278-9 (this edition is not annotated).

[4] See Christine Gerrard, *Aaron Hill: The Muses' Projector 1685-1750* (Oxford: Oxford University Press, 2003), p. 41. It is scarcely decisive (since the occupation was a common one) that John Skerratt of Petty France, a tallow chandler, was listed among Westminster constables in 1738: see *The Historical Register for the Year 1738* (London, 1738), p. 101.

[5] Howard William Troyer, *Ned Ward of Grub Street; A Study of Sub-Literary London in the Eighteenth Century* (Cambridge, MA: Harvard University Press, 1946), pp. 169, 175.

[6] *TE* 5: 87.

[7] Quoted by Troyer, *Ward*, p. 201.

[8] Troyer, *Ward*, p. 179.

[9] *TE* 6: 37-8, 59-60, 123. Ozell was still in Pope's sights in *The Dunciad*, when a boastful notice in a newspaper by the translator is reproduced in the Errata (*TE* 5: 92-3, 198).

[10] See Howson, *Thief-Taker*, pp. 51-2. According to Jonathan Wild's own narrative, Hitchen was an habitué of the most famous of all the "molly houses", that of Mother Clap (Howson, *Thief-Taker*, pp. 62-5). For fuller information on all these matters, see Rictor Norton, *Mother Clap's Molly House* (London: Gay Men's Press, 1992). For an account of Hitchen's activities within the wider context of crime and punishment in this period, see J.M. Beattie, *Policing and Punishment in London, 1660-1750: Urban Crime and the Limits of Terror* (Oxford: Oxford University Press, 2001), pp. 252-6.

[11] See for instance the trial of William Brown on 11 July 1726, in *The Proceedings on the King's Commission of the Peace, and Oyer and Terminer, and the Jail-Delivery of Newgate, held for the City of London, and County of Middlesex, at Justice-Hall, in the Old Baily* (London, 1726), p. 8.

[12] John Strype, *A Survey of the Cities of London and Westminster, brought down from the Year 1633 to the present Time*, 6 pts in 2 vols (London, 1720), 6: 75. In 1742 Ned Ward's *The Cudgel*, containing an attack on Pope and dating originally from 1728, was reprinted and said to be sold at the author's house in Vinegar Yard, near Drury Lane. Ward had died years before.

[13] *Proceedings. . in the Old Baily* (London, 1724), p. 6. For a witness who was obviously a receiver of stolen clothing in Vinegar Yard, see the *Proceedings* for 1746, p. 294. Oswald Dykes, *English Proverbs, with Moral Reflexions: In Imitation of Sir Roger L'Estrange's Æsop* (1713), p. 115, has a passage on would-be gentlemen such as "Mr. such a one, TAYLOR of Thieving-Lane, *Squire* PORTER of Pimp-Alley, *Sir Edward* SPENDTHRIFT of Vinegar-Yard, *my Lord* CROOK-BACK of the Livery-Stables."

[14] Thomas Gordon, *The Humourist: being Essays upon several Subjects*, 3rd edn (1724), pp. 167-8.

[15] Pope *Prose*, 1: 283.

[16] *TE* 5: 111.

[17] Gerrard, *Hill*, p. 73.

[18] An alternative candidate might seem to be Barnham Goode, who has generally been described as a master at Eton College. But this was really Francis Goode (1674-1739), a Fellow of King's College, Cambridge, and teacher at Eton from 1720 (second master by 1727): he may have been a brother. Barnham (d. *c.*1750) was a journalist residing in Westminster, and he associated with fellow dunces such as Lewis Theobald, Giles Jacob, Dennis and Thomas Cooke. Pope accused him in *The Dunciad* of writing "many anonymous Libels in Newspapers for Hire," but these appear to date from the 1720s. Curll told Robert Walpole that Goode had interceded on his behalf to have "some provision" made for him (*TE* 5: 163; *Gentleman's Magazine*, 68 (1798), 190).

[19] *TE* 6: 137-9.

[20] T.B. Macaulay, *The History of England*, 3 vols (London: Everyman, 1906), 1: 290.

[21] Rowell served as Rector of Great Cressingham in Norfolk until his death in 1718. His receipt for work on the translation is dated 2 June 1713 (British Library, Add 38728, f.185(b).). He may have been related by marriage to Curll, whose first wife was Anne Rowell of St Martin's in the Fields – the parish where Exeter Exchange stood.

[22] Pope mentions one of these books in *A Full Account* (Pope *Prose*, 1: 260).

[23] For a description of the Exchange, see Hugh Phillips, *Mid-Georgian London: A Topographical and Social Survey of Central and Western London about 1750* (London: Collins, 1964), p. 160. Its reputation had once been more dubious: *A Trip from St. James's to the Royal Exchange* (1744) called it "a Place which is said to have formerly to have furnished the Men of Quality with most of their Mistresses." However this "trade" had now moved to Tavistock Street, and "the chief Apartments converted to more *serious* and *solemn Uses*," that is the business of funeral undertakers. See the reprint in *Tricks of the Town*, ed. Ralph Straus (London: Chapman & Hall, 1928), p. 216.

[24] *The Works of John Dryden*, vol. 8, ed. John Harrington Smith and Dugald MacMillan (Berkeley: University of California Press, 1962), pp. 59-60.

[26] William Stow, *Remarks on London: being an Exact Survey of the Cities of London and Westminster, Borough of Southwark* (London, 1722), p. 80); James Granger, *A Biographical History of England, from Egbert the Great to the Revolution: Consisting of Characters Disposed in Different Classes*, 4 vols (London, 1779), 4: 221. Granger was writing about the late seventeenth century, and claimed to have used state poems in manuscript belonging to the Duchess of Portland (daughter of Pope's friend Lord Harley). It will be obvious that three of the four places named figure among the locations for Pope's authors. One of the whores listed in Thomas Berington, *New from the Dead* (1756), p. 123, is "*Foggibissa* in *Dog* and *Bitch*-Yard in *Long Acre*." This is plainly the same location, as Long Acre is the next street to the south.

[25] *Proceedings. . .in the Old Bailey* (London, 1726), p. 6.

[26] *TE* 5: 92.

[27] Swift *Prose*, 2: 37. Toland studied at Glasgow, Edinburgh (where he obtained a Master of Arts), Leiden, and briefly at Oxford (though not as a member of the university), as well as the Franciscan College at Prague.

[28] "Some Memoirs of the Life and Writings of Mr. John Toland," in Toland, *A Collection of Several Pieces*, ed. Pierre Des Maizeaux, 2 vols (London: J. Peele, 1726), 1: ix

[29] British Library, Add MS 4295, f. 25. In 1718 Curll reprinted Toland's *Description of Epsom* (1711) in his edition of John Aubrey's *Natural History of Surrey*.

[30] See Alan Harrison, "Notes on the Correspondence of John Toland," *I Castelli di Yale*, Anno IV, *John Toland torna a Dublino* (1999), pp. 182-200.

[31] Toland, *Collection*, 2: 484. The writer's letters were directed from Putney in the last three years of his life, January 1719 to March 1722. See also Des Maizeaux, "Memoirs," 1: lxxxviii.

[32] As the home of one of the four original freemasons lodges who combined to found the first Grand Lodge in June 1717, the Apple Tree Tavern had hosted a meeting to arrange the union. See James Anderson, *The New Book of Constitutions of the Antient and Honourable Fraternity of Free and Accepted Masons*, p. 109. It was thus involved in another pioneering secret society at the very same moment. Toland has been claimed as a freemason by Margaret Jacob, but the evidence seems inconclusive. None of the details regarding the foundation of the druidical "Bond" can be regarded a dependable: however, the connection with the Apple Tree tavern is among the more plausible parts of the story.

[33] *TE* 5: 144.

[34] Like scores of Curll's pamphlets, this carries the name of James Roberts on the title-page. However, Roberts was merely a distributor, and it is certain that in these cases Curll was the true agent of publication, as his advertisements and catalogues abundantly demonstrate.

[35] Pope *Prose*, 1: 263.

[36] Howson, *Thief-Taker*, pp. 44-7, 134-5. The association of thief-taking with this particular area is confirmed by references in the Old Bailey *Proceedings*: to give a single instance, a defendant charged with assault and robbery in late 1732 gave evidence that one of his gang "made an Agreement with *Kirk* and *Brock, Will. James*, and the Rest of the Thief-Takers in *Drury-Lane*." In 1726 Margaret Howel was convicted of keeping a disorderly house in Lukenor's Lane, where she entertained "lewd and disorderly Persons" (*British Journal*, 5 March). She was fined only 1*s.* on account of her poverty, but whipped at the cart's tail around the Drury Lane area, and sent to the house of correction for three months.

[37] Quoted by Howson, *Thief-Taker*, p. 119.

[38] Pope *Prose*, 1: xcix-c. For a freely imaginative account of "Thomas Pureney," see Charles Whibley, *A Book of Rogues* (London: Macmillan, 1921).

[39] See for instance the trials of Benjamin Goddard (1724), Thomas Morris (1736), Joseph Shaw (1737), and James Wint (1739) in the Old Bailey *Proceedings*. (In some cases there were multiple defendants: the first name in the charges is cited here.) The first named was arrested while drinking at "the *Farthing Pye-house* near *Moorfields*."

[40] Pope *Prose*, 1: 259. Somehow Pope had managed to get the jump on Oldmixon, whose recent activities are retailed in embarrassing detail in the *Full Account* (see Pope, *Prose*, p. 265). Moreover, Pope knew of a work called *The Conduct of the Earl of Nottingham*, which he mentions in both pamphlets as unpublished. In fact this work by Oldmixon was suppressed owing to family pressure, and never came before the public. For a fuller analysis of the entire episode, see Pat Rogers, "The Conduct of the Earl of Nottingham: Curll, Oldmixon and the Finch Family," *Review of English Studies*, 21 (1970): 175-81.

[41] A satire on Oldmixon in Mist's *Weekly Journal* for 26 July 1728 alleged that he had "lately retired from his Garret and trade of Drawing up Indexes, making Ballads, and writing of Strange Relations."

[42] Pope *Prose*, 1: 282; *TE* 5: 146.

[43] See John Wilson Bowyer, *The Celebrated Mrs. Centlivre* (Durham: University of North Carolina Press, 1952), pp. 192, 207-08.

[44] While the sex of the author is not revealed in most cases, it looks as if Centlivre was the only woman on the porter's schedule. Among other clues is a reference in *A Full Account*, where Curll is made to bequeath "a Week's Wages Advance to each of his Gentleman Authors, with some small Gratuity in particular to Mrs. *Centlivre*" (Pope *Prose*, 1: 265.)

[45] Curll himself would become familiar with the operations of shifty characters such as the mistress of the Bull Tavern in the Mint: this is when he was incarcerated in a sponging-house in the vicinity of the King's Bench prison during his legal troubles in the middle 1720s.

[46] See H.G. Paul, *John Dennis: His Life and Criticism* (New York: Columbia University Press, 1911), pp. 59-60.

[47] *TE* 5: 135. In the 1743 version of the poem, the role of Milo was transferred to Oldmixon: there were good reasons for this, in that Dennis had been dead for several years, while Oldmixon had emerged in the 1720s as a critic, and he had himself now reached his seventies.

[48] Pope *Prose*, 1: 158. In this pamphlet Dennis is given a different residence, with "Lodgings near *Charing-cross*, up three Pair of Stairs" (p. 157).

[49] Quoted by M. Dorothy George, *London Life in the 18ᵗʰ Century* (New York: Capricorn Books, 1965), p. 82. George points out that "the Field Lane district was intersected by the filthy channel of the Fleet ditch (called in 1722 'a nauceious and abominable sink of nastiness')" (p. 85). All readers of Swift and Pope will be familiar with the use they made of this material. For Strype, see his edition of John Stow, *A Survey of the Cities of London and Westminster*, 2 vols (London: A. Churchill and others, 1720), 1.iii: 256.

[50] *Proceedings. . .in the Old Baily* (London, 1726), p. 6.

[51] See his letters to Matthew Prior, written from Bull Head Court off Jewen Street in 1721, in Historical Manuscripts Commission, *Calendar of the Manuscripts of the Marquess of Bath*, vol. 58 (London: HMC, 1908), 3: 506-7.

[52] *TE* 5: 92.

[53] *TE* 6: 142.

[54] One of the resolutions taken by the assembled group is to abuse Pope at ladies' tea tables: but "that in Consideration our Authors are not *well dress'd* enough, Mr. C--y be deputed for that Service." This must mean Walter Carey (1685-1757), a well known courtier and MP. Pope called him "a fond Fop" in a poem "To Eustace Budgell, Esq." (*c*.1714) which also sneers at Boyer, Gildon, Ozell and Philips. See *TE* 6: 123, as well as other references, pp. 112, 141, 172.

[55] *TE* 6: 283. In addition, Sewell was collecting material for a translation of Ovid's *Metamorphoses*, intended by Curll as a counterblast to the high-prestige version edited for Tonson by Sir Samuel Garth. Pope actually had a section on Vertumnus and Pomona reprinted in Sewell's edition, which appeared in October 1716. Some of Curll's team figure in the poem Pope composed about the Garth version, *Sandys's Ghost* (c.1717).

[56] Toland had a low opinion of Oldmixon, whom he called "one of the despicable tools of the late poetical ministry" (letter to the Earl of Oxford, *c*.1712, in Historical Manuscripts Commission, *Manuscripts of the Duke of Portland*, vol. 29 (London: HMC, 1899), 5: 260). But then Oldmixon despised Pittis. In real life

Curll's hacks seldom acted with the cooperative zeal they show in the later section of the pamphlet: more representative is their behaviour in the earlier part of the text, where they glance suspiciously at one another on entering Curll's shop.

[57] This may account for the omission of Thomas Burnet and George Duckett among others. They were certainly scourges of the poet at this date, but they did not regularly produce material for Curll, and seem to fit none of the descriptions in the text.

CHAPTER SEVEN

"A STRANGE AND WONDERFULL RELATION": JOHN GAY, POPE, AND THE MASQUERADE

Not far short of forty years ago, the late P.J. Croft published the text of a poem which had been almost entirely unknown hitherto, with a photographic facsimile of the holograph manuscript by John Gay.[1] This appeared too late to be used in the standard edition of Gay's *Poetry and Prose* (1974), and to date the item has not been brought fully into the Gay canon.[2] In his brief introduction, Croft remarked, "this 'Excellent New Ballad' can be enjoyed without the detailed annotation to which it might no doubt be subjected." True enough, but the work makes considerably more sense if its precise context is delineated and its verbal surface explored: its subject-matter (fashionable masquerades in London) indicates a very particular historical situation around 1717-19.

My aim here is to take up the implied invitation offered by Croft. In the opening section, I shall describe the background to the poem, and after this the poem is printed, as set out by Gay in what is apparently a revised draft. Textual variants have been listed in Croft's transcript, and they are visible in his facsimile version. Here I record only the few significant alterations Gay made in his draft. Thirdly an attempt is made to provide thorough annotation, and then lastly some tentative conclusions are offered on issues of attribution and dating, as well as the place of the work within the canon of Scriblerian writing.[3]

The draft is found in the Portland manuscripts, now preserved in the University of Nottingham Library (MS Portland Pw V351). It is written in Gay's hand on a single sheet of paper folded to make two leaves. There is no sure way of dating the item exactly. The subject, that is the fashion for masquerades in the Haymarket which had been under the supervision of Johann Jakob Heidegger since 1713, points to a date from 1717, when these assemblies began to attract increased attention on a regular basis. Croft quoted a letter from Pope to Lady Mary Wortley Montagu in June 1717 which alludes to the craze,[4] and also mentioned a draft in Pope's hand of two stanzas (12 and 9) which survives among the Homer manuscripts in the British Library (Add MS 4808, f. 117). These lines had been printed, with some inaccuracies, in a volume of *Additions to the Works of Alexander Pope* (1776), and previous students naturally assumed that this indicated Pope's authorship.[5] It was only Croft's discovery of the fuller draft which pointed to Gay as the writer. The position of the poem within the Homer manuscripts might suggest that Pope's draft was written around late September 1718, and Croft accordingly proposed that the poem "was probably composed in the autumn of 1718 while [Gay] was staying in the country with Pope." However, the reference to Thomas Killigrew's play *Chit Chat* in l. 45 indicates a date no earlier than February 1719. As regards Pope's draft, Volume V of the *Iliad,* on which he was working at this period, did not appear until May 1720, so it is conceivable that he was composing the relevant section of his translation some time later than September 1718. Another possibility is that the fairly extensive revisions which apparently went on (as can be seen by comparing Gay's draft with the two stanzas Pope wrote out) proceeded into 1719, while Pope transcribed an earlier version in 1718.

Such an account rests on the assumption made by Croft, namely that the existence of the poem in Gay's hand establishes his responsibility for the work. However, a close study of the text leaves open the possibility that Pope had at least some share in its composition. This was a period when the two men had often collaborated, most obviously in the assistance Gay admitted to have received from Pope and Arbuthnot in his farcical play *Three Hours after Marriage* (1717). In addition, Gay had used lines from Pope's version of Homer in the libretto he most likely provided for Handel's *Acis and Galatea*, which is a work that can be closely connected with the time Gay spent with Pope in Oxfordshire from June to September 1718. But quite apart from such external evidence, a number of phrases in the poem directly echo usages in Pope's work at this time. There remains, too, the question as to why Pope should have written out two stanzas and two stanzas only, in a different order from that of the complete draft.[6] This issue will be taken up again later on, in the light of evidence to emerge in the course of discussion.

For the text of Pope's draft, see Nokes, "Pope and Heidegger," p. 312. If we compare this draft (*P*) with Gay's transcription (*G*), the most notable differences are these:

(1) The first stanza in *P* corresponds to stanza 12 in *G*, but it is labelled "13". On the other hand, *P*'s stanza "8" corresponds to *G*'s stanza 9. It is possible that stanzas were dropped during revision, but since the alterations move in an opposite direction, it seems likely that some kind of renumbering went on.

(2) In stanza 8, the second included in *P*, the opening line reads, "Then all like an ---a Devil appeared." As appears below at line 54, *G* fills out the blank with "Actress."

(3) In the fifth line of the same stanza in *P*, the word "Shape" was first written, before it was crossed out and "Face" inserted, as in *G* at line 59. The joke on Heidegger's evil countenance was made once more in *The Memoirs of Martinus Scriblerus*, ed. Charles Kerby-Miller (New York: Oxford University Press, 1989), p. 169. The fact that *G* adopts the revised reading might suggest that *P* represents the earlier version, but this is not conclusive.

Nokes's conjectural readings, especially as regards what became line 73 in *G*, have been vindicated by the discovery of the fuller draft. A number of minute discrepancies between the two drafts, in matters such as capitalization and punctuation, are not recorded here.

The transcript of Gay's holograph which follows contains no editorial interference, except for the suppression of a few cancelled words of no discoverable significance, and for the addition of line numbers. A notable feature of the style is a heavy reliance on proverbial usages relating to the devil; "Tilley" in the annotation refers to Morris P. Tilley, *A Dictionary of Proverbs in England in the Sixteenth and Seventeenth Centuries* (Ann Arbor: University of Michigan Press, 1950).

***

A Strange and Wonderfull
Relation how the Devill
Appeared last night
At the [Opera House *del.*] Masquerade
In the
Hay-market.
And how he carry'd away several People together with the
Roof of the House, to the great Astonishment of all the
spectators.
An Excellent New Ballad,
To the Tune of the Cutpurse

1.
A House in the Hay-market yesterday stood,
(And if it now stands 'tis a pity it should
For 'tis a vile place,
And Folks void of
Go thither to show something else, than their Face.
There Hei---r, H---r, he was so wicked,
To let in the Devil without ee'r a Ticket.

2.

For Satan the younger came to his old Sire,
Who sat with his children all around the Coal fire;
Let me go, quoth Hell's heir,   10
To yon Masquerade rare,
Which is such as would make your own Saucer Eyes stare.
And He---er, H---r, he is so wicked
He'll let in the Devil without e'er a Ticket.

3.

The Suit it was granted unto the brave boy,
Then all like a Puppy his tail wagg'd for joy
He wash'd from his breech
All the Brimstone and pitch
Lest the Ladys should smell it and think he'd the Itch.
An Attorney did offer to forge him a Ticket,   20
Nay fye, quoth the Devil I'll not be so wicked.

4.

Full tight at his Buttocks he roll'd up his Tail,
And went for to draw in his horns like a Snail;
Nay let that alone,
Quoth He to his son;
Horns, there are so many, you'll never be known.
And H---r &c.

5.

Then sprung up the Devil slabdash into Air:
Like a Gentleman called, and bilked his Chair;
But first he did go 30
To Lady B-s-w,
And to good Lady M—n's, whom so many folk know.
Then whipt to the House, show'd his horn for a Ticket,
Bless your Honour quoth H—r, open the Wicket.

6.

First he bows to a conjuror with a white stick
Then cry'd to a Lawyer hoh, hoh Brother Nick!
Knew his friends in a Trice,
Ask'd each man his Price,
And whisperd some folk who act by his Advice.
Oh H---r Hei---r, thou wert so wicked   40
To let in the Devil without e'er a Ticket.

7.
Though the room was such swearing such Bawdy, such nonsense,
That though just come from Hell, it much troubled his conscience.
But, when wit round him flew,
[The Chit-chat he knew *del.*] Some false, & some true,
Odso, cry'd the Devil, here's my K—ll—w.
Oh Hei---r &c.

8.
He tempted in all shapes, Maids, Widows, and Wives,
Who neer did such frolicks before in their lives.
And, as they tell me,   50
Some husbands still see
The print of his black hand above their Wive's knee.
Oh He---- &c.

9.
Then all like an Actress the Devil appeard,
And strait the whole house took the Dev'l by the beard;
Then a friar, then a Nun,
And then he put on
A face all the company took for his own
Ev'n thine, O false H---r, who wert so wicked
To let in &c.   60

10.
Next comes a brisk spark, and accosts him just so,
You're an Angell above, but have Hell fire below.
Quite dumb was he struck,
At this his ill luck,
And thought himself known till he call'd him B-lle C—ck
Oh Hei---r &c.

11.
Who took him for Woman, might find by the smell
That their fingers had been in the Devil of hell.
If Man's shape he chose,
And touch'd a Belle-chose   70
He burnt Lady's smocks, And sing'd their Dominos.
Oh H---r &c.

12.
Then he went to the side-board, and call'd for much liquor,
And glass after Glass, he drank quicker and quicker;
So that H---r quoth,
Nay, Saith on his Oath,

Of two hogsheads of Burgundy, Satan drank both.
But 'twas his own fault; for why was he so wicked
To let in &c.

13.
And now at the Gaming-board he took his place, 80
Then clink went his purse, as he sat by her Grace;
But how vex'd must he be,
To find ev'ry body,
Cog and palm his own bones, so much better than He!
Oh H---r &c.

14.
The Gamesters had set him; they butter'd, they tricked,
Then rap went the Box, and the Devil was nick'd.
In a rage up he flew,
All the Waxlights burnt blew,
And Dammee, he roar'd, give the Devil his due. 90
Oh H---r &c.

15.
Shelves sashes, and glasses came clatt'ring like thunder,
Then rattled the Tiles, the whole roof split asunder;
So away did he bear
All the whores that were there;
And Astrologers saw fiery tails in the Air.
Oh He---r, H---r, thou wert so wicked
To let in the Devil without e'er a ticket.

***

Annotation

Title. The King's Theatre in the Haymarket, which had become the
London home for Italian opera, under the management since 1713 of John
James Heidegger. Masquerades were held regularly there from 1717. Pope
wrote to Lady Mary Wortley Montagu, then in Constantinople, about the
time that the third volume of the *Iliad* translation was published, 3 June
1717: "We have Masquerades at the Theatre in the Haymarket of Mr
Heideker's institution; they are very frequent, yet the Adventures are not
so numerous but that of my Lady Mohun still makes the chief figure. . .
.The Political State is under great divisions, the Parties of Walpole and
Stanhope as violent as Whig and Tory. The K[ing] and P[rince of Wales]

continue Two Names: there is nothing like a Coalition, but at the Masquerade. . ." (Pope *Corr*, 1: 407).

Masquerades first attracted wide notice after the French ambassador, the Duc d'Aumont, gave a number of masked balls at his apartment in Somerset House, beginning in May 1713. One of the most constant critics of such events was Joseph Addison, who wrote an amusing account of a masquerade at the ambassador's in *Guardian* no. 154 (7 September 1713).[7] The narrator, who signs himself "Lucifer," attends the occasion in the guise of the devil, complete with a long tail. Among the revellers he encounters are a magician with a wand and "Ladies of the Night [transformed] into Saints." In describing "Such a Confusion of Sex, Age and Quality,"[8] Addison anticipates some of the material of the ballad; but this is exactly typical of Scriblerian satire, which commonly replays the themes of gentle Spectatorial humour in a harsher key.

Pope's letter refers to a time when political divisions caused the opera programme to be suspended and Handel to go abroad (see below, p. 149). However, the masquerades continued at first without any break: six were held in the winter of 1719/20. It was not until January 1721 that press announcements informed subscribers that "at the Instances of the Bishops, who waited on His Majesty, the masquerades are prohibited during this Winter." The campaign had been led by the Bishop of London, Edmund Gibson: nevertheless, Heidegger found ways to circumvent the ban, and William Law was still assailing the practice in 1725. When describing the "great New Theatre" in his *Tour* of Britain in the same year, Defoe wrote sourly, "These Meetings are called BALLS, the Word *Masquerade* not being so well relished by the *English*, who, tho' at first fond of the Novelty, began to be sick of the Thing on many Accounts."[9] Still in 1725, however, Lady Mary Wortley Montagu told her sister, "Public places flourish more than ever; we have Assemblies for every day in the week besides Court, Operas, and Masquerades" (*Complete Letters*, 2: 46). In fact the masquerade survived as a major social activity for the remainder of the century.[10]

The classic analysis of this fashionable amusement is Terry Castle, *Masquerade and Civilization: The Carnivalesque in Eighteenth-Century English Culture and Fiction* (Stanford: Stanford University Press, 1986). One of the fullest contemporary accounts from this period is to be found in Mist's *Weekly Journal* (dated by Michael Kelly 15 February 1718). Reprinting this description, Otto Erich Deutsch points out that Mist's does not contain such an item on this day. See *Reminiscences of Michael Kelly*, ed. T.E. Hook (New York: Da Capo, 1969), p. 414: Deutsch, *Handel: A Documentary Biography* (London: Cassell, 1955), pp. 80-1. As noted, the entertainment had been known in London for some years, at least since 1712, and Pope refers to masquerades twice in *The Rape of the Lock* (1: 72, 108). Further references occur in "A Roman Catholick Version of the First Psalm" (1716) in *TE* 6: 164; and in a letter to Martha Blount around March 1716 (Pope *Corr*, 1: 339).

The "tune of the Cutpurse" refers to a song in Ben Jonson's *Bartholomew Fair*, but in fact it is identical (save for not repeating the first and second lines) with the best known of all ballad melodies, that of "Packington's Pound." See Claude M. Simpson, *The British Broadside Ballad and its Music* (New Brunswick, NJ: Rutgers University Press, 1966), pp. 564-70. It is used as Air XLIII in *The Beggar's Opera*, and as "the Cutpurse" in Gay's "Newgate Garland" (*Poetry and Prose*, p. 287). Swift had also written "A Ballad to the Tune of the Cutpurse" in 1702-03.

l. 1 The "house" was the King's Theatre, built on the west side of the Haymarket by John Vanbrugh, and opened in 1705. For contemporary views of the exterior, as well as a portion of Hogarth's "Masquerades and Operas" (1724), see Hugh Philips, *Mid-Georgian London* (London: Collins, 1964), pp. 88-93: masquerade scenes are shown on p. 91. In Hogarth's design, the hard-featured impresario looks down from a window as masqueraders line up to enter the building, headed by a devil and a jester whose headdress appears to sprout horns. Full commentary is provided by Ronald Paulson, *Hogarth*, 1: 74-90. Another print of *c.*1724 shows Heidegger seized by Hercules (his lion's skin ending in a long tail), while Britannia, Minerva (?) and Piety look on together with a clergyman (possibly Bishop Gibson). The line of masqueraders is chained up outside the theatre. A more literal depiction of the scene at the Haymarket, also dated *c.*1724, is found in Giuseppe Grisoni's oil painting (now at the Victoria and Albert Museum). For these images, see Celina Fox and Aileen Ribeiro, *Masquerade* (Museum of London, 1983).

Masquerades were normally held in the Long Room, alongside the main auditorium on the western side of the building. Sometimes the opera shared its space with masquerades: thus, Handel's *Amadigi* was put on "without Scenes, the Stage being in the same magnificent Form as it was in the Ball" (i.e. the masquerade held on 21 February 1717).[11] Lotteries were also drawn on the stage of the theatre: one in 1723 attracted "a great Appearance of Nobillity and Gentry."[12] This would have interested Gay, who became a commissioner for the official state lottery in the same year.

From its inception, the playhouse had a Whiggish emphasis: "The new theatre was certainly viewed at one time as a Kit-Cat venture. . . . The. . .Club was to be a major source both of moral support and at least of financial promises."[13] Most of the backers were prominent Whig peers, including Lord Hervey, later Earl of Bristol (see note to l. 26 below). When the foundation stone was laid, Tory critics had made fun of the ceremony, which involved Lady Sunderland, a daughter of the Duke and Duchess of Marlborough. The Churchill family were regular targets of Scriblerian onslaughts at this date (see also note to l. 81 below).

l. 5 Contemporaries often expressed outrage at the disguise element in masquerades, which promoted anonymous sexual affairs as well as the concealment of class, age and gender characteristics. The poem also suggests that masked faces went with revealing costume on the body below. See Terry Castle, "The Culture of Travesty," in *Sexual Underworlds of the Enlightenment*, ed. G.S. Rousseau and R. Porter (Chapel Hill, NC: University of North Carolina Press, 1987), pp. 156-80.

l. 6 Johann Jakob Heidegger (1666-1749), lessee and manager of the theatre. An impresario from Zürich whose family had Bavarian origins, he was known at one time as "the Swiss Count", and later satirized by Fielding as "Count Ugly." He was also pictured in a caricature by Pope's friend the Countess of Burlington, which shows the Haymarket superstars Cuzzoni and Farinelli. His career in opera can be traced in Deutsch, *Handel*, passim. Heidegger subscribed to Gay's *Poems* (1720).

Opera tickets were available at White's chocolate house in St James's Street (then a Whig gambling centre) until 1723, when the Royal Academy of Music began to sell them at their office in the Haymarket. (Only gallery seats were sold on the night, at a price of 2s.6d. or 5s.) It appears that masquerade tickets were also sold at White's. The charge for a single ticket to a ball is sometimes quoted as one guinea (date not supplied): by comparison a "passo tempo" with music, in the Long Room, cost 5s. in 1723. From 1722 "ridottos" were held on the stage, following a concert of operatic items, at a price of one guinea per ticket. Generally such ventures were supported by subscription: the rate for subscribing to masquerades at this date has eluded discovery, although twelve "barefaced" balls run by Heidegger in 1727 cost ten guineas each. Tickets for opera were often traded at a rate above their official price, and this may have been true of masquerade tickets also. See Deutsch, *Handel*, for relevant details.

Pope makes constant play of the devil, especially in shorter works. He was well aware that popular usage identified the Pope with Satan – hence the line in Scriblerian verses, "He that's named next to the Devil," as a way of indicating his own name (*TE* 6: 116). Another ballad in the Portland manuscripts at Nottingham ends with a wish that God will bless the King, "the Duchess fat" [Kendal], and the Prince of Wales, "and give us grace for to defy / The devil, and the Pope."[14] It was common to curse by invoking Satan, e.g. "wishing the Pope and the Devil take me." This was in an era when Reginald Scot's description had not altogether faded from the popular imagination: "An ugly devil having horns on his head, fire in his mouth, and a tail in his breech, eyes like a basin, fangs like a dog, claws like a bear, a skin like a Niger and a voice roaring like a lion."[15] Innumerable anti-Catholic polemics continued to forge a connection between the papacy and the diabolic: astrologers like John Partridge even found High Church doctrine to be "only Pop'ry by another name. . .Sa[chevere]ll's brimstone church is nothing less."[16] Often pictured by his enemies as a monstrous and diabolical figure, Pope responded by describing the bizarre metamorphoses of the great and powerful: "Did ever Proteus, Merlin, any Witch, / Transform themselves so strangely as the Rich?" (*TE* 4: 291). But he also wrote in a more self-implicated way when a beautiful woman was suggested to him as an eligible bride, "I did not care to force so fine a woman to give the finishing stroke to all my deformities, by the last mark of a Beast, horns" (Pope *Corr*, 2: 431). This letter was written to the Blount sisters in September 1717, at a time when the ballad was possibly in the process of composition.[17]

l. 12 Saucer eyes: "an eye as large and round as a saucer, generally ascribed to spectres and ghosts" (*OED*, citing Matthew Prior's "Hans Carvel," where the devil appears out of his usual guise "without Saucer Eye or Claw.") However, Pope uses the expression of a ghost, "with saucer Eyes of Fire," in a ballad called "Sandys's Ghost" (*c*.1716-17): see *TE* 6: 171.

l. 16 In the next stanza of the same ballad, Pope compares a young aspirant for literary honours to a "Puppy tame" (*TE* 6: 171).

l. 19 Compare the proverb, "The devil always leaves a stink behind him" (Tilley D224). The itch: scabies (also found in "The Court Ballad"). Pope rhymes "Br—" and "Itch" in "Bounce to Fop" (1736): see *TE* 6: 182, 367. There is an obvious pun on *itch* in the sense of (sexual) urge or yearning.

l. 20 Attorneys were a lower category in the legal profession and had a dubious reputation, particularly after some well-publicized cases involving fraud. See Paul Baines, *The House of Forgery in Eighteenth-Century Britain* (Aldershot, 1999), p. 10. The ballad almost anticipates one event reported in the *Daily Post* on 27 February 1720, when John Waterlidge was committed to Newgate "for forging Masquerade Tickets, under the head of Mr.Heydiger. He endeavoured, with one of his sham Tickets, to pass into the House, in the Habit of a Shepherdess, but was detected at the third Door" (quoted by Elizabeth Gibson, *The Royal Academy of Music 1719-1728: The Institution and its Directors* (New York: Garland, 1989), p. 131).

l. 23 A proverbial expression (Tilley H620).

l. 25 Summoned a sedan-chair and then avoided paying for it.

l. 26 Elizabeth Hervey, Countess of Bristol (1676-1741), wife of the first Earl, and mother of Pope's adversary Lord Hervey. She was a friend of Lady Mary Wortley Montagu, who often referred to her fondness for cards. Appropriately, Lady Bristol was portrayed as Cardelia in Lady Mary's "The Basset-Table" in *Court Poems* (1716). Lady Mary wrote to her sister in June 1722: "The Countesse is come out a new Creature; she has left off the dull Occupations of Hazard and Bassette, and is grown Young, blooming, Coquette and Galante; and to shew she is fully sensible of the errors of her past life, and resolv'd to make up for time mispent, she has 2 lovers at a time."[18] Four letters survive which Lady Mary sent to Lady Bristol, dating from 1716 to 1718 during her trip to Constantinople. For the Countess's reputation as gossip and gambler, see Robert Halsband, *Lord Hervey: Eighteenth-Century Courtier* (Oxford: Clarendon Press, 1974), p. 21.[19] She had taken a great interest in Italian opera at the Queen's Theatre from its inception (sometimes holding private performances at her home), and continued to do so into the 1720s.

Lady Bristol's town-house in St James's Square stood handily placed for the Haymarket playhouse. Her family associations were Whiggish: her father, Sir Thomas Felton, had been Master, and then Comptroller, of the Household in the early years of Queen Anne, and supported the anti-Junto Whigs.[20] Her husband was a follower of the Duke and Duchess of Marlborough. For Lady Bristol's position at court under George I, see the discussion below, p. 143.

l. 26 Cuckold's horns: moralists condemned masquerades as an opportunity for untramelled adultery. Underlying this stanza is the proverb, "The devil is known by his horns/tail/claws" (Tilley D252).

l. 28 *OED* does not record this variant of "slapdash."

l. 32 Elizabeth Mohun (d. 1725), widow of the notorious rake Lord Mohun, and mother of the court ladies Elizabeth Rich and Anne Griffith. Pope refers to all three in the letter from June 1717, quoted in the opening discussion above: "The Adventures are not so numerous but that of my Lady Mohun makes the chief figure. Her marriage to young Mordaunt, & all its circumstances, I suppose you'll have from Lady Rich or Miss Griffith" (Pope *Corr*, 1: 407). Lady Mohun's new husband was Colonel Charles Mordaunt, grandson of the first Viscount Mordaunt of Avalon, and thus a nephew of the Earl of Peterborough, who was to become a close friend of Pope around 1723.[21] In a letter also dating from June 1717 Lady Mary imagines a round of social pleasures in London, which includes the engagement, "*Tuesday*, Lady Mohun's" (Pope, *Corr*, 1: 412).[22] Lord Mohun, who had been a member of the Kit-Cat Club along with Lady Mary's father, inherited Macclesfield House in Gerrard Street, conveniently situated in a fashionable quarter within a short walking distance of the Haymarket theatre.[23]

There is a further odd connection here. In *Sober Advice from Horace* (1734), Pope writes, "A Lady's Face is all you see undress'd; / For none but Lady M-show'd the Rest." When the poem appeared in the collected *Works* in 1738, the verb "show'd" was altered to "shows." According to John Butt in the Twickenham edition, the change "suggests that Pope was once more thinking of Lady Mary," something that is plausible in view of the bitter turn which their relations had taken by that date. However, a manuscript note in a copy belonging to the second Earl of Oxford recounts an episode involving Lady Mohun. According to this story she was caught by her husband with some men in a hackney coach, and bared her posteriors to him out of the window in order to satisfy his curiosity as to who was in the coach.[24] In 1717-19, Pope and Lady Mary were of course on highly amicable terms, but Lady Mohun's reputation (and by association that of her former husband, the rake and multiple duellist) would make her an apt subject for the innuendo at any date. She was a vehement Whig who "sponsored an annual orgy of bell-ringing on the King's birthday."[25] Pope, who relayed a story about Lord Mohun's antics at the Kit-Cat Club, would have considered his widow a true inheritor of his disreputable mantle.[26]

In 1717 a pamphleteer alleged that Gay had received a gift from three Maids of Honour at court, including Miss Griffith: in return Pope had agreed to mention these ladies in a ballad.[27] In fact all of them turn up in "The Court Ballad," written by Pope at the start of 1717, as well as in a short epigram he composed about the same time (*TE* 6: 180-3, 185). Lady Rich, the wife of a senior officer since 1714, also figures in the ballad, in terms suggesting she was not noted for chaste behaviour.[28] Perhaps in concert with Lady Mary Wortley Montagu, Pope wrote to Lady Rich around July 1716 (Pope *Corr,* 1: 345-6). Three letters survive from Lady Mary to Lady Rich, written during her sojourn at the Turkish embassy (*Complete Letters,* 1: 269, 287, 438). In addition, Lady Louisa Stuart recounts an occasion on which Lady Mary (grandmother of the anecdotist) mocked the ignorance and affectation of her "former friend" Elizabeth Rich.[29] The other sister Anne Griffith is mentioned in several letters by Pope from this period. She married William Harrington, later first Earl of Harrington, in 1718, but died in childbirth on 18 December 1719.[30]

ll. 35-6 Conjurors and lawyers were among the popular costumes: for example, Boswell attended a masquerade in 1773 as "a dumb conjuror." The overtones of this disguise are Faustian; cf. *The Dunciad* (1729), where "a sable Sorcerer" is glossed as "Dr. *Faustus*". The white stick also suggests a symbol of political power, the best known example being the staff of the Lord Treasurer: see for example Swift's "The Virtues of Sid Hamet the Magician's Rod" (1710), which refers to Godolphin's "brethren of the conjuring tribe" (see Chapter 1 above). The treasury was at the date of the ballad in commission, with Sunderland/Stanhope and Walpole/Townshend factions competing for power. If an individual is meant, this might be James Stanhope, First Lord of the Treasury from 15 April 1717, and the King's most trusted servant until he died in 1721.

However, a rod of white wood was also "a sign of office carried erect by an officer of the Court of Justice" (*TE* 6: 224). Pope would shortly utilize this detail in his satire on Nicholas Lechmere (1675-1727), who was Solicitor-General (1714-18) and Attorney-General (1718-20). From 1718 he was also Chancellor of the Duchy of Lancaster. The lawyer appears as "*Nic.* of *Lancastere*" in another of the poet's ballads on topical themes, 'Duke upon Duke' (*c.*1719-20):

From out the Boot bold *Nicholas*
Did wave his Wand so white. (*TE* 6: 222)

He became a Privy Councillor on 1 July 1718, an honour mentioned in "Duke upon Duke," line 92. "Nick" is of course proverbial for the devil (Tilley N161), but Pope's line certainly glances at Lechmere, whom the Duchess of Marlborough called "the worst man that ever I knew in my life."[31] In 1719 Lechmere married Lady Elizabeth Howard, daughter of the Earl of Carlisle: she was an early friend of Lady Mary Wortley Montagu, who had stayed with her at Castle Howard in 1714. Later heavy gaming losses by Lady Lechmere were reported by Lady Mary (*Complete Letters,* 1: 210; 2: 57). In 1726 there were (false) rumours that she had poisoned herself after running up huge debts at Bath.

His offences, from the Scriblerian point of view, are described in the next essay in relation to "Duke upon Duke." In 1716, Lechmere joined in two controversial measures with Lord Coningsby, a renegade Whig whom Pope attacked elsewhere: see Pat Rogers, *The Life and Times of Thomas, Lord Coningsby: The Whig Hangman and his Victims* (London: Continuum, 2011). The second was designed to strengthen the protestant interest by enforcing the laws against papists: Lechmere spoke so virulently on this matter in the House of Commons that a number of Catholics and non-jurors felt they would have to leave the country. This was the juncture when Pope's family were forced to leave their home in Windsor Forest, as Catholics were driven from their estates by measures such as the act requiring registration of all property (1 Geo. I, st. 2, passed on 26 June 1716). Lechmere was the most vehement proponent of these measures.

An even more specific circumstance underlies the mention of Lechmere here. During the summer recess of parliament in 1716 "he joined with the Duke of Argyll in caballing against the Government; supplied Argyll with precedents to show that the Prince's powers as Regent were not as ample or honourable as in previous cases; and promoted congratulatory addresses to the Prince on his appointment to be Regent, with a view to masking the mischief between him and his father. At the end of 1716 it was reported that he was to be head of Argyll's party in the House of Commons" (Romney Sedgwick, *The House of Commons 1715-1754*, 2 vols (London: Oxford University Press for the History of Parliament, 1970), 2: 203). In other words, Lechmere had been active in the quarrel whose beginnings Pope had jokingly exploited in "The Court Ballad," and had espoused the party of the Prince of Wales, led by the Duke of Argyll.

For the association in proverbs between the devil and lawyers, see Tilley D256.

l. 37 "Do you know me?" was the stock greeting at masquerades: see for example Byrd's comment in Tinling (ed.), *Correspondence of Byrds*, 1: 413.

l. 38   The phrase "Every man has his price" has no known origin in folk expressions, and its currency grew when it was attached to Robert Walpole, largely by posthumous and apocryphal sources. See also *The Oxford Dictionary of English Proverbs,* 3rd edn, ed. F.P. Wilson (Oxford, 1970), p. 229.

l. 42 "There is an absolute Freedom of Speech, without the least Offence given thereby; while all appear better bred than to offer at any thing profane, or immodest, but Wit incessantly flashes about in Repartees, Honour, and good Humour" (Mist's account, quoted by Deutsch, *Handel*, p. 80).

ll. 45-6 Thomas Killigrew the younger (1657-1719), gentleman of the bedchamber to the Prince of Wales, and author of the comedy *Chit Chat*. This was performed at Drury Lane on 14 February 1719, and published by Bernard Lintot, the bookseller of both Pope and Gay, with a dedication to the Duke of Argyll. The Duke is reported to have been "a great Friend to the Author" and to have ensured that Killigrew cleared over a thousand pounds from the play. In the service of the Prince and Princess, Killigrew was a colleague of the three Maids of Honour recently celebrated by Pope (see note to l. 32 above); and the Duke of Argyll "is

known to have been on the friendliest terms with the three Maids."[32] The circle of
Argyll provided extensive materials for Scriblerian satire at this date, and the dig at
Killigrew seems to be connected with this body of allusion.[33]

l. 48 For the devil's ability to counterfeit human shapes in order to tempt people,
see Thomas, *Religion and Magic*, pp. 564-6.

l. 49 Pope writes of himself as "frolick with my Foes," in "A Farewell to London,"
TE 6: 130.

l. 52 "Black as the devil" (Tilley D217), one of several traditional formulations
linking Satan with blackness.

ll. 54-5 A number of actresses were well known to both writers at this period. Gay
mentions the "frolick" Margaret Bicknell and her sister Elizabeth Younger as
friends in "Mr. Pope's Welcome from Greece" (1720), and Pope similarly includes
them in "A Farewell to London" (1715): see *Poetry and Prose*, 1: 257, and *TE* 6:
129. Each woman had taken a leading role in Gay's dramas. Another member of
the cast of *Three Hours After Marriage* was Anne Oldfield, whom Pope often
mentioned in a tone of admiration for her acting mixed with reprobation for her
sexual activities, which exhibited an ability both "to ruin, and to please" ("Sober
Advice from Horace," in *TE* 4: 75).
    In transcribing the draft in Pope's hand, Nokes found a blank, "an —", instead
of the word "Actress." He commented that the line employs a stock expression, to
take by the beard (that is, to attack), and added that those handling the devil in this
way would find that even his beard was part of a false disguise. The sense of l. 55
becomes more complicated with the word spelt out in full, and may perhaps be
paraphrased "attempted to assault."

l. 56 Both were especially common as masquerade costumes. See Aileen Ribeiro,
The Dress Worn at Masquerades in England, 1730-1790 (New York: Garland
1985), passim.

l. 58 This might mean that he appeared to don the "disguise" of the devil, perhaps
the most ubiquitous of all costumes,[34] but the next line suggests that he was
mistaken for the villainous-looking Heidegger ("ugly as the devil" being another
stock expression). According to one contemporary pamphleteer, "Mr. *Heyd-g-r*
had, at the slender Appearances of his *Balls* and *Opera*, so distorted his
Countenance, that he was scarce known by his most intimate Friends and
Acquaintance."[35] One of the key figures in the opera world, Paolo Rolli, wrote to
Giuseppe Riva in July 1720 of Heidegger as "[il] *Proteo alpino*" (quoted by
Gibson, *Royal Academy*, p. 137).

l. 62 Echoes proverbial formulae such as "All saint without, all devil within."
Compare the line on the women of the town at another notorious pleasure palace,

"They're Saints without, but D-s all within" in *Belsize-House. A Satyr* (London: T. Warner, 1722), p. 17.

l. 65 Presumably "Belle Chuck [Cook *or* Coke]": not positively identified, but this must refer to a woman of the town. See Castle, "The Culture of Travesty," pp. 167-8, on prostitution at the masquerade. Most likely she is "Bell Chuck, a blackamoor girl, in high keeping, who was first kept by Lord Orrery," and the mistress of a peer in 1714. She had been put to bed with "Lord B" by Lords Bathurst and Jersey – the former a close friend of Pope by the time of this ballad. See *The Wentworth Papers 1704-1739,* ed. J.J. Cartwright (London: Wiley, 1883), p. 395. The name is also used in a biography of the courtesan Sally Salisbury: here it seems to derive from "Chuck-Hole" = vagina. See "Capt. Charles Walker," *Authentick Memoirs of the Life Intrigues and Adventures of the Celebrated Sally Salisbury* (London, 1723), p. 68.

l. 68 "Hell" was a slang usage for the female pudenda, from the sense "a yawning depth, an abyss" (*OED*). Pope uses "the Dev'l of Hell" in his short squib, "The Six Maidens" (*c.* 1732): see *TE* 6: 341. The wit of this poem plays around "Hell fires" and "Angells" as well; the text suggests that the maids of honour now serve "a new Lord and Master", who is Frederick Prince of Wales but, just as obviously, the devil.

l. 70 *Belle-chose*: vagina (*OED,* "chose", 3).

l. 71 A domino was the long cloak worn at masquerades, "with a small mask covering the upper part of the face, by persons not personating a character" (*OED*). Originally black, it was found in other colours later in the century. Here the word is stressed on the second syllable.

l. 73 "On the Sides are divers Beaufets, over which is written the several Wines therein contained," including champagne and burgundy. See Mist's account, quoted by Deutsch, *Handel,* p. 80.

l. 77 Burgundy: Addison's Lucifer figure (see note to title, above) praised the "Goodness" of the champagne and burgundy at the Duc d'Aumont's masked ball. Initially masquerades were regarded in England as frenchified occasions (despite their Venetian origin), and the discovery in 1716 of secret correspondence between the Duc and British Jacobites may have strengthened the connection. Thereafter efforts seem to have been made to anglicize, or in some ways germanize, the institution.

l. 80 See Deutsch, *Handel,* p. 80, on the gaming room.

l. 81 The teasing generality incites speculation, as it resists a firm identification. It is unlikely, though just possible, that Gay was recalling affectionately his former employer, the Duchess of Monmouth. As for the Duchess of Queensberry, although she and her husband were among subscribers to the *Poems* in 1720, Gay's role as their client was only just beginning at this date: moreover, the Duke was abroad on his Grand Tour up to August 1718, and the couple did not marry until March 1720. Equally, contemporary readers might have filled in the implied blank with names such as the Duchess of Ormonde or the Duchess of Buckingham, both of whom were well known to Pope. It would have been tactless to mention the second wife of the Duke of Kingston (Lady Mary's estranged father).[36] None of these women had any strong links with the world of the Haymarket at this date. On the other hand, the Duchess of Shrewsbury (wife of the former Lord Chamberlain and a Lady of the Bedchamber) did take a role in operatic affairs, but had no ascertainable link with masquerades.[37]

If the draft is contemporary, then the phrase cannot refer to Henrietta Godolphin, eldest daughter of the Duke of Marlborough, who inherited the duchy on his death in 1722. Otherwise she would be a highly plausible candidate: a woman noted for her sexual affairs, for her love of ombre, and for her links with the Whig aristocracy surrounding the Kit-Cat Club: when the Queen's Theatre was opened in 1705, she had been celebrated in a prologue to the first performance. She had a longstanding interest in opera, and Heidegger dedicated to her the book of a pasticcio named *Arminio* in 1714.[38] When Handel's *Water Music* was first performed in July 1717, she was on the royal barge, together with Mme Kielmansegg and great ladies such as the Duchess of Bolton and her own newly married daughter, the Duchess of Newcastle (see below, p. 146). Mme Kielmansegg, later Countess of Darlington, was the King's half-sister and a major figure in Court life.[39] This was the authentic panoply of Hanoverian womanhood. Appositely, Henrietta lived at Godolphin House, on the western side of St James's Palace.

For several years the Countess had been closely involved with one of the Kit-Cat luminaries, William Congreve, who was a long-established friend of Pope by 1718.[40] According to her mother, the implacable Sarah, the fondness which Henrietta Godolphin had for the company of writers led her to give a hundred guineas to "a very low poet" – that is Gay, who spent the summer of 1722 at Bath with the Duchess, Congreve and their physician Arbuthnot.[41] When in the following year the Duchess gave birth to her daughter, generally believed to be Congreve's, Lady Mary wrote that "her poor Freind" had in this way "expos'd her self to the most violent Ridicule." From now on each party discovered slights perpetrated by the other, and the pair became, in Lady Mary's words, "2 people that are resolv'd to hate with Civility" (*Complete Letters*, 2: 30, 52). There is some background to this breach: when the Wortley Montagus got back to London on 2 October 1718, it was to find that Congreve had now embarked on a full-fledged liaison with Lady Godolphin. This may for a time have eclipsed Montagu's close relations with Congreve.[42] Accordingly she would perhaps not have been averse to a dig at her supposed rival, and Pope appears to have held a low opinion of the Duchess.[43] However, the reference seems almost friendly – and if the draft really dates from the proposed period, this rules out Henrietta Godolphin.

The overwhelming probability is that "her Grace" means Elizabeth Douglas, Duchess of Hamilton (1682-1744). During the year 717 Pope in particular had extensive contacts with this lady, while Gay was in France with William Pulteney. Writing to Gay on 8 November, for example, Pope mentions a letter his friend had sent to the Duchess, and goes on to refer to her in relevant terms: "Her Grace has won in a Raffle a very fine Tweezercase." In the previous month Pope had reported to the Duchess on Gay's experiences in France (Pope *Corr,* 1: 450, 438).[44] At this very time he commissioned a portrait of the lady, very likely by his friend Charles Jervas: this picture hung in the great parlour at Twickenham, according to the inventory taken at the time of the poet's death.[45] It was probably in this summer that the Duchess invited Pope (then staying at Jervas's home in St James's) to join her barge for a music party on the Thames. Characteristically a retainer has to write the letter, the Duchess claiming to be too drunk to do so.[46] On another occasion, perhaps in October, the Duchess waited to meet Pope in "St Albans street": this ran just to the west of Haymarket and gave direct access to the opera-house (Pope *Corr,* 1: 439).

It is the same woman who appears as "the chearful Dutchess" in Gay's "Welcome to Mr . Pope" (*Poetry and Prose,* 1: 256). Swift had met her in 1711, and in the following year he had comforted her after the death of her husband in the notorious duel with Lord Mohun. At that time he had said of her, "She has abundance of wit and Spirit; about 33 year old, handsom, and airy, and seldom spared any body that gave her the least Provocation."[47] Known for her free ways in company, she had actually been involved in a public slanging-match at a playhouse in March 1712, as Lady Mary had herself reported (*Complete Letters,* 1: 118). Horace Walpole recalled her sitting up all night drinking before attending his father's levee, and called her "a Woman of great Debauchery and Wit."[48] Formerly the Duke and Duchess resided at an imposing house in St James's Square, near to the Earl and Countess of Bristol (see note to l. 26 above); the Duchess moved to Bond Street in 1716.

There is a still more crucial consideration: the Duchess was an old enemy of Lady Mohun – indeed, the families had been at odds over an inheritance long before the fatal duel. Moreover, the women were divided by irreconcilable differences in politics (Lady Mohun as a Whig and Hanoverian, her adversary a Tory and probably a Jacobite). At the time of the ballad, these two were *still* engaged in a longstanding lawsuit concerning property, which outlasted Lady Mohun and remained unsettled when Elizabeth Douglas died in 1744.[49] Lady Mohun's reputation was such that the phrase "whom so many folk know" would certainly convey the sense of sexual libertinage; whereas the Duchess was noted for her unconventional freedom of manners, rather than for any unchaste behaviour. All these factors suggest that the expression "her Grace" must have meant the Duchess of Hamilton to any insider – and the poem may have been intended only for the eyes of a limited coterie of friends.[50]

The long battle between Hamiltons and Mohuns cast its shadow over many corners of life in early eighteenth-century England. Congreve actually found himself as defendant in a Chancery suit by the Duchess, since Lady Mohun in her will had named him among trustees for her estates, along with the Duke of Argyll, the Duke's brother Lord Ilay, and her husband Charles Mordaunt.[51] Argyll had long been an adversary of the Hamiltons, who had used his considerable clout on the side of Lady Mohun. Equally, the politics of the duel refused to go away. Hamilton's second, Colonel John Hamilton, lost his commission as soon as George I acceded to the throne, and died in obscurity not long afterwards. Meanwhile George Macartney, Mohun's second, prospered under the patronage of the King and the Duke of Marlborough, receiving promotions and places in abundance.[52]

l. 84   *OED* quotes a sixteenth-century source, "To shake the bones and cog the crafty dice," as well as a work from 1755, "To use my Hands to palm an Ace or cog a Dice." Gay writes of "Cogging of Dice" in his ballad "Newgate's Garland," in *Poetry and Prose,* 1: 287. "Bones" had long been used for dice; *Poor Robin's Almanack* in 1678 described cards and dice as "the devil's books and the devil's bones." Underlying this stanza is a proverb, "The devil is in the dice" (Tilley D250).

Cf. Pope's address to Lord Hervey, "A Letter to a Noble Lord" (1733): "Did I . . . ever throw *a false Dye*, or palm *a foul Card* on you?" (*Prose Works*, 2: 445).

l. 86   "Set" means marked down as a prey. To butter was "to increase the stakes every throw or every game" (Johnson).

l. 87 A pun on "nick", variously to cheat, to catch unawares, and make a winning score at hazard (dice). Pope, writing in the person of a maid of honour, describes how the lady had interrupted a game of hazard: "Lord H. would say I came in the Nick" (Pope *Corr,* 1: 381). Arbuthnot noted how Pope had become addicted to punning when in the company of Lady Mary in the summer of 1719 (Pope *Corr,* 2:10). We might also recall that Sir Plume "rapp'd his Box" (in this case a snuffbox) in *The Rape of the Lock*, 4: 130.

l. 89 Candles were said to burn blue "as an omen of death, or as indicating the presence of. . .the Devil" (*OED*, citing Defoe's *History of the Devil*: "When the candles burn blue the Devil is in the room"). But again a closer parallel exists with Pope's ballad "Sandys's Ghost," l. 36: "While as the Light burnt bluely" (*TE* 6: 172). For the "five hundred Waxlights" at the Haymarket, see Deutsch, *Handel*, p. 80. There is also a recollection of the "numerous Wax-lights" blazing in *The Rape of the Lock*, 3: 168.

l. 90 Playing on the familiar proverb, "Give the devil his due" (Tilley D273). This occurs in the Epilogue to *Three Hours after Marriage*: see Gay's *Dramatic Works*, ed. J. Fuller, 2 vols (Oxford: Clarendon Press, 1983), 1: 262.

ll. 92-4 See Thomas, *Religion and Magic*, p. 560, on the ability of the devil to provoke high winds and thunderstorms, as well as to snatch sinners and fly off with them through the air.

l. 96 Part of the long campaign waged by the Scriblerians against astrologers, starting with John Partridge (compare the scene with the "radiant *Trail of Hair*," observed by Partridge, in *The Rape of the Lock* 5: 123-39). By this date the target had widened to include the theories of William Whiston on comets: see "A True and Faithful Narrative" in Gay, *Poetry and Prose*, 2: 464-73. Whiston was patronized by the Princess of Wales, another reason for the Scriblerus faction to attack him.

Recent celestial events had afforded opportunities both to soothsayers and to serious astronomers: thus, Edmond Halley reported in turn on a total eclipse in April; 1715 (the first seen in London since the Middle Ages), a display of aurora borealis in March 1716, and "a small telescopical comet" seen at London on 10 June 1717. He also observed "an extraordinary meteor" in March 1719. Arbuthnot had known Halley for many years and may have helped to spark Pope's own interest in astronomy, which developed after the poet attended lectures by Whiston in 1713.

Another work which certainly derived from the Scriblerian camp[53] was a short squib attributed to "E. Parker, Philomath," and entitled *Mr. Joanidion Fielding His True and Faithful Account of the Strange and Miraculous Comet which was seen by the Mufti of Constantinople*, dating from the end of 1716. Two of the prophecies here have an immediate relevance: "He that frequenteth *He*----'s Masquerade, shall not piss the easier," and "Thrice shall *Heideker* beshit himself, without changing his Countenance or his Linen." At this date Pope was following Lady Mary's journey to Constantinople, and fantasizing about her experiences when she reached Turkey (see for instance his letter of October 1716, in Pope *Corr,* 1: 363-4). In fact it was May 1717 before she arrived at Constantinople.

Commentary

The evidence is not sufficient to establish authorship with any certainty. As regards external factors, it is obvious that Gay and Pope moved in such a similar world that their individual interests can hardly be disentangled. Thus, Gay entered the milieu of Italian opera, where Heidegger occupied a central place, through his contacts at Burlington House; but Pope too spent much time with Lord Burlington around 1716, enjoying the "ravishing" music Handel provided (Pope *Corr,* 1: 338), just as Gay paid tribute to these "melting strains" in *Trivia*, published in January of that year. Here the friends would have met many of those connected with the opera, including the Italian musicians who performed in the Haymarket orchestra. (It is most likely, although not provable, that both writers encountered Heidegger at this time.) In addition, Pope was a neighbour of the Earl at Chiswick, and he also had Dr John Arbuthnot as informant on matters musical. It has generally been thought that Gay wrote the libretti of *Acis and Galatea* and *Esther,* to be set by Handel, when the composer worked for James Brydges (soon to be created Duke of Chandos) at Canons around 1718. However, recent commentators speculate that "a club of composers" including Arbuthnot aided in this process. Contemporaries certainly named both Gay *and* Pope as having been lined up to furnish the libretto for *Acis and Galatea*.[54] What this means is that almost every aspect of this milieu likely to be known by Gay would also have been familiar to his friend.

Dr Arbuthnot could have conceivably had a hand in the composition of the ballad, as he did with other Scriblerian squibs. He is believed to have been the prime author of *Annus Mirabilis* (1722), although many attributed the work to Pope.[55] At this time Pope wrote to Gay, then at Bath with the doctor and the Duchess of Marlborough, "Dr Arbuthnot is a strange creature; he goes out of town, and leaves his Bastards at other folks doors" (Pope *Corr*, 2: 133). The immediate relevance of *Annus Mirabilis* is that the central event in this satire takes place when the audience at the opera undergo a collective sex-change, an idea which echoes the devil's gender transformations in the ballad – and of course matches the reversals in appearance which opponents of masquerade so much disliked.[56] (Meanwhile at the Haymarket opera, the principal male roles in Handel's most popular opera, *Rinaldo*, were often taken by altos, either women or castrati.)[57] See also Chapter 3 above.

Arbuthnot was the one Scriblerian with strong musical credentials, and he was the lone member of the group who became *immediately* involved with Heidegger as a director of the opera company from late 1719. Not surprisingly, it was Arbuthnot who was deputed by the Court of the Academy to ask Pope to propose "a Seal with a Suitable Motto for it," something the poet seems never to have done (Deutsch, *Handel*, p. 97). However, the doctor spent a long period in Paris and Rouen with members of his family in 1718, visiting the exiled Bolingbroke, and he was not available when an attempt was made to reform the Scriblerus Club that summer.[58] Consequently it would be hazardous to speculate that he had any involvement in the ballad.

Both Pope and Gay of course knew Lady Wortley Montagu, who was perfectly equipped to supply information and gossip. (See Isobel Grundy, *Lady Mary Wortley Montagu* (Oxford: Oxford University Press, 1999) for the fullest account of her life.) It has been thought probable that she was one of the two ladies, along with a lord, whom Pope was to present to Gay in April 1715 (Pope *Corr*, 1: 288). She is named in Gay's *Welcome to Mr Pope*, along with Mary Lepell (later Hervey) and other persons who have turned up in the annotation to "A Strange and Wonderfull Relation": portraits of both Lady Mary and Lady Hervey hung in Pope's "best room fronting the Thames" until his death.[59] All three writers whom we are considering took some part in the six "town eclogues," three of which first appeared as Edmund Curll's clandestine *Court Poems* in March 1716, although Montagu was probably responsible for the original composition of all these items.[60] At this date she was living in Duke Street on the south side of the Park, another address which gave convenient access to the opera-house.[61] However, she had left for Constantinople in August of the same year, and thereafter it was Pope who maintained a close relation by means of letters. These often included allusions to Lady Rich, and at least once accompanied a letter she herself had written to Lady Mary. As observed in the note to l. 32 above, Lady Mohun's family regularly figures in the correspondence passing between Turkey and England, and so on occasion does Lady Bristol. The latter was appointed a Lady of the Bedchamber in March 1718, after years of fruitless effort to achieve such a post. One of her attempts to gain favour at court had been to attend the opera at the Haymarket in company with Mme von der Schulenberg, the King's mistress (whom Lady Mary regarded as supremely dull). The Scriblerians never aimed their shots at a venture: here it seems likely that their best informant must have been Lady Mary, an old acquaintance of Lady Bristol. If so, Pope is more likely than Gay to have been the conduit of such personal details.[62]

We need to consider, too, what seems to be the next act of collaboration between Gay and Pope, in the years following the date of this ballad. This relates to the epilogue to Gay's tragedy *The Captives*, which Anne Oldfield delivered after the play was first presented in January 1724. Pope refers to this epilogue in a letter hastily dashed off to Jacob Tonson, and it is hard to resist the conclusion that he himself was its author. The lines ironically suggest that masquerades, operas and harlequinades all offer more to the contemporary audience than mere tragedy: "Since Masquerades must give more feeling pleasure, / Where we meet finer sense and better measure." Married women, coquettes and prudes are all able to take advantage of the ballroom for their own purposes. The case which has been made by Norman Ault for Pope's authorship of this epilogue seems strong; but it is not unimpugnable, and the only obvious candidate otherwise is Gay himself.[63]

The textual evidence carries more convincing and suggestive weight. Both writers composed ballads to match well-known tunes, well before *The Beggar's Opera* appeared. However, Pope was more active in this area during the first years of the Hanoverian regime. The verbal parallels noted which link this poem with works such as "Sandys's Ghost," "The Court Ballad" and "Duke upon Duke" take on added interest in the light of this fact.[64] An unmistakable reference to Lechmere as "Nick", complete with an allusion to the white wand of office (ll. 35-6), creates a direct link with "Duke upon Duke." There are also more echoes of the ballad on Heidegger in Pope's correspondence than in that of Gay, although it is true that far more survives of the former than of the latter. More generally, the construction of a ballad around proverbial lore (though chiefly associated with Swift) is more characteristic of Pope than of Gay: see for example the end of "Duke upon Duke", as well as "The Discovery" (1726), in *TE* 6: 223, 259-62.

If we consider the matter of dating, it is important to remember that Gay was on the continent from July 1717 to May 1718. This means that he was out of touch with day-to-day events in England, and unlikely to have executed the entire poem, on his own, in this period. It is possible that he began it before he left and worked on revising the text while abroad. Otherwise the date must be put forward to the period in 1718 when he was with Pope, or even into 1719. In the event that we postulate a collaborative work, which much of the evidence examined here suggests as likely, then a more sustained sequence of composition and revision might be conceived. The natural time for beginning the poem would be 1717, when the craze for masquerades was at its height, and when Pope expressed to Lady Mary his interest in these events. In November of that year Pope was staying with Charles Jervas at Cleveland Court, his usual base in town: this lay on the northern side of St James's Palace, adjacent to the Park, and put him only a gentle stroll of five minutes down Pall Mall from the Haymarket opera-house.[65] In the following February he called on Lord Bathurst, whose town-house stood in St James's Square, a stone's throw from the theatre.[66] It was only a couple of weeks later that the Hanoverian courtier von der Schulenberg (half-brother of the King's mistress) wrote bemusedly back from London to his chief minister, commenting on the rage for masquerades.[67] At this very time, it happens that Pope was planning to build a house on the other side of Piccadilly, in land behind Burlington House (Pope *Corr*, 1: 516): but for the anti-Catholic laws, he might well have become a resident of the West End, rather than Twickenham. [68]

As we have seen, however, the period of most prolonged contact between Gay and Pope occurred when they were at Stanton Harcourt and Cirencester for much of the summer of 1718. Their host for part of this time was Bathurst, who maintained an up-and-down relationship with Lady Mary. It was actually during a lull in the Oxfordshire sojourn that Pope and Gay, back in London, tried to revive the cooperative enterprise of Scriblerus, together with Parnell and Lord Oxford.[69] While the pair were in the country, Pope maintained a regular correspondence with both Blount sisters - we might recall that, until the young women went down to stay with John Caryll in Sussex, they were living at the top of St James's Park in Bolton Street, perfectly placed to hear the gossip of the West End.

On 17 September Pope wrote to Martha Blount in a rather Addisonian accent of the blessings of pin money, "In thee are comprised fine clothes, fine lodgings, fine operas, fine masquerades, fine fellows." Three weeks later, he set out the obligatory concerns of a young lady on her return to London: "Balls, plays, assemblies, Operas, &c." (Pope *Corr*, 1: 512, 515). Evidently these were among the things on Pope's mind during his stay at Cirencester.

This juncture, then, would have offered the best opportunity for resuming collaborative work. In the second half of 1719 Gay was back in France, perhaps for reasons of health, and perhaps also in order to accompany Burlington on his way to Italy. He is unlikely to have taken any active role in composition beyond the date of his departure.[70]

II

To all appearances the poem conveys no overt political point, but it would be unlike the Scriblerians to pass by an opportunity of mischief-making. We have seen that Pope referred to "great divisions" in the state when he wrote to Lady Mary about the rage for masquerades. This disunity at court would come to a head when the Princess of Wales gave birth to a son on 20 October 1717. Although the baby lived for only a few months, his arrival was to precipitate a widening of the breach between the monarch and his heir, and between the government and its opponents. The Prince and Princess were ejected from St James's Palace, and in a short time moved to Leicester House, which subsequently became a focus of opposition. It is just possible that the exposition of the ballad hints at the elder George as an "old Sire", with Prince George as a puppyish "Satan the younger' and "Hell's heir." We have plenty of evidence outside Pope's innuendo that the king and other members of the royal family sometimes attended masquerades; and it has been stated by the leading modern authority on George I that these assemblies "appealed to him, reminiscent as they were of the Hanover carnival."[71] Certainly, he was at the Haymarket on 4 February and again on 6 June in 1720, the latter time "in the habit of a Venetian nobleman."[72]

As leading supporters of opera, both the King and the Prince of Wales bestowed patronage on Heidegger in another direction, by instituting command performances and other means. Annual grants from the Treasury of £1,000 were made to the opera in the reign of both George I and George II. Moreover, £500 was paid to Heidegger "as a Present from His Majesty" in 1721 (Deutsch, *Handel*, p. 124). But we now are aware that the King also made regular payments from the Privy Purse, rather than public treasury funds: thus he subscribed fifteen guineas for Heidegger's benefit on 17 April 1717. This is just one of many such payments – on 6 July 1718, for instance, a further 24 guineas were paid to the impresario. As regards the taste of the regime, it has been shown from the same source that George I went to the Haymarket several times a year from the beginning of his reign, and attended about half of the Royal Academy operas after its inception in 1719. Just before the opera closed down in 1717, the King was at the theatre on 30 May and 29 June. Moreover, the royal taste for water parties saw at least fifteen such occasions on the Thames in 1715-17: usually the musicians were drawn from the Haymarket orchestra, though the King seems not always (if ever) to have contributed towards their payment.[73]

The most noteworthy statement in this area occurs in a report to Berlin which was filed by the Prussian Resident in London, Friedrich Bonet, on 19 July 1717. This has often been cited, as it contains major evidence on the first performance of Handel's *Water Music* two days earlier. Bonet's account can been challenged on details, but it may reflect widespread perceptions even where it is inaccurate:

> A few weeks ago the King expressed to Baron Kilmanseck His desire to have a concert on the river, by subscription, similar to the masquerades this winter which the King never failed to attend. The Baron accordingly applied to Heidecker, – a Swiss by origin, but the cleverest purveyor of entertainments to the Nobility. The latter replied that, much as he would wish to comply with His Majesty's desires, he must reserve subscriptions for the great events, namely the masquerades, each of which brings him in three or 400 guineas net. Observing His Majesty's chagrin at these difficulties, M. de Kilmanseck undertook to provide the concert on the river at his own expense.
>
> (Deutsch, *Handel*, p. 77)

Comic as Heidegger's belief must appear, that his assemblies were the great events - *not* the performance of what has proved to be an enduring item in the musical repertoire - we may admire his effrontery in so casually refusing, in effect, a royal command. The satirists chose well when they referred to the impresario's "face." Bonet's report also states, "Neither the Prince nor the Princess took any part in this festivity," a further indication of the disunity which Pope had mentioned to Lady Mary on 3 June.[74]

III

One episode serves to crystallize the issues under discussion. This occurred in March 1718, when the King was forced to apologize to the Archbishop of Canterbury, after Colonel Charles Churchill appeared at a ball in the dress of a bishop: the reason was that the monarch had himself been present.[75] The colonel (*c.*1679-1745) was the illegitimate son of General Charles Churchill, a younger brother of the first Duke of Marlborough; he acted as a pallbearer at Congreve's funeral, and was remembered in the will of Henrietta, Duchess of Marlborough. His mistress was the noted actress Anne Oldfield, for whom Pope had a low regard in personal terms (see note to ll. 45-6). Churchill was a man of business to Robert Walpole (whose illegitimate daughter he married), and he would play a clandestine role in breaking up the Atterbury plot. Dispatched to Paris in April 1722, he negotiated with the Earl of Mar to find incriminating evidence against the bishop, a particularly dear friend of Pope. His conduct at this time would not have endeared him to the earl's sister-in-law, Lady Mary Wortley Montagu: as it happened, she heard of Churchill's activities at first hand, when she met the colonel at the Haymarket opera in July of that year (*Complete Letters*, 2: 19). In later years Lady Mary composed verses satirizing the ageing roué (*Essays and Poems*, p. 294).

Years before, Churchill had been involved in the preliminaries to the duel between Mohun and Hamilton, as a friend and neighbour of George Macartney, Mohun's second (see note to l. 81 above).[76] Also involved was another officer, Robert Rich – soon to marry Elizabeth Griffith (see note to l. 32). Every one of these men – Mohun, Macartney, Churchill, Rich – had many features in common: they were soldiers, rakes, and rabid Whigs. Each achieved high military office (brigadier at least); all served under Marlborough. Once the Hanoverians arrived, Churchill and Rich both entered parliament for safe, and corrupt, Whig seats, and they both joined the retinue of the Prince of Wales as Grooms of the Bedchamber in 1718.[77] Aptly, Churchill has been described as "a hard drinking, hard hunting, half-literate friend of Walpole," who was one of the minister's "most devoted and loyal allies" - much of this applies to the other individuals within the group.[78] By way of example of their style, we might consider Macartney, who was dismissed by Queen Anne after bring accused of a rape. Briefly restored to command, he lost it again when he launched drunken curses on Robert Harley and the Tory ministers. As soon as the Hanoverians came to power, his outlawry was reversed and he was given a batch of posts as governor and commander. Years later it came out that he had plundered every fund entrusted to him and raided every store of money designed for his troops. The career of these men resembles that of Colonel Charteris, the arch-villain of Scriblerian satire. That the devil should call at the home of Lady Mohun (personally linked to each of them) before moving on to the King's Theatre now emerges as deeply appropriate. Her house seems, on the evidence of Lady Cowper, "to have been a place of resort for the Whigs, more especially those of less rigid morals."[79] All the identifiable figures - if we exclude the conjectural presence of the Duchess of Hamilton – belong to a group of seedy but successful hangers-on, mostly connected to the court of the Prince of Wales. The masquerade has become part of squalid Whig exploitation of the English people under the rule of Hanover.

On the accession of Prince George to the throne in 1727, it was Heidegger who supervised the coronation banquet and became Master of the Revels.[80] The new monarch continued to attend events at the Haymarket – a circumstance not lost on Hogarth, who produced a *Masquerade Ticket,* recalling the refrain of this earlier ballad. The face of the impresario is depicted on a clock at the top of Hogarth's design: the royal insignia have become his own, as the supporters on the King's coat of arms (lion and unicorn) gambol obscenely.[81] As late as 1735 there is reference to an episode at the Haymarket during one of a series of masquerades attended by the King, and allegedly set up for his personal pleasure.[82] And of course the opera-house was at least in name "the King's Theatre." If the poem happened to be in the throes of composition or even revision during the early months of 1718, as other clues indicate may have been the case, then it would be difficult altogether to suppress any recollection of this royal taste.[83]

The Scriblerians, it may be said, took no definite side in the struggle between father and son, even though their contacts at court tended to fall chiefly among the Prince's party – this was more a matter of age and propinquity than of ideological alignment. A close friend of Pope and Gay, James Craggs, the younger, served as Cofferer to the Prince of Wales from 1714 to 1717. He was identified chiefly with the Stanhope-Sunderland faction, deriving from the Marlborough connection, but he retained office under the opposing group of Whigs led by Walpole and Townshend. It was Argyll, however, who served as the focus of Prince George's party, when the King forced his resignation as Groom of the Stole to the Prince. Tories had briefly hoped that the heir to the throne would lead their own broken ranks into a major political force once more, but this unrealistic dream was already seen to be doomed.

In the summer of 1718 Pope wrote to Lady Mary what looks like a revealing passage: "Our Gallantry and Gayety have been great Sufferers by the rupture of the two Courts here. Scarce any Ball, Assembly, Basset table, or any place where two or three are gathered together" (Pope *Corr*, 1: 470).[84] It is true that he had described the solitude at court in almost identical terms, when writing to the Blount sisters in the previous September; and the evidence suggests that any halt to the round of pleasures in the capital was short-lived. However, the reference does confirm the closeness of public entertainments to court politics, and makes it even less likely that Pope could have taken any share in a ballad on this theme without paying heed to the political context. The reading of the poem offered here suggests that it may have constituted a blow on the side of the Duchess of Hamilton against her enemy Lady Mohun (see notes to ll. 32, 81): certainly the reference to "her Grace" is as lacking in animus as anything in the entire text, conveying a sense of cosy familiarity as the devil joins the Duchess at the gaming table.[85] Since Argyll supported Lady Mohun against the Hamilton cause when it came before the Privy Council in 1714, there may very well be another thread of innuendo here.[86] It can scarcely be an accident that the ballad singles out for attention Nicholas Lechmere, who had become one of the most reviled politicians with the High Church and Catholic communities, since Lechmere had emerged as Argyll's principal lieutenant in the House of Commons.

To read the poem in this way strengthens the argument for dating its inception to 1717, when masquerades were most in the news, and when topical political events existed to give the satire more point. This in turn reinforces the judgment that Pope must have had a large share in the original conception of the ballad, and probably in its execution: matters such as the Hamilton/Mohun quarrel and the intrigues of the Duke of Argyll related more directly his concerns than to those of Gay. The reading offered here would also position the satire in familiar Scriblerian politics, deriving ultimately from the bitter party battles in the last four years of the reign of Queen Anne. Moreover, as we have seen, the references to Lechmere and to Killigrew's play - apparently rescued by a gift from Argyll - link the work with other items such as "The Court Ballad" which deal with the events surrounding the clash between the King and the Prince of Wales (see note to ll. 45-6). After the Prince was obliged to go into a kind of internal exile, the ladies in waiting to Princess Caroline faced an awkward situation, since they would make themselves *personae non gratae* if they tried to keep in contact with both courts. Among the devices they used to get round this problem were secret meetings at the masquerade.[87]

IV

We can point to one circumstance which might explain the survival of the poem in Gay's hand, even on the assumption that it was the product of collaborative authorship. During the main phase of Scriblerian activity, we have it on Pope's own authority that Gay "often held the pen", and served as "secretary" to the project.[88] Old habits die hard, and it is plausible that Gay should have taken responsibility for transcribing a poem of which he was only part-author. Apparent confirmation lies in the fact that he copied out a full version of the verses "To Mr. John Moore," in a letter to Parnell dated 26 March 1716 (Gay, *Letters*, pp. 30-1), since the piece in question is always considered to be largely, if not wholly, the work of Pope. This suggested history would also explain why Pope might have written down two stanzas, in a slightly different form and *out of order* – something which is easier to reconcile with a work of two hands that underwent revision, than with an act of composition by Gay alone.

In his article David Nokes suggested that the ballad may "very possibly" have been intended "as a witty bagatelle for inclusion in a further letter to Lady Mary." Now that we have the full text of the poem, this speculation appears still entirely valid. The evidence assembled here shows that many of the identifiable personages within the text were intimately acquainted with Lady Mary. (Only the Duchess of Hamilton, assuming that this is the point of l. 81, moved out of her orbit, in a group hostile to the Kit-Cat ascendancy.) As one who had been almost born into the Kit-Cat Club, she possessed a familiarity with the court circle which went back longer than that of Gay or Pope. By this date she almost certainly knew their friend, the author and physician John Arbuthnot: the doctor had a long association with the Earl of Mar, whose second wife was Lady Mary's sister Frances.[89] For a time, it has been suggested, "she became almost a Scriblerian."[90]

To go a little further, it is conceivable that she actually had a hand in composing the ballad. She was able, for example, to refer knowingly to the world of operas and masquerades, including mention of Heidegger, in an essay in *Common-Sense* (1738); while she could always recognize Lord Hervey (Lady Bristol's son) at a masquerade, according to one story, no matter what disguise he had donned.[91] In her letters there are several references to masquerades she had attended; and a contemporary versifier linked her obliquely with such events:

> In Masquerades I go well drest
> And talk so very pretty
> That by the crowd I am confest

Like Lady Mary witty.[92]

In company with Flavia in her owntown eclogue, "Saturday," she had known a time when "Opera Tickets pour'd beneath [her] Feet" (*Essays and Poems*, p. 201). Apart from this, her adoption of Turkish dress and her depiction in that guise helped of course to introduce one of the most popular of all masquerade costumes.[93] Equally, her enduring friendship with Congreve, one of the original managers of the Haymarket theatre, would cement her knowledge of playhouse doings. From a literary standpoint, too, there are some relevant considerations: Montagu had collaborated with Gay and Pope on the eclogues in 1715-16 (though the poems as we have them seem to be largely her work), and she wrote some verses to existing ballad tunes – the best known example is "Virtue in Danger" (1721). Many of her productions were collected by Lady Oxford, a close friend, and her daughter the Duchess of Portland – who is the proximate source of the manuscript now at Nottingham.

There are two difficulties with this suggestion. The first is that Lady Mary was abroad (as well as giving birth to her daughter, also Mary) for most of the likely period of composition.[94] What is not altogether beyond the bounds of probability is that she was involved in some kind of revision after her return in October 1718. By this time Pope had decided to settle in Twickenham: the move was made at an unspecified date around March 1719. In the following June, the Wortley Montagus were planning to move into Savile House, not very far away, and renting a temporary home in the village. By the end of the year Pope had started to contemplate a portrait of Lady Mary, which he commissioned from Kneller. There would certainly be opportunities for the two writers to get together in the spring and summer. However, nothing in the text directly points at this possibility, unless it is the puns they shared that year (see note to l. 87).

The second objection lies in the nature of the ballad. Its target is an institution chiefly associated with Whiggery and the surviving Kit-Cat legacy - Pope's persistent urge to make fun of this club, as the breach with Addison and Steele grew wider, is shown by an epigram he wrote in 1716 (*TE* 6: 177). The ballad may even cast the Prince of Wales as Satan the younger: it certainly derides a social practice which enjoyed considerable royal support. Lady Mary Wortley Montagu would scarcely have minded thrusts at the notorious Elizabeth Mohun, and she is unlikely to have resented the suggestion that the devil's first port of call lay at the home of the Countess of Bristol. Nor would friendship have precluded sallies of wit against the unpopular lawyer to whom Lady Lechmere was married. However, Lady Mary was herself "Whigissima", and far too closely linked to the grandees who patronized Heidegger to have felt altogether comfortable with this poem – one that so patently identifies folly and dissolute living with the Hanoverian court and its hangers-on.

V

We should not make much of the fact that the poem remained unpublished in the lifetime of all the personages connected with it: sheer accident might have produced this result. Nevertheless, ballads of an equally scabrous nature did eventually find their way into print, and even into collections of the Scriblerian authors. Gay's draft survives in the Portland papers, which suggests that this version, at least, never left England - as it survived among a major trove of manuscripts relating to Pope and his circle, handed on by the Earl and Countess of Oxford to their daughter. Beyond that, the suppression of the work is still a matter of mystery.

In any case, the interest of this poem extends well beyond questions of attribution, of circulation or of exact dating. The "Excellent New Ballad" represents an early skirmish in the campaign against fashionable entertainments which was to reach its most developed stage with *Gulliver's Travels*, *The Beggar's Opera* and *The Dunciad*. Some years before Hogarth satirized "the Bad Taste of the Town" in his print of "Masquerades and Operas," the Scriblerus group had identified Heidegger as the purveyor of a noxious innovation in social activity – later on, the impresario makes a fleeting appearance in Book I of *The Dunciad* and in Chapter XVII of *The Memoirs of Martinus Scriblerus*. Blessed with royal and aristocratic patronage, supported by the corrupt circle of Lady Mohun, this Mephistophelean figure will lure the nation into ruin, just as the court poet and "Lord Chancellor of Plays" Colley Cibber will bring England to its knees in a later satire. Witty and adroit in wordplay, the ballad makes a worthy addition to the corpus of Scriblerian literature, no matter who precisely was responsible for its contrivance.

Notes

[1] P.J. Croft, *Autograph Poetry in the English Language*, 2 vols (London: Cassell, 1973), 1: 63-7.

[2] See Gay, *Poetry and Prose*. For brief commentary on the poem, see David Nokes, *John Gay: A Profession of Friendship* (Oxford: Oxford University Press, 1995), pp. 281-2.

[3] I am grateful to the Manuscript Librarian at the University of Nottingham for providing a photographic copy of the work, and for permission to reprint.

[4] Pope *Corr*, 1: 407.

[5] See David Nokes, "Pope and Heidegger: A Forgotten Fragment," *Review of English Studies*, 23 (1972): 308-13.

[6] It is of course within the bounds of possibility that Pope wrote the *entire* ballad and Gay transcribed it for him. This seems rather unlikely in view of the alterations in the draft. Moreover, Pope would probably have retrieved the item for future publication, as he did with other poems and letters. It should be emphasized that the draft is a rough working copy; it does not resemble the fine calligraphic transcripts which Pope made of his own poems or of Lady Mary Wortley Montagu's town eclogues. For the latter, see *Court Eclogs, Written in the Year, 1716*, ed. R. Halsband (New York New York Public Library, 1977).

[7] In fact Addison had written a satirical piece on midnight masquerades in a very early issue of the *Spectator*, no. 8 (9 March 1711).

[8] *The Guardian*, ed. J.C. Stephens (Lexington, KY, 1982), pp. 501-04.

[9] Daniel Defoe, Letter I in *A Tour*, Vol. 2 (1725) in Defoe, *Tour*, 2: 114.

[10] "These diversions will still subsist, in spite of the bishops, who. . .own very freely, that their whole bench don't do half as much good as Mother Heydecker dos harm" (William Byrd II to Mrs Armiger, 25 June 1729). See *The Correspondence of the Three William Byrds of Westover, Virginia 1684-1776*, ed. M. Tinling, 2 vols (Charlottesville: University of Virginia Press, 1977), 1: 413. The editor suggests that this refers to Heidegger's (non-existent) wife: it plainly alludes to his sexually ambiguous persona. He serves as a bawd or mother midnight figure (see also on this Castle, *Masquerade*, p. 31).

[11] Advertisement in the *Daily Courant*, cited by Winton Dean and John Merrill Knapp, *Handel's Operas 1704-1726* (Oxford: Clarendon Press, 1995), p. 288.

[12] See Paulson, *Hogarth*, 1: 79.

[13] Kerry Downes, *Sir John Vanbrugh: A Biography* (New York: St Martin's Press, 1987), p. 255.

[14] Quoted by Mark Blackett-Ord, *Hell-Fire Duke: the Life of the Duke of Wharton* (Windsor: Kensal Press, 1982), p. 80. For an example dating from November 1716, see Pope *Prose*, 1: cxiii. 1719 is the year usually assigned for the Hell Fire Club, in which Wharton is alleged to have taken a prominent part. It is said to have met at this date in Bury Street, just off St James's Street. Lady Mary certainly knew of the young Duke's profligacy: see *The Complete Letters of Lady Mary Wortley Montagu*, ed. Robert Halsband, 3 vols (Oxford: Clarendon Press, 1965-67), 2: 38-40.

[15] Keith Thomas, *Religion and the Decline of Magic* (London: Penguin, 1991), pp. 566, 606-07.

[16] Partridge's *Merlinus Liberatus* for 1706, quoted by Bernard Capp, *English Almanacs 1500-1800: Astrology and the Popular Press* (Ithaca: Cornell University Press, 1979), p. 248.

[17] For Pope and the monstrous, see Dennis Todd, *Imagining Monsters: Miscreations of the Self in Eighteenth-Century England* (Chicago: University of Chicago Press, 1995); and Helene Deutsch, *Resemblance and Disgrace: Alexander Pope and the Deformation of Culture* (Cambridge, MA: Harvard University Press, 1996).

[18] *Complete Letters*, 2: 17.

[19] The suppression of the ballad may help to account for the fact that Lady Bristol and her husband both subscribed to the *Odyssey*. So (shortly before her death) did Lady Mohun, who also subscribed to Gay's *Poems*.

[20] R.O. Bucholz, *The Augustan Court: Queen Anne and the Decline of Court Culture* (Stanford: Stanford University Press, 1993), p. 72.

[21] Pope followed happenings in the family: after Colonel Mordaunt's suicide on 7 May 1724, he incorporated a reference to this event in some verses commemorating his own birthday: see Ault, *New Light*, p. 203. Robert S. Forsythe, *A Noble Rake: The Life of Charles, Fourth Lord Mohun* (Cambridge, MA: Harvard University Press, 1928), p. 140, appears to confuse him with another Charles Mordaunt.

[22] For Lady Mohun's career as a *grande dame* of Whig society, see Victor Stater, *Duke Hamilton is Dead! A Study of Aristocratic Life and Death in Stuart Britain* (New York: Hill and Wang, 1999), esp. pp. 278-81 (although Stater wrongly identifies Lady Mohun's bridegroom as Peterborough's brother). In 1718 Lady Mohun received the huge sum of £53,000 when she sold the ancestral seat at Boconnoc in Cornwall to Thomas Pitt.

[23] An obscure couplet published by Edmund Curll in 1717 suggests that Pope and Gay frequented some unknown address in Gerrard Street, well known to the court ladies (*TE* 6: 186): this most likely refers to Macclesfield House, where Miss Griffith's mother resided.

[24] *TE* 4: 85. Professor Niall Rudd points out to me that the line may pun on "moon" in the sense of "to present one's bare buttocks," although *OED* treats this as a modern usage.

[25] Stater, *Duke Hamilton*, p. 279.

[26] *Anecdotes* 1: 51.

[27] See Nokes, *John Gay*, pp. 239-40, 250. One of these three, regularly mentioned by Pope, was Mary Lepell, who in 1720 became Lady Bristol's daughter-in-law on marriage to John Hervey. The two women were often at odds (see Lady Mary's comments, *Complete Letters*, 2: 45). In December 1716 Pope had told Martha Blount, "Gay dines daily with the Maids of honour" (Pope *Corr*, 1: 379).

[28] "Lady Rich is happy in dear Sir Robert's absence," Lady Mary told her sister in 1723 (*Complete Letters*, 2: 23).

[29] Lady Mary Wortley Montagu, *Essays and Poems: with "Simplicity", A Comedy*, ed. Robert Halsband and Isobel Grundy (Oxford, 1977), pp. 44-5. As late as 1727 Lord Hervey told Lady Mary that he found only three people he knew at Bath: the "young" Duchess of Marlborough, her lover Congreve, and Lady Rich (*Complete Letters*, 2: 52). Lady Rich regularly subscribed to musical books, and she was still attending Handel's oratorios and operas at the Haymarket in 1734. Horace Walpole called her "a great patroness of operas": see *The Yale Edition of the Correspondence of Horace Walpole*, ed. W.S. Lewis *et al*, 48 vols (New Haven: Yale University Press, 1937-83), 30: 295. Lady Rich's elder daughter Elizabeth (d. 1795) became the second wife of Lord Lyttelton, Opposition politician, poet and friend of Pope.

[30] Horace Walpole linked Anne Griffith with the character of Calypso in Pope's "Epistle to a Lady," but there seems little to support this (*TE* 6: 53). See also Pat

Rogers, "Wit, Love and Sin: Pope's *Court Ballad* Reconsidered," in *Eighteenth-Century Encounters* (Brighton: Harvester, 1985), pp. 56-74. Lady Rich's husband subscribed to the *Iliad* in 1715.

[31] Quoted by Downes, *Vanbrugh*, p. 488. See further Chapter 8 below.

[32] See *TE* 3.ii: 174, where the editor associates a passage in Pope's imitation of Horace, *Epistle I. vi*, ll. 85-8, with Argyll and the court ladies.

[33] See "Pope and Argyle," in Ault, *New Light*, pp. 172-85; and Rogers, "Wit, Love and Sin," pp. 56-74.

[34] See Castle, *Masquerade and Civilization*, p. 64, on the diabolic origins of the masquerade.

[35] *Tricks of the Town: Eighteenth Century Diversions*, ed. Ralph Straus (London: Chapman and Hall, 1927), p. 175.

[36] The Duke married Lady Isabella Bentinck on 2 August 1714. Another new bride was Jane, wife of the Duke of Argyll since June 1717: see Rogers, "Wit, Love, and Sin," pp. 69-70, as well as the note to ll. 45-6 above. The Duchess of Ormonde was addicted to cards, but preferred to give parties in her own home.

[37] Lady Mary presents the Duchess as a woman of low morals (*Essays and Poems*, p. 184). Pope visited the Duke of Shrewsbury's home in July 1717 (Pope *Corr,* 1: 417).

[38] During the 1720s the Duchess would take the side of Bononcini against Handel in the famous operatic *querelle*. "In the summer of 1721 Bononcini, [Guiseppe] Riva, Peterborough, Anastasia [Robinson], Pope, and Mary Wortley Montagu were living in close proximity at Twickenham" (Dean and Knapp, *Handel's Operas,* p. 306). They formed the support-base of the Bononcini cause, which the Duchess most actively promoted. See also Grundy, *Lady Mary*, p. 226, for Montagu's support of the opera.

[39] Two months later Pope wrote to the Blount sisters, that he knew of no assemblies "except Mad. Kilmanzech's, to which I had the honour to be invited, & the grace to stay away" (Pope *Corr,* 1: 427).

[40] Lady Godolphin subscribed to the *Iliad*. Pope's friend Charles Jervas had painted her, while Pope himself had attempted under the tutelage of Jervas to make portraits of her sisters Elizabeth and Mary.

[41] Nokes, *John Gay*, p. 330, takes a reference in Gay's letter to Burlington, dated 3 October 1722, to refer to the Duchess of Queensberry, but it is almost certainly Henrietta whom Gay means.

[42] See Grundy, *Lady Mary*, p. 181.

[43] Tradition associates the Duchess with the portrait of Philomedé in Pope's *Epistle to a Lady*, but the evidence is inconclusive: see *TE* 3.ii: 56.

[44] Pope had paid a visit to the Duchess in July, around the possible inception date for the ballad (*Corr* 1: 411, 417).

[45] See Maynard Mack, *The Garden and the City: Retirement and Politics in the Later Poetry of Pope 1731-1743* (Toronto: University of Toronto Press, 1969), p. 252. The Duchess subscribed to the *Iliad* and the *Odyssey*, as well as to Gay's *Poems*.

[46] See Pope *Corr,* 1: 404. It is not quite certain that the duchess in question was Elizabeth Douglas, but all the signs indicate as much. Pope was to meet her at her

home in Bond Street (where she now had her town-house), and then to embark at Whitehall – the starting-point for the King's boat trip on 17 July 1717, when Handel's *Water Music* was first performed. We should remark too Sherburn's note: "From its place in the Homer MSS. . .one might place this letter as late as 1718 or 1719," despite the clues which point to 1717. The same logic might apply to the draft of the ballad which Pope made (see pp. 123-4 above).

[47] *Journal to Stella,* 2: 573-4. He also commented on her 'diabolical temper.'

[48] Quoted in *TE* 3.ii: 54. Walpole's suggestion that the Duchess served as a model for Pope's character "Sylvia" seems to have little basis (*TE* 6: 286-7).

[49] See Stater, *Duke Hamilton*, pp. 278-81, on the lawsuit and the hatred between the two women.

[50] The reference to "her Grace" in Lady Mary's town eclogue, "Tuesday," is one of studied vagueness, in keeping with the rest of the poem (*Essays and Poems*, p. 184). The speaker is alleged to be Jackie Campbell, who married Mary Bellenden in 1720, and later succeeded as fourth Duke: Pope dined with him in December 1716. The eclogue is set at St James's coffee- house, as fashionable society gets ready to attend the nearby opera.

[51] For the Duchess's bill of complaint and Congreve's response, see William Congreve, *Letters & Documents*, ed. J.C. Hodges (New York: Harcourt Brace, 1964), pp. 136-9, 143-4.

[52] See Stater, *Duke Hamilton*, pp. 274-6.

[53] As first suggested by George Sherburn, *The Early Career of Alexander Pope* (Oxford: Clarendon Press, 1934), p. 182.

[54] See Donald Burrows, *Handel* (New York: Schirmer, 1994), pp. 81-97, for a summary of evidence concerning the possible activity of "a Cannons literary syndicate" in these productions.

[55] A mock letter from the star opera singer Senesino, published in Mist's *Weekly Journal* on 12 January 1723, indicates that *Annus Mirabilis* was "the Contrivance of two *Wits* in *Conjunction*," i.e. Pope and Arbuthnot.

[56] See Castle, *Masquerade and Civilization*, pp. 46-7, 63-4. Shortly after *Annus Mirabilis,* a poem appeared exploiting the same conceit, "An Epistle to the Most Learned Doctor Woodward": this is usually believed to be a joint production of Gay and Arbuthnot. The poem, concerning one of those transformed at the opera house, plays with ambiguous genitalia somewhat in the manner of the ballad on Heidegger (see Nokes, *John Gay*, p. 329).

[57] Thus Nicolini played the hero in a revival of the opera in January 1717, with two other castrati in the cast. Gay doubtless knew *Rinaldo* well, as he was working for its librettist Aaron Hill when it first appeared at the Haymarket in 1711.

[58] See Swift *Corr*, 2: 278. Arbuthnot was asked by the Royal Academy to treat with Anastasia Robinson in 1719 (National Archives, LC 7/3, quoted by Gibson, *Royal Academy*, pp. 328, 330). Gay had already praised the singer in his verse epistle *To William Pulteney* (written 1718), and she was almost certainly an intimate of the Scriblerian group by that date. For relations at Twickenham in 1721, see Gibson, *Royal Academy*, p. 151; and *Complete Letters*, 2: 13.

[59] See Mack, *Garden and City*, pp. 249-50. All three were intimately acquainted with Charles Jervas.

[60] For the text, see *Essays and Poems*, pp. 182-204. For a full discussion of the poems and their authorship, see Grundy, *Lady Mary*, pp. 103-12.

[61] Matthew Prior was another resident and invited Pope there in 1718. The street should not be confused with Duke Street, St James's, near the opera house: Vanbrugh was living here in early 1717.

[62] Lady Mary's family made a noble showing in the subscription for Gay's *Poems* in 1720: she is listed herself, along with her sisters Lady Mar and Lady Gower, as well as her father and step-mother the Duke and Duchess of Kingston. Despite this, she seems to have moved out of Gay's orbit for the duration of her sojourn abroad.

[63] See Ault, *New Light*, pp. 207-14.

[64] Pope pays a studied compliment to Lady Mary's intellectual powers in "Sandys's Ghost" (*TE* 6: 173).

[65] Lady Mary's old friend Dorothy Townshend (sister of Robert Walpole) lived next door with her husband, the second Viscount. Pope refers to Townshend's political reverse in "The Court Ballad." Also resident in Cleveland Court was Richard Hill, a friend of Sir William Trumbull whom Pope had known since 1714. In March 1718 Martha Blount was 'picking up a large collection of libels' to send to John Caryll (Pope *Corr*, 1: 472): no verse by Pope which fits this description is known from that precise juncture.

[66] Sir Samuel Garth, who lived in St James's Street until his death in January 1719, was still in regular touch with Pope. In 1715 Gay once dropped Garth off at the Opera House (Pope *Corr*, 1: 305).

[67] See Ragnhild Hatton, *George I: Elector and King* (Cambridge, MA: Harvard University Press, 1978), p. 266.

[68] Gay was fated to die very close to this spot, in the town-house of the Duke of Queensberry in Burlington Gardens.

[69] Nokes, "Pope and Heidegger," p. 313, suggests that the attempt to revive the Club may have been the occasion for writing this ballad: the existence of Gay's draft makes this more likely rather than less.

[70] He did write to Mrs Howard from Dijon in September 1717, asking to be remembered to Mary Lepell and Mary Bellenden, but the letter shows him as totally cut off from a remote-seeming London: Gay, *Letters*, pp. 35-7.

[71] Hatton, *George I*, pp. 134, 265-6.

[72] Newspaper report cited by Gibson, *Royal Academy*, p. 131.

[73] Information in this paragraph is based on material in the Niedersächsisches Hauptstaatsarchiv, belonging to Prince Ernst August of Hanover. It is assembled in a most important article by Donald Burrows and Robert D. Hume, "George I, the Haymarket Opera and Handel's Water Music," *Early Music*, 19 (1991): 323-43.

[74] According to Bonet, the King sometimes attended the opera icognito, accompanied by Mme von der Schulenberg (Deutsch, *Handel*, p. 72). The ballad possibly gives him another disguise.

[75] From the diary of John Perceval, later Earl of Egmont, quoted by Hatton, *George I,* p. 292. Oddly, a few years later, "at the last Ridotto or Ball at the Opera-House in the Hay-Market, a Daughter of his Grace the Archbishop of Canterbury won the highest Prize" (*Daily Journal*, 11 February 1723).

[76] Some of these deliberations went on in White's chocolate house in St James's Street and others in the Queen's Arms in Pall Mall. Contemporary accounts refer merely to "Colonel Churchill"; this could indicate Joshua Churchill (no relation), who also later became a Whig MP. Presumably drawing on the accounts of John Hamilton's trial, Stater speaks of "Col. Joseph Churchill - a kinsman of Marlborough," but no such figure is known. It was Charles Churchill who was the Duke's nephew, and who was connected with Macartney and Rich. Lady Mohun's first husband, Col. Edward Griffith, had earlier been married to Barbara Jennings, sister of Sarah Churchill. He owed his position at court to his interest with the Marlborough connection (cf. Stater, *Duke Hamilton*, p. 172).

[77] The King had opposed his appointment to court office in 1714 on account of his illegitimacy: but significantly pleas on his behalf were made by both Marlborough and Argyll. See J.M. Beattie, *The English Court in the Reign of George I* (Cambridge: Cambridge University Press, 1967), p. 139. Churchill (1720-22) and Rich (1740-68) also served in turn as Governor of Chelsea Hospital, an office controlled by Walpole, whose chief London home adjoined the hospital. Rich was one of the victims of the Berkshire Blacks, as a Whig "interloper" in Windsor Forest: see E.P. Thompson, *Whigs and Hunters: The Origins of the Black Act* (Harmondsworth: Penguin, 1977), pp. 109-10.

[78] J.H. Plumb, *Sir Robert Walpole: The King's Minister* (London: Cresset, 1956), p. 42.

[79] Forsythe, *A Noble Rake*, p. 139.

[80] The post at this date was held by Charles Killigrew, brother of the dramatist Thomas, mentioned at ll 45-6: their father had also been Master of the Revels under Charles II.

[81] See Paulson, *Hogarth*, 1: 168-9.

[82] Diary of the Earl of Egmont, quoted by Mack, *Garden and City*, p. 129.

[83] As Prince of Wales, George built in 1724 the four houses known as Maids of Honour Row at the west end of Richmond Green, for the occupation of Caroline's attendants. After his ascent to the throne, in 1744, none other than Heidegger came to live in one of these houses.

[84] The Italian opera managed by Heidegger had collapsed in June 1717 after heavy losses: this was only partially related to the quarrels at court. See Burrows, *Handel*, p. 78; Dean and Knapp, *Handel's Operas*, pp. 163-7. In 1720 the new Royal Academy of Music began operations at the Haymarket, with Burlington, Vanbrugh and Arbuthnot among its directors: Heidegger also attended meetings of the Court of this body, which was a joint stock company. Others with close links to Pope and Gay who served as directors in the early years were Brigadier James Dormer, the Duke of Queensberry and William Pulteney.

[85] It would perhaps have been too close to *lèse majesté* for the ballad to indicate Mme von der Schulenberg, created Duchess of Munster in the Irish peerage in 1716. In any case the Duchess of Hamilton makes more poetic sense.

[86] The Duchess hated Argyle's first wife and once described her as resembling "a fat hog in armour" (quoted by Stater, *Duke Hamilton,* p. 306).

[87] Hatton, *George* I, p. 208.

[88] See *Anecdotes*, 1: 46; and Pope *Corr*, 1: 250.

[89] In 1716 the Earl asked Arbuthnot to keep an eye on his son Thomas, Lord Erskine, then a pupil at Westminster; Lady Mary attended the Westminster English play in 1720, and praised young Erskine's performance. See L.M. Beattie, *John Arbuthnot: Mathematician and Satirist* (Cambridge, MA: Harvard University Press, 1935), pp. 28-9: and Grundy, *Lady Mary*, p. 188.

[90] Valerie Rumbold, *Women's Place in Pope's World* (Cambridge: Cambridge University Press, 1989), p.134.

[91] Grundy, *Lady Mary*, p. 336. It has been suggested that Lady Mary contributed a letter on masquerades to the *True Briton* in 1724, but no evidence is adduced: see Blackett-Ord, *Hell-Fire Duke,* pp. 106-07.

[92] Quoted by Grundy, *Lady Mary*, p. 261.

[93] See Fox and Ribeiro, *Masquerade*, p. 11.

[94] In January 1718 Lady Mary sent Congreve a letter, now lost, which is summarized by its writer: "Why he lets P[ope] make lampoons" (*Complete Letters*, 1: 374). In fact Congreve spent much of 1718 and 1719 nursing his fragile health at Lord Shannon's house, Ashley, in Walton on Thames: his firsthand contacts with Pope seem to have been few (Congreve, *Letters & Documents*, pp. 72, 123, 229-31).

CHAPTER EIGHT

DUKE UPON DUKE:
SATIRIC CONTEXT, AIMS, AND MEANS

Hardly any branch of Pope's writing stands more in need of reappraisal than his range of ballads on topical themes. Items such as *Moore's Worms* (1716), *Sandys's Ghost (c.*1717), *The Court Ballad (c.*1717), *The Discovery* (1726), and *Bounce to Fop* (1736) may not rank among his greatest works from a literary standpoint. Nor are they all immediately attractive to a modern reader, in view of their dependence on a wealth of reference to fugitive events. However, even this apparent disincentive can be overcome, as shown by Dennis Todd's recent use of *The Discovery* (possibly co-written by Pope and William Pulteney) in his analysis of the famous episode involving the "rabbit woman", Mary Tofts.[1] We should recall, too, that these were among the most frequently reprinted of Pope's poems in their time: indeed, *Moore's Worms* was "probably the most popular poem (at least in his own day) that Pope is supposed to have written" (*TE* 6: 163).

Perhaps the most effective of these items is a ballad entitled *Duke upon Duke* (1720). Pope told Joseph Spence that he was the principal author: that is, in the precise words of Spence's report, "Good part of the ballad on Lechmere and Guise was written by Mr. Pope" (*Anecdotes* 1: 152). In 1742 it was included in the Pope-Swift *Miscellanies,* although (as usual with this series) without any indication of authorship. Here it was described as "*An excellent new* Ballad. *To the Tune of* Chevy Chase." Gradually the piece slipped out of the canon, having been once included in an edition of John Gay, and elsewhere attributed to Swift or Arbuthnot. It was not until 1949 that Norman Ault mounted a decisive case for Pope's authorship, and not until 1954 that it appeared in Pope's collected works for the first time.[2]

Three editions of the ballad came out in 1720, two containing music by "Mr. Holdecombe". The exact priority of the earliest editions has not been established: D.F Foxon lists six printings.[3] An advertisement by the fictitious publisher A. Moore indicates that one of the Holdecombe versions came out on 15 August (*Daily Post*). It may in fact have been a reissue of a printing from earlier in the summer: such a dating would square with the known facts more adequately. On 18 August "Moore" was warning the public against one of the other editions, stating that "The great Demand there is for this Ballad has tempted some Pyrates to print a Grub-street Copy of it."[4] One can easily believe that sales were brisk for this risqué, topical, and amusing poem. Further confirmation comes in a news story which appeared on 27 August:

> On Monday night a Female Hawker going through the Temple, crying the Celebrated Ballad of *Duke upon Duke*, a Friend of his to be meant therein, fell upon the Woman, tore her Papers, and was for beating her, but that she demurred, having *Vox Populi* on her Side, she assailed her Combatant with such Fury, that the Man retired in as precipitate a Manner as 'tis said somebody else did from Kensington.[5]

As we shall see, "some body else" points to Nicholas Lechmere, the absconding "hero" of Pope's ballad. The Tory journalist Nathaniel Mist also lands a sideswipe with a reference to *VoxPopuli, Vox Dei*, a Jacobite pamphlet which a year earlier had led to the trial, conviction and execution of a teenage printer – an affair in which Lechmere took a leading role.

Another reprint of *Duke upon Duke* with a musical setting appeared in 1723. The poem with or without music was reissued in at least six miscellanies between 1724 and 1752, disregarding its inclusion in the Pope-Swift volume. Previously the author of the earliest musical setting has not been named, but he can be identified as Henry Holcombe (*c.* 1693-1750), singer and composer, who published a number of popular songs, including *Arno's Vale,* an extremely common anthology piece in the second half of the eighteenth century.[6] A further indication of the currency of Pope's ballad exists in the shape of an *Answer to "Duke upon Duke"*, advertised by the ubiquitous A. Moore just a week after the original work appeared (*Daily Post*, 22 August 1720). The threepenny reply carries on its title-page the name "B. Moor" instead: again Holdecombe's music is added. Significantly, this response addresses Pope as the known author of the first poem.

Despite the clear merits of *Duke upon Duke,* it has received little attention for one obvious reason. The ballad concerns a supposed duel between Nicholas Lechmere, the prominent Whig lawyer and politician, and a backwoodsman in the House of Commons, Sir John Guise. As Ault was forced to admit, "documentary evidence of the cause of the trouble" between the two men "appears to be entirely lacking" (*TE* 6: 189). The duel almost certainly never took place: indeed, it is averted within the text of *Duke upon Duke*. The principals managed to keep the basis of their quarrel out of the public prints: like Ault, I have conducted a search of newspapers in the relevant period (mainly the summer of 1720) without coming up with any allusion to this episode. That the quarrel existed at all is attested, outside the ballad and the reply, by only one piece of independent evidence. Just over a year later, Pope was staying at the Guise family home, Rendcomb, north of Cirencester in Gloucestershire. From here he wrote to his friend Edward Blount, whose wife Annabella was a sister of Sir John: "I fear none so much as *Sir Christopher Guise,* who being in his Shirt, seems as ready to combate me, as her own Sir John was to demolish Duke *Lancastere.*" Again the joke has not been properly explained. Pope writes of being "directed by [Mrs Blount's] Ancestors, whose faces are all upon me" (Pope *Corr*, 2: 85-6).[7] His reference is to a portrait of Sir John's grandfather Sir Christopher (d. 1670), the first baronet. On one occasion this ancestor provided a source of the dynastic pride which helps to explain Pope's use of the title "Duke", for Sir Christopher had noted the heraldic account of his family origins as "descended from a brother of the Duke of Guise who was a companion of William the Conqueror".[8] This was probably a myth, but as will emerge it fitted the poet's purpose.

In fact, we can understand the main drift of the poem without having to know all the details of the quarrel, or even needing to be sure that a duel was ever really threatened. The ballad and the reply contain enough clues to make the intent of *Duke upon Duke* almost wholly transparent. Up to now, however, one of the pervasive strains in the poem has been missed: an undertow of references echoing the famous border ballad *Chevy Chase*. In exploring the work, it is natural to start with the protagonists.

I

The career of Sir John Guise (1677-1732) is easier to summarize, as he passed most of his life in obscurity.   Succeeding as third baronet in 1695, he served as an MP in the reign of Queen Anne and again during the 1720s. He started out as an independent Whig, but played no significant role in national politics. Guise emerges from the poem with less discredit than Lechmere, but still cuts a rather foolish figure. Ault suggests that Pope gave him the style of a "Duke" from the title of a play by John Dryden, *The Duke of Guise,* but as just noted the word hints at family notions of historic grandeur. In fact the Guise lineage was one of substantial gentry: they held the manor of Enmore from the time of Henry III, and acquired their seat at Rendcomb in 1635. However, it suits Pope's aims, for a poem set in a world of mythical medievalism, that there should have been alleged links to the feudal aristocracy. Annabella Guise married Edward Blount *c*.1700: their four daughters were brought up as Roman Catholics and three would marry into the Catholic aristocracy. Meanwhile Sir John stuck to Protestantism, and regarded his sister's conversion to "the popish religion" with disfavour. He also discouraged her literary pursuits.[9] We have no evidence of his relations with Pope, other than the fact of the poet's visit to Rendcomb, but Sir John did subscribe to the *Odyssey* in 1725.

After the accession of the first Hanoverian, George I, in 1714, Guise described the regime as one of "bad subjects and worse rulers". He vainly attempted to heal the breach between the King and his son and daughter-in-law, the Prince and Princess of Wales, in 1717. According to Guise's son, the fourth baronet, his father had been "too indolent and unhealthy to pursue a court intrigue and of too honest open a temper to have kept any power there". Another observer described him as deliberately crossing a fellow MP for Great Marlow: "for Sir John was of such a spirit of controversy and delighted in it that right and wrong it was all alike to him".[10] The picture of Guise which emerges from *Duke upon Duke* shows the same characteristics: he is crotchety, perverse, and cantankerous, but also "guileless" and gout-ridden (lines 49-52).

By contrast, the strident Whig lawyer and politician Nicholas Lechmere (1675-1727) maintained a far more visible presence on the national stage. Since the Hanoverian accession he had been in turn Solicitor-General and Attorney-General, and was still chancellor of the Duchy of Lancaster (hence his naming in the poem as "Nic of Lancastere"). He became a privy councillor on 1 July 1718, an honour mentioned in *Duke upon Duke,* line 92. Following the change of regime in 1714, he had been one of the most ardent in bringing to book those Tories who had served in the Harley administration: for this service and others in the Whig cause, he was rewarded in 1721 with a barony. Two years earlier Lechmere had married Lady Elizabeth Howard, daughter of the Earl of Carlisle: she was an early friend of Lady Mary Wortley Montagu, who had stayed with her at Castle Howard in 1714.[11] It helped Pope's purposes that his grandfather, also Nicholas, had served as a baron of the exchequer from 1689, even though this was a judicial title only. Like the Guises, the Lechmeres were an ancient but not noble family, settled at Hanley Castle, Worcestershire, at least from the time of Edward I: they also claimed to have been granted land by the Conqueror.[12] Nicholas represented the nearby borough of Tewkesbury in parliament until 1721. The poem depicts Lechmere as passionate and capricious in his behaviour, as he was known to be, and also suggests his cowardice in avoiding the duel with Guise. As we saw in Chapter 7, an almost contemporary Scriblerian satire provides another passing reference:

First he bows to a conjuror with a white stick
Then cry'd to a Lawyer hoh, hoh Brother Nick![13]

"Nick" is of course proverbial for the Devil,[14] but the line certainly glances at Lechmere, whom the Duchess of Marlborough called "the worst man that ever I knew in my life".[15]

From the Scriblerian point of view, Lechmere's offences began with his role in the trial of Dr Sacheverell in 1710, when he had been among the Whig managers, and had led the assault in a hectic manner on the very first day of proceedings. This made him hugely unpopular among Tories. When he went out on circuit after the trial, Lechmere found himself the target of violent acts of reprisal: the windows of his lodgings at Hereford were smashed, and the mob hissed and jeered him at Shrewsbury.[16] Swift's *Examiner* no. 26 in January 1711 predicted that Lechmere would bring in a parliamentary bill to allow freethinkers, deists, and atheists such as John Toland and Anthony Collins to serve in any official position.[17] Equally, a satire usually attributed to Swift, "A Fable of the Widow and her Cat" (1712), singles out Lechmere for his readiness to speechify.[18] In early 1714 the lawyer had given Richard Steele some help in writing *The Crisis,* a pamphlet so offensive to the ministry that its author was expelled from the Commons.

After George I came to the throne, the rising politician was in the forefront of promoting measures against opposition groups. A client of the hated Earl of Wharton, he inherited the mantle of the Earl, who died in April 1715.[19] Very soon Lechmere made himself the most reviled member of the government in Tory eyes. Within a few months he served on the secret committee into the conduct of Robert Harley's government; helped to draw up the articles of impeachment against Viscount Bolingbroke and the Duke of Ormonde; oversaw the prosecution of the Jacobite lords implicated in the 1715 rising; and personally led the indictment of Lord Derwentwater. In the course of his arraignment of the peer, Lechmere asserted with some intemperance that the new King had done "more for the honour of the Church, and the true interest of his kingdom, than any of his predecessors, in three times the number of years".[20] He was also mainly responsible for the suspension of Habeas Corpus.[21] All these measures struck at Pope's family, friends, allies, and co-religionists: Derwentwater was a young Catholic lord, beheaded at Tower Hill -as it happens, a few months after he had been listed as a subscriber to Pope's translation of the *Iliad.* Pope also enjoyed the friendship of Lady Swinburne, a member of the Englefield family from Whiteknights, near Reading: the Swinburnes were closely related to the Earl of Derwentwater.

That same year, 1716, Lechmere joined with Lord Coningsbv, a renegade Whig whom Pope attacked elsewhere, in two controversial measures. One was aimed against the former Tory ministers, including Lord Oxford. The second was designed to strengthen the Protestant interest by enforcing the laws against Roman Catholics: Lechmere spoke so virulently on this matter in the House of Commons that a number of Catholics and nonjurors felt they would have to leave the country. This was the juncture when Pope's family were forced to give up their home in Windsor Forest, as Catholics were driven from their estates by measures such as the act requiring registration of all property (1 Geo. I, s. 2, passed on 26 June 1716). Among all the Whigs, Lechmere was the most vehement proponent of these measures. A year later, he defended Lord Cadogan, "a coarse, bull-necked Irishman", who was accused by Walpole of embezzlement. By now Lechmere was firmly leagued with the Sunderland faction of Whigs against his old boss. Pope's scornful reference to Cadogan in the *Epistle to Bathurst,* lines 1-92, shows the depth of his dislike for this successful careerist, a bitter opponent of the poet's friend Atterbury.[22]

Then, as Attorney-General, Lechmere led the prosecution of High Church "martyrs" such as the printer John Matthews in 1719, briefly mentioned above. He secured a conviction for high treason against Matthews, who was still not out of his teens, on the basis of a Jacobite pamphlet he had printed, *Vox Populi, Vox Dei.* The outcome was that the youth was sentenced to be hanged, drawn, and quartered at Tyburn; many considered this little better than judicial murder.[23] Leading for the defence was John Hungerford, a well-known Tory MP and lawyer.[24] The two advocates were bitter enemies: Hungerford would head a parliamentary inquiry into fraudulent insurance companies, set up in February 1720 and reporting in April of the same year. Among the allegations surfacing was one that Lechmere had been implicated in some of the muddy dealings.[25] Amazingly, the Solicitor-General, Sir William Thompson, had hinted that his senior colleague Lechmere had accepted bribes to grant charters to the burgeoning number of joint-stock companies. On this occasion Lechmere was exonerated by the House of Commons, but some of the mud stuck.[26]

An even more specific circumstance underlies Pope's treatment of Lechmere here. During the summer recess of Parliament in 1716 he "joined with the Duke of Argyll in caballing against the Government; supplied Argyll with precedents to show that the Prince's powers as

Regent were not as ample or honourable as in previous cases; and promoted congratulatory addresses to the Prince on his appointment to be Regent, with a view to masking the mischief between him and his father. At the end of 1716 it was reported that he was to be head of Argyll's party in the House of Commons."[27] In other words, Lechmere had been active in the quarrel whose beginnings Pope had jokingly exploited in *The Court Ballad,* involving the faction of the King and that of the Prince of Wales, led by the Duke of Argyll. As we have seen, Guise had also made an effort to intervene in this dispute. It happens that Pope's contacts with the Prince and Princess of Wales were much closer than those with the King; but he found the whole episode irresistibly comic, and satirized both parties to the quarrel more than once. When Lechmere was removed from his post as government lawyer in April 1720, it was possibly because the Prince and Princess had returned to the fold after their split— for this was a price the King might have been able to exact from them. After his dismissal Lechmere continued his vendetta against Walpole, now back in power, and became one of the fiercest critics of the ministry during his spell in the Lords from 1721 to 1727.

So much for the background. If we turn to the poem itself, we find that Pope concentrates nearly all of his firepower on Lechmere, leaving a supporting role to the insignificant Guise. In forty-seven ballad stanzas, he takes the opportunity to utilize his familiar repertoire (in the ballad form) of pun, proverb, and bawdy language, with witty innuendoes concerning the principals. An alternative title found in one of the early printings, "Pride will have a Fall", accurately describes the comic plot. The phrase actually occurs in the last line of the opening stanza, and forms the very last line of the poem (lines 4, 148). The use of a stock proverb is a common element in broadside ballads, but rarely does an author top and tail his work so neatly with such an expression.[28]

II

At the start Pope adopts the mock-archaic diction which he sometimes affected in his more demotic works, appropriate here to a faux-medieval narrative. In the manner of one of the Robin Hood ballads, he addresses "Lordings" who feast "In Bower or Hall", and promises to reveal "what befel *John* Duke of *Guise,* / And *Nic.* of *Lancastere*" (lines 7-8). This formula might recall *Robin Hood and the Butcher,* for example, which opens, "Come all ye gallants, and listen a while / . . .That are in the bowers within".[29] Invoking in ballad style the reign of Richard Cœur de Lyon, the poet states that in those days the barons "rag'd and roar'd"—something for

which the soon-to-be Baron Lechmere of the eighteenth century was
notorious. In the next stanza Pope hints at two standard expressions:

> A Word and Blow was then enough.
> (Such Honour did them prick)
> If you but turn'd your Cheek, a Cuff,
> And if your A—se, a Kick.
>
> (13-16)

This abbreviates "A word to the wise is enough" (Tilley W781) and
incorporates the biblical "turn the other cheek". In those days the
combatants fought "from head to Foot", i.e. with every part of their body
(OED, s.v. "head", 40). The proudest of these warriors was the Duke of
Lancaster: if that reminds us of the Wars of the Roses, then the first line of
the next stanza recalls the verse "I saw young Harry with his beaver on"
from *I Henry IV* (IV. i. 105): "Firm on his Front his Beaver sate" (line 25).
Nic dyes his complexion to a swarthy hue and pomades his hair: though
short in stature, he stands as tall as possible, merely nodding where other
dukes give a full bow. Yet he behaves in a "courteous, blithe, and
debonair" manner towards Guise, and there seems no reason to quarrel.
Capriciously, "having no Friend left but this", he resolves to challenge the
other man. The absurd pretext is an invitation from Lechmere to a game of
whist (hardly a medieval pastime), which "the guileless *Guise*" declines
owing to gout. This provokes the main action.

Nic drives fiercely though "Kingly *Kensington*" from his house at
Campden Hill, and then assaults Guise.[30] Bearing in mind Pope's known
habits of writing, it can be no coincidence that Guise had taken "a little
house at Kensington" in 1715, and had entertained George I to supper
there around 1718 or 1719.[31] The outcome is not what Lechmere expected:

> But mark, how 'midst of Victory,
> Fate plays her old Dog Trick!
> Up leap'd Duke *John,* and knock'd him down,
> And so down fell Duke *Nic.*
>
> (61-4)

"To play a dog trick" (Tilley D456) was a very familiar expression
meaning to act meanly by anyone: Swift uses it in his poem *Upon the
Horrid Plot,* just two or three years later. The point of the next stanza is
less clear:

> Alas, oh *Nic* Oh *Nic,* alas!
> Right did thy Gossip call thee:

> As who should say, alas the Day,
> *When John* of *Guise* shall maul thee.
>
> (65-8)

The godmother ("gossip") has christened Lechmere "Nick", and this apparently suggests the crucial opportunity (as in "nick of time") which Guise seized to "maul" him (or possibly grab, as in "to nick", a long-established usage by this time). The victor sits on his vanquished opponent, and appears likely—by the rhyme at any rate—to be about to shit on his adversary. The threat is averted, and Guise triumphantly scoffs at his victim: "No *Sheet* is here to save thee."

Indignantly, Lechmere asks if Guise knows who he is, one who has brawled and quarrelled more than "all the Line of *Lancastere*". He proceeds:

> In Senate fam'd for many a Speech,
> And (what some awe must give ye,
> Tho' laid thus low beneath thy breech,)
> Still of the Council Privy.
>
> (89-92)

This wickedly precise stanza alludes to Lechmere's known predilection for long speeches in parliament and, as already remarked, to his continuing place on the Privy Council. The mechanism is of course a pun on "privy", following on the scatological language of the preceding stanzas. Next the speaker reminds us of another of his perquisites:

> Still of the *Dutchy* Chancellor,
> *Durante Life* I have it;
> And turn, as now thou dost on me,
> Mine A—e on them that gave it.
>
> (93-6)

The verses deftly integrate a technical term, *durante vita,* referring to an appointment granted for life, which was precisely the basis on which Lechmere had acquired a virtual sinecure in June 1717—one that he duly held until his death in 1727. The phrase about turning his arse on those who bestowed the appointment refers to the politician's break with his former allies, mentioned above. In particular, it recalls his recent invective during a parliamentary debate over the South Sea bill in January 1720. One part of his speech severely criticized a plan which had been put forward by Robert Walpole, giving the Bank of England a greater role in financial reconstruction at the expense of the South Sea Company.

Walpole was now out of major office, but he had been leader of the Prince of Wales's party previously. We should remember that *Duke upon Duke* came out in the very midst of the South Sea year: if the ballad had contained no reference to the dominant news story of the decade, it would have been unique among such verses.[32]

At this juncture servants enter, and Lechmere proposes that the duel be fought "under the Greenwood Tree", another preposterous pseudo-feudal touch, drawn especially from the Robin Hood ballads. In Pope's day real duels were waged in Hyde Park or another convenient part of London where a measure of privacy was possible: they did not take place in some rural nook.[33] So "the valiant *Guise*" sets out that evening for the appointed meeting, with his sword "at Saddle Bow". Another deliberate archaism is introduced: "Full gently praunch'd he o'er the Lawn' (line 109). At length he catches sight of the "Merry- men brown" (normally the companions-in-arms of a knight, here presumably liveried servants) with Lechmere's coach and four. At first it seems his opponent is intent on going ahead with the duel, as he points out "the gloomy Glade" where it should be held with his "Wand so white"—his staff of office, but here also connected with pretended conjurors and charlatans. Suddenly Lechrnere turns tail and heads for New Court, in the Middle Temple, where his chambers were, on the pretext that "business must be done", another evasive cliché. He then slinks back by Brompton Park, best known at this time for the large nursery of the landscape gardener Henry Wise, and along "the Gore" (Kensington Gore) to his home at Campden House.[34] Guise is left fretting in the evening dew with no adversary. He goes home, resolving to put Lechmere's name on every "Pissing-Post" for each "Pisser-by" to use appropriately The ballad concludes with a stock formula, "Now God preserve our gracious King", and expresses the hope that his nobles will all learn a lesson from Duke Nic: "That *Pride will have a Fall*". In the text Lechmere's fall is literal: in the wish-fulfilling ideology of the poem, it will be a descent from his arrogant use of power.

III

Some of the issues at stake are illuminated by *An Answer to "Duke upon Duke"*. Ault dismisses this retort in a few words: "As an answer it is not a success; as a poem it is a tedious failure." Although its forty-one stanzas are "redeemed by never a spark of wit or life", the poem leaves no doubt about "the person it attacks for having written *Duke upon Duke*".[35] In my opinion this is doubly wrong: the reply exhibits a good deal of imaginative energy. and it does not really attack Pope. The work might be regarded as a kind of prolongation of the original ballad, with no more than a few mild and good-humoured references to Pope. Five such allusions are cited by Ault, but none of them indicates real hostility. The opening stanza is indicative:

> Thou Pope, oh Popery burning hot.
> For none but Papists would
> Enter into a cursed Plot,
> 'gainst Protestant so good.
>
> (1-4)

If we harbour any doubt that this is ironic, then the later poem makes it clear that Lechmere is no Protestant hero of the author, whoever he was.

Indeed, Ault's comments miss the central point of the poem, which is a dramatic monologue in the voice of Lechmere himself. Thus the "attack" on Pope comes from a wholly unreliable source; and ultimately the real target is Lechmere. A single stanza will illustrate the satirical approach:

> Take heed thou Satan's crooked Rib,
> For, though not Tall, I'm strait;
> That thou, like me, not bilk thy Crib,
> Like me, repent too late.
>
> (17-20)

The first verse here plays on the stock idea of Adam's rib; while the third line alludes to a gambling expression used in cribbage.[36] Clearly, we are meant to suppose that Lechmere has been caught cheating and made to suffer the consequences. In the fourth verse comes a reminiscence of one more proverbial idea, "Repentance comes too late".[37] There is, too, an odd parallel with Pope's own line "I cough like *Horace,* and tho' lean, am short" *(Epistle* to *Arbuthnot,* line 116). The *Answer* suggests that since the lawyer lost his post as Attorney-General in April 1720 ("cashiered like me", line 34) he has lost all favour at court. As a result, he has become anxious about his continuing hold on the Duchy of Lancaster. He may need to ask his wife to ensure that "her Sire, in Upper House", i.e. the Earl of Carlisle, should take his side. A further reference brings in a certain "Sir R — t", described as "of Law the very Pride" (line 74), and obviously Sir Robert Raymond, the man who had succeeded Lechmere as government lawyer.

More significantly, the *Answer* makes a glancing allusion to the "Knight of *Ipswich* Town" (line 103), who can be identified as Sir William Thompson, Solicitor-General from 1717 to 1720, and MP for Ipswich from 1715 to 1729, as well as Recorder of the City of London. This draws

attention to another salient episode in Lechmere's career about which
Duke upon Duke had surprisingly said nothing: that is, the allegation of
corruption levelled against him by his government colleague. As we have
seen, the charge was dismissed after an inquiry by the House of Commons,
and Thompson lost his job. When the committee's report was published
after its presentation to Parliament in April 1720, some compromising
facts became available to Lechmere's critics. The most likely explanation
for Pope's silence is that he did not wish to highlight an episode from
which his prime target had emerged relatively unscathed. Thompson
himself had a sullied reputation, and when Walpole came to the power he
served as the prime minister's main law enforcement operator through
most of the 1720s and 1730s. Tactically it would have been unwise for
Pope to lay emphasis on his brush with Lechmere.[38]

The *Answer* extends not just the subject matter but also the methods of
its predecessor. Like *Duke upon Duke,* it employs what might be termed a
topic proverb, i.e. a saying which encapsulates the meaning of the whole
poem: in this case, the expression is "Little said's soon amended" (Tilley
L358). Other stock expressions found are "live and learn" (Tilley L379),
"ill jesting with an edged tool" (Tilley J45), "pull someone down a peg"
(Tilley P181), and "Tewkesbury mustard" (Tilley M1333).[39] Another neat
verbal manipulation occurs when Lechmere wishes he had held his tongue,
and "To cool my Porridge, sav'd my Breath" (1. 15), utilizing Tilley
W422. While the formula "a lucky hit" was not exactly proverbial, it had
wide currency as a cant phrase of the day, and a particular favourite of
Pope himself.[40] All this helps to confirm the view that the retort comes
from a source hostile to Lechmere, and probably friendly to Pope. It is not
wholly out of the question that the *Answer* was written by one of the
Scriblerian group or their close associates.

Pope's poetry in the ballad form is marked by a striking idiolect, which
differs from the habitual linguistic tone and texture of his other verse. A
closer similarity lies with the register found in Swift's poems "The Virtues
of Sid Hamet's Rod" and "Dialogue between Captain Tom and Sir Henry
Dutton Colt" (both 1710). In these cases the trick is to find details about
the satiric object (in terms of his or her career, or character and reputation)
which can be made to play into trite and familiar word patterns. Both *Duke
upon Duke* and, rather less nimbly, the *Answer,* exhibit this technique.
Among the predominant devices are puns, as in the joke on "Council
Privy" already quoted; neologisms and distortions, as in "Pisser-by"; and a
species of zeugma, as in "As if he meant to take the Air, / Or only take a
Fee" (lines 123-4). The poet draws in the victim's conduct to an existing
hoard of worldly-wise maxims or pre-packaged formulas. Thus when

Lechmere is made to say, "I will not cope against such Odds" (line 99), he appears distinctly unheroic, lacking even the braggadocio of Falstaff: behind the wording lie clichés such as "two (or three) to one is odds" (Tilley T644). Repeatedly language enacts a judgment on the material in this way.[41]

In *Duke upon Duke*, too, the pervasive use of archaisms helps to create a linguistic template, absurdly costuming the participants in antiquated dress. As we saw earlier, in the *Miscellanies* Pope subtitled the work "*An excellent new* Ballad. *To the tune of* Chevy Chase". This was of course one of the most popular of all such musical settings; but the allusion does more than reinforce the spurious sense of medieval balladry.[42] Since the time of Joseph Addison's influential *Spectator* paper no. 70 in 1711, the original *Chevy Chase,* after which the tune was named, had been the most widely admired of the Border ballads. According to Addison, "The old Song of *Chevey Chase* is the favourite Ballad of the common People of *England;* and *Ben Johnson* used to say he had rather have been the Author of it than of all his Works."[43] It had been retold in numerous broadside versions throughout the seventeenth and early eighteenth centuries. The poem often surfaces under alternative titles, such as *The Hunting of the Cheviot* (Child 162). One of the most familiar versions of this poem begins "God prosper long our noble king", which, as we have seen, is almost identical with the formula used at the close of *Duke upon Duke*.

The endings are suspiciously similar. This is the conclusion of the Child ballad:

> God save our King, and bless this land
> With plenty, joy and peace,
> And grant henceforth that foul debate
> 'Twixt noblemen may cease!
>
> (133-6)[44]

Compare Pope's closure:

> Now God preserve our gracious King!
> And grant, his Nobles all
> May learn this Lesson from Duke *Nic.*
> That *Pride will have a Fall.*
>
> (145-8)

Besides this, there are other details which amount to direct parody: thus, *Chevy Chase* employs a stock formula borrowed by Pope: "The rest were slain in Chevy Chase Under the greenwood tree" (lines 523-4). The phrase *merry men* appears in the older work at line 90. At the same time, Pope's subject is about as far as he could get from the elemental passions of the original. Instead of courageous and generous combatants like Earl Percy and Earl Douglas, we have two bickering commoners. The scene is set not in desolate Northumbrian moorland, but in the well-manicured outskirts of London, around "kingly Kensington". Lechmere arrives for the joust, not "well mounted on a gallant steed", but in a coach and four, the symbol of conspicuous consumption in that South Sea year. Through echoes of *Chevy Chase,* Pope creates a kind of mock-heroic effect: just as an implied comparison with Homeric figures diminishes the stature of Belinda and the Baron in *The Rape of the Lock,* so the duellists in *Duke upon Duke* look puny beside the brave medieval combatants. Their dealings involve ridiculously obsolete English, with words like *certes* and *Caitiff,* and they address one another in the antiquated second person singular.

This use of archaism has a particular point, in view of the Guise family legend about the Conqueror, and the Lechmeres' belief that their roots went back to the Domesday Book. As we saw, Nic boasts to his opponent of outdoing "all the Line of *Lancaster.*" Sir John's grandfather had claimed that he could establish his pedigree "without going to the Heralds Office". Among his papers he found "more certain lights of my own evidence" which traced the estate at Elmore to Anselm Guise, whose "office in Edward I. time in the Gloucestershire book, in the Tower of London, I have seene". He also had a charter "very fayre written with [a] large seale" relating to this matter.[45] At the same time Lechmere's grandfather maintained that his forebears "came in wth the Conquest, as appeareth in an authentick record in fflaunders, the copy whereoff I have inserted in this booke" (a family historv).[46] This desperate urge to "authenticate" their feudal past characterized both the Lechmeres and the Guises, and it gives added point to the pseudo-medieval manner of the ballad. Similarly the invocation of barons' wars, with its recollection of contests in the time of Richard Cœur de Lyon (lines 9-11) points up the triviality of the squabbles among modern "barons", as well as the less than lion-hearted display put up by the principal satiric target. Lechmere, too, is implicitly belittled by comparison with such legendary figures as John of Gaunt, Duke of Lancaster in the fourteenth century – much as Guise shrinks alongside Claude of Lorraine, Duke of Guise, soldier and regent of France, and grandfather of Mary Queen of Scots.

IV

Pope's ballad celebrates the "fall" of Lechrnere, i.e. his loss of political office. That event occurred in April 1720, and this is one reason for suspecting that the work originated not in August but up to four months earlier. The second reason is the absence of any up-to-date reference to the affairs of the South Sea Company, whose stocks reached their peak on to July and began their own precipitous "fall" in the second half of August. Instead, *Duke upon Duke* fixes on a minor quarrel between two men not known to be centrally involved in the Bubble.[47] As we have seen, Guise was merely a bit-part player in Pope's narrative; and he was in any case likely to be spared as the brother-in-law of one of the poet's closest friends among his co-religionists, Edward Blount. All the animus of the poem is concentrated on Lechmere, a long-time *bête noire* of the Tories, who had been satirized by Swift almost a decade earlier. For his conduct in 1715 and 1716, Lechmere became especially obnoxious to the family and friends of Robert Harley: that he was already unpopular in the Harley country of Hereford and Shropshire is shown by the treatment he received from pro-Sacheverell mobs round these parts in 1710, an episode touched on above. By 1720 Pope was very closely tied to the Harleys.

The ballad portrays Duke Lancaster as "Paramount in Pride" (line 22). Here the key word carries a fearful sting, because Lechmere had just lost his job and would not become a baron, let alone a "lord paramount," for another year. Even then he never regained under Walpole the influence he had formerly wielded in Whig counsels. Despite his split with the ministry, he retained his old hatred for Atterbury: he spoke in favour of the bill of pains and penalties which the Lords brought against the bishop after the Jacobite plot came to light. Nor, we should note, did the lawyer's humiliation in this fracas with Guise do anything to cool his temper. In 1723 he challenged a former ally Lord Cadogan to a duel after some fisticuffs outside parliament when Lechmere tried to run over Cadogan with his carriage, at which Cadogan beat his adversary's coachman with a cane and called his master a rascally lawyer. They met in St James's Park, when the old soldier used "only a hunting knife to parry the blows, disarmed this opponent and went off laughing."[48] It sounds almost like a replay of the events in 1720. A ballad predictably followed, on the model of *Duke upon Duke*, under the title *A Fight and no Fight*.

Within Pope's poem, Duke Lancaster's choleric nature consorts with the fact that the real Lechmere would ultimately die at Camden House "of apoplexy, while at table".[49] Equally, the poem depicts Lechmere as cowardly and disloyal, someone always willing to turn on his friends: "He

kick'd and cuff'd, and tweak'd, and trod / His Foes, and Friends beside"
(lines 23-4). Here, the inversion of the expected order "friend or foe"
produces the meaning "he attacked his foes and *even* his friends". This
simple but effective device utilizes the small shifts in grammar at which
the poet was so adept. Again, an implied contrast with historic warriors
such as Earl Percy helps to produce the desired effect. Contemporaries
would easily recall that a year before Lechmere had been instrumental in
sending a fatherless boy to Tyburn, even though in the end Matthews'
body had not been quartered. This puts the clumsy corporeality of the
encounter in *Duke upon Duke* into a still more ignominious light.

Pope makes the starting-point of his work a trifling brush between the
two politicians, rather than one of the better-known scandals in
Lechmere's career. However, a careful reading prompts the view that the
ballad enlists a much more widespread resentment, which had been
building up for years in Pope and his allies. Like other ballads, it is a *pièce
d'occasion* which takes us well beyond the immediate occasion.

Notes

[1] Dennis Todd, *Imagining Monsters: Miscreations of the Self in Eighteenth-Century England* (Chicago: University of Chicago Press, 1995), pp. 72-4.
[2] See Ault, *New Light*, pp. 186-94; and *TE* 6: 217-24. In his copy the antiquarian
Maurice Johnson implausibly attributed the poem to James Craggs (not otherwise
known to have written any verse), with revision by Thomas Tickell. The inclusion
of this item in the *Miscellanies* renders Johnson's attribution untenable.
[3] See D.F. Foxon. *English Verse, 1701-1750: A Catalogue of Separately Printed
Poems with Notes on Contemporary Collected Editions,* 2 vols (Cambridge:
Cambridge University Press, 1975), items D502-07. A further variant printing at
the Bodleian Library is listed in the online *English Short Title Catalogue,* item
N71066. One of the characteristic features of Pope's ballads is that, if they appear
in an early printing, it is always through some illicit or clandestine outlet, such as
"Moore" or Edmund Curll.
[4] *Post Boy,* 22 August 1720, quoted in *TE,* 6: 186.
[5] Mist's *Weekly Journal,* 27 August 1720.
[6] For details on Holcombe, see *The New Grove Dictionary of Music and Musicians,*
ed. Stanley Sadie, 20 vols (New York: Grove, 1995), 8: 643.
[7] Pope knew Sir John's uncle, John Grubham Howe MP, and stayed with Howe's
son in 1728 at Stowell, Gloucestershire, just five miles from Rendcomb.
[8] Quoted by Felicity Heal and Clive Holmes, *The Gentry in England and Wales,
1500-1700* (Stanford, CA: Stanford University Press, 1994), p. 37. After reading of
his family's antiquity, Sir Christopher went on to review deeds among his
muniments showing that the Guises had held their Gloucestershire estates since the
thirteenth century. See above, p. 174.

[9] See *Autobiography of Thomas Raymond and Memoirs of the Family of Guise of Elmore, Gloucestershire,* ed. Godfrey Davies (London: Royal Historical Society, 1917), pp. 142-3; and *Eighteenth-Century Women Poets,* ed. Roger Lonsdale (Oxford: Oxford University Press, 1990), p. 186.

[10] Romney Sedgwick, *The House of Commons 1715-1754,* 2 vols (London: HMSO for the History of Parliament Trust, 1970), 2: 89-90.

[11] Later Lady Mary reported heavy gaming losses by Lady Lechmere. See *The Complete Letters of Lady Mary Wortley Montagu,* ed. Robert Halsband, 3 vols (Oxford: Clarendon Press, 1965-67), 1: 210; 2: 57.

[12] Two generations later, in the main line through Nicholas's elder brother Anthony, the family was awarded a baronetcy which survives today. The barony expired on Nicholas's death.

[13] 'A Strange and Wonderfull Relation how the Devill Appeared last night at the Masquerade in the Hay-market", University of Nottingham Library, MS Portland Pw 35 i. For the authorship of this item, see Chapter 7 above.

[14] See Tilley N161.

[15] Quoted by Kerry Downes, *Sir John Vanbrugh: A Biography* (New York: St Martin's, 1987), p. 488. It has been conjectured without very much evidence that the character of Flavia in Pope's *Epistle to a Lady* refers to Lady Lechmere: see *TE* 3.ii: 57.

[16] See Geoffrey Holmes, *The Trial of Doctor Sacheverell* (London: Eyre Methuen, 1973), pp. 235-6.

[17] *Swift* vs. *Mainwaring: "The Examiner" and "The Medley",* ed. Frank H. Ellis (Oxford: Clarendon Press, 1985), p. 195.

[18] Swift also expressed the Tory line in "The Faggot" (1713), line 48: "A Fig for *Lechmere, King,* and *Hambden*" (Swift *Poems,* 1: 191). These three were all Whig lawyers and politicians who had been active in the Sacheverell affair.

[19] Lechmere was one of the guardians of the Whig leader's son, Philip (later Duke of Wharton), who was only sixteen when he succeeded to the title.

[20] Quoted from *Parliamentary History* by Wolfgang Michael, *England under George I,* 2 vols (New York: AMS Press, 1970), 1: 208.

[21] In addition, he was centrally involved in introducing the Riot Act, about which Pope made a bitter little joke shortly after its introduction in July 1715 (Pope *Corr,* 1: 311).

[22] On Cadogan see E.P. Thompson, *Whigs and Hunters: The Origin of the Black Act* (Harmondsworth: Penguin, 1977), pp. 100-02, 202-04. For Pope's reactions, see *TE* 3.ii: 97; and *Corr,* 2: 386-7.

[23] The proceedings are reported in T. B. Howell and others, *A Complete Collection of State Trials,* 33 vols (London, 1809-26), 15 (1812): 1323-1403. According to the under-secretary of state, Charles Delafaye, this great show trial lasted from 10 a.m. until past 11 p.m. (National Archives, SP43/63).

[24] Hungerford subscribed to the *Odyssey* in 1725, as well as to volumes by Matthew Prior (1719) and John Gay (1720). He opposed the bill of pains and penalties against Atterbury, as well as a special tax on Catholics in 1722, and defended the ill-starred agent of the Atterbury plot, Christopher Layer. All these

represent the negation of Lechmere's posture, and in most cases indicate Pope's own outlook on events.

[25] See Carswell, *Bubble*, p. 138. In Sedgwick, *House of Commons*, 2: 161, the date is wrongly given as February 1721.

[26] There is no doubt that in 1718 the entrepreneur Case Billingsley offered both Thompson and Lechmere's predecessor Sir Edward Northey one thousand guineas each, if his marine insurance company charter was granted. He cheerfully admitted this to the Commons investigative committee, stating that he had not regarded it as a bribe. Billingsley was perhaps the most notorious company promoter of the Bubble era: he was a close associate of Thompson, and worked hard on Lechmere to get official backing for his schemes, such as the York Buildings Company. See also David Murrav, *The York Buildings Company: A Chapter in Scottish History* (1883; repr. Edinburgh. Bratton, 1973), pp. 27-9. Eventually the insurance scheme went ahead. In 1722 Billingsley launched the Harburgh Company, with the Prince of Wales as governor, in which Lechmere (now out office) took part: it turned out to be a spectacular fraud. See A.J.G. Cummings and Larry Stewart, "The Case of the Eighteenth-Century Projector: Entrepreneurs, Engineers, and Legitimacy at the Hanoverian Court in Britain", in *Patronage and Institutions: Science, Technology, and Medicine at the European Court, 1500-1750*, ed. by Bruce Moran (Ipswich: Boydell & Brewer, 1991), pp. 235-61.

[27] Sedgwick, *House of Commons*, 2: 203.

[28] For the proverb, see Tilley P581.

[29] *English and Scottish Ballads,* ed. by Francis James Child, 8 vols (Boston: Little, Brown, 1859), 5: 33.

[30] Kensington was of course "kingly" on account of its royal associations, in fact the palace had become a great favourite with George I: it had recently been out of bounds to the Prince, and so it was part of the monarch's territory during their battle of wills. In addition, William Benson had begun improvements to the state apartments in 1718, as part of a series of measures to make the house and gardens more regal; but the new rooms were badly designed and "in need of repair not long after their completion in 1722" (Ragnhild Hatton, *George I: Elector and King* (Cambridge, MA: Harvard University Press, 1978), pp. 262-3). Pope's patron Lord Burlington recommended William Kent to carry out restorative work in 1722. In *The Dunciad*, 1: 321 Pope would criticize the elevation of the amateur architect Benson, a Whig politician, to replace Christopher Wren at the Board of Works.

[31] *Memoirs of the Family of Guise,* ed. Davies, pp. 153-5. The date of this event is not given, but the likeliest time would be the late summer of 1719. This is another touch suggesting insider information, of a sort which Pope (but not Swift or Gay, for example) might have possessed.

[32] In any case, before the South Sea episode, Lechmere had become known for a lack of reliability: thus he had introduced a wrecking amendment to the Septennial Act in 1716, even though this was proposed by the leader of his own faction of the Whigs, James Stanhope. See Basil Williams, *Stanhope: A Study in Eighteenth-Century War and Diplomacy* (Oxford: Clarendon Press, 1932), p. 197.

[33] It was in Hyde Park that the most famous duel of recent times, that between the Duke of Hamilton and Lord Mohun, had taken place in 1712. Some details of the

poem - the mention of the road to Kensington, the waiting coach - recall descriptions of the Hamilton duel. See also Chapter 7.

[34] Camden House was a Jacobean mansion, destroyed by fire in 1862. According to Austin Dobson, Lechmere bought it from the Noel family in 1719, and lived there for several years. See Leigh Hunt, *The Old Court Suburb: Memoirs of Kensington, Regal, Critical and Anecdotal,* 2 vols (London: Constable, 1903), 2: 200. I do not know the evidence for this.

[35] Ault, *New Light,* p. 188.

[36] "Sometimes it so happens that he is both bilkt in hand and crib" (quoted from Charles Cotton's *Compleat Gamester* (1680) in *OED, s.v.* "crib", 16).

[37]*The Oxford Dictionary of English Proverbs,* ed. by F.P. Wilson, 3rd edn (Oxford: Clarendon Press, 1970), p. 672.

[38] In addition, Thompson had been one of the managers of the Sacheverell prosecution, and taken part in prosecuting the Jacobite lords. From the Tory viewpoint he was not a whit better than Lechrnere. On his career generallv, see J.M. Beattie, *Policing and Punishment in London 1660-1750: Urban Crime and the Limits of Terror* (Oxford: Oxford University Press, 2001), pp. 424-62. For the bad blood between Lechmere and Thompson, see a letter from the solicitor general dated 12 September 1718, complaining that he had been treated by Lechmere as "Mr. Attorney-General's footman" (National Archives, SP 35/18/15).

[39] The joke here, in the last line, is that Lechmere was MP for Tewkesbury.

[40] See Howard Erskine-Hill, "The Lucky Hit in Commerce and Creation," *Notes & Queries,* 14 (1967): 407-08.

[41] The prime sense of *upon* in the title is "into contact or collision with, esp. by way of attack" *(OED,* "upon", 15); but the wording also recalls phrases like "age upon age". There was a maxim, used by Swift, "Metal upon metal is false heraldry" (Tilley M906), which might be applicable to the pretensions of these "dukes".

[42] See Claude M. Simpson, *The British Broadside Ballad and its Music* (New Brunswick, NJ: Rutgers University Press, 1966).

[43]*The Spectator,* ed. by Donald F. Bond, 5 vols (Oxford: Clarendon Press, 1965), 1: 298.

[44] Child, *Ballads,* 7: 54.

[45] *Memoirs of the Familv of Guise,* ed. Davies, pp. 107-08. As Davies says, such pedigrees were often compiled with the help of "those mythical genealogical trees which began to appear in Elizabeth's reign" (p. 85).

[46] [E.P. Shirley], *Hanley and the House* of *Lechmere* (London: Pickering, 1883), p. 52.

[47] In fact Lechmere seems to have supported the interests of the South Sea Company against rival companies promoted by men like Thompson and Case Billingslev. His own sister-in-law reported rumours that he deliberately stayed out of the firing line when the Bubble investigations were going on in 1721: "He is so little beloved that I believe he has many undeserved reflections cast on him. 'Tis said Mr. Knight's going off [i.e the absconding of the South Sea Company's cashier] is very serviceable to him since there would have been some discoveries made not much to his honour had Knight stayed' (quoted in Sedgwick, *House of Commons,* 2: 204).

[48] Eveline Cruickshanks and Howard Erskine-Hill, *The Atterbury Plot* (Basingstoke: Palgrave, 2004), p. 206.

[49] [Shirley], *Hanley,* p. 56.

CHAPTER NINE

PLUNGING IN THE SOUTHERN WAVES:
THE IDIOM OF SWIFT'S POEM ON THE BUBBLE

Swift produced few more characteristic works in verse than *The Bubble*, which he composed towards the end of the baneful South Sea year of 1720.[1] By this I do not mean simply that the poem brings together a number of the author's favourite strategies and verbal devices, enlisting a variety of different idioms (heroic, satiric, political, biblical, proverbial) and crossing tonal registers from flippant to corrosive. What makes it equally representative of Swift's poetry in general is that *The Bubble* takes on a large contemporary issue which formed the subject-matter for many contemporary effusions by writers great and small. Moreover, Swift chose a form, the broadside ballad, which was precisely the one most popular with other writers dealing with the topic. This provided a marked contrast with Pope, who waited several years before he tackled similar themes in a sustained fashion. We have to wait until 1733 for Pope's own treatment of this issue: the *Epistle to Bathurst* (1733) is a complex and richly orchestrated composition, not wholly remote from popular idiom but oblique and allusive rather than direct or univocal. For all the variety of its means, *The Bubble* operates essentially on a monothematic level. The rhetoric of Pope's epistle enjoins a process of standing back, where that of Swift's poem embraces the topical, the sense of the moment. *The Bubble* is composed in a familiar ballad stanza; significantly, an abridged version soon appeared, with the text accompanied by a satiric print.

I

The difference in method points to fundamental disparities in outlook and approach between Swift and Pope, which have been explored in recent years by Carole Fabricant, Ellen Pollak, and other scholars. In this essay the emphasis will lie on Swift alone. What matters for my reading of the poem is that *The Bubble* belongs, as the *Epistle to Bathurst* does not, to the huge array of satire (graphic as well as literary) provoked by the collapse of the South Sea Bubble in the autumn of 1720. This consideration goes beyond the fact Swift wrote his poem at the height of the national furore occasioned by the Bubble; it is also related to his choice of verse-form, metre, imagery, and reference. Hardly any poem in the canon better illustrates his ability to occupy the same imaginative space as the Grub Street writers whom the Scriblerians often derided; hardly any other poem shows more clearly his ability to transcend by emulating, or his capacity to make an artistic virtue out of circumstantial necessity. Swift belongs with Kipling or Joyce in this respect, rather than with Pope or Eliot: the demotic element energizes his words and gives buoyancy (not weariness) to the rhythms. *The Bubble* is a self-contextualizing work, which may be why it has not received much attention in the grand reassessment of Swift's verse. Unlike *Verses on the Death of Dr. Swift* it relies on the quarrel with others more than the quarrel with the self, and in this it resembles most popular literature. It is, of course, a highly sophisticated piece of work, intellectually dense and verbally inventive; but it possesses at the same time some of the unmediated gusto and the plain rudeness of hack writing on the subject. The Bubble was an easy target, and that suited Swift, who generally had simple feelings about large issues.

The few commentaries on this poem usually enlist a sentence in a letter which Matthew Prior wrote to Swift in February 1721, a few weeks after *The Bubble* first appeared: "I am tyred with politics and lost in the South Sea: the roaring of the Waves and the madness of the people were justly putt together."[2] Prior is alluding to Isaiah 5.30: "And they [the people] shall roar against them in that day like the roaring of the sea: and if one look unto the land, behold darkness and distress, and the light is darkened in the clouds thereof." This is much to the purpose, for *The Bubble* is (like much of Swift) prophetic in the Old Testament manner rather than apocalyptic. We might usefully recall the end of the preceding verse: "Yea, they shall roar, and lay hold of the prey, and carry it away safe, and there shall be none to deliver." The raging seas do not enter the poem in a fully explicit way until near the end, but the idea of a prey is called up in the opening lines, whilst the hope of deliverance is enshrined in a climactic passage. It is also valuable to consider the succeeding phrases in Prior's letter: "I can send you no sort of News that holds either Connexion or sense,'tis all wilder than St Anthony's dream, and the Bagatelle is more solid than any thing that has been endeavoured here this Year." This suggests the flux and discontinuity of Swift's own poem, but also the scenes of chaos exemplified in Hogarth's print of the Bubble and other graphic satires at this time. It should be remembered, too, that the edition of the poem garnished with prints was entitled *The Bubbler's Medley*. This might fashionably be described as the charivari motif; more simply, the design of Swift's work (much less carefully integrated than that of most of his poems, for all the care we know that he bestowed on it)[3] reflects the widespread sense of confusion in the aftermath of South Sea.

Swift begins with relatively homely detail, that is his old favourite topic from the *Tale* onwards, tricks of a mountebank. But by the end of the third line Swift has interpolated the central trope of the poem: just as he made the idea of "banks" crucial to *The Run upon the Bankers* (1720), so the literalising of "South Sea" stands at the heart of *The Bubble*:

> What Magick makes our Money rise
> When dropt into the Southern Main.
>
> (2-3)

This act of reification is the more effective because of the fiction built into the very name of the South Sea Company, a putative trading corporation which had actually been set up primarily to fund the national debt. By this stroke Swift is able to insinuate the bogus nature of the enterprise from its outset; by making the South Sea actual waves, actual rock-strewn water, actual *wetness*, he is revealing what was in his view the fundamentally fraudulent nature of the new financial structures   - much as Pope was to turn "Blest paper credit" into real sheets of paper, wafted about on the breeze.

Swift moves on rapidly from the notion of alchemical transformation, which had been used in other ballads, such as one carrying the subtitle *The Grand Elixir, or the Philosopher's Stone Discover'd*. The delusion changes to the frenetic vision of a desperate bankrupt, who

> Puts all upon a desp'rate Bett,
> Then plunges in the *Southern* Waves,
> Dipt over head and Ears - in Debt.
>
> (22-5)

The commonplace figurative expression "over head and ears" was set for enough centuries to have earned a listing in dictionaries of proverbs: it is Tilley H268, and Swift indicatively drops it into the banal sociobabble of *Polite Conversation*. This may appear a familiar and unremarkable sort of cross-reference, but such convergences are surely worthy of note. If one imagines the solemn puerilities of *Bouvard et Pécuchet* transplanted wholesale into *Madame Bovary* one may get a better sense of the imaginative trick involved: Emma certainly thinks in clichés, but these do not typically have the precise verbal outline of a stock expression or catchphrase. The underlying effect of Swift's procedures is identifiable enough: it involves a laying bare of reality, a stripping of the protective abstract clothing which everyday phrases tend to wear, just because they call for so little examination in their ordinary context. Indeed, one could describe the process as that of anti-metaphor: a reversal of the primal poetic urge, substituting the literal for the symbolic, the tenor for the vehicle.

Next Swift employs the figure of a calenture or fever to describe the mania, appropriately insofar as this was incident to sailors in tropical seas. Once again the image reminds us of the actual South Sea, that is the very Pacific latitudes which the Company professed to trade in (though in practice it did so inadvertently or irrelevantly). Then follows the first mythic episode, likening hopeful investors to Icarus, with his *"Paper Wings"*, plunged at the end into "Southern Seas". Precise geography is unimportant, compared to the indefeasible wateriness of the ocean. This element is intensified by mention of a "dang'rous Gulph" (whirlpool), and then the River Severn, in which geese swim without wetting a feather. The point of this last reference is to illustrate a true Swiftian mock-proverb: *"Fools* chiefly float, the Wise are drown'd." Here we have almost the cadence of numerous sayings recorded in the collections, along lines like "A wise man by night is no fool by day" (Tilley M173).

The first direct opprobrium fixed on the peccant directors of the Company is found in a succeeding stanza, in lines foreshadowing the celebrated passage on fleas in *On Poetry: A Rapsody*:

> As Fishes on each other prey
> The great ones swallowing up the small
> So fares it in the *Southern* Sea
> But Whale *Directors* eat up all.
>
> (65-8)

For good reasons Swift's mind was drawn to whales, sometimes identified as the dragon in the sea with whom Pharaoh is linked in the prophetic books (Swift had likened the deluded investors to Pharaoh in a stanza following line 32, omitted in the standard version of the poem). Pharaoh's Egypt as a land of devastation and waste underlies many descriptions of England in the wake of the Bubble. At line 77 we get a direct allusion to the Day of Judgement, not lingered on as the phrase carries its own urgency. Much of the Old Testament idiom seems to be present as a kind of back-up, as though Swift wanted to displace feelings of anger and desire for retribution on to an outside source. This in turn enables him to preserve in his own narrating person a measure of geniality and even suavity, since the harsher implications of his language are, so to speak, the work of others. It seems as if Swift often needed some such displacement to preserve his own state of contentment as a writer.

Following stanzas put further emphasis on the "moistned Wings" of fish, and then on the image of Venus for once not arising from, but descending to, the sea, "searching the Deep for Pearl and Coral". After this, another high Swiftian touch:

> The Sea is richer than the Land,
> I heard it from my Grannam's Mouth,
> Which now I clearly understand,
> For by the Sea she meant the *South*.

(97-100)

I do not know of the prior existence of such homely wisdom, but once more the formula is out of the common stock (compare Tilley's item S177: "Praise the sea, but keep on land"). Admittedly such antithetical couplings are hospitable to versification by any Augustan poetaster; nevertheless, it was Swift far more than anyone else who made the leap. Perhaps Byron is the writer when he injects into *Don Juan* familiar-looking tags filling the space of an orthodox saw or motto. Underlying all these manipulations of household words is the covert sense, "it must be so because we have, or almost have, or should have, a proverb to cover it." A few lines further on Swift insinuates a real proverb, "all is not Gold that glisters"; the potential triteness of this manoeuvre is reduced by the fact that it occurs in the third line of the ballad stanza, with a more openly thematic line following ("Ten thousand sunk by leaping in").

The two notions of gold and water (specifically "washing", as in an alchemical bath) are intertwined in the immediately succeeding stanzas. The directors, masquerading as "Patriots", are invited to *"wash their Hands"* in the sea; the italicized phrase obviously recalls Pilate's gesture of self- exculpation (Matthew 27-24). Swift's mind darts rapidly from this allusion to the fable of Midas, which he had used as the basis of a political ballad at the start of 1712; much of the verbal play in *The Bubble* goes back to Swift's earlier attacks on Godolphin and Marlborough. Further alchemical language in the passage beginning in line 113, with mention of "magick Virtue", recalls an analogous use of wit in *Sid Hamet's Rod* (see Chapter 1). On this occasion the key attribute of gold is its materiality, that is its heaviness: a quality more commonly associated with the base metals, such as lead. *The Bubble* is above all a treatise on the art of sinking, and just as Pope's Dulness with its peculiar gravity draws everything down into the "profound", so the South Sea is a vortex into which money is irresistibly attracted:

> Upon the Water cast thy Bread
> And after many Days thou'lt find it,
> But Gold upon this Ocean spred
> Shall sink, and leave no mark behind it.

(133-6)

Swift makes explicit reference to Ecclesiastes at the start is explicit; and this not the only point in the poem where he enjoys himself in metrical paraphrase. There may be a more glancing allusion to Prospero in the last verse of the stanza, apt if present because *The Tempest* is certainly the play closest to Swift's concerns here.

The note deepens as Swift's mythologizing imagination comes into full play with a vision of Change Alley as a narrow sound, where subscribers "fish for Gold and drown"; meanwhile a group of wreckers lie in wait on "GARR'WAY Clifts". Garraway's was a coffee-house which operated as a centre of trading activity in the Alley, but the name may also suggest "Galloway", a coast noted for smuggling and lawlessness. What cements this vision is another stanza devoted to straight metrical paraphrase, this time a word-by-word version of Psalm 107.26-27:

> *Now bury'd in the Depth below,*
> *Now mounted up to Heav'n again,*
> *They reel and stagger too and fro,*
> *At their Wits ends like drunken Men.*

(149-52)

"Like a drunken man" in the Psalmist's picture of the storm is in effect a dead metaphor; when Swift reapplies the image it is closer to a literal similitude, since the investors are shown to be intoxicated by their delusive hopes of gain. Swift soon has another shopsoiled byword ready to draw on and reanimate in use:

> While some build Castles in the Air,
> *Directors* build 'em in the Seas;
> *Subscribers* plainly see 'um there,
> For Fools will see as Wise men please.

(165-8)

The identification of directors with the wise is ironic, but it is easily accepted as the subscribers genuinely qualify as fools and the proverbial formula calls for an equivalent body of the sagacious. Swift had exploited the implications of "castles in the air" on previous occasions, notably in a poem from 1708, *Vanbrug's House* (Swift *Poems,* 1: 179). Yet again the trick is to make concrete an expression which had fallen into amiable and hazy abstraction. By a natural transition Swift moves on to *"Earl Godwin*'s Castles", that is, the supposed buildings which were alleged to lie beneath the Goodwin Sands and to disturb sailors by reappearing like the submerged cathedral of Ys.

As the poem approaches its climax, its virtuosity increases, so that there is a characteristic double impression, of heightened intensity along with a kind of detached artistic pleasure to be derived from the ingenious connections forged. Three successive ballad stanzas picture first the directors as hungry sea-monsters; then the long proverbial "Dogs of *Nile*", snapping up water on the move so as not to risk an encounter with crocodiles; and finally the story of Hercules and Antaeus. Swift's sources here include Lucan and Phaedrus, but there is no parade of learning; the intent is to naturalize or domesticate classical idiom. What happens to the dogs of Nile is entirely typical of Swift's working methods. Phaedrus has in his fable the lines "Canes currentes bibere in Nilo flumine, / A crocodiles ne rapiantur, traditum est". The story also occurs in Pliny: a proverb evolved, *ut canis e Nilo*, meaning to do something too hurriedly. In that form it appeared in the Adages of Erasmus, and a later English version, "Like a dog at the Nile", crops up intermittently over the centuries (*ODEP* 194). What Swift does is to reverse the proverb-creating process, and expand from a phrase to an incident; his mind continually reasserts the actual, reactivates the physical.

II

So we move towards the remarkable culmination of *The Bubble*, in which Swift draws together the scattered implications of a rhetorical attack mounted over the preceding lines. Two stanzas are devoted to a straightforward joke which consigns the directors to a fate which Swift probably thought they deserved in sober reality:

> Directors thrown into the Sea
> Recover Strength and Vigor there,
> But may be tam'd another way,
> *Suspended for a while in Air.*

> *Directors*; for tis you I warn,
> By long Experience we have found
> What Planet rul'd when you were born;

We see you never can be drown'd.

                                                            (185-92)

First, to explicate the joke: the passage depends on an unexpressed
thought, that is, a proverb not directly quoted: "He that is born to be
hanged will never be drowned" (Tilley B139). There cannot be a shadow
of doubt that this was familiar to Swift: he actually cites it in *Polite
Conversation*, and it is indeed one of a number of stock expressions
involving dogs and hanging which figure his work (Swift *Prose*, 4: 147).[4]
The best-known literary exploitation of this idea occurs, significantly, at
the start of *The Tempest*. Comic wordplay goes on resolute, there amid the
danger and confusion, and Gonzalo's comment on the boatswain carries
more wit than may be readily apparent today: "I have great comfort from
this fellow: methinks he hath no drowning mark upon him; his complexion
is perfect gallows. . .If he be not born to be hanged, our case is miserable
(I.i.32). There are other examples in Shakespeare, and one of Defoe's
many proverbial allusions in *Colonel Jacque* turns on the same expression.
But there is a second issue to confront, critical rather than merely
expository: that is, the tone and drift of the passage in *The Bubble*.
Contemptuous, mocking perhaps, it is also sublimely confident in its way
(the planet ruling at line 191 must be Mercury, who presided over thieves;
"who being as I am, littered under Mercury, was likewise a snapper-up of
unconsidered trifles"). Yet there is possibly something too unthreatening
in enemies so easily consigned to perdition. Pope's elaborate catalogue of
the failings of his South Sea villains, John Blunt and the rest, gives us no
certainty that they will be brought to book. By comparison Swift's brisk
popular style has the strengths and weaknesses of what might be called a
literary version of tabloid journalism. Swift's vein is not so much
prophecy in the sense of prediction as that of wish-fulfilment; he appeals
to the stock of inherited language to make proverb-lore convict the villains
out of its own mouth.

The peroration is still couched in this vein, but it gains strength, that is
both polemical force and artistic cogency, from a series of theological
references. We start with a mode of compressed litany:

Oh, may some *Western* Tempest sweep
These *Locusts* whom our Fruits have fed,
That Plague, *Directors*, to the Deep,
Driv'n from the *South-Sea* to the *Red*.

May He whom Nature's Laws obey,
Who *lifts* the Poor, and *sinks* the Proud,
Quiet the Raging of the Sea,

And *Still the Madness of the Crowd.*

(205-12)

This breathtaking chain of allusions can scarcely be paralleled elsewhere in Swift's poetry. The first stanza takes us back to Exodus 10.12-19: Swift may have thought of the episode principally because of the "exceeding strong wind" which God called up to drive out the locusts, or more likely because of the simple Red Sea/South Sea transposition. The second stanza contains echoes both of the Prayer Book and of the Bible. Line 210 recalls the Magnificat, but also neatly reasserts the idea of sinking which has permeated the entire poem. Lines 211-12 bear chiefly on the Psalms, and perhaps especially the form of prayer to be used at sea. There are also Gospel sources, extended in the next stanza, which hinges on the story of the Gadarene swine from St Mark:

> But never shall our isle have Rest
> Till those devouring *Swine* run down,
> (*The Devils leaving the Possess't*)
> And headlong in the Waters drown.

(213-16)

This episode in the Gospel narrative follows the account of Christ stilling the storm; it is idle to conjecture what set of mental associations brought Swift to make the same transition in his poem. It was not unusual for conservative moralists to interpret the whole South Sea mania as a kind of "possession" by unclean spirits; Swift is as often swimming with the tide of popular opinion.

So to the concluding stanza, which is a perfect embodiment of the strategies that have been pursued all along.

> The Nation too too late will find
> Computing all their Cost and Trouble,
> *Directors* Promises but Wind,
> South-Sea at best a mighty BUBBLE.

(217-20)

The last line has the air of a truism. What else should the famous Bubble be but a bubble? But "Bubble", as a licensed and, so to say, official expression, lost particularity as it adopted a capital letter. The metaphor is quiescent, if not totally dead. By aligning the term syntactically with "Wind" Swift gives back to the word its original semantic weight. We are to picture a real envelope of film, a giant soap-bubble which can only burst and shower the nation with a useless froth. Nobody will emerge dry from the South Sea experience; the image universally applied to the episode is (by a paradox that underlies much of Swift's dealings with language) as-it-were literally true: as-it-were literally, because the South Sea Company will plunge everyone into debt even though it has effectively no ocean-going or maritime role. The name of the corporation is actually a misnomer, but it still manages to spill the entire beans. For Swift, you have to peel off the fictive or figurative exterior, and then you see that the fiction or the figure is indeed the truth. In this case the point of visualizing the Bubble (proper noun) as a bubble (common noun) is to gain the recognition that the South Sea undertaking really does have no more substance than the figure of speech implies.

To say that *The Bubble* is one of the most characteristic poems Swift ever wrote may seem no more than a polite evasion, an oblique admission that it is not among his greatest works. One can acknowledge that *The Bubble* is unlikely to achieve the sort of currency which better-known items have now achieved, that it will not promote the hectic controversy which surrounds the "excremental" group, and that its subject-matter is too narrowly timebound to excite general interest. Nevertheless, it is a poem which displays an important facet of Swift as a poet in its most fully developed expression. It shows him prising open the cant idiom of political debate, reappraising the shibboleths of public argument, and exploring the premises of topical discourse.

Earlier on, I made a brief mention of *A South Sea Ballad, subtitled Merry Remarks upon Exchange-Alley Bubbles, to a new Tune, call'd The Grand Elixir: or, The Philosopher's Stone Discover'd*. This was actually the work of Ned Ward, and it is far from an incompetent performance.[5] Some of its language resembles that of Swift: we have Spanish dogs, leaping into South-Sea water; fishing for golden frogs; South-Sea Babel; and (most indicative) "When all the Riches that we boast / Consist in Scraps of Paper". Ward even glances at a proverb used by Swift: "The Losers then must ease their Gall / By Hanging or by Drowning." But Ward can write of treasure in the clouds without seizing on the precise verbal formula that unveils the reality behind a conventional thought, where Swift selects the individual turn of speech which exposes this reality. Similarly, Ward's application to alchemy is illustrative, almost decorative, where Swift's is fully integral. Ward expresses disapproval towards certain kinds of behaviour or social attitudes; Swift anatomizes the way we perceive and register these things.

For *The Bubble* could be called without affectation a kind of metapolitical ballad. The economic case behind it is that the credit structure has become unreal, and that modern finance rests on the empty promises of credit instruments. Analogously, Swift shows, language fails to live up to its promissory function until we restore the sound money of literal reference. There is a streak in Swift which constantly demands hard cash of figurative language. In restoring a truth-function to metaphors such as the Bubble, or in reifying the pious abstractions of South Sea, Swift is performing a highly relevant linguistic task. The nation, he asserts with other balladeers, needs a restoration of financial probity, which will involve demolition of many castles in the air that have deluded gullible investors. To assert this political "truth", language itself must have its credit restored. To depict the South Sea as actual water, and the Bubble as actual gas, is to call in the cash loans of metaphor, a form of parsimony to which Swift was never averse.

Notes

[1] References follow the text supplied in Swift *Poems,* 1: 248-59. For the historical background, the best survey remains Carswell, *Bubble.*

[2] Swift *Corr,* 2: 368.

[3] See Swift *Corr*, 2: 353.

[4] For a number of instances, drawn from several parts of Swift's work, see my essay, "Swift and the Reanimation of Cliché," in *The Character of Swift's Satire: A Revised Focus* (Newark: University of Delaware Press, 1983), pp. 203-26. For discussion of another poem using a chain of proverbs in close succession, see my essay, "'Dog-Logick' in Swift's *Upon the Horrid Plot*," in *Eighteenth Century Encounters*(Brighton: Harvester, 1985), pp. 29-40.

[5] See D.F. Foxon, *English Verse 1700-1750*, 2 vols (Cambridge: Cambridge University Press, 1975), 1: 865 (item W177). Passages from Ward's poem are cited, anonymously, in Howard Erskine-Hill, *The Social Milieu of Alexander Pope* (New Haven: Yale University Press, 1975), pp. 186-7. Erskine-Hill provides valuable background to Swift's poem in his chapter on Sir John Blunt, pp. 168-203, and also in his essay "Pope and the Financial Revolution", in *Writers and their Background: Alexander Pope*, ed. Peter Dixon (London: Bell, 1972), pp. 200-29.

CHAPTER TEN

MACHEATH AND THE GAOL-BREAKERS: ROGER JOHNSON, WILLIAM PITT, AND THE BACKGROUND OF *THE BEGGAR'S OPERA*

It has scarcely gone unnoticed that Macheath leads a charmed life in *The Beggar's Opera*. According to Michael Denning, "There are three escapes in the play, one at the end of each act, and they definitely establish Macheath as a Jack Sheppard, the escape artist."[1] In fact the first of these is not strictly an escape, rather a timely get-away from the clutches of Peachum, thanks to aid from the thief-taker's daughter Polly. As for the final scene, this involves a reprieve from the gallows, mockingly presented as a requirement of "strict poetical justice" as acted out in conventional operas (3: 16). This ending has received a good deal of critical comment, but less attention has been devoted to the end of Act 2. Here Macbeth is actually sprung from gaol by a second heroine, Lucy Lockit, daughter of his other nemesis, the keeper of Newgate.

This essay aims to look at the background of the second and most authentic case of the three. In the process, I shall suggest first that Sheppard is not a plausible model for Macheath, and that other escapees such as the well-known criminal Roger Johnson fit the case more squarely. Second, that a wider history of gaol-breaking, from the time of the Jacobite lords, underlies the use of this motif in Gay's drama. Third, that a real-life model for Lockit can be found in the career of the contemporary keeper of Newgate, William Pitt. A conclusion that can be drawn is that the satiric economy of *The Beggar's Opera* depends, more than has been recognised, on an undertow of reference to these issues. A major thrust of the satire relates to intervention by the authorities in prison-breaks, whether through incompetence, benign neglect, or deliberate collusion in perversions of the judicial process.

I

The first matter, involving Jack Sheppard, is the easiest to deal with, because this lends itself most readily to analysis in terms of precise historical events. Certainly Sheppard's exploits still haunted the public mind in 1728, when the play came out, even though Sheppard had been executed four years earlier. There is perhaps some exaggeration in Peter Linebaugh's claim, at the start of his discussion of "Jack Sheppard and the Art of Escape," that Sheppard "was once the single most well-known name from eighteenth-century England," but the criminal's renown scarcely diminished at all in the short span of time before the *Opera* arrived on the scene.[2] However, in terms of the supposed identification, all the signs are contra-indicatory. For one thing, Sheppard did not operate as a highwayman, like Macheath, but as a smalltime housebreaker who gained notoriety almost entirely through his exploits as an escapologist. Unlike Gay's hero, he did not lead a gang, but worked alone or with a single accomplice. Sheppard was physically unprepossessing, and had no great taste for finery, again unlike Macheath, whose attractions to women are constantly stressed: "I see him already in the car," says Polly, "sweeter and more lovely than the nosegay in his hand. . .What vollies of sighs are sent from the windows of Holborn, that so comely a youth should be brought to disgrace."[3] (Beyond this, Sheppard was afflicted with a stammer, unlike the verbally deft Macheath.) An excited throng of bystanders attended the road which Sheppard took to Tyburn, but they were mostly hoping for another disappearing act on the part of the leading man. In the event the crowd did keep his corpse from the anatomists, when they dragged it away to the Barley Mow ale-house in Long Acre, but unlike the fictional criminal he was granted no last-minute reprieve.

A more crucial consideration lies in the manner of his escapes. Sheppard normally worked alone, with only limited help from others: his skill appeared in adroit use of tools (such as a saw, hammer, chisel and gimlets), as well as his strong hands and nimble body. Finally, he was the agent of his own liberty. Once he was out and on the run, he generally camouflaged himself in the clothes of menial tradesmen (butcher, porter, carpenter) and even once as a beggar. To find a suitable disguise, he robbed the shop of a dealer in Monmouth Street, the centre of the second-hand clothes market. By this means he managed to hide undiscovered for long periods, even when the entire forces of authority were bent on his capture. It is impossible to imagine Macheath deigning to take on the beggar's rags in a night-cellar, or melting into the crowd when he is with the other gentlemen of the road. Nor would he have sunk to robbing a pawnbroker's shop in Drury Lane. These differences point to a basic fact about the play: Macheath is basically a supine character, bought and sold by other characters, and never seen in the commission of a successful crime. In a direct reversal of the dramatic plot, Sheppard impeached fellow-criminals, and rescued his mistress Edgeworth Bess from St Giles's Roundhouse - where the house-breaker was later confined after his own brother betrayed him. Sheppard belonged to a genuine subculture within criminal London, and was treated as such when he reached Newgate: he had double fetters to fix him to the floor of the cell, and weights of 300 pounds attached to him. Against this Macheath is offered the choice of the lightest chains, if he will pay for the privilege (2: 7). In his operatic role he never has to fear any of the real dangers which Sheppard encountered, such as being arrested at gun-point.

As Denning remarks, the ending of the *Opera* represents an over-determined closure, with poetic justice and the taste of opera audiences enabling Macheath to get away with his crimes, although realism would have dictated a harsher conclusion. (He does not escape scot-free of course, since the sequel *Polly* shows him transported to the West Indies.) One reading of the play in the light of the historical background just established would be to see the happy ending as a kind of dramatic wish-fulfilment, designed to placate those who regretted that Sheppard had gone to his death.   Many people held such a view, especially because he first entered Newgate at the instance of the unpopular Jonathan Wild, who had refused to do more than promise the condemned man a decent execution. But Sheppard, however much of a crowd-pleaser, could not have hoped to escape the gallows: he had after all confessed to the lone charge which stuck, when he faced prosecution at the Old Bailey on 12 August 1724.[4] His subsequent escape from Newgate - itself a repeat offence - served to aggravate the crime. The key point is that his career as an escape artist touched on a raw nerve, since all too many prisoners had managed in recent years to free themselves from custody, especially at Newgate. In fact a current scandal had come to public notice when Gay was writing his play, and it involved Roger Johnson.

II

In a cheap biography of Johnson (*c*.1695-1740) that appeared after his death, the author remarks in his opening homiletic: "No one hath been more conspicuous in the World, for a long Series of Tricks and Impostures."[5] He would fit well enough into the gang of robbers in *The Beggar's Opera*. For one thing, he was a member of Jonathan Wild's criminal circle, running a kind of import/export business in clandestine goods at one time, and a malefactor of astonishing versatility. Like Macheath, he was said to have a taste for fine clothes and, most important, he died with his boots on - at least he mysteriously avoided hanging.

Johnson started out helping to run a brothel in Drury Lane, the location in which the women of the town operate in Gay's drama. Later he became involved in coining and narrowly escaped the gallows for passing false coin. After this he branched out into various forms of confidence tricks, and became known as "the most dextrous and polite Pick Pocket in Town."[6] In October 1718 he was actually convicted at the Old Bailey of stealing seven pairs of silk stockings, valued at five pounds, and sentenced to death. Somehow he seems to have evaded justice. Within a few days he was released on bail (Applebee's *Weekly Journal*, 18 November). Even this early, there were signs that he had his protectors:

> This Week one Roger Johnson who had been formerly condemned, was committed to Newgate by the Bench of Justices, for what is called in Jonathan Wild's Dictionary, *the Kid Lay*; in our Tongue, Shoplifting. He is likewise reckoned the most dexterous and polite Pick pocket in Town, and by his Industry that way, has acquired too great a Fortune (as his Friends say) to be hanged.
>
> (*London Journal*, 5 November 1720)

Perhaps the most famous exploit in Roger's life of crime occurred in 1724, when Wild arranged a series of robberies during a Garter installation at Windsor: this was almost as favourable an opportunity for his business as the Coronation, which Peachum regards as a major source of booty (3: 5). Johnson is said to have gained entry to the court by bribery, and then relieved those attending the ceremony of valuable jewellery. One dubious anecdote has it that he "succeeded in picking the Prince of Wales's pocket by 'accidentally' tripping him up as he passed through the crowds."[7] The unreliable Alexander Smith, in his life of Jonathan Wild, has Johnson executing one of his thefts on the steps of St George's Chapel, the nerve centre of national chivalry.[8] According to some accounts, he had got away with goods to the value of about £3,000. At the same time, we learn that "Madam Johnson, the Wife of the famous Roger Johnson, a Burgher of Rotterdam. . .has been committed to Clerkenwell Bridewell, where she lives in the most splendid Manner, being, as we hear, attended by several Servants, among whom is a French Cook" (*Daily Journal*, 7 May 1725). The wife had been caught at a house in Tyburn Road: meanwhile her husband had fled the coop, his escape "beyond Sea [having been] forward'd by J[onathan]. W[ild]." She was transferred to Newgate, and charged with a felony, but never shows up in the Old Bailey proceedings.

Johnson was now deemed "one of the greatest Robbers History has known" (Read's *Weekly Journal*, 1 May 1725). Much embellishment has obviously gone into all this, but some underlying evidence supports such grotesque events. It is a pattern of activity closer to that of Peachum's men than are most of the exploits attributed to Sheppard. According to a later newspaper story, Gay himself had gone to Windsor for the installation and there became acquainted with "the genuine Peachum," who let slip a number of the tricks of his trade. This is deeply implausible, but it shows what kind of basis in fact the audience of the *Opera* might countenance.[9]

Eluding punishment once more, Johnson cropped up as the master of a ship owned by Wild, which carried a contraband lace from Flanders and took out the products of the thief-taker's activity in London.[10] He also smuggled people and property to and from Ireland, but eventually he was caught bringing in black-market goods when his sloop was boarded by the authorities in the Thames estuary. Again Johnson found himself in desperate trouble, when he was seized outside an ale-house in the Strand, but Wild had contrived to get a tame JP under his influence to procure the release of his comrade. A little later, on the road at Stratford to the east of London, the robber was caught by an old adversary, a man named Edwards who specialized in robbing wagons: somehow Wild started a disturbance which allowed Johnson to get away. When the thief-taker was arrested in 1725, one of the original charges against him was that he had contrived "the Escape of Roger Johnson, a notorious Thief, when he was beset by the Constables" (*Newcastle Courant*, 27 February1725). Johnson managed to stay out of trouble, probably because he had already decamped to the Low Countries (perhaps Rotterdam). The relations of the two men had often been strained, in line with the *sauve qui peut* spirit which informs *The Beggar's Opera*. Significantly, however, Wild never once appeared to give evidence in any of the trials in which Johnson was involved. He did make court depositions when Sheppard and Joseph "Blueskin" Blake, with other well known criminals, were facing justice.

After the great rogue went to the gallows, Johnson continued on his habitual way. He was betrayed by one of Wild's old gang and sent to Newgate. While in gaol he bought his way into the Master's Side and was granted the liberty of the Press Yard, where the most expensive accommodation could be found. Some of his victims, at least, were anxious to see the rogue brought to justice, even if the legal system displayed less urgency. We can tell this from one press advertisement:

Roger Johnson, formerly convicted of Shoplifting, and since Partner to
the late Jonathan Wild, and who has for many Years both in Town and
Country, defrauded several Persons, upon Pretence of pawning broad
Pieces, and getting Guineas for Silver, and changing bad broad Pieces and
Moidores, is now (with several of his Accomplices) in Newgate, and
stands charg'd with the abovemention'd Crimes, as also with Gilding,
Washing, Diminishing and Counterfeiting the current Coin of this
Kingdom.

N.B. He was formerly a Holland Trader in Partnership with the said
Wild and others, and such Persons as have been defrauded as above, are
desir'd to give Notice by Letter or otherwise to Mr. Thomas Jones, at Old
Parr's-head, Middle-row, with an Account of their Damages, and the best
Descriptions they can of the Persons who injur'd them.

(*Evening Post*, 11 May 1727)

Shortly afterwards, we learn that Johnson's wife *and* father have been
taken to the New Prison, on a charge of "putting off Counterfeit Money"
(Read's *Weekly Journal*, 27 May 1727). Evidently they wished to keep it
in the family. But some of the usual evasions ensued: when a certain
Christopher Johnson was moved to Newgate, Anne Johnson, alias
Dowling, was left where she was temporarily, having conveniently just
given birth to a child (*Daily Post*, 24 July). She was eventually transferred
to await trial in August. In early September she, her father–in-law and now
her sister were, surprisingly, admitted to bail – Rumpole of the Bailey
could not have done better for his regular clients, the recidivist Timpson
family. On 17 October, "Anne Johnson , alias Bewley, Christopher
Johnson, and Mary Williams, were indicted for High Treason, in filing and
demolishing the current Coin of this Kingdom, but for want of sufficient
Evidence they were all acquitted."[11]   I am not sure whether these really
were Roger's family; but such episodes occur regularly enough to instill
doubt over the view of the criminal law system as a brutal regime where
poor and hapless victims stood no chance against the might of the
prosecution mounted against them.

Back in 1718, Eleanor Johnson, wife of Christopher Johnson, had been
convicted of coining and sentenced to be burnt at the stake. "Being a little
too old to plead her Belly," Applebee's *Weekly Journal* starkly asserted on
26 April, "'tis believed she will be demolish'd." The pseudonymous
biographer of criminals, Captain Alexander Smith, whom we need not
trust, says that Johnson had saved his own life by swearing his mother to
be a coiner, truly the behaviour of a Jemmy Twitcher, but he wrongly
states that she died in Newgate before coming to trial. The Old Bailey
records show this is false, and also indicate that the panel of matrons did
find Eleanor to be "with quick Child".[12] We might add here that

Christopher Johnson, said in the account by the Ordinary of Newgate to be the son of Roger, and conceived in the prison, was dispatched to Tyburn in 1753. He had been active as a conman and thief, but he was convicted of murder following a robbery that went wrong. The magistrate who examined him after his arrest was Henry Fielding.[13]

Soon after the notice by Thomas Jones appeared, in the early summer of 1727, Roger had contrived yet again to make his escape. For immediate purpose this was among the most significant of the many occasions when he eluded the grasp of the law. This time he got away in the company of an alleged murderer named Henry Fisher, who fled abroad, and eventually claimed to have taken up a penitential life as servant to a monk in Florence (*British Journal*, 16 December 1727). On 27 May, the *Daily Journal* related, the fetters that Johnson and Fisher had worn were mysteriously found in a field at Edmonton. In righteous outrage, the Lord Mayor and aldermen of London set up a committee of inquiry, to be described in due course. The natural object of suspicion was the keeper, William Pitt, of whom we shall also hear more shortly; but Pitt, too, was a survivor, and in the end he kept his job.

A barrage of press notices makes clear the degree of insecurity felt by the authorities about gaol-breaks, just a few months before *The Beggar's Opera* had its premiere. They put a reward of £50 (later upped to £60) on Johnson's head, only half what they offered for the capture of Fisher. A description of both men appeared in several announcements that appeared in the press. It was claimed that Johnson sometimes posed as a minister and sometimes as a quaker (*Daily Post*, 18 May-29 May, 31 July 1727; *Daily Journal*, 19 May; *Daily Courant*, 20 May, 2 June). He was alleged to have written to the keeper of Newgate offering to shop Fisher to the authorities if assured of a pardon, by a notice inserted in the *London Gazette* (*British Journal*, 27 May 1727). This may or may not be true. Another better-founded report claims that Johnson was quickly recaptured in Shropshire, after he had cheated a gentleman of 28 pounds with a counterfeit note. He was arrested and committed by the magistrates to Shrewsbury gaol, but managed to escape from the local Dogberry who had been deputed to take him to prison (Read's *Weekly Journal*, 8 July 1727). He had prevailed on the constables to go with him to an alehouse, where he plied them with drink, and he easily got away. The head constable was later bound over to appear at Shrewsbury assizes (*Evening Post*, 6 July). Rumours spread, too, that Roger had committed a number of frauds in the west of England, around Shaftesbury and had been caught before managing to make off, but these may be panic sightings.

After this he remained on the lam for just over a year until he was caught in the cellar of a tavern in Newcastle upon Tyne where – fortuitously, it is suggested - he was seen by two gaolers from the London area who recognized him, despite his disguise in a clergyman's habit (*British Journal*, 22 June 1728). It was later found that he carried deacon's orders in his pocket, along with money. He naturally tried to bribe his captors with a purse of guineas, but they refused to comply. When he got back to London he claimed the escape had been arranged by Fisher, and that they parted the moment they got down the ladder after scaling the prison wall. He was visited in his new heavy duty fetters by a noble lord, who pointed out his folly in not leaving the country after "so successful an Enterprize." Johnson replied (or so the papers assure us) that "Nothing but the Love of his native Country had brought him to the Gallows" (*London Evening Post*, 20 June 1728). At this juncture the new keeper of Newgate issued a press notice, alleging that the escape may have been helped by some workmen who had been carrying out construction work in the gaol (*Daily Journal*, 10 July 1728). He also presented the two men who had caught Johnson with an engraved silver tankard apiece. Subsequently the authorities returned the convict in irons to the foul vermin-infected Common Side, where Sheppard had lain: but even here was able to bribe the keeper to get him out of the Stone Hold. There was, as we shall see, a consequence to this escape.

Around this time an unknown author submitted a modest proposal to the City of London on street robberies. In this he mentioned "the indirect practices of your Newgate Sollicitors" who induced victims "not to appear to prosecute" by a sum in hand. This proposal was reprinted in the newspapers, with a gloss, "Roger Johnson's Secreting, and keeping out of the Way, the Witnesses against him (as is suppos'd)" (*Stamford Mercury*, 10 October 1728). But could he have done this without help?

III

Events would now move beyond the time-frame imposed by *The Beggar's Opera*. In September Johnson was arraigned at the Old Bailey on a new charge for stealing £20, but the trial was deferred until the next sessions, the evidence "being absent" (*British Journal*, 7 September 1728). Perhaps the idea was simply to keep him in custody. The grand jury indicted him for breaking gaol, deemed a felony under an ancient act when the original offence for which the prisoner was committed fell into this category. But nothing happened, though every few weeks droves of miserable petty malefactors were being dispatched to Virginia or to kingdom come. By now we can anticipate the result: "it appearing to the Jury, that Fisher (charged with Murther, who made his Escape out of Newgate at the same Time) broke out first, and that the said Johnson was not privy to his breaking out, he was acquitted" (*Daily Post*, 22 October 1728). They relied on the testimony of one Mrs Burney, whom others described as having "but a very indifferent Character." When the verdict of not guilty was announced, "one Carroll an Irishman, a Soldier, clapp'd his Hands for Joy, whereupon he was committed for *Contempt of Court*" (*British Journal*, 26 October 1728). Liberal thinkers used to celebrate the development of the jury system as a prime component in the growth of liberty, and Roger might have shared their view.

Later in the same year he was to taken to the King's Bench bar, to contest an outlawry carrying a death sentence for "flying the Kingdom," imposed at the Old Bailey. He produced two parchments alleging that he was out of the country when the outlawry was pronounced, had surrendered himself within a year and had then pleaded not guilty to the charge of high treason. He also claimed that he ought to be allowed to have counsel for his defence, and Abel Kettleby (who had been given the impossible task of defending Wild) supported this with an argument that one of the charges allowed him under common law to have the benefit of counsel. Various legal niceties were raised, which caused the attorney general some perplexity, and the case was adjourned for a few days. At length the matter came to a resolution on 25 November with a predictable outcome: its being "proved that he was then out of the Kingdom," the King's Bench granted a writ of a certiorari to remove the judgment, and he gained one more acquittal. Someone appears to have got at the jury once more. "But he was afterwards arraigned at the Motion of Mr. Attorney-General in diminishing the Coin" (*British Journal*, 2, 9, and 30 November 1728; *Daily Post*, 18 November). So it went on: one legal authority would arraign him, another (probably with government connivance) would see that he got off the charges.

What seems to have happened is this. In August, a certain Henry Kelley had written from confinement to Sir Andrew Fountaine, collector, numismatist and fiend of Swift, who had just become warden of the Royal Mint on the death of Isaac Newton in 1727. Kelley states that he had given information for high treason against Roger and for petty treason against Anne his wife, whom the court acquitted "as only deling under her Husband." Since Roger's escape and recapture, Mr Pinkney, the deputy warden, had "Dropt the Prosecution, and left both King and Country neglected." As Kelley was in custody, he could not pursue the prosecution himself, he urges Fountaine to command Pinkney to carry it forward, or to send someone to him (Kelley) to ensure that Johnson was tried at the next sessions. A copy of the letter was also sent to the secretaries of state.[14] This action may have got things moving, because a few days later Johnson signed a note stating that he intended to take his trial at the Old Bailey on 28 August. But when on that day Johnson entered a plea to be bailed, tried, or discharged, he was simply "still order'd to remain," that is remanded in custody (*Daily Post*, 29 August). Next day he was to have been arraigned on the recent theft charge, but the principal witness for the crown was still unaccountably absent, so that too was deferred.

The coining charge, itself a capital offence amounting to high treason, stayed on ice until February 1729 when Roger was tried before the Lord Chief Justice in the King's Bench and a special jury. (Also sitting on the bench was the notorious Judge Page, familiar to readers of Pope and Fielding.) A constable who searched Johnson's lodgings deposed that he had found gold dust and files after a tip from an informant – no other than Henry Kelley, who gave evidence in court. But this informant, a thief who had been the chief evidence against Jonathan Wild, lost all credit when witnesses reported that he had gone round saying that he would "hang Roger Johnson to gain his own Liberty" (*Craftsman*, 8 February 1729). After a five hour trial, the prisoner was yet again acquitted by the jury. His counsel recommended that his fetters should be removed, but no order was made as other felony charges remained, as the keeper of Newgate told the court. The gaoler doubtless recalled "how that ingenious Artist had formerly made his Escape from him" (*Daily Post*, 5 February 1729). A month later Johnson appeared again the Old Bailey, this time charged with stealing twenty guineas from a French apothecary near Soho Square. By now it will be no surprise to find that he was acquitted "for want of sufficient Evidence" (*British Journal*, 8 February, 8 March 1729; Read's *Weekly Journal*, 8 March 1729). As the Old Bailey proceedings drily put it, "by some Management or other no Prosecutor appeared." Just one day later, he faced the indictment of felony theft, but again he was ruled not guilty. We shall come back to these cases.

Still, he remained in prison, by reason of an unpaid debt of £800 due to the exchequer, imposed for running brandy. Soon afterwards Johnson was accused of leading a prison conspiracy and sentenced to remain a close prisoner *sine die*. His efforts to sell his jewels, rings and plate in 1730, to pay his fine apparently came to nothing. He duly made intercessions to compound for the debt, but this does not seem to have worked (*British Journal*, 3 January 1730; *London Evening Post*, 19 March). In December he was tried for theft yet again, a case we shall return to presently: it would not be spoiling the story to reveal the outcome at this point. After this he was returned to the Master Debtors' side and took on informal supervision of the gaol. This is close to the role which Fielding would allot him in his *History of the Life of the late Mr. Jonathan Wild the Great* (1743), and though the treatment of Johnson in that book is almost entirely fictional it serves to confirm that Roger was still a well-known name. When parliament set up a committee under James Oglethorpe to investigate abuses in the prison system, an episode to be described shortly, Johnson was carried up from Newgate to Westminster in order to testify (Read's *Weekly Journal*, 2 May 1730). He could certainly claim to be an expert witness. But he proved, as we might expect, no respecter of persons, and his name is found along with that of his wife Anne among a list of "infamous and profligate" persons to be committed to Newgate for a conspiracy to vilify the lord chief justice of Common Pleas (*Monthly Chronicle*, May 1730; *London Evening Post*, 7 May 1730). Since he was already an inmate of the prison, this seems an odd decision.

Nothing could rid him of his persistent ways, which throw Macheath into the shade. As the vigilant journalists recorded:

> Yesterday the famous Roger Johnson, now a Prisoner in Newgate, brought a *Habeas Corpus* to be carried to Serjeants-Inn, Chancery-Lane, in order to surrender himself, as he pretended, before Mr. Justice Probyn in Discharge of his Bail; but before he was brought quite to the Inn, be made his Escape from the Officers that had him in their Charge, and ran down the Temple-Lane; but being pursued, he was retaken, and carried back to his former Lodging in Newgate.
>
> (*Daily Courant,* 11 November 1730)

This led to a further trial at the Old Bailey on 4 December, to which we shall return in due course. One might have thought people dealing with Johnson would have learnt their lesson by now. But there was more to follow. In 1731, after a raid on his cell by customs officers, Johnson was charged with making "mould candles" inside the prison, and thus "defrauding the King of his Duty" to the value of £300: the outcome does not appear (*London Evening Post*, 20 May 1731).

Next came a major episode in the criminal history of the day. This was the trial at the Old Bailey in 1733 of the notorious Sarah Malcolm, immortalized in Hogarth's portrait: she was a Catholic aged just twenty-two, working as a laundress in the legal chambers at the Temple. She was accused of slitting the throats of three women, a rich old widow and two maid-servants, but the trial proceeded on only one of the indictments. None other than Roger Johnson now came forward to explain in court how he had discovered on Malcolm's person the property she had stolen from the victims. He relates how on reaching the gaol she asked to go to the debtors' quarters, and he told her that this would cost her a guinea, "and she did not look like none that could pay so much." He then took her to another room, "where there was none but she and I." Since there was reason to suspect she was guilty of the murder, Johnson continued, "therefore I have Orders to search you (tho' indeed, I had no such Orders) and with that I begun to feel about her Hips, and under her Petticoats. She desir'd me to forbear searching under her Coats, because she was not in a Condition, and with that she shew'd me her Shift, upon which I desisted." This was important because in her spirited defence (she didn't have a lawyer) Sarah would argue that blood on her shift could only be her own menstrual blood and nothing to do with the victims.   However the self-appointed body-searcher soon found a bag of money under her cap. Sarah said that it came from one of the victims, but she would give it to Johnson if he would keep quiet, asking only for threepence or sixpence a day until her trial came on. Roger's eyes must have lit up when he counted up the haul of gold coins - including 36 moidores and 18 guineas, five broad pieces worth between 23s. and 25s., along with smaller denominations. He locked her up and went to a gaoler, who interviewed Sarah while Johnson hid "in a dark place" to observe the interrogation. It was a long and complex trial with many witnesses, but in the end it took the jury only fifteen minutes to convict her. She was hanged a few days later on a portable gallows set up near the scene of the crime, in Fleet Street opposite Mitre Court.[15]

According to the evidence Malcolm gave, Johnson had told her that "he would be cleared and get out of Goal (*sic*) on that Account" (*Craftsman*, 17 March 1733). Eventually he did indeed obtain an amnesty, and in early 1737 was freed from custody. During his last years he lived "honestly as a Pawn-broker" in Round Court, which lay not far from St Martin's in the Fields near the wretched slum district of Porridge Island. He died there in August 1740, when his body was carried away for burial in a hearse with six horses, as well as a coach and six attending (*London Evening Post*, 26 August 1740). Crime seems to have paid quite well. Immediately he became the subject of a catchpenny life, published by Charles Corbett, who was issuing work by Fielding at this date including *The Champion*. The pamphlet came out in plenty of time to be utilized in *Jonathan Wild*.

These closing phases of Johnson's life relate to the *Opera* only in contingent ways. But much earlier we can discern a pattern according to which Johnson, by bribery, connections or threats, was able to evade the justice meted out to so many other hapless individuals. The newspaper writer who described Johnson in 1720 as the most skilful of shoplifters and pickpockets could not resist adding that by his "Industry in that Way" Johnson had "acquired too great a Fortune (as his Friends say) to be hanged." An examination of surviving records indicates that this was more than idle gossip. Many of the stories appear to belong to a picaresque novel or rogue's biography, but they can often be confirmed from legal documents, prison records and government papers. As we have seen, Johnson had already beaten the rap on the coining charge, after receiving a death sentence. On later occasions he benefitted from the help of Wild: in the case of the arrest at Stratford this allegedly involved an attack on the constable with pistols. But more often Johnson appears to have suborned the authorities, in particular the prison staff at Newgate. This is different from what happened with Sheppard, whose escapes were generally conceded (with one possible exception, to be considered shortly) to have been effected without such help. Consequently, the gaol-breaks with which Johnson was associated carried far more potential for embarrassment, as reflecting either incompetence at best, or complicity at worst, on the part of those administering justice. Thus they met Gay's aims more directly: they led in the direction of explicitly political discourse, as they could be construed as failures of the system. Sheppard relied largely on his native wit and his prowess as an escape artist, but Johnson repeatedly gained his freedom by underhand methods. This became particularly obvious in the case of the break Johnson made with Henry Fisher in 1727, which was a hot issue when *The Beggar's Opera* appeared.

IV

For some time people had been concerned about a spate of well-publicized events involving the escape of prominent persons (as Roger Johnson had now become). Quite recently, one of the minor players in the Atterbury Plot, Rev. Philip Neyno, had managed to get out of the custody of a messenger at a time of heightened national paranoia about security issues. Swift refers to Neyno, a nonjuring Irish clergyman, in his poem "Upon the Horrid Plot" (*c.*1723): "Besides this horrid Plot was found / By *Neno* after he was drown'd" (Swift *Poems*, 1: 299). Neyno had eluded his captor by climbing out of a third-floor window after tying sheets and blankets together, and clambering along a wall to the Thames. He then jumped into the full-flowing river to try to attain his freedom: unfortunately he could not swim and perished in the water.

Well before Sheppard and Johnson were familiar names to everyone, a few notorious instances had come to general attention. Some of these occurred in the aftermath of the Jacobite rising in 1716, when rebel leaders managed to evade punishment. The most famous episode concerned the Earl of Nithsdale, who got out of the Tower by changing clothes with his wife, and made his way to safety on the continent. In fact he had been reprieved from execution on the previous evening, along with three other lords, but had not yet learnt of this. The Earl had many friends at court, and even the wife of Lord Chancellor Cowper (who had presided at the trial) wrote in her diary of the affair, "I hope he'll get clear off. I was never better pleased at Anything in my Life and I believe Everybody is the same." The king is said to have flown into a rage, and declared that he had been betrayed, "for it could not have been done without some confederacy."[16] The facts appear to support this: Nithsdale had not even bothered to shave off his beard, so that it would not have required meticulous inspection to penetrate his female disguise.

Not long afterwards, the Earl of Winton also got away. He had been the only one of the rebels to plead not guilty, and had conducted his defence in such a bizarre fashion that some felt he was feigning outright madness. Even before his trial in March, as contemporary reports made known, he had been making efforts at gaining his liberty. "One of the Bars of a Window in the Earl of *Winton*'s Apartment was brought into Court," a pamphlet informed the public, "which had been filed off (as is supposed by the Spring of a Watch) in Order for the Earl's making his Escape."[17] In any case Winton was convicted and in theory still faced the death penalty for treason. However, this was not to be. "At the beginning of August, and thanks to his early and unusual training as a blacksmith, his lordship filed through a bar in the window of his apartment (Lady Cowper declares he did it with a watch-spring) and, with the help of a little bribery, got clean away." This time Lady Cowper was irritated, since she disliked the mad act Winton had put on at Westminster Hall. But what is truly unusual is not the Earl's skill in smithery (a watch-spring would be secretly passed in to Sheppard, as well), but the fact that he was able to accomplish this get-away in exactly the manner which had been foretold in the public prints five months earlier. Winton, also, made tracks to the Stuart court.

It was widely believed at the time that these escapes could not have been carried out without complicity on the part of the authorities. Only two of the condemned lords had gone to the scaffold on Tower Hill, the Earls of Derwentwater and Kenmure. As is common knowledge, Derwentwater in particular had left a considerable impression by his bearing: an eloquent dying speech, in which he declined to recant, had declared the Pretender to be his "rightful and lawful sovereign." Plainly, the Hanoverian ministry feared that he would be the first in a line of martyrs proclaiming their unchanging faith, so that even before his execution they changed course and took a rapid decision to spare the remainder of the lords. Among the other rebels, Lord Nairne was reprieved on the intervention of James Stanhope, the secretary of state, who had been his schoolfellow at Eton, and who supposedly threatened to resign should the sentence be carried through. According to Lady Cowper, it was the Princess of Wales who interceded on behalf of Lord Carnwath. Along with Lord Widdrington, (who was a cousin of Lady Cowper), these men were granted reprieves as arbitrary in their way as that of Macheath at the end of the play. Although they suffered forfeiture of their estate and titles, these disabilities were effectively removed by a later Act of Grace. It was an odd-looking reversal, since none of them had offered much more of a defence than the two lords who suffered the extreme penalty.

Then came the affair of Thomas Forster. He was the hapless "general" of the English forces, chosen mainly on the grounds of his protestant faith (necessary to drum up support for the rising in the North of England) and his connections - his aunt was married to Nathaniel Crewe, a high churchman (and undoubtedly a Jacobite) who held the palatial bishopric of Durham. Forster himself, though an MP since 1708, was little more than a country gentleman from an ancient but impoverished line, with no credentials as a military man. All along the choice of Forster was unpopular with the Scottish rebels, and it proved to be disastrous. His feeble capitulation at Preston drove the last nail into what may have already been a doomed enterprise, and when the bedraggled prisoners reached London he was singled out for scorn on all sides. A further insult was the fact that he was sent to Newgate, the gaol reserved for the commoners, instead of the Tower, where the rebel lords were imprisoned. But already rumours had got about that there was no great stomach to carry out this prosecution. Lady Cowper claimed that she received a 'strange offer' from Mlle Schutz and Baron Bothmar, key figures in the king's entourage, 'to let Tom Forster escape, if I had a mind, while upon the road.'

The trial was none the less scheduled for 18 April; but a few days before this Forster found means to gain his liberty from Newgate. The romantic story attached to this event gives the credit to Tom's sister Dorothy, who is said to have ridden through the snowy winter from Northumberland to London, accompanied by the local blacksmith. With the calm heroism of a Jeannie Deans, she infiltrated a duplicate key, made by the blacksmith, into the prison, so that Forster could lock up the keeper, William Pitt, in one of the rooms and so effect his break-out. Like several of the rebels, he went across to the Jacobite court, and later served as a steward to the Pretender. Again this get-away looked all too easy, and unsurprisingly "it was whispered that the Government had connived in it, having no wish, after the Wintoun trial, to have another Anglican in the dock."[18] None the less, the government made apparent efforts to recapture the fugitive, issuing a description of Forster and placing a reward of £10,000 on his head - although they had already discovered his escape-route to France.

Some of this material is familiar to all students of the period. But historians have said little about the climate of opinion engendered by such suspicious escapes. Furthermore, it has not been possible until now to see a link to the immediate context of *The Beggar's Opera*. Such a connection is provided by William Pitt, whose name scarcely figures in the burgeoning historiography of crime, and who has received less attention than the ordinaries of Newgate, such as Paul Lorrain and Thomas Purney. His grimy career has been overshadowed by the more heavily publicised travails of Thomas Bambridge, notorious as a brutal warden of the Fleet Prison. In 1729 Bambridge, who had bought the office in the previous year for £5,000, was sent to Newgate after allegations of brutal conduct against prisoners (one of those making these accusations was Roger Johnson). He was suspected of having caused the death of the architectural writer Robert Castell, a friend of James Oglethorpe, who instigated parliamentary enquiries.   The sittings of the committee of the House of Commons were depicted in a famous picture by William Hogarth, and the miserable regime of Bambridge and his predecessor John Huggins have come down in the annals of criminal history.[19] In fact the scandals which surrounded the management of debtors' prisons like the Fleet and the Marshalsea, exposed by Oglethorpe's enquiry, were matched by equally corrupt practices in Newgate: an official investigation into the gaol as far back as 1702 had itemised the ways in which prisoners unable to pay so-called garnish money on admission were "stript, beaten and abused in a very violent manner."[20] Pitt is perhaps a more representative figure than Bambridge or Huggins, though he never had to suffer public exposure on quite the same scale. Nevertheless, evidence survives to document some facets of his career. For present purposes, the key issue concerns the fact that he was the gaoler involved when first Forster and then, eleven years later, Johnson each made their get-away - never mind Jack Sheppard.

V

Following the escape of Thomas Forster, Pitt's own life had been on the line He was indicted at the Old Bailey on 14 July 1716 before a panel

headed by the Lord Mayor, Sir Charles Peers, and including Lord Chief
Baron Sir Thomas Bury, Judge Robert Tracey (who had tried the rebels at
Carlisle), and the Lord Chief Justice, Sir John Pratt. Also on the panel was
the Recorder of London, Sir William Thompson (or Thomson), who later
played a large part in the downfall of Jonathan Wild, presiding at his trial
and pronouncing the death sentence. The jury for its part was headed by
Sir Daniel Wray, knight. These judges represented the civic and legal
establishment in its most obvious form during the early Hanoverian years.
On the surface they would have appeared to have every reason to uphold
the law in its most stringent modes, as Forster had been the ostensible
leader of a treasonable conspiracy against the state. And indeed the
charges laid against Pitt were extremely severe, as much so as those the
rebel leaders had faced:

> William Pitts, of London Gent. Indicted for High Treason; for whereas he
> being Keeper of the Gaol of Newgate, on and before the 8th of December
> last, and whereas Thomas Foster, jun. A false Rebel and Traitor to his
> Excellent Majesty King George, was on the Day aforesaid committed to
> him the said Prisoner, to be kept close and secure in the said Gaol till he
> should be discharged by due Course of Law, he the said Prisoner on the
> 11th of April last, not having the Fear of God in his Heart, but being moved
> and seduced by the instigation of the Devil &c. as a false Traitor, &c. did
> permit, aid and abett the said Foster to make his Escape out of the said
> Goal, Contrary to the Duty of his Allegiance &c.[21]

The proceedings were lengthy, occupying the whole of the Saturday
session - more protracted than some of the state trials in this era. At the
start delays were caused by the defendant's challenge to twenty-three
jurors, and then by disputes over the legality of the warrant for Pitt's
arrest, issued by the secretary of state, Lord Townshend. For present
purposes it will be enough to pick out a few salient details.

Opening for the prosecution was the "council for the King," who
seems not to have been the attorney-general (at this date Sir Edward
Northey). The first witness was Mr Rewse, a keeper, who described how
the escape was detected.[22] This witness went to great lengths to emphasise
that "his Master was always very diligent in performing his Duty," and to
set out the precautionary measures which had been taken. He deposed that
"Mr. Foster's Room was very strong, and more secure than any other
Room in the prison; and that he could make no Noise nor Disturbance
without waking his Master, who lay upon the same Floor, a Partition being
only between them."[23] Other witnesses testified that Pitt had impressed on
his servants that they must take no bribes, although the rebels were "very

free to offer them," up to a sum of thousands of pounds. All the prison staff toed the same line, and in effect sought to exonerate Pitt, as well as themselves, by reference to the "false key" which the prisoner had somehow obtained. (No one in the trial mentioned the story that Pitt had himself been locked up.) Evidence was also given by Samuel Buckley, the official who ran the government's secret service operations, and Temple Stanyan, the under-secretary of state, but they were only able to report on what they were told when they went to the prison following the break-out. However, both men did refer to an admission that Pitt and another prisoner had been sitting with Forster "over a flask of wine" immediately before the escape. Those testifying earlier had managed to play down this damaging evidence.

The defence then called its witnesses, including Pitt's maid-servant, the clerk of Newgate and a former keeper, Mr Fells.[24] They testified to his good conduct, and to the fact that it had been the practice for decades to keep the most important prisoners where Forster had been confined. After this "several Honourable and Worthy Persons" appeared to speak in favour of the prisoner's reputation, notably eight individuals with a knighthood, all grandees of the City and in four cases very recent Lord Mayors.[25] Each of them gave Pitt "the Character of a very careful, fair, honest Man." Such a description hardly squares with some of the stories which had gone around: "It was estimated in during three or four months in 1716 . . .[Pitt] cleared some £3,000 or £4,000 from his Jacobite prisoners 'besides valuable presents given in private'."[26] But he did not get as much as he expected, according to one account. Nine Scottish prisoners, including the veteran conspirator Mackintosh of Borlum, managed to get away on the day before they were to stand trial in May 1716. It was alleged that they had vandalized new bedding that Pitt had been forced to provide, and had refused to pay anything towards their maintenance, as was customary. "Others, mostly Scotsmen, were too poor to contribute anything anyway."[27] This was not what the court heard. However, such rumours probably reached Gay's ears: it was, after all, in August 1716, just a month after the trial,   that Swift wrote to him proposing the subject of "a Newgate pastoral, among the whores and thieves there," a reflection of the topicality of these issues.

After the defendant had spoken to maintain his total innocence, the government prosecutor replied. He pointed out in convincing detail the implausibility of some of the defence arguments, and indicated a number of ways in which a greater wall of security might have been erected to prevent all possibility of an escape. Counsel also found it significant that the prisoner had appeared reluctant to testify on oath, a matter which had come up during Buckley's evidence. On the face of it, the case looks almost impenetrable, and to any amateur jurist it seems as safe a conviction as one could hope to achieve. None the less, when Lord Chief Baron Bury had summed up the evidence, "which he did very fully," the jury retired, "and being return'd Acquitted the Prisoner." Not everyone expressed total confidence that the right decision had been made. Witness the heavily ironic flavour of this report in *Annals of King George*, a publication which generally toed the government line:

> Mr. *Pitts*, the Keeper of *Newgate*, under whose Management so many Prisoners had made their escape out of that Prison, esteemed before the strongest Prison in *England*, was tryed for High Treason, but was acquitted after a   full Hearing, and return'd to his Charge, where he had not been many Days, but Mr. *Bruce* and Mr .   two other Prisoners, made their escape out of the same Prison, and almost in the same manner.

The report goes on to describe the successful escape of five prisoners in the Fleet gaol, while "one Dr. *Garns*, a Doctor of Physick, did the same at *Edinborough*, having disguis'd himself in his Sister's Cloaths." Finally, the account mentions the episode of Earl of Winton. Plainly some anxiety existed about these gaolbreaks and the ease with which they had been accomplished.[28]

We could speculate at length on how this verdict was arrived at: political bias, jury subornation, deference to the opinion of the aldermen who had spoken for Pitt, a reluctance to convict on a charge of high treason (where there could be no remission for benefit of clergy, and death was the only sentence allowed). Juries consisting of ordinary members of the public sometimes acquitted, even where the prisoner had been proved guilty, because they considered the offence too light for the punishment enjoined by the law; and they sided occasionally with those cocking a snook at authority. But we could hardly see the keeper of a prison renowned for its wretched conditions and brutal regime as the sort of defendant likely to benefit from such lenience. Pitt's challenges to the jury may have packed the panel in his favour, while the prosecution witnesses were reluctant to show him in a bad light. It is hard to stifle a suspicion that the whole proceedings may have been a charade, to keep up the fiction that Forster was a figure of great standing whose flight had been a disaster to the nation.

The Whig press blamed Pitt for further gaol-breaks in the aftermath of the rising, including that of the Jacobite author of "the Treasonable Libel, call'd *The Shift Shifted*," George Flint, and did not scruple to indicate that such mishaps occurred because of the keeper's favouring the Pretender's cause.[29] One author gave a detailed account of the way in which Forster had been allowed to get away, and attributed the failures in the prison system to Pitt's designedly liberal regime. The Lord Mayor of London actually reinstated some more diligent guards at Newgate who had taken a tough line with the prisoners while Pitt was out of commission during his trial.[30]

Before two years were out Pitt found himself in trouble again. This time the matter related to the confusingly named James Shepheard, an apprentice coach-painter aged just eighteen, who was accused of writing a letter in which he set out his intention of killing the king. For the government this illustrated "the hellish Machinations" of their opponents; for the Jacobites, it turned Shepheard into an overnight hero. After a show trial at the Old Bailey, he was convicted of high treason, and sentenced to death by the Recorder of London. The identity of the presiding justice will arouse no astonishment: it was William Thompson. Soon afterwards in March 1718 the prisoner was dispatched at Tyburn, and rapidly portrayed as a martyr for the Stuart cause. While in custody he had received the ministrations of a nonjuring priest by the name of Robert Orme, who probably wrote the incendiary dying speech attributed to the hapless apprentice. Orme was held in gaol for some time, with complaints made about "his unwarrantable Conduct in Visiting and Absolving *Shepherd*." As for Pitt, the privy council summoned him to appear before them so that he could| explain how he had permitted the priest access to Shepheard's cell. Somehow he wriggled out of the accusations.[31]

On the showing of his trial in 1716, Pitt was either remarkably incompetent; open to a bribe from the Jacobite leaders; or else conniving in an official plot to let go some of those who had inconveniently allowed themselves to be swept into the net at Preston. Eight years later, when Sheppard twice escaped from Newgate, the last possibility can be discounted, and bribery is much less likely. This time, it seems as though the prison authorities were genuinely surprised by the house-breaker's ability to turn his hand to gaol-breaks. All the same, there were those who thought that Pitt may have been complicit in these escapes, too. This becomes clear from *The History of the Remarkable Life of John Sheppard*, a hastily compiled life which John Applebee managed to get out even before the execution - in hopes, no doubt, of good sales on the Tyburn holiday when Sheppard went to the gallows. It is a strange production, culminating in a riot of punning based on the criminal's flight through London ("it had so intirely *Stranded* my reason, that by the time I came to *Half-Moon-Street* end, it gave me a *New-Exchange* to my Senses, and made me quite Lunatick").[32] The pamphlet is commonly attributed to

Daniel Defoe: this is possible, but not really likely.[33] The point of interest here is the author's repeated efforts to exculpate Pitt from charges of complicity which had evidently been made against him.[34] The narrative stresses the alarm which the custodians at Newgate felt when Sheppard got away for the first time in September. Instead detailed information is provided on the tools which were smuggled in to him, and they help he received from other prisoners, including one Stephen Fowles, "whom he most ungenerously betray'd to the Keepers after his being retaken, and the fellow was severely punish'd for it." Far from being involved in the break-out, the narrator states, the prison staff were guiltless:

> The Keepers of *Newgate*, whom the rash World loaded with Infamy, stigmatiz'd and branded with the Title of Persons guilty of Bribery; for Connivance at his Escape, they and what Posse in their Power, either for Love or Money did Contribute their utmost to undeceive a wrong notion'd People. Their Vigilance was remarkably indefatigable, sparing neither Money nor Time, Night or Day to bring him back to his deserv'd Justice.

After Sheppard was caught with an accomplice, he was taken back to prison and chained to the floor "with double Basels about his Feet." In addition, when the accomplice Page was committed to Newgate by Sir Francis Forbes, "the Prudence of Mr. *Pitt* caus'd a Separation between him and his Brother the first Night, as a Means to prevent any ensuing Danger." The joy at Newgate at this turn of events was "inexpressible," and *"Te Deum* was Sung in the Lodge." [35]

Although the authorities had sent Sheppard on his return to what was in effect the high security wing of Newgate, the Castle, he still made efforts to regain his freedom, by unlocking a padlock with a nail and trying to sneak up a chimney. Defeated by some iron bars, Sheppard "finding this Attempt entirely frustrated" revealed to "Mr. *Pitt*, the Head Keeper, and his Deputies" how he had loosed himself from his irons. Accordingly he was hand-cuffed and "more effectually Chain'd." Clearly we are meant to feel that the prison staff were on top of their job: examinations were performed by outsiders to ensure that sufficient restraints were in place. However, as we know, Sheppard did manage to make one more bid for freedom, to the consternation of all at the gaol. After his disappearance, "Infinite Numbers of Citizens came to *Newgate* to behold *Sheppard's* Workmanship, and Mr. *Pitt* and his Officers very readily Conducted them up Stairs, that the World might be convinc'd there was not the least room to suspect, either a Negligence, or Connivance in the Servants. Every one express'd the greatest Surprize that has been known, and declar'd themselves satisfy'd with the Measures they had taken for the Security of their Prisoners." The exact methods used by the escapee remain, we are told, a secret, but some details are given of a possible route. The narrator returns to his theme: "it will perhaps be inquir'd how all this could be perform'd without his being heard by the Prisoners or the Keepers." A not wholly persuasive answer is given, involving the distance from Sheppard's place of confinement to other parts of the prison, and the fact that the deed was done in the utmost dark of night. Then:

> The Jaylors suffer'd much by the Opinion the ignorant Part of the People entertain'd of the Matter, and nothing would satisfie some, but that they not only Conniv'd at, but even assisted him in breaking their own Walls and Fences. . . .This is indeed a fine way of Judging, the well-known Character if Mr. *Pitt* and his Deputies, are sufficient to wipe of (*sic*) such ridiculous Imputations; and 'tis a most lamentable Truth, that they have often-times had in their Charge Villains of the deepest Die; Persons of Quality and great Worth, for whom no Entreaties, no Sums how large soever have been able to interfere between the doleful Prison, and the fatal Tree.

This section concludes, "The Officers have done their Duty, they are but Men, and they have had to deal with a Creature something more than Man, a *Proteus*, Supernatural, Words cannot describe him."[36]

At this date we cannot determine if Sheppard got any degree of help from the prison warders. What appears certain is that the *Narrative* served as a whitewashing exercise, whether written by Defoe or another. But who was being protected? Pitt may have had well-placed friends who were ready to come to his defence. However, we might equally deduce that the need had arisen to save the keeper's face so as to shield others higher up in the system who had a corrupt role in the administration of justice: Sir William Thompson's role in the prosecution of Wild suggests he might be such a person. He was, we recall, on the panel of judges at Pitt's trial in 1716. After the Forster episode in 1716, Thompson had gone on to serve as solicitor general under Stanhope and Sunderland, but he was dismissed when accusations of corruption he made against his own colleague, the attorney general Nicholas Lechmere, were found to be groundless by a parliamentary committee. Be that as it may, the *Narrative* clearly shows that there was anxiety in the public: this focussed on the ease with which Sheppard had made his successive escapes from larger and larger places of confinement, starting with the flimsy roundhouse at the top of St Giles's and moving on to the formidable bastions of Newgate. This was a form of disquiet on which Gay could play in the *Opera* - and things had got worse in the interim.

VI

We saw earlier that Roger Johnson escaped from Newgate on 17 May 1727. He had been committed in "a violent Suspicion" of having stolen a large sum of money, the property of Thomas Hayn [or Hale], in the house of Thomas Overbury. Committed to the New Prison by Justice Broughton, he was later transferred to Newgate, where he bought himself out of the Common Side, and had been allowed the liberty of the Press Yard by "the New Keeper," Thomas Allen. From here, together with the prisoner on a charge of murder, Henry Fisher, he managed to climb out on to the leads and jump across a narrow alleyway. The two men were able to get through Phoenix Court into Newgate Street, and then vanish into the city. As we have seen, Johnson was recaptured and brought back for trial at the Old Bailey on 16 October 1728: this was nine months after *The Beggar's Opera* premiered, but the affair had already had its repercussions. Soon after the break-out, on 30 May 1727, the court of aldermen of the City of London had appointed a committee to investigate what had happened. This body issued a long report on 20 July, and after taking advice from the attorney general (Sir Philip Yorke, better known later as Lord Hardwicke) the aldermen decided that Pitt should be prosecuted. These circumstances were first set out by C.A. Rivington, who noted also that the keeper's methods in some ways prefigured those of Lockit, so that "Pitt can be taken to be the original on whom the character, Lockit, is at any rate partly based." Rivington went on to suggest that Gay may have been given facilities to see the inside of Newgate by John Barber.[37] The reasoning behind this is that Gay had known Barber for many years (he was invited to the mayoral feast in the following year): moreover, Barber as an alderman had been involved in the administration of Newgate, and actually served on the committee looking into the affair of Johnson and Fisher.

What happened about the supposed prosecution of Pitt remains a mystery. There is no record in the court of aldermen's books, and nothing has turned up in the archives of the common law-courts. From the reference to "Mr. Allen," it appears that Pitt was undergoing some form of suspension in October 1728. We might surmise that the keeper's chequered past had finally caught up with him. But it is risky to make such assumptions with respect to the judicial system in past centuries. The keeper still held his office in November 1730, when he signed a document setting out his answer to complaints made by prisoners. One charge related to the "taps" kept within the gaol by turnkeys' wives for liquor sales. Pitt argued that, "as escapes are often contrived in the Gaol of Newgate, the turnkeys' wives, being constantly there, do often prevent their villainous designs by giving timely notice to their husbands."[38] Or not. Then, in 1732, the *Gentleman's Magazine* in 1732 recorded the death, on 16 May, of Mr Pitt, at his house in Newgate Street. He was identified as "Head Keeper of Newgate." His post was freehold, once purchased, so that it would take an earthquake to remove him. Later that year, during John Barber's mayoralty, the aldermen decided to abandon such sales of the office in future.

What of the equally resilient Johnson? At his trial in 1728, the counsel for the crown undertook to prove that "the Prisoner had broken Goal, and by a Statute made in the first Year of Edward the Second, it was enacted. That if any person should break any Goal, and it should appear that he was committed to the said Goal. For Felony, or nay capital Offence, he should lay under the same Judgment for breaking Goal, as if he had been convicted for the Crime for which he was committed." Later in the century, Sir William Blackstone discussed this statute, "*de frangentibus prisonam*" (1 Edw. II, s.2), and he added a telling observation: "But the officer permitting such escape, either by negligence or connivance, is much more culpable than the prisoner; the natural desire of liberty pleading strongly in his behalf, though he ought in strictness of law to submit himself quietly to custody, till cleared by the due course of justice."[39] Insofar as this is orthodox doctrine, one might expect the courts to come down hard on those who permitted an escape such as that of Johnson. But there was no need to worry. The trial transcripts reveal that a "dispute" arose, "Whether the said Roger Johnson broke Goal, or whether it was broke by one Fisher, who escaped at the same Time; and a Witness appearing, who depos'd, That the Goal was broke by Fisher, the Jury acquitted him, though that Witness, one Mrs. Burney, had but a very indifferent Character."

Even that was not the end of this particular story. On 26 February 1729 Johnson was back at the Old Bailey, charged with the original offence of stealing from Thomas Hale: but "by some Management or other no Prosecutor appeared, and he was acquitted." On the same day he was also indicted for stealing twenty guineas from John Sudoe: "but the chief Evidence who should have appeared against him was gone or sent into the Country a Year since, upon which he had the good Fortune, once more to be acquitted." Seldom do the formal transcriptions give vent to such open sentiments.[40] A year later, Johnson was arraigned for a highway robbery, carried out in the somewhat unlikely location of Chancery Lane. According to evidence in court, Mordecai Pitts, a serjeant of the Poultry Compter, was bringing Johnson to appear before Lord Chief Justice

Raymond in his chambers. While waiting they took a drink in a tavern, and then they set off for their appointment, when suddenly four men with clubs appeared. Johnson allegedly threw snuff in the face of Mordecai Pitts before making his escape. In the process Pitts' wig and hat were snatched off, and these were the items of property occasioning a charge of robbery: wig, valued at 30s., and hat, 10s. This time the key witnesses did appear against the defendant, but he also found a compliant witness of his own. The results were much as before: "It appearing by the Evidence to be rather a Riot in order to an Escape than a Robbery, the Prisoner was acquitted."[41] Hardly any charge would stick to Johnson. The newspapers, perhaps weary by now of his escapades, reported his acquittal without comment.

Perhaps this is not such a mystery after all: one factor unites every case in which he got off lightly - as with the gaol-breaking charge, the thefts from Hale and Sudoe, the attack on Pitts, and the trial of Sarah Malcolm. This is the presence on the panel of judges of Thompson, who against custom continued to serve as Recorder even after he became a Baron of the Exchequer in November 1729. It is most unlikely that Thompson took his place on the bench for every session at the Old Bailey, but this *eminence grise* was present everywhere if seldom visible. J.M. Beattie has shown just how central he was to the development of a "new penal order" in the 1720s and 1730s, and how well connected to the central government.[42] Unquestionably he played a key role in combating day to day crime in the capital. Modern penologists have tended to look for faults in the system of eighteenth-century justice, rather than heaping blame on individuals. But someone with the confidence of Walpole was deeply involved in the wheeling and dealing which went on around the courts. The only plausible candidate is Thompson, who was a noted hard-liner on most penal issues - Beattie refers to him as "clearly a man who strongly valued both the stern punishments and the wider discretion the [Transportation] Act put into the hands of the bench."[43] On the bench he was totally deaf to the appeal for mercy which Sheppard had made after his conviction in August 1724.[44] What is more significant here is his approach to court-room accommodations. As Recorder, he argued that in cases of assault it was better for the defendant or his friends to speak with the prosecutor before the trial, "and then if he forbears to appear and prosecute [the defendant] will be discharged, and all the charges of a Tryal saved, which would be a great expence."[45] One wonders whether the defendant in Thompson's court had a timely word with the prosecutors when Johnson's alleged victims unaccountably took a trip into the country.

Johnson, indeed, was a serial escapee. Somehow he evaded the consequences of his actions, time and time again. When Wild's henchmen were rounded up, he was safely out of the way, probably in the Low Countries.[46] As we saw, his own wife, who had close ties with Wild, was arrested in May 1725, and committed to Clerkenwell Bridewell; but her husband made his escape.[47] Later he was held in Newgate for several years, as described earlier, but after he gave crucial evidence against Sarah Malcolm, he was allowed to go free. While Johnson never became as famous as Sheppard or Wild, it must have been obvious to many that he had the protection of someone powerful in the legal or political world. As for William Pitt, his entire career shows that it was almost impossible to obtain a conviction against a figure in his position - even Thomas Bambridge, for that matter, was acquitted in 1729, in a better publicized case, although he was disabled from holding office. Both Pitt and Johnson belonged to a milieu where there were more ways of evading justice than filing through the bars of a cell - but where that might be an acceptable means of escape, in the right circumstances.

VII

Most commentary on penal matters in this age has concentrated on the ordinary workings of the system in attempting to regulate crime and punishment. Scholars have debated such issues as who committed offences; how they were prosecuted; what sentences were imposed; when they were acquitted or reprieved, and so on. The administration of justice has been the focus of important work by J.M. Beattie and others, while numerous historians have followed the lead of E.P. Thompson in seeking to uncover the ideology underlying contemporary penal practice. Emphasis has lain on the commission of the crime, the trial and the punishment imposed. What the facts presented here suggest is that we may need to incorporate a new element within the discourse: the post-arrest phase, when accused persons were held in custody awaiting trial, and when break-outs generally occurred. This issue is quite distinct from matters such as of formal pardons or constructive mitigation of offences by an indulgent jury.

It is evident that escapes had loomed large in the national consciousness for some years- as far back at least as the time of Forster and the Jacobite lords. Gay was able to draw on a ready understanding of the issues when he brought this motif into his plot.[48] What linked many of the most prominent cases was the involvement of William Pitt, and it is hard to oppose the suggestion by Rivington that much of Lockit's characterisation picks up on aspects of the keeper. From his first entrance on the stage, when he welcomes Macheath as his "lodger" to the prison, Lockit is concerned with fees and garnish (2: 7).[49] We know from independent evidence that Pitt had a reputation for extracting the maximum fees for his services.[50] The famous quarrel between Peachum and Lockit later in this act (2: 10) has most often been discussed in terms of a political analogue, the currently bad relations of Walpole and Townshend. But it reveals also that the keeper was toying with criminals like Ned Clincher, whose arrest he could speed or delay; that he was paying an informant, Mrs Coaxer, for leads towards apprehending other thieves; and that he was regularly claiming the reward for providing evidence which helped to gain convictions on capital offences. However, the most explicit commentary is found a little later in the play (2: 12), when Macheath tells Lucy that her father has his price:

> But if I could raise a small sum - would not twenty guineas, think you, move him? Of all the arguments in the way of business, the perquisite is the most prevailing. Your father's perquisites for the escape of prisoners must amount to a considerable sum in the year.[51]

Nobody had ever successfully hung such an accusation on Pitt, yet the odour must have clung to him after the disappearance of Johnson in the previous year and the investigation by the city authorities.[52] According to a pamphlet published in 1717, Pitt had paid £5,000 for his office (quite a smart deal, by contemporary standards), and he needed to recoup this money.[53]

True, Lockit has no complicity when the break is made in the *Opera*: at the crucial moment, he is in a stupour after drinking with the prisoners, and Lucy manages to sneak away the keys.[54] This must have reminded many in the audience of that old story about the time when Pitt and Thomas Forster shared drinks, prior to the Jacobite's well-publicized escape. Still, the keeper's reaction on learning what has happened tells all: "Did he tip handsomely? How much did he come down with? Come hussy, don't cheat your father. . .Perhaps, you have made a better bargain with him than I could have done." Lucy insists that she has taken no money, which provokes her father to scorn. Of course, on a warm-hearted reading of the play, to arrange an escape for love displays a better motive than any other; but this is not the way most of the characters look at matters. Shortly afterwards Lockit assures Peachum that they will soon be able to recapture Macheath, to which the thief-taker replies, "But what signifies catching the bird, if your daughter Lucy will set open the door of the cage?" In due course, Macheath is betrayed, and Lockit complacently tells him, "You have neither the chance of love or money for another escape, for you are ordered to be called down upon your trial immediately." After his arrest, Macheath utters a remark which illustrates the centrality of this entire theme in the workings of justice and in the play: "For my having broke prison, you see, gentlemen, I am ordered immediate execution." [55] This, then, is the immediate cause of the hero's downfall: not his offstage doings as a highwayman, not his dealings with the prostitutes - but his flight.

Still, as we know, Lockit's prediction will prove false, when the absurd catastrophe is substituted for the real-life fate which would be meted out to the characters: for, as the Beggar says, "the audience must have supposed they were all either hanged or transported."[56] The ease with which this ending is switched parodies capricious means of escape, as exemplified by the seeming ease with which Nithsdale, Winton, Forster and recently Johnson had flown the coop, without any need for the elaborate props and skills utilised by Sheppard. Gay's audience must have seen this as an allusion to convenient escapes, engineered by one means or another, when the authorities had no desire to keep a prisoner locked up. They may perhaps have remembered, too, certain timely fugues, such as that of the South Sea cashier Robert Knight - not to mention the large number of Jacobites who had been able to get away to the continent in the wake of the rising. Yet one more timely escape would have struck the first-night audience, though it occurred too late to have been in Gay's mind when he wrote. On 11 December 1727 Richard Savage had been brought from Newgate to the bar at the Old Bailey, where five days earlier he had been convicted with James Gregory for murder: he was sentenced to death. The sequel is well known: "The Queen having been graciously pleased to grant a pardon to Messrs Savage and Gregory, they were admitted to bail on the 20th of January, 1728, in order to their pleading that pardon; and accordingly, on the 5th of March following, they pleaded to the said pardon, and were set at liberty."[57] Many of those assembled in the theatre at Lincoln's Inn Fields on 29 January must have been aware of this sensational trial and its aftermath. If Savage could cheat the gallows, thanks to royal intervention, why not the hero of this play?

Some have wondered whether *The Beggar's Opera* really operates as an explicitly political statement, to the extent that we have generally supposed. Once we look into the story told here, we may see in the play a critique of systematic misuse of the judicial system by the authorities, at one level or another. We do not have to regard the official apparatus of law as merely analogous to the criminal world; in the person of men like Johnson and Pitt the two worlds commingled and attained something like homology. The *Opera* feeds off a rich collective memory, and Macheath's career as an escapee calls up many episodes of recent history. Assuming that the "vehicle" of the play is the underworld, as Denning argues,[58] then we need to extend that milieu from the doings of Wild and Sheppard to the ongoing story of William Pitt and Roger Johnson, along with their shady political ties.

Notes

[1] Michael Denning, "Beggars and Thieves," *Literature and History,* 8 (1982), 41-55, reprinted in *John Gay: The Beggar's Opera*, Modern Critical Interpretations, ed. Harold Bloom (New York: Chelsea House, 1988), pp. 99-116.

[2] Peter Linebaugh, *The London Hanged: Crime and Civil Society in the Eighteenth Century* (Cambridge: Cambridge University Press, 1992), pp. 7-41.

[3] John Gay, *The Beggar's Opera*, ed. Bryan Loughrey and T.O. Treadwell (London: Penguin, 1986), p. 64. All references are to this edition: act and scene numbers are cited in the text, as "1: 3."

[4] His name was wrongly given as "Joseph Sheppard" in the semi-official court reports: see *The Proceedings on the King's Commission of the Peace, and Oyer and Terminer, and the Jail-Delivery of Newgate, held for the City of London, and County of Middlesex, at Justice-Hall, in the Old Bailey* (August 1724), p. 7. He was acquitted on two other charges of housebreaking and theft, on the grounds of insufficient evidence.

[5] *A Full and Particular Account of the Life and Notorious Transactions of Roger Johnson* (1740), p. 4.

[6] Howson, *Thief-Taker*, p. 144. This book provides the fullest details of any modern authority: the author draws on many of the early sources, which include a short life published in 1740, as well as collections of criminal biographies by authors such as "Captain Alexander Smith." None of these is wholly dependable, but a reasonable approximation to the main course of Johnson's career can be established on the basis of the materials provided by Howson, along with fresh documents quoted here.

[7] Howson. *Thief-Taker*, p. 214.

[8] "Capt. Alexander Smith", *Memoirs of the Life and Times, of the Famous Jonathan Wild, together with the History and Lives, of Modern Rogues, that have been Executed before and since his Death* (London, 1726), p. 30.

[9] The story is quoted from the *Flying Post*, 11 January 1729, by Howson, *Thief-Taker*, pp. 214-15, who states that "it is the kind of story which could just be true." This is uncharacteristically indulgent on the part of a writer who elsewhere shows a due degree of scepticism on such points. It should be recalled that the events were by this time almost five years old.

[10] On this account, unlike Sheppard, Johnson is occasionally referred to as "Captain" - though Macheath's adoption of this title probably relates to an older tradition which saw highwaymen as quasi-military men.

[11] *The Proceedings at the Sessions of the Peace, and Oyer and Terminer, For the City of London. And on the King's Commission of Goal-Delivery of Newgate, held at Justice-Hall in the Old-Baily; for the City of London, and County of Middlesex. On Tuesday, Wednesday, and Thursday, the 17th, 18th and, 19th of October, 1727* (1727), p. 3.

[12] "Smith", *Memoirs of Wild*, p. 29.

[13] See *The Ordinary of Newgate's Account of the Behaviour, Confession, and Dying Words, of the three Malefactors, who were executed at Tyburn on Monday the Twenty-third of June, 1753* (1753).

[14] National Archives, SP 36/8/45-48, 69.

[15] For a full account of the trial, see *The Proceedings at the Sessions of the Peace, and Oyer and Terminer, for the City of London, and County of Middlesex; on Wednesday the 21st, Thursday the 22d, Friday the 23d, and Saturday the 24th of February 1733* (1733), pp. 73-95. Johnson's deposition appears on p. 89.

[16] Quoted by Ralph Arnold, *Northern Lights: The Story of Lord Derwentwater* (London: Constable, 1959), p. 149. Lady Cowper was a member of the Clavering family of Northumberland, heavily implicated in the rising, but there is no reason to suppose she had strong sympathy with the rebels at large.

[17] *An Account of the Proceeding to Judgment against George Earl of Winton, Impeached for High Treason* (1716). This is a single sheet with no place or date of publication. What seems to be a unique copy is held in the McLaughlin Library of the University of Guelph: I am grateful to the library staff for help in obtaining a photocopy of this item.

[18] Arnold, *Northern Lights*, pp. 128, 169.

[19] For a summary of key events, see Paulson, *Hogarth*, 1: 188-95. A fuller narrative will be found in Roger Lee Brown, *A History of the Fleet Prison: The Anatomy of the Fleet* (Lewiston, NY: Edwin Mellen, 1996), pp. 64-90.

[20] Greater London Records Office, Middlesex County Records, Sessions Book 597, quoted by Maureen Waller, *1700: Scenes from London Life* (New York: Four Walls Eight Windows, 2000), p. 310.

[21] *The Proceedings on the King's Commission of the Peace, and Oyer and Terminer, and Gaol-Delivery of Newgate, held for the City of London, and County of Middlesex, at Justice-Hall, in the Old Bayley* (July 1716), p. 3ff.

[22] "Mr. Reuse" was still a keeper at the time of Sheppard's execution in 1724 (*Daily Journal*, 17 November). He is mentioned under the guise "Mr. R---se" as one willing to treat suitable, i.e. well-heeled, prisoners in a humane fashion, in *The History of the Press-Yard* (1717), quoted by Charles Gordon, *The Old Bailey and Newgate* (London: T. Fisher Unwin, 1902), pp. 100-03. ("Gordon" was a pseudonym for the well known writer of popular social histories, John Ashton.) He can be identified with Bodenham Rewse or Rouse, active in the campaign of the Society for the Reformation of Manners in the 1690s, especially against coiners and loose women, and a thieftaker. He bought the post of head turnkey, or deputy keeper of Newgate in 1701. See J.M. Beattie, *Policing and Punishment in London, 1660-1750: Urban Crime and the Limits of Terror* (Oxford: Oxford University Press, 2001), p. 239.

[23] Rewse justified the fact that Forster was confined in the prisoner's house (that is, the keeper's lodging) on the grounds that "Count Guiscard" had been confined there, "it being thought by the then Ministry to be the safest Place, and Mr. Harvey for High Treason." The allusions are to the adventurer Antoine de Guiscard, who had attempted to assassinate Robert Harley in 1711, and Edward Hervey of Combe, implicated as a Jacobite in the recent rising. According to a contemporary pamphlet, *The History of the Press Yard* (1717), the "Governor" offered a Jacobite prisoner "a Habitation in his House, for so the *Press Yard* was called" (quoted by Gordon, *Old Bailey*, p. 103).

[24] In fact this was James Fell, who had been convicted in 1696 of "conniving at the escape of one of his prisoners in return for a financial reward." However, "the offence does not seem to have been considered especially grave for the sentence of the court was postponed indefinitely and Fell was allowed to retain the keepership." See Anthony Babington, *The English Bastille: A History of Newgate Gaol and Prison Conditions in Britain 1188-1902* (London: Macdonald, 1971), p. 65.

[25] Another of the group, Sir William Stewart, would achieve the mayoralty in 1722. "Sir Richard Houte" is certainly Sir Richard Hoare, and "Sir Francis Ferves" must actually be Sir Francis Forbes, Lord Mayor in 1726. Information on these men, who were mostly Whigs of one description or another, can be found in A.J. Henderson, *London and the National Government, 1721-1742: A Study of City Politics and the Walpole Administration* (Durham, NC: Duke University Press, 1945).

[26] Christopher Hibbert, *The Road to Tyburn: The Story of Jack Sheppard and the Eighteenth-Century London Underworld* (Cleveland: World Publishing Company, 1957), p. 137. Hibbert does not give his source, and his accompanying statement that Pitt had paid just a thousand pounds for the keepership conflicts with other evidence.

[27] Leo Gooch, *The Desperate Faction? The Jacobites of North-East England 1688-1745* (Birtley, Durham: CASEC, 2001), p. 94.

[28] *The Annals of King George, Year the Third* (London: A. Bell 1718), p. 14.

[29] Flint himself was sent to Newgate in January 1716 for seditious publications. When he fell ill, his wife employed the usual gaol-breaking manoeuvres to get out of her incarceration in the Fleet, so that she could visit him. She then petitioned to join her husband in Newgate, and this was granted. In 1717, unsurprisingly, after he was sentenced to death, she contrived it for her husband to escape to the Continent. As an act of reprisal, Pitt had her moved to the common side of the prison, where she caught a potentially fatal dose of the plague; but ultimately she was released and could join George in Calais. See Gooch, *Desperate Faction*, 146-7.

[30] *The Secret History of the Rebels in Newgate. Giving an Account of their Daily Behaviour, from their Commitment to their Goal-delivery* (London, 3rd edn: J. Roberts, A. Dodd, J. Harrison, [1717]), passim.

[31] *The Annals of King George, Year the Fourth* (London: A. Bell, 1718), pp. 33-49; *Read's Weekly Journal*, 22 March 1718.

[32] *Selected Prose and Poetry of Daniel Defoe*, ed. Michael F. Shugrue (New York: Holt, Rinehart and Winston, 1968), p. 267.

[33] P.N. Furbank and W.R. Owens, *Defoe De-Attributions* (London: Hambledon Press, 1994), pp. 136-7, reject the attribution on fairly solid grounds.

[34] Hibbert, *Road to Tyburn*, p. 161, writes that Pitt had "recently been tried twice on charges of accepting bribes from rich prisoners and allowing them to escape." He adds that though Pitt was acquitted, "his assistants knew more than they had admitted at the trials and were consequently very uneasy about what might come out at a future inquiry and interfere with a useful source of income." Hibbert does not identify the second trial, and I have been unable to find any details about it.

[35] Defoe, *Selected Prose*, pp. 246, 251. When Page came up for trial on 4 December, one of the charges was that "well knowing the said John Sheppard to be convicted as aforesaid, did notwithstanding, on the 10th of Sept. last, receive, comfort, and harbour the said John Sheppard." The defendant admitted that "he had kept Sheppard Company ever since he broke out of Newgate." He was sentenced to transportation. See *The Proceedings on the King's Commission of the Peace, and Oyer and Terminer, and Gaol-Delivery of Newgate, held for the City of London, and County of Middlesex, at Justice-Hall, in the Old Baily* (December 1724), p. 8. On this day no fewer than 97 cases were heard, a sharp contrast to the protracted trial of Pitt in 1716.

[36] Defoe, *Selected Prose*, pp. 257, 260, 262-3. For mythical or magical comparisons used of Sheppard, see Linebaugh, *London Hanged*, p. 37.

[37] Charles A. Rivington, *"Tyrant": The Story of John Barber 1675-1741* (York: William Sessions, 1989), pp. 132-3, citing Guildhall Record Office, Repertories of the Court of Aldermen, vol. 131.

[38] Quoted by Babington, *English Bastille*, pp. 116-17 (the source not listed, but seems to be Corporation of London Record Office, *Answer of the Keeper of Newgate Gaol to Articles Exhibited against him re Debtor Prisoners*).

[39] William Blackstone, *Commentaries on the Laws of England*, 4 vols (Oxford, 1769; rptd Chicago: University of Chicago Press, 1979), 4: 130-1. The basis of the law was that no one who broke from prison was subject to conviction as a felon, unless the original offence for which he had been committed itself constituted a felony. However, Blackstone goes on to say that "Officers. . .who, after arrest, *negligently* permit a felon to escape, are also punishable by fine; but *voluntary* escapes, by consent and connivance of the officer, are a much more serious offense: for it is generally agreed that such escapes amount to the same kind of offense, and are punishable in the same degree, as the offense of which the prisoner is guilty, and for which he is in custody, whether treason, felony, or trespass. And this, whether he were actually committed to jail, or only under a bare arrest." This is obviously the basis on which Pitt was charged with high treason after Forster's escape.

[40] *The Proceedings on the King's Commission of the Peace, and Oyer and Terminer, and Gaol-Delivery of Newgate, held for the City of London, and County of Middlesex, at Justice-Hall, in the Old Baily* (March 1729), p. 6.

[41] *The Proceedings on the King's Commission of the Peace, and Oyer and Terminer, and Gaol-Delivery of Newgate, held for the City of London, and County of Middlesex, at Justice-Hall, in the Old Baily* (December 1730), pp. 11-12.

[42] See J.M. Beattie, "William Thomson and Transportation," in *Policing and Punishment*, pp. 424-62.

[43] J.M. Beattie, *Crime and the Courts in England 1660-1800* (Princeton: Princeton University Press, 1986), p. 507. For other examples of Thompson's severity towards criminals, see pp. 510, 517. Accusations of corruption against Thompson were common (see Howson, *Thief-Taker*, p. 241), and while this may have been unavoidable for a man in his position there are plausible signs that he was able to influence the behaviour of the turnkeys at Newgate.

[44] Thompson recused himself from presiding at the trial of Bambridge for theft in July 1729, on the grounds he had been a member of the Commons committee investigating the gaoler. This may have resulted from genuine scruples on his part: it did not stop from trying Wild, whom he had been pursuing for years. Bambridge was eventually acquitted, as he had already been for the murder of Castell. Thompson was also absent from the trial of Huggins, when the jury brought in a special verdict.

[45] Quoted by Beattie, *Crime and the Courts*, pp. 457-8.

[46] Wild reached Newgate in February 1725 on a committal by Sir John Fryer and Sir Gerald Conyers, charged with "rescuing one Roger Johnson, a felon Convict, from a Constable who had him in Custody." However, the warrant of detainer prepared by Sir William Thomson shortly afterwards does not mention such an action among the myriad offences it lists; and when Wild appeared before Sir William at the Old Bailey this charge had been dropped. See Howson, *Thief-Taker*, pp. 235, 238-40.

[47] Henry Kelley, the principal witness at Wild's trial, deposed that he had gone "to see Mrs. Johnston, who then lived at the Prisoner's House: Her Husband brought me over from Ireland" (*The Proceedings on the King's Commission of the Peace, and Oyer and Terminer, and Gaol-Delivery of Newgate, held for the City of London, and County of Middlesex, at Justice-Hall, in the Old Baily* (May 1725), pp. 5-7.

[48] Newspaper regularly printed stories about attempted gaol-breaks, some successful, some not. In 1725 Mist's *Weekly Journal* several such cases: one reported on 4 September concerned twelve convicts scheduled for transportation, who "found an opportunity to cut the chain that fasten'd the main door on the common side of Newgate, and to make their escape, the lock and keys having been sent to be mended above ten days before; and if the lower door had not been immediately secured, many more would have escap'd, and had a gaol delivery their own way." Next year, Edward Burnworth, the youthful highwayman whose gang had many links with Wild, led a mass attempt to break out of the condemned hold at Newgate, but the plan was forestalled by the turnkeys; Burnworth had shot his way out of the New Prison in 1725. Burnworth was promptly fitted with "very ponderous irons" (see Read's *Weekly Journal*, 26 February, 19 March, 9 April 1726). In fact, Burnworth and his accomplices were being held awaiting trial at Surrey assizes, where they were convicted. One of this number, Emanuel Dickenson, had been acquitted of highway robbery as of "good Character" at the Old Bailey in 1722: Thompson was on the judicial panel at this session.

Such escapes continued after the *Opera* came out: in 1730 it was the turn of Moll Harvey, the most notorious female criminal of the day, to arrange a rescue from custody by a gang. Like Johnson, he fled first to Rotterdam. Recaptured on return to England, she escaped from the New Prison in male disguise. Then in 1731 six inmates hacked their way through the floor of their dungeon and got into the sewer below. Four managed to crawl through to Fleet Lane, but two either suffocated or drowned in the attempt (Babington, *English Bastille*, p. 116).

[49] In *The History of the Press-Yard* (1717), a Jacobite prisoner arriving at Newgate reports that "the Great Mr. *Pitt*. . .gave orders for furnishing me a Bed with clean Sheets, after I had pay'd the Woman that brought them to my Garret of a Chamber in the *Press Yard*. . .Five Shillings" (quoted in Gordon, *Old Bailey*, p. 103).

[50] See his bills for providing convicts as bonded laborers (*c.*1717) in Peter Wilson Coldham, *Emigrants in Chains: A Social History of Forced Emigration to the Americas of Felons, Destitute Children, Political and Religious Non-Conformists, Vagabonds, Beggars and other Undesirables, 1607-1776* (Baltimore: Genealogical Publishing Co., 1992), pp. 59-60. He charged £32.8.0 for 54 hand and feet irons, which recalls Lockit's comment on fetters, "We have them of all prices, from one guinea to ten" (*Beggar's Opera*, p. 80). It is noteworthy that the Transportation Act of 1718 (4 Geo. I, c.11) which gave Pitt some lucrative new opportunities was introduced by Sir William Thompson: see A. Roger Erdlich, *Bound for America: The Transportation of British Convicts to the Colonies 1718-1775* (Oxford: Clarendon Press, 1987), p. 17; and Beattie, *Policing and Punishment*, pp. 424-32.

[51] *Beggar's Opera*, pp. 88-9.

[52] Another illustration: in December 1724 a court order was issued by the Middlesex authorities requiring Pitt and "Bosenham Rews his Turnkey" to attend at Hick's Hall. This was in order to show why they "refused or wilfully avoided" to inform the justices of the peace that a prisoner in Newgate had formerly been in gaol there for a felony, and had returned illegally from transportation (quoted by Howson, *Thief-Taker*, p. 230). The criminal, Thomas Butler, was an associate of Wild, who shortly afterwards was allowed to go free in order to give evidence against him. On 7 April 1725 Butler "pleaded to his Majesty's most Gracious Pardon" at the Old Bailey. The court order was signed by Peter Walter, who had recently been appointed Clerk of the Peace for Middlesex. Walter was often aligned with Robert Walpole and Jonathan Wild: for this satiric triad, see Howard Erskine-Hill, *The Social Milieu of Alexander Pope: Lives, Example and the Poetic Response* (New Haven: Yale University Press, 1975), p. 256.

[53] *The History of the Press-Yard* (1717) gives this information: see Gordon, *Old Bailey*, p. 103. According to a work quoted in the same source (p. 89), the going rate had been £3,500 as far back as 1696. One pamphlet stated in 1708 that the keeper of Newgate "holds that place of great trust under the Queen, giving £8,000 security" (quoted by Babington, *English Bastille*, p. 73). In a spirited attack on the system, emphasizing the harsh treatment meted out to poor debtors, Thomas Baston deplored the fact that the keeper paid to get his position at Newgate (he names a sum of £3,500). He argues that as a consequence this made the place "an *Asylum*, or rather a Garrison for Thieves," who were let out "at certain Seasons" to carry out depredations on the public, after which they passed on their plunder to

"an Officer they have among them, call'd a Thief-Catcher." As a result the prison, "instead of being a Punishment, is a Sanctuary." See [Baston], *Thoughts on Trade, and a Publick Spirit* (2nd edn, 1728), pp. 206-07.

[54] Of course it was not unknown in real life for women to assist prisoners to escape. For example, one of Wild's gang, the highwayman William Burridge, got away from the New Prison in 1722 with another man after a female acquaintance brought in a rope and tools.

[55] *Beggar's Opera*, pp. 96, 104, 113, 118.

[56] *Beggar's Opera*, p. 120.

[57] *Newgate Calendar*, 3: 42.

[58] Denning, "Beggars and Thieves," p. 100.

CHAPTER ELEVEN

POPE AND THE MAYPOLE IN THE STRAND

London's famous maypole in the Strand was finally taken down in 1718. It had been erected in 1661 to replace one smashed up by the Puritans during the Civil War. A well known reference to the latest of these events is found in a Byronic couplet by James Bramston: "What's not destroy'd by Times devouring Hand? / Where's *Troy*, and where's the *May-Pole* in the *Strand*?"[1] However, there had been at least two earlier allusions. One occurs in a source contemporary with the action, the *Weekly Journal* of Nathaniel Mist. The other comes a decade later in the second book of Pope's *Dunciad*. Both draw attention to the fact that the first of the new "Queen Anne" churches had been erected on the site where the maypole had stood. In order to understand what Mist and Pope were saying, we need to explore some of the context. This relates, first to the political history of maypoles; second to the fortunes of this particular pole in the Strand, including its curious after-life; and thirdly to the church of St Mary le Strand, designed by James Gibbs, which rose on this site.

I

For many decades the maypole had been associated by puritans with the pagan ceremonies of ungodly England, and the Elizabethan moralist Philip Stubbes had famously described it as a "stinkyng idoll." Throughout the seventeenth century, some of the main culture wars had raged over the conflict in attitudes held by the parliamentarians and their opponents to "maying" and other festive customs. A culminating action occurred when the Lords and Commons passed an ordinance banning maypoles in April 1644, describing them as "a heathenish vanity, generally abused to superstition and wickedness." On the other hand the Stuarts had always identified themselves with such folk rituals as maying games: both James I, in 1617, and Charles I, in 1633, had issued a so-called "Book of Sports" (1633) which specifically licensed "May Games, Whitsun Ales, Morris Dances, and the setting up of Maypoles."[2] Indeed the King's obstinate loyalty to these ordinances had been one of the issues on which his opponents worked to erode his authority in 1640. For the royalists, David Underdown has remarked, the maypole was "a natural symbol."[3]

At the same time, the monarchy needed to steer clear of the less salubrious side of Maytime fun and games. In France, as Mikhail Bakhtin pointed out, this date was marked by "popular-festive" customs over which Misrule presided: on May Day eve, prostitutes enjoyed special privileges and even authority.[4] (Pope's reference to the "saints" of Drury Lane obscurely recalls this.) London itself had to endure the notorious excesses of May Fair, held annually for two weeks from 1 May: it took place from 1686 on a site to the north of Piccadilly. Almost every year the courts had to deal with riots and tumults there, and not infrequently killings. In 1702 the Queen issued a proclamation after riots involving "rude soldiers" and "lewd women," offering a pardon and £50 reward to anyone giving information about a murder at the fair. Seven years later the Grand Jury of Westminster issued a presentment regarding the "vice and debauchery" witnessed at this time, and recommending that the example of the City of London be followed in banning stage plays and gaming at Bartholomew Fair. A proclamation to this effect was issued on 30 April, and the fair collapsed almost overnight.[5] Luckily the maypole in the Strand was geographically remote enough to avoid identification with the fair and its disorders.

After the change of dynasty in 1714, even the innocent maying had to stop. A latter-day John Selden might have said, "there never was a merry world since the [young people] left dancing."[6] For the dancers and their garlands suggested at some imaginative level a golden world, pre-Reformation in its absorption of pagan rites, pre-Calvinist in its unashamed sexuality, and pre-Hanoverian in its self-consciously "English" roots. "I wish you a merry May-day, and a thousand more," wrote Jonathan Swift to Stella on 1 May 1712, a greeting as old-fashioned as it was genial (*Journal to Stella*, 1: 258). It was not a formula the Dean used in later years.

II

The fall of the maypole marked the end of a traditional way of life. Since the sixteenth century, the original pole had stood in the Strand, on what had been a "green" near the junction with Catherine Street, until its demolition in 1644. The replacement was set up on 14 April 1661 with elaborate ceremony, as a prelude to the upcoming coronation festivities. The King's brother, the Duke of York, commanded twelve seamen who brought the massive log up from the Thames in two sections, with the help of cranes, blocks and tackles. It was carried up the Strand amid cheering crowds. At the site it took four hours to raise the pole in a gesture of monarchical potency. The two parts were joined with iron bands, and a richly gilded "vane" on the top surmounted by the royal crest. Garlands were placed to the accompaniment of trumpets and drums, and flowers strewn in the familiar fashion - for this was also a cult of Flora. In what was doubtless a staged display, morris dancers, "fairly deckt," cavorted around the pole. Among bystanders, the young were said to rejoice while the old reflected that golden days had come again. "A week later Charles rode past on his way to be crowned," as Ronald Hutton writes, "and [the maypole] formed a focal point for the celebrations of the people of London and Westminster that summer and for fifty years after."[7]

The new maypole was destined to enjoy its garlands for a brief period, like the dynasty for which it stood. In 1672, according to John Aubrey, a gale had sheared off the topmost third. By 1713, as the Stuarts' hold on the throne wobbled to a close, it had further decayed and was broken almost to ground level. A new pole was to be set up, a short distance to west along the Strand.[8] Its erection would take place "against the Thanksgiving Day," that is at the grand ceremony already mentioned, marking the successful outcome of the peace in July 1713. On this occasion the children of the charity school sang loyal hymns lauding the Queen, and offered the vain hope that the Lord would grant her his "saving health." In fact Anne felt too sick to attend the service, although the hymns were still performed: within thirteen months, she was dead. If a replacement maypole was actually put in place, it lacked stability. At the time it came down in 1718, John Strype reports, only the bottom twenty feet were still standing: but, if not upright, the timber must have been in a state to be reused. Allegedly it was made of cedar and 134 feet long. In any case, this was not a site of historic interest on which the Whig regime intended to place a preservation order.

This brings us to the bizarre fate of the famous pole. At the end of 1717 or the start of 1718, it was bought by Sir Isaac Newton. Accordingly a few weeks later workmen lugged the pole off on an oversize carriage, and placed it in the park of Lord Castlemaine - a rich and dependable Whig - at Wanstead, Essex, where a showy mansion by Colen Campbell was then under construction. So it came into the hands of the rector, Rev. James Pound, and entered into its final role as the prop to a telescope. This was the largest in Europe at this date, with a focal length of 123 feet: according to some reports, it had been presented to the Royal Society by a French gentleman, "M. Hugon." Newton knew James Pound, FRS (1669-

1724), who had achieved renown as an astronomical observer. In addition, Pound was the uncle of James Bradley, soon to become Savilian Professor at Oxford and later Astronomer-Royal, who took over the observatory after Pound's death. By 1719 Pound was reporting to the Royal Society observations he had made on the so-called "Hugenian" (*sic*) telescope.[9] In any case, an obvious reason to remove the maypole had arisen, as the adjoining ground was now occupied by St Mary le Strand, one of the new Queen Anne churches. It is this linkage of maypole and church on which both Mist and later Pope capitalize.

III

On 8 March 1718 the *Weekly Journal* carried a poem entitled "The Welsh Hero." These obscure lines refer to the fact that on St David's Day, a week earlier, "wags" had put up a puppet figure of the poet laureate, Nathaniel Rowe. Neither Rowe nor any of the chief figures involved in the maypole affair was Welsh: the demonstration seems to have been politically motivated, since Rowe was a Whig favored by the Hanoverian court, and Mist's was a staunchly Jacobite organ. The relevant lines run:

> Just where, to the Fame
> Of GREAT ANNA's bright Name
> Stands a Church, bless'd be her Intention,
> There (famous of old)
> Is a May-pole now sold,
> As a damn'd Anti-Christian Invention.

This passage may have been in Pope's head when he was writing the earliest version of *The Dunciad*, published in 1728. He describes the dunces assembling for their "heroic" games under the eye of Dulness:

> In that wide space the Goddess took her stand
> Where the tall May-pole once o'erlook'd the *Strand*;
> But now (so *ANNE* and Piety ordain)
> A Church collects the saints of *Drury-lane*.

(2: 11-14)

Despite the obvious differences in meter and linguistic texture, the parallels are very close. Each poet locates the action with a "where" clause; each mentions the Queen by her name; each refers to her pious "intention" ordaining the new London churches; and each evokes the former position of the maypole ("of old," "once"). There is also an inadvertent chime of *stands/ stand*. By 1728 the removal to Wanstead was stale news, and whatever topical incident had implicated Rowe (who died later in the same year) was long off the political screen. Nevertheless most of the central ideas are the same in both cases.[10]

The location was certainly a "wide space," forming a broad portion of one of the broadest streets in London.[11] On this stretch of the road a grandstand, more than six hundred feet in length, was erected when the procession for a service of thanksgiving for the peace made its way along the Strand in July 1713: four thousand charity school children, fitted out in new clothes, were placed here to sing hymns blessing the Queen.[12] Three years earlier, it was here that some of Dr Sacheverell's supporters congregated when the High Church preacher rode triumphantly past in his coach to his trial at Westminster Hall. This was also one of the sites where the pillory was set up, and that demanded a space large enough for a good-sized crowd to gather, armed with suitable missiles. On the south side of the street throughout the 1720s the notorious Edmund Curll had his shop, "over against the Catherine Street in the Strand" (see also Chapter 6). Thus Pope locates the action on the doorstep of a principal actor in this section of *The Dunciad* - the very one who will lead off the first of the duncely games, in a passage of the poem which immediately follows the lines quoted.[13] As for the prostitutes from Drury Lane, they were of course no invention of the poet's. As we saw in Chapter 5, his friend John Gay had mentioned them in *Trivia* (1716), referring to "The Harlots' guileful Paths, who nightly stand, / Where *Katherine-street* descends into the Strand" (3: 261-2). The rhyme words are identical, and so is the topographical siting.[14]

The original plans for St Mary's had not called for a steeple. Rather, there was to be a small campanile together with a separate column, to be surmounted by the Queen's statue, with inscriptions on the base to commemorate the building of the fifty churches.[15] This column would be set up opposite the entrance to Somerset House, about a hundred feet down the street from the church, close to where the old maypole stood. James Gibbs, a surveyor to the churches along with Nicholas Hawksmoor, duly submitted a design for a Corinthian pillar, rising to 250 feet in height, and fifteen feet in diameter. When Anne died in August 1714, the scheme for the church was revised, with a steeple restored to the plans, and Gibbs proposed that a statue should be placed on the western portico instead.[16] This too was abandoned, and when St Mary's was built in the years 1714-1724, a flaming urn was substituted.[17] Most of the structure had been completed by 1717, with the steeple completed on 7 September in that year, and this made it highly inappropriate for a maypole to remain in place only a few yards west of the new church. The Commissioners had formerly ordered "bricks and stones" to be removed, and "all rubbish to be cleared as soon as possible."[18] For the new body of overseers, this term probably included the maypole.

The analogue with Mist's paper, previously overlooked, helps to reveal that there is more animus in Pope's lines than has been suspected. The poet has the dunces congregate at a spot from which the maypole, a symbol of the old pre-Commonwealth England, had been removed. As an acquaintance of Gibbs, who was a fellow Catholic, the poet must have known that the Queen's effigy had also been banished from this site. The published designs for the church show the statue of the Queen positioned above the west porch; but as we have just seen this was replaced by an urn. Gibbs had prepared a wooden model of the original pillar, which was presented to Anne, and was approved by the Commissioners for the Fifty New Churches. After the Queen's death, work on the column was halted, although the foundation had been laid. In the following year, a new commission came into office, with the members' sympathies closer to the newly knighted John Vanbrugh than to Gibbs. It soon became evident that "their business was only to provide places of worship and not monuments to the late Queen."[19] They did not stop at abandoning the revised plan for a statue on the portico: Gibbs himself was dismissed as surveyor to the new churches in January 1716.[20] When the main part of the building was completed in 1717, the Hanoverian arms were set on a pediment above the nave. One of the so-called "Queen Anne churches" had been accommodated to a new reality.

Confirmation that Pope was aware of these matters comes from another piece of evidence which has been overlooked until now. None of the biographers of Dr John Arbuthnot, the poet's close friend, reveal his close connection with the building of St Mary's. It now appears that Arbuthnot served on the Commission for the New Churches from 1713 to 1715. Moreover, he wrote a letter of recommendation for Gibbs to act a surveyor.[21] Still more to the point, the minutes disclose that he was appointed to a committee on 1 July 1714 to consider a model of the proposed pillar, and was then allotted an even more important role: "to wait upon the Queen with plan of ground near the Maypole in the Strand and design of a pillar to be erected there." A week later, the response came through: "Bishop of Hereford [Philip Bisse] reported that he and Arbuthnot had waited upon the Queen, who thought pillar intended to be erected in the Strand ought to be 50 ft from the church and not directly against the Somerset House Gate." A distinguished committee, including Sir Christopher Wren and Edmond Halley as well as Arbuthnot, was formed to "direct laying of the pillar's foundation."[22] On 21 July directions were given for the foundation for the pillar to be laid. The Queen died on 1

August; and with immodest haste this last direction was rescinded juts four days later: "No more stone to be laid in for foundation of the pillar intended to be erected in the Strand until further notice."[23] When the new Commission took charge in January 1716, Arbuthnot lost his place along with Bisse, Bingley and several other politically unacceptable figures - not to mention the departure of James Gibbs.

Pope must have learnt at least something of these transactions from Gibbs, who was shortly to start work remodeling the villa at Twickenham to which the poet moved around May 1719.[24] But his contacts with Arbuthnot were so intimate throughout this entire period that he must have known all about the church, the pillar and the statue. Most likely he knew what was going on from 1713, when he and Arbuthnot came together in the Scriblerus Club. Nor was the connection with the maypole remotely arcane: the Commissioners generally referred to St Mary's in early planning stages as the "new church near the Maypole in the Strand." Significantly, the Queen "required to be informed about her interest in site before she could answer [the Commissioners'] request about the Maypole in the Strand." Only then did she agree.[25]

IV

For Nathaniel Mist, an unreconstructed Jacobite, this marked an epoch in political history: Gibbs's column had been levelled before it could even be set up. Under Anne not much had been heard of May Day. She had "studiously avoided any ostentatious celebration of the great - but increasingly partisan - political anniversaries of Augustan England," such as Restoration Day, that is 29 May. Instead, the Queen "chose to emphasize those anniversaries personal to her and her rule."[26] This may have had something to do with the distinctly sober and un-merry tone of the court in her reign. But it was partly because she needed to separate herself from the excesses of her father, and wished to keep a distance from any perceived connection with her half-brother the Pretender. Even in moments of national rejoicing, when the bonfires and the bells were in full evidence, the maypole was not brought out.[27] Undoubtedly 1 May 1707 was chosen as the day on which Great Britain came into existence, through the union of English and Scottish parliaments, because it was felt to be an auspicious date, but this had nothing to do with maypoles, milkmaids or games. After 1715, as the Jacobite cause began to appropriate a number of the icons of Merry England, an increasing tendency emerged to transfer May Day ceremonies to Restoration Day.[28] Yet, if this had become a moveable feast, the maypole remained a symbol of allegiance to the exiled

family. When George II came to the throne in 1727, Mist's *Journal* printed
a story that maypoles had been set up and decorated in the traditional way
at various towns in the Midlands. Troops were sent down to discourage
this show of "loyalty."[29]

Pope, too, knew that the Stuarts' pole had fallen. Anne's church-
building scheme, a Tory initiative dreamt up by Francis Atterbury and the
lower house of convocation in 1711, had been hijacked by the new Whig
Commissioners, who disapproved of the dazzling ornamentation Gibbs
introduced into St Mary's. Gibbs had been ousted, partly because of "St
Mary's blatantly Roman associations"[30]: he was replaced by John James,
more tractable and safely protestant. In 1713 Pope had looked forward to
the creation of a brilliant new London skyline under Anne's beneficent
care for the church:

> Behold! *Augusta*'s glitt'ring Spires increase,
> And Temples rise, the beauteous Works of Peace.[31]

There would be less glitter from now on. At the same time, the old
Queen's "piety" had given way to the pallid Lutheran faith of George I,
the cheerful agnosticism of his son, and the skeptical permissiveness of his
daughter-in-law Caroline. By expunging the maypole, the puritans may
have hoped to assail High Church idolatry, and further the rule of the true
saints. But the saints who show up for the service are prostitutes from
Drury Lane, and the only game in town is the sports day of the dunces,
held on the very site where morris-men had once led the royalist dance.
Part of the joke is that Pope selects a site associated with the symbol of the
innocent frolicking of milkmaids and traditional rural sports. At this place
the dunces meet, ready to vie in contests of gross physicality, which enlist
the urban squalor that surrounds them (for example, diving in the foul
recesses of a London sewer).

Proverbially, May was the merry month. It thus served the ideological
purposes of one who sought to present himself as the merry monarch - and
one who by chance had been born and had undergone his miraculous
"preservation" on what became Oak Apple Day, 29 May. This was also
the month in which Charles had come back to claim his kingdom.[32] More
generally, an attempt was being made to reinstate an ancient symbolic
order. The May games had celebrated the return of spring, and so in 1718
Jacobites could dream that their exiled leader might also enjoy his own
once more.[33] According to the social anthropologist N.J.G. Pounds, "The
Lenten, Mayday and harvest rituals became shells which people could fill
with whatever meaning and significance they chose."[34] Supporters of the
Stuarts chose to invest the rites of May Day with a meaning emblematic of

the new "restoration" they desired. In this light, they would look at the decay of the maypole in the Strand, and its unceremonious sale to shore up a piece of scientific equipment, as the work of more than time's devouring hand. The flowers were gone along with the pole, and January had supplanted May. Equally, the dismissal of Anne's effigy from the same location must have seemed like banishing the Queen of the May - for in the mentality of the Jacobites, however unrealistically, she operated as her uncle's successor in this regard. Once the new regime had dismantled this totemic maypole, the Stuart revels were all but over.

Notes

[1] *The Art of Politicks* (London, 1729), lines 71-2. Bramston's work was issued by Lawton Gilliver, the young publisher whom Pope had recently set up in business.

[2] See David Cressy, *Bonfires and Bells: National Memory and the Protestant Calendar in Elizabethan and Stuart England* (Berkeley: University of California Press, 1989), pp. 22-3.

[3] David Underdown, *Revel, Riot, and Rebellion: Popular Politics and Culture in England, 1603-1660* (Oxford: Clarendon Press, 1985), p. 177.

[4] Mikhail Bakhtin, *Rabelais and his World*, tr. Hélène Iswolsky (Bloomington: Indiana University Press, 1984), pp. 257-63.

[5] *Post Man*, 15 January 1709; 3 May 1709.

[6] *Table Talk: being the Discourses of John Selden, Esq;* (London: White, 1786), p. 101. Selden of course wrote "fairies' rather than "young people."

[7] Ronald Hutton, *The Rise and Fall of Merry England: The Ritual Year 1400-1700* (Oxford: Oxford University Press, 1996), pp. 225-6.

[8] See Joseph Addison, *The Guardian* (Lexington: University of Kentucky Press, 1982), ed. J.C. Stephens, p. 696.

[9] *Philosophical Transactions*, 30 (1717-19): 900-02. By this Pound meant a telescope using the lens developed by Christian Huygens, and it seems likely that the putative donor "M. Hugon" is a ghost figure.

[10] No evidence exists that Pope ever wrote for the *Journal*, which indeed was publishing attacks on him by Lewis Theobald in 1728, all duly noted by the poet and mentioned in *The Dunciad* (for example at 1: 194). It is clear that Pope was a regular reader of the paper.

[11] In *The Dunciad Variorum* of 1729 and subsequently, the opening four words are replaced by "Amid that Area wide." The noun here has the older sense of "a vacant piece of ground, a level space not built over or otherwise occupied" (*OED*, "area," 1).

[12] For contemporary descriptions of the ceremony, see John Ashton, *Social Life in the Age of Queen Anne* (London: Chatto & Windus, 1883), pp. 15-17; and Addison, *The Guardian*, p. 695. The scene was depicted in an engraving by George Vertue, which has often been reproduced.

[13] This episode also contains a joking reference (2: 64) to a more respectable bookseller, Jacob Tonson senior. Since October 1710 Tonson's business had also been established "at Shakespear's Head over-against Catherine-street in the Strand." This stood adjoining Duchy Lane on the south side of the Strand: see Hugh Phillips, *Mid-Georgian London: A Topographical and Social Survey of Central and Western London about 1750* (London: Collins, 1964), pp. 167-8. Tonson was elected as a vestryman for St Mary's in 1724: see *The Commissions for Building Fifty New Churches: The Minutes Books 1711-27, A Calendar*, ed. M.H. Port (London: London Record Society, 1986), p. 112.

[14] Many cases at the Old Bailey refer to assignations and robberies involving prostitutes in Catherine Street. For a criminal case on 26 May 1748 mentioning a bawdy house, the Queen's Arms, "in Catherine-street, in the Strand," see *The Proceedings at the Sessions of Peace* [Old Bailey sessions records] (1748), p. 194.

[15] For the order on 29 April 1714, see *Commissions*, ed. Port, p. 32.

[16] Before the Queen's death, it had been intended that a statue should be set up in a "conspicuous" position at every one of the new churches. Designs were to be furnished by Grinling Gibbons and Francis Bird. In fact Bird, a Catholic, was known personally to Pope, and carved the memorial to his parents at Twickenham. Subsequently John Talman arranged for a Florentine sculptor to carve a bronze statue, for which the later Commissioners were blatantly unwilling to pay. See *Commissions*, ed. Port, pp. 21, 82-5.

[17] See Terry Friedman, *James Gibbs* (New Haven: Yale University Press, 1984), 40-53. Friedman does not mention the maypole.

[18] *Commissions*, ed. Port, p. 37. We are told that "the citizen walking in the Strand found his path encumbered by huge blocks of stone, as St Mary's progressed towards completion": see E. Beresford Chancellor, *The XVIIIth Century in London: An Account of its Social Life and Arts* (London: Batsford, n.d.), p. 192.

[19] Kerry Downes, *Sir John Vanbrugh: A Biography* (New York: St Martin's, 1987), p. 364.

[20] At the time he gained the church commission, Gibbs's main patron had been the Jacobite Earl of Mar, soon to lead the doomed Rising in 1715-16. Gibbs was himself suspect as a Catholic and a Scot. In addition he had become surveyor thanks to the influence of Robert Harley, Earl of Oxford, who had been released from the Tower in 1717 but was still in official disgrace.

[21] This was presented to the Commissioners by Christopher Wren junior, Chief Clerk of the Board of Works on 13 August 1713, along with one from Lord Bingley: *Commissions*, ed. Port, pp. 24-5. Gibbs had a strong supporter in Robert Benson (1676-1731), chancellor of the exchequer in the Harley administration, who had been created Baron Bingley in July 1713. He was a noted architectural patron, and created the house and gardens at Bramham Park, Yorkshire.

[22] *Commissions*, ed. Port, p. 36. The other members were Bisse, Bingley, Sir John Vanbrugh, Thomas Archer (the other architect involved in the project), and Christopher Wren junior.

[23] *Commissions*, ed. Port, pp. 35-6. Friedman does not mention Arbuthnot's role.

[24] The most reliable account is Anthony Beckles Willson, *Mr Pope & Others* (Twickenham, priv. ptd, 1996), pp. 68-84. Pope knew several members of the

Commission: Bingley subscribed to the *Iliad*, and entered his name for ten copies of the *Odyssey*.

[25] *Commissions*, ed. Port, pp. 17-20. The parish clerk in his description of the church stated that "it is situate on the easterly side of the *Strand*, where the *Maypole* stood formerly." See *New Remarks of London* (London: E. Midwinter, 1732), p. 286.

[26] R.O. Bucholz, *The Augustan Court: Queen Anne and the Decline of Court Culture* (Stanford: Stanford University Press, 1993), p. 213.

[27] Nicholas Rogers notes that the Pretender's birthday bought "very occasionally, as at Ipswich in 1713, a maypole revel amid fireworks and 'other Demonstrations of Joy'." See Rogers, *Crowds, Culture, and Politics in Georgian Britain* (Oxford: Clarendon Press, 1998), p. 27. Such events seem to have been rare indeed.

[28] R.W. Malcolmson, *Popular Recreations in English Society 1700-1850* (Cambridge: Cambridge University Press, 1973), pp. 29-30. Malcolmson suggests that this process began "after the Restoration," but the evidence suggests it accelerated markedly after 1714, when it became a gesture of opposition to the ruling dynasty.

[29] Quoted by Paul Kléber Monod, *Jacobitism and the English People 1688-1788* (Cambridge: Cambridge University Press, 1989), p. 203.

[30] Friedman, *Gibbs*, p. 51. Note also, "[A] Stop should be put to the extravagt. Carvings within" (surveyors' report, 1718, quoted by Friedman, p. 50).

[31] *Windsor-Forest*, lines 377-8 (*TE* 1: 187).

[32] "Charles II was the May king, born in that month, and re-born to his kingdom, ever to be associated with maypoles and the revelling good fellowship of his father's and grandfather's Book of Sports" (Cressy, *Bonfires and Bells*, p. 171).

[33] As early as 1660, a puritan clergyman had claimed that, of two maypoles set up in his parish, one was stolen, and the other "given by a profest papist." Quoted by Joseph Strutt, *The Sports and Pastimes of the People of England* (London: Tegg, 1850), p. lvii.

[34] N.J.G. Pounds, *The Culture of the English People: Iron Age to the Industrial Revolution* (Cambridge: Cambridge University Press, 1994), p. 417.

CHAPTER TWELVE

APOCALYPSE THEN:
POPE AND THE PROPHETS OF DULNESS

Like other dissidents, heretics have enjoyed a good scholarly press in recent years.[1] Yet perhaps heresy needs to be reconceptualized, or at least to be reconfigured historically. We have not always seen the extent to which heresies have existed in competition -- unavoidably so since heretics are often self-defined, and what is heretical is contested by those within unorthodox faiths as well as by those outside them. One preliminary step is to abandon the model, derived from Michel Foucault, of a crushing power system which creates categories of the marginal and rigidly defines the normal. This model relates chiefly to the highly centralized absolutist states of Europe, particularly France, with their organized and bureaucratically effective church— though it may also fit New England to some extent. It applies much less well in other places, notably in the case of early modern Britain. Over the course of the long eighteenth century, the British experience involved an almost permanently contested orthodoxy, in matters of political, constitutional, and religious opinion, and so heterodoxies were constantly shifting in their nature and influence. This is not to say that minorities could never be left out or oppressed, especially on economic grounds. But the foundations of the state had been regularly challenged and indeed overturned under the Commonwealth, with the supreme symbol of monarchical power executed. They were put in doubt once more in 1688-89, when the king was ejected, and yet again during the early Hanoverian years, when a constant threat of another seismic disturbance hung over the nation. Meanwhile, the established Church found itself beset by rivals, whether dissenters, or freethinkers, and often had to extend a more or less reluctant tolerance towards such groups.

In this context, the situation of Alexander Pope is both exceptional and exemplary. He often took the role of an outsider. As a Catholic, he belonged to an effectively proscribed religion. As an invalid he was subjected to extensive somatic prejudice. As a freemason, who knew a good deal about Rosicrucianism and other branches of "ancient knowledge," he was potentially suspect to those who upheld the ruling orthodoxies. And even if he was not an active Jacobite (though that is a questionable assumption), he emphatically held deep sympathy with the dying spirit of the Stuart cause as the dynasty faded into the margins of history. It is true that he was not anxious to persecute dissenters: indeed, he showed himself tolerant and sympathetic towards individual members of the nonconformist church. Yet he did take a stand, with his friend Swift, against enthusiasm and the practices of extremist protestant sects. (There can be debate, of course, as to what is extreme in this context and what constitutes a sect.) All this is the more notable because Pope was clearly in other respects a true insider, who attain a relation of almost camaraderie with dukes and duchesses, and who had access even to Robert Walpole. If he had chosen to compromise his personal values and sense of vocation as a writer, he could actually have operated legitimately as court poet and spokesman for the establishment—almost the last author of genuinely high talent of whom this might be said.

We can clarify the attitudes Pope displayed if we look at *The Dunciad* in the context of three historical phenomena. They might variously be described as ideologies, discursive practices, or modes of heretical testimony. Each promised in its own way a new world. Each offered a promise of a transformed Britain, allegedly based on some kind of ancient prophecy, and each defined an orthodoxy from which Pope would be specifically excluded. The first was the continuing strain of militant protestantism which the experience of defeat in the Civil War had quite failed to destroy. Second was the brief incursion of a group of French prophets into the nation, during the reign of Queen Anne. The third was the unceasing barrage of anti-catholic propaganda distributed to a section of the population by the almanacs of men like John Partridge—a figure with a longer-lasting relevance to Pope than to a more familiar adversary, Swift.

I

Recent scholarship has conclusively demonstrated that Spenser, Milton, and Marvell have important roots in chiliastic and apocalyptic beliefs of their age.[2] Milton and Marvell died in the decade before Pope was born, and thus they were no more remote to the poet as he formed his identity as an author than T.S. Eliot would be to a young writer in his or her thirties today. Pope's own father (a Catholic convert) was born in 1646, his mother in 1643; even his nurse, the other key member of the household during his childhood, came into the world as early as 1648. The poet's most important mentor, Sir William Trumbull, was old enough to retain boyhood memories of the Civil War, since he first saw light in 1639. Young Alexander's early development and reading were supervised by men of this generation: among his other mentors at this stage were William Wycherley, born about 1640, and Thomas Betterton, born about 1635. The sponsors of his *Pastorals* included another dramatist, Thomas Southerne (b. 1659); the Marquess of Dorchester (b. *c*.1665); Lord Wharton (b. 1648); Sir Samuel Garth (b. 1661); Sir Henry Sheeres (b. *ante* 1650); and the Duke of Buckingham (b. 1648). All members of this group were at least fifteen years senior to Pope. His new literary friends around 1712-13 included Swift (b. 1667), Arbuthnot (b. 1667) and Prior (b. 1664). The dedicatee of *Windsor-Forest* was George Granville (also b. 1667), himself a seventeenth-century poet. Most, though not all, of this group came from a royalist background: it is just as significant that they belonged to a cohort who had lived through the contentious aftermath of the political and religious struggles of the mid-seventeenth century. This is of course to leave aside Pope's poetic father John Dryden (b. 1631), another writer whose concerns with what might be called political astrology are now fully documented. Such men laid down the intellectual and literary coordinates within which Pope came to maturity.

Two ways of approaching the millenarian tradition immediately suggest themselves. We might consider the growth in the sixteenth and seventeenth centuries of an aggressive protestant ideology, at the heart of which lay an eschatological account of the way in which the English became the chosen people, preordained to accomplish God's purposes, and the instrument of a providence which would extirpate the Antichrist. According to this doctrine, the Reformation had enabled England to lead the process by which the domination of Rome would be brought down. Even the Civil War had been no more than a stage on this, as Christ came to liquidate the king. It was, Keith Thomas observes, "the execution of Charles I which left the way open for King Jesus."[3] The coalition that fought the war was soon to split up, and at the radical end many of the individual sects were to have a short effective life. But the Ranters and Levellers and Diggers lived on as their ideas were expressed both in politics and in religious dissent.

The Ranters in particular have received sympathetic treatment from Clement Hawes, but it is the Fifth Monarchy Men who are the most immediately to our purpose.[4] Scholars usually trace their beliefs back to Nebuchadnezzar's dream in the second book of Daniel as this was interpreted by the prophet. The four biblical empires (sometimes identified with Persia, Media, Egypt and Greece, with Rome often substituted for

Media) were to be succeeded by the fifth kingdom of God. The crucial instrument of these communities of belief was the use of prophecy. This comes out not just directly in the astrological tradition as developed by men like William Lilly, but also in the practice of searching out ancient myths that would sustain the ideology of overthrowing the monarch. As Lilly declared, "All or most of our ancient English, Welsh and Saxon prophecies had relation to Charles Stuart, late King of England, unto his reign, his actions, life and death, and unto the now present times wherein we live, and unto no other preceding kings or times whatsoever."[5] Thus millennial hopes regularly led to a politics of social revolution: what may not be so obvious is that they could just as easily be subsumed in a theology of anti-popery. The innumerable appeals to Geoffrey of Monmouth and other stores of Celtic mythology (Pope, we recall, was well versed in this author),[6] the tendentious usc of Arthurian legend and tile endless repetition of the deeds of Merlin as satirized by Swift in his poem "The Windsor Prophecy" (1711) - all testify to this hunger for mythical precedents. Indeed, what Thomas calls "the appeal to the past" is among the most vital constituents of tile millenarian mindset.[7] It is surely no accident that *The Dunciad* is littered with references to a similar obsession on the part of the dunces—deriving from their conviction that they are accomplishing the *predestined* conquest of the nation: "This, this is he, foretold by ancient rhymes: / Th' Augustus born to bring Saturnian times" (3: 319-20).

However, a more general context of apocalyptic and chiliastic thinking exists. For instance, the Jewish tradition had enshrined a very old idea concerning the great sabbath, according to which the world would last six thousand years and then enter a final age of one thousand years, when the people would come into their own. Etymologically, *shabbath* means simply "rest" in Hebrew: Pope's joke is to literalize this, so that when the godly people of *The Dunciad* take over, it will be one long snooze: "See Christians, Jews, one heavy sabbath keep, / And all the western world believe and sleep" (3: 99-100). This plot is acted out most obviously in the climactic scene following the great .yawn of Dulness in the last book. Before *Oblomov,* before *Bouvard et Pécuchet,* before *Ulysses,* Pope had intuited that the ultimate step into dehumanized chaos might be taken out of a kind of sloth, more than from greed, tyranny, or ambition.

As most people know, all sorts of millennial sects flourished in medieval Europe. Some were actually stigmatized by the church as heresies *eo nomine*. An example is the movement of the Free Spirit, a frequent victim of the Inquisition, and one whose adepts rejected all rules and restraints in the name of spiritual emancipation. This sect has been

studied along with other groups of holy beggars and mystical apostles by
Norman Cohn, in his classic (the more so, because controversial) book *The
Pursuit of the Millennium*. Some of these movements had a profound
social impact, and some led to major uprisings, including the Peasants'
Revolt—an event still recalled in the almanacs of Pope's day. Most of the
groups envisaged a new order which would emerge from some great
cataclysmic event, such as the appearance of the New Jerusalem following
upon the Day of Wrath. With such a future to be expected, it was natural
to place great emphasis on portents and prodigies, especially those
expressed in the heavenly language of comets and meteors.[8]

Almost every one of these features is echoed in *The Dunciad*. The
social unrest, the abandonment of restraint, the prophecies, thee portents
are all present. As for the rejection of all restraint, this is palpably a goal of
the dunces throughout, but it can be seen at its most explicit in a passage
from the third book:

> All crowd, who foremost shall be damn'd to Fame.
> Some strain in rhyme; the Muses, on their racks,
> Scream like the winding of ten thousand jacks:
> Some free from rhyme or reason, rule or check,
> Break Priscian's head, and Pegasus's neck;
> Down, down they larum, with impetuous whirl,
> The Pindars, and the Miltons of a Curl.

(3: 158-64)

However, the similarities between millenarian activity and duncely
activism can easily be occluded, because we have tended to concentrate on
the classical mythology underlying the poem, whether it be the first book
of the *Metamorphoses* or Virgil's eclogue to Pollio. In fact, there were
other versions of the golden age, neo-platonized or translated into
alchemic terms, which intervened between Ovid and Pope, as we need to
recall in reading lines such as those which invoke "a new Saturnian age of
Lead" (1: 28). In addition, the phrase had acquired a specifically political
usage, available to royalists as well as republicans. When Pope writes of
"*Albion's* Golden Days" (*Windsor-Forest*, 424), he may be remembering
the Golden Day which Catholics had imagined more than a century earlier,
and which would see Elizabeth brought down and the monasteries
restored. For the most part such applications to the myth by royalists
tended to be narrowly concerned with the restoration of a particular
dynasty: ostensibly at any rate, they did not incorporate a long-term
theology of rebirth as did the radical versions — though it is possible that

a wider politics was obfuscated or mystified in conservative treatment of the golden age.

A compelling section of Norman Cohn's book deals with the prophetic background to the Crusades. Even before Urban II urged the ranks of Christendom to regain the Holy Land, at the end of the eleventh century, hordes of common people were gathering to implement this programme, under the leadership of inspired *prophetae* like Peter the Hermit. For the common people, the Crusade was "an armed and militant pilgrimage, the greatest and most sublime of pilgrimages."[9] It was through the teachings of such mystics that so many became convinced that they were destined to share in the overthrow of the Antichrist, as the long-anticipated hero known as the Last Emperor led his forces to Jerusalem. The theme of *The Dunciad*, of course, lies in the effort of Dulness to restore her "old Empire" (1: 17). In the augmented four-book version, Cibber is bizarrely cast as the heaven-born leader, fated to revive this "good old Cause" (1: 165), and presented to tile people as their savior: "And the hoarse nation croak'd, 'God save King Log!'" (1: 330). At the same time, the "Chosen" among his followers behave as the elect always do, self-righteously confident of their mission to eradicate other groups, whether Moslem, Jewish, or Catholic. Just as the medieval hordes set out on their mission to massacre the ungodly, so the modern dunces rolling through the city in a "black troop" (2: 360) embark on their own pogrom to eliminate the negative: "How keen the war, if Dulness draw the sword!" (3: 120). Behind all their insights ("barb'rous civil war," 3: 176) and their orgiastic practices, the Dunces cling on to their crusade to "MAKE ONE MIGHTY DUNCIAD OF THE LAND" (4: 604). In the action of the poem, a conventional epic property—the vision of a prophecy to be fulfilled—is linked to messianic ambitions: Dulness repossesses "her ancient right" (1: 11) as she persuades her puppet Cibber and the rest of her followers to clothe her in glory:

> And see, my son! the hour is on its way,
> That lifts our Goddess to imperial sway;
> This fav'rite Isle, long sever'd from her reign,
> Dove-like, she gathers to her wings again.
> No' look thro' Fate! behold the scene she draws!
> What aids, what armies to assert her cause!
>
> (3: 123-9)

One famous episode, above all, seems to fit the anti-milleniary purposes of *The Dunciad* most squarely. This occurs with the "messianic reign of John of Leyden," as Cohn describes it—that is, the uprising by Anabaptists who seized the city of Münster in 1534, and set up a kingdom of Zion, which enforced a nakedly communist regime as well as a system of polygamy.[10] The movement was led by a tailor of twenty-five, Jan Bockelson, who named himself king of Israel and the chief of his fifteen wives Divara. We have positive proof that the Scriblerians were well aware of Jack of Leiden, as he was generally known by this date. He is present as a fanatic in the "Digression on Madness" in *A Tale of a Tub*, where one of Jack's nicknames in the allegorical narrative is "Dutch Jack."[11] Moreover, at the start of the *Memoirs of Martinus Scriblerus*, we learn that the home of the hero's father, Cornelius Scriblerus, is Münster, and this same Cornelius is a devotee of every bogus arcane craft. It is worth reminding ourselves that Pope was busy preparing the *Memoirs* for their first appearance in print among his collected works in 1741, at a juncture when he was also completing the four-book version of *The Dunciad*.[12]

The occupation of Münster lasted little more than a year before the city was besieged and taken by the bishop of the diocese. Jack himself underwent torture and death in public. Nevertheless, the entire episode, culminating in atrocities on both sides, took a strong hold on the European historical imagination. It is hard to read any account of the events, such as the graphic description by Cohn, without being constantly reminded of *The Dunciad*. For example, the Anabaptists declared that the unlearned were chosen by God to redeem the world, with the result that "when they sacked the cathedral they took particular delight in defiling, tearing up and burning the books and manuscripts of its old library."[13] All books save the Bible were banned—the dunces do not make even this exception. The episode anticipates *Fahrenheit 451*, but it resembles in much closer detail Settle's inspired vision of the triumph of Dulness, based on the destruction of the wisdom of centuries: "And one bright blaze turns Learning into air" (3: 78).

Jack was solemnly anointed and proclaimed king of the New Jerusalem; this is pretty well exactly what happens in the first book of Pope's poem, with Cibber substituting as monarch and the empire of Dulness equated with Jerusalem. Equally revelatory is Cohn's description of the magnificently dressed Jack on his throne among his suite of courtiers: "In the market place a throne was erected; draped with cloth of gold it towered above the surrounding benches which were allotted to the royal councillors and the preachers. Sometimes the king would come there to sit in judgement or to witness the proclamation of new ordinances. Heralded by a fanfare, he would arrive on horseback, wearing his crown and carrying his sceptre." There followed "a long line of ministers, courtiers and servants."[14] All this is faithfully replicated in *The Dunciad*, with its picture of Cibber resplendent "High on a gorgeous seat" and surrounded by his peers (2: 1-12). The queen promptly proclaims "by herald Hawkers" the games to follow (2:18), and the later part of the poem supplies the approach of courtiers at a royal levee. Furthermore, we are told that preachers identified Bockelson as none other than the Messiah foretold by the prophets in the Old Testament. This blasphemous thought is never far from the surface in *The Dunciad*, first because Pope replays with parodic force lines from his own *Messiah*, but mainly because the language of the millenarians hovers over the diction of the poem.

Jack was said to be strikingly handsome and endowed with "an irresistible eloquence." From his youth, he had delighted in writing and acting plays: as Cohn says, at Münster he was able "to shape real life into a play, with himself as its hero." When the siege took effect, he devised more fantastic entertainments to distract the populace: "On one occasion the starving population was summoned to take part in three days of dancing, racing and athletics [again, precisely the plot of Book 2] . . . Dramatic performances were staged in the cathedral: an obscene parody of the Mass, a social morality based on the story of Dives and Lazarus."[15] It needs no emphasis that the actual Colley Cibber was actor, playwright, and theatrical impresario, or that these occupations are central to the role Pope allots to Cibber in the poem, as the showman of state fit to rule over Walpole's England. He is also in a technical sense the "hero" of the epic, with his perverse suitability for the office set out in a lengthy segment of the preliminaries; and his self-regarding vanity expresses the narcissism of power. Like other messianic leaders, Cibber bases his authority on personal glamour and unlimited confidence rather than solid achievement. He resembles the "amoral supermen" studied by Cohn, with their easy routes to self-deification: "What then remains? Ourself. Still, still remain / Cibberian forehead, and Cibberian brain" (2: 217-18).

It would be impossible to sustain the claim that Cibber *is* Jack of Leiden, or that *The Dunciad* constitutes a direct replay of the terrors of Münster. Instead, Pope's vision of Duncehood reinscribes actual heresy, as some saw it, on the republicans and extreme radicals of his day. The Scriblerians, like other conservative thinkers, feared the element of social disruption that such prophets inspired, with their charismatic egocentricity and innocence. Beyond this, Pope cannot have failed to observe that the millennial creeds nearly always involved a pollution of hallowed rites, as with the obscene parody of the mass at Münster. It is scarcely a coincidence that Jack began with a sort of ethnic cleansing: all Roman Catholics and Lutherans who remained in the town were compelled to go through a ceremony of rebaptism. It became a capital offence to be unbaptized. The others were driven out as godless. This was done in the name of achieving a community of true believers, the children of God. In Jack's world the new age was to be "the age of vengeance and triumph of the Saints."[16] Pope could not have heard such phrases without trembling, in the awareness that there were homebred "saints" who thirsted for revenge and whose triumph would mean suppression of the old faith. Whether it was Bockelson running naked through the streets of Münster in a state of mystical ecstasy or the Dunces claiming the West End of London for their own savage rituals, the result would be the same—true piety would be mocked, reason abjured, and vengeance taken against the ancient bastions of civilization. It sounds like a melodramatic view of the world to us, but then we are not beleaguered Catholics surrounded by a lurid anti-papist rhetoric, put about by those whose recent ancestors had suffered humiliation and contempt alter the failure of their own constitutional experiment.

II

If, as a young man, Pope had wanted a real-life demonstration of enthusiasm at work, he had before his eyes the amazing descent of the so-called French prophets in London from 1706. This has been the subject of an excellent book by Hillel Schwartz, whose account provides some necessary analytic insight into a series of events striking enough in their narrative interest. The complex background to this sudden eruption of religious feeling can be briefly summarized here. Its story began with a Protestant rising in the Cevennes following the revocation of the Edict of Nantes in 1685. At first the Huguenots envisioned their delivery in 1689, and after that hope failed they looked to a new judgment day in 1700. When this equally declined to materialize, the movement pressed on regardless, and the *inspirés* toured the country to bring the breath of the divine spirit to their persecuted co-religionists. A full-blown revolt was mounted by the Camisards in the summer of 1702. The royal troops proved unable to crush this rising for two whole years, a period which witnessed a violent series of ambushes and atrocities. In December 1702, for example, more than two hundred churches in the Cévennes were burnt down. Inevitably, the authorities responded with equal savagery. Then, in 1706, three of the prophets arrived in London, to proclaim the Second Coming, and received a warm welcome from the descendants of those millennial groups (notably the Philadelphians, under the direction of Jane Lead) that had flourished in England in the 1690s. Gradually their appeal widened, even among Anglicans: they proved able to attract a large number of women followers in particular, under the leadership of an Englishman of genteel origins named John Lacy.[17]

For the next two years, the prophets were the talk of the town. Swift mentioned them in the Bickerstaff papers, as well as slipping in allusion to them in his attack on the displaced lord treasurer, Godolphin (see Chapter 1, above). Mary Astell wrote a condemnatory pamphlet. There can be no doubt that Pope was well aware of their activities, for the group prompted a somewhat paranoid reference in a letter from his elderly friend Wycherley in late 1707:

> For Agitation is now the word, because they work out their Damnation here, with fear, and trembling, as the Quakers did formerly; and they are seised, with a Spiritual Ague; which turns to such a Feaver, in their Brains, that they are hot-headed to the degree of Fanatical Prophecy; and so great a Faith, that 'tis said, they believe themselves what they say; and pretend to working Miracles also.
>
> (Pope *Corr*, 1: 35)

Everything here could be paralleled in the numerous alarmist pamphlets that greeted the arrival of the French devotees. What may strike us most is the assimilation of this group into a tradition of inspired prophecy, reaching back—significantly—to the inception of the Quaker movement just half a century before. Pope made no direct response in his extant correspondence, but he continued to joke about prophets, as he would for the remainder of his life. At the height of the affair, on 30 October 1707, his close adviser Sir William Trumbull received news of the doings of John Lacy—a sign of how anxious the conservative heartland of the nation was growing by this time.[18] Distant as the events were by 1728, still more by 1742, he poet must have kept stored up in his mind when he came to write *The Dunciad* a recollection of this briefly celebrated episode of "Fanatical Prophecy."

One small circumstance provides a piquant addition. The most interesting of the three prophets who came to trial in England was Nicolas Fatio de Duillier (1664-1753), a notable Swiss astronomer and physicist, and friend of both Isaac Newton and David Gregory. In addition, he had served as tutor to the Earl of Arran, brother of the great Duke of Ormond, and this led the duke to take steps to ensure that the three men were treated with a measure of lenity after their conviction. Arran was a Catholic, a Jacobite, a subscriber to the *Iliad*, and a neighbour of Pope's sister and brother-in-law in Windsor Forest whom Pope would visit in years to come. Here was another possible reminder of the French Protestants.

Ultimately, three of the Camisard devotees were put on trial and sentenced to the pillory in December 1707 for their "wicked and counterfeit prophecies." They stood on the scaffold at Charing Cross, and the populace duly pelted them with mud and stones. Not surprisingly, this made martyrs of them, a necessary prelude as they saw it to the coming of the New Jerusalem. A more serious reversal occurred when one much-heralded miracle, involving the raising of the dead Thomas Emes, a follower of the prophets, failed to materialize. On schedule, the event would have taken place in May 1708 at Bunhill Fields—an area associated with Milton, Bunyan, and Defoe. Swift was one of those to note the failure of this resurrection with satisfaction: a reference also appears in Defoe's *Review*.[19] For a few more years the cult continued to win some adherents, but it gradually faded into obscurity, and by 1715 it was effectively finished as a popular movement.

The prophecies of the group, with its pervading ethos of cataclysm, had taken a familiar form: "The Trumpet is ready to sound. Fire, Lightning and Thunderbolts are prepared for thine Enemies." A day of vengeance was foretold: pestilential fogs and mists would sweep away the inhabitants of London "like a Plague," just what the "cloud-compelling Queen" of Dulness (1: 79) brings to the capital.[20] There would be many portents such as comets and eclipses, anticipating the Scriblerian satires against men like William Whiston in years to come (see Chapter 3), and pointing towards the cosmic upheavals of *The Dunciad.* Remarkably, the *inspirés* prophesied while asleep, an accomplishment to be envied by the inhabitants of Dultown:"Hence, from the straw where Bedlam's Prophet nods, / He hears loud Oracles, and talks with Gods" (3: 7-8). There are further odd contiguities: Lacy rented a building in tile Barbican to serve as an officially licensed meeting-place for the French prophets, and it remained the centre of their operations throughout their stay: hostile observers termed it their "Shop of *Inspiration.*"[21] Likewise the dunces met in the very same quarter of the city, and before that, in the chief literary model of Pope's poem, Dryden had described Shadwell's imperial residence at the start of *Mac Flecknoe:* "An ancient fabrick . . . / There stood of yore, and *Barbican* it hight." The prophets, it emerges, hung out just down the road from Grub Street.

Here then was a concrete historical case that attracted the attention of Pope and his friends. It was a recrudescence of the kind of popular prophetic movement that had been so visible in England during the seventeenth century and about which Pope's elders perhaps muttered warnings to the young boy. It could be enlisted by the poet to align millenarian causes with virulent anti-Catholicism and with social upheaval. Nothing quite like this had erupted in the intervening years up to the composition of *The Dunciad*. Schwartz remarks on the various forms anti-Catholicism took in the early eighteenth century, which could be shared by "all levels of English society."[22] He also cites a playbill for an opera performed at Bartholomew Fair during Anne's reign, with a spectacular apocalyptic finale of the very kind that Pope satirizes in the third book of his poem (3: 253-72). Again we find Dives along with Herod as a personification of the cruelty, tyranny, and pomp of the papist church. In such a climate, the proclamation of doom towards Catholicism uttered by the prophets could count on a sympathetic hearing from a large segment of the population. If Alexander Pope did not immediately feel his heart turn cold, he was astonishingly resilient.

We need not recite here all the evidence which scholars have assembled to show that Pope as a young man was deeply scarred by the treatment he and his family received at the hands of authority. Born to Catholic converts at the very moment when papists were least popular, forced into a kind of internal exile by the recusancy laws, driven out again after the Hanoverian accession from his paternal home in Windsor Forest (which remained a lost domain in his imagination ever after), required officially to declare his allegiance to the new regime, not to mention taxed in a discriminatory way—such a life experience could scarcely leave him unaffected.[23] In 1715 his friends and relatives were implicated in the Old Pretender's rebellion: many of those who subscribed to the *Iliad* translation of that year found themselves banished, stripped of their estates, or sent to the Tower—one of their number, the Earl of Derwentwater, actually went to the block. (The Earl was also, as contemporaries defined these things, the brother-in-law of Pope's close friend Martha Blount.) Without melodramatizing these events, there are moments when we might recall the pursuit of Edmund Campion a century and a half before. The Elizabethan recusant spent his last few days of freedom at Stonor, the family home of Pope's friend and neighbor Thomas Stonor. Of course, the Hanoverians would not succeed in repressing members of the Catholic faith quite as brutally as the Elizabethans had done—but that may be because they lacked such effective means of repression.

III

For certain, plenty of respectable ways existed to foment anti-papist feeling in Pope's lifetime. Beyond any of these, one discursive site contained a more durable and pervasive strain of hostile feeling. This was the domain of the almanac, a branch of literature that has received much more attention in recent years in the wake of Bernard Capp's valuable survey, hut which still tends to be unduly neglected in attempts to understand the *mentalité* of early modern Britain. That Pope was aware of the almanac literature proves very little — every sentient being was familiar with these ubiquitous organs of popular expression.

Even before he met Pope, of course, Swift had involved himself with John Partridge, in the Bickerstaff papers of 1708-9. As for Pope, his own most famous reference occurs at the end of *The Rape of the Lock,* when Belinda's lock is carried up to the heavens as a new astral phenomenon for the soothsayers to interpret:

> This *Partridge* soon shall view in cloudless Skies,
> When next he looks thro' *Galilæo*'s Eyes;
> And hence th' Egregious Wizard shall foredoom
> The Fate of *Louis,* and the Fall of *Rome.*

(5: 137-40)

Partridge was by no means the only protestant astrologer to foretell the death of Louis XIV or to herald the destruction of the Roman Catholic Church. At the very time of Pope's birth, the almanacs had joined in decoding the victory of William III over James II as a sign that the new king would act as "umpire" of Europe, by "destroying the pope and his champion, Louis XIV.[24] But Partridge was notorious for the virulence with which he pursued this theme: he had fled abroad at the accession of James, and when the Revolution came in 1689 he gave an "astrological guarantee" that the change was permanent. It happens that *The Rape of the Lock* supplies further evidence that Pope was fully cognizant of the astrological calendar, especially the bad or "dismal" days, to which Ariel refers in canto 1 and Belinda in canto 4.

We have received an impression of Partridge as a hapless, well meaning man who unluckily found himself embroiled with Swift. In truth he was well able to look after himself. He spent decades fomenting religious and political warfare, and he had traded blows with all the leading astrologers, notably John Gadbury. While exiled in Holland, he had revealed that according to the stars James II might be dead by October 1688, which was a remarkably good guess as far as the king's political survival was concerned. If the wind had not turned in the wrong direction, William's expeditionary force would have set out before the end of that month: it actually made its first abortive attempt on October 30, and then set sail on its successful campaign on November 10. Until this time, Partridge had been firmly republican in his views, asserting that "a

commonwealth's the thing that kingdoms want.'' Opposing almanac
writers accused him of being involved with the Duke of Monmouth and
the Rye House Plot to kill the king.[25] It is true in any case that prophecy
had always been linked with conspiracy and rebellion: long before,
Thomas Nashe had declared that "all malcontents intending any invasion
against their prince and country run headlong to [the astrologer's]
oracle."[26] Even those who disbelieved in astrology reprinted Partridge's
works on the Revolution for their political and propagandistic value.
Throughout the seventeenth century, Protestant eschatology as represented
in the almanacs had interpreted events (both topical and historical) as
predicting the fall of Rome: William Lilly had said this about the Plague
of 1665 and the Great Fire of London a year later. Totally characteristic, in
an almost banal way, is the bill of fare offered by the *Protestant Almanack
for the Year 1684,* which promises readers an account of "The Bloody
Aspects, Fatal Oppositions, Diabolical Conjunctures, Inhuman Revolutions,
and Pernicious Designs of the *Papacy,* against the Lord's Anointed," as
well as "Popish Gulleries and Fopperies," aimed at deluding the common
people.

Most almanacs also ran a chronology of leading events in British
history, which must have constituted the major source of information for
many humble people. The *Protestant Almanack* lists these in terms of the
time gap since a given event: thus, Martin Luther wrote against the Pope
168 years ago. The final entries relate to "Our deliverance from Popery by
Queen *Elizabeth,*" then "The horrid design of the Gun-Powder Plot,"
followed by "The Burning of the City of *London"* (no need to allot
explicit blame), and "Our miraculous Deliverance from Popery, by K.
William." We shall find it hard to recover in our mind the insidious effect
of such messages on the literate population, repeated as the onslaught was
every single year. In book 3 of *The Dunciad,* the prophetic vision of Settle
concerns the destruction of imperial Rome; but it is impossible to doubt
that Pope is encoding a message simultaneously about the fall of Rome, in
the sense that Lilly used it, or as it appears in *The Rape of the Lock.* Settle,
we may recall, was most celebrated "For writing Pamphlets, and for
roasting Popes" (3: 284). Besides, it was in predicting the *destruction* of
cities and empires that Lilly's specialty had lain.[27] Like Cibber, in the
demented vision of Settle, astrologers were for Pope "born to see what
none can see awake" (3: 43).

On one occasion in 1702, the journalistic prophets were able to detect a
propitious sign as Saturn and Jupiter came into conjunction:

> It remained an article of faith in the almanacs that the pope was Antichrist,
> and that his fall was at hand. Many compilers offered a glorious

millenarian future. Moore drew on the Sybilline oracles, the prophecy of the Northern lion, and Nostradamus. He envisaged a messianic English conqueror sweeping through Europe to destroy the pope and Turk, and recall the Jews. . . . Partridge in 1702 spoke of a millennium due to dawn in the following year and to reach perfection in 1778; his definition of the Antichrist widened generously to embrace almost all "priests of all persuasions". . . Tanner anticipated a glorious age of sabbatism, Kendal, a "peaceable and happy time," Salmon looked for a messianic *Pax Britannica.*[28]

Several details here recall *The Dunciad,* for example the moment when Cibber is led on his visit to the Elysian shades by "a slip-shod Sibyl" (3: 15), or the triumphant progress of barbarism through Europe, culminating in the "conqu'ring tribes" of Mahomet: "See Christians, Jews, one heavy sabbath keep, / And all the western world believe and sleep (3: 99-100). More generally, the poem enacts the success of Dulness in erasing the world of learning as this is accomplished through tyranny, inundations of barbarians, and superstition (see Pope's note to 3: 67). This last phase shows ''Rome, the Mistress of Arts, described in her degeneracy," quickly to be followed by Britain, "the scene of the action of the poem." In fact, the text of the poem at this point draws on Bayle's *Dictionary* to show the medieval popes as presiding over a superstitious process of converting pagan symbols into Christian artifacts: "Till Peter's Keys some christen'd Jove adorn" (3: 101). Notoriously Pope had written in the *Essay on Criticism* that "the *Monks* finish'd what the *Goths* begun" (692). He accepted the conventional view of his time that the election of Leo X in 1513 instituted a great revival in the arts and marked the end of an obscurantist and backward-looking papacy.

With the defeat of Stuart hopes on the accession of George I, the Whig astrologers knew their moment of triumph. As Capp tells us, Partridge made 1 August, when the king acceded, "a red-letter day of thanksgiving for deliverance from 'popery, French slavery and English traitors'." During the reign of Anne, almanacs like those of Partridge and Francis Moore had kept up a barrage against the French and Jacobitism linked to a general attack on the Catholic faith: Partridge's had long contained a section called "The Protestant Remembrancer," which held up Catholic beliefs and practices to ridicule. The editor warned that the Old Pretender was nothing but "a pupil of Jesuits, and tool of Rome." His elevation to the throne would mean that the Church reclaimed all the valuable lands that had been confiscated in the Reformation. More crucially still, Capp reminds us that "anti-popery was linked, almost inevitably with millenarian excitement."[29] Indeed it could be argued that millenarian zeal survived in the eighteenth century (as it did, to some extent) largely through the preservation of its hopes in the enduring discourse of almanacs.

A few almanacs still remained that took the opposing stance. From the 1690s George Parker had kept up a campaign against the "Villany" of Partridge in *Mercurius Anglicanus; or, the English Mercury,* but this ran out of steam in the new century. For Pope, the most significant of the remaining Tory organs was probably the *Oxford Almanack* which clung on to the dream of a Stuart restoration longer than most. In the later years of Anne, this publication featured an annual cover design presenting an allegorical version of Jacobite politics. These designs provided an iconographic basis for *Windsor-Forest,* with its symbolism of a beneficent Stuart rule protecting the grateful nation.[30] But for the most part the astrological field was left to the victors, whose triumphalist copy reached almost every segment of society. As scholars including Patrick Curry have shown, a stubborn core of astrological belief persisted in the mind of individuals such as Pope's acquaintance William Stukeley.[31] The predictions of William Whiston - a frequent butt of the Scriblerians, as we saw in Chapter 3 - joined those of Nostradamus in the almanac-makers' repertory of unlikely and ambiguous prophecies. To quote Capp once more:

> The fall of Rome and the Turk were still at hand, and the descent of the New Jerusalem must surely follow. In the 1750s the editor of Moore cited the great earthquake at Lisbon as marking the fall of Antichrist (for the city had been inhabited by "most bigoted" papists), and mentioned a triumphant piece of Whig theology, by which the Young Pretender, Charles Edward, was unveiled as the little horn of the beast of Daniel.[32]

As it turned out, Pope died a year too soon to witness the rebellion of the Young Pretender, but the rising led by Charles Edward's father a generation earlier had provoked equally virulent claims and equally implausible applications to the prophetic books of the Old Testament.[33]

Not that almanacs provided the only source where Pope could have found lurid accounts by soothsayers of the course of English history. The Cheshire prophecies of Robert Nixon were supposed to date from the reign of Edward IV, although Nixon himself lived in the early seventeenth century. They foretold the destruction of popery and were interpreted in 1714 as a sign of the triumph of protestantism after the arrival of the Hanoverian regime. The prophecy went through innumerable printings right into the nineteenth century: five came out by the end of 1715, and a few months before Pope died in 1744 the so-called "thirteenth" edition appeared. The rising of 1745 brought the tally up to twenty editions. Many of these reprints carried the name of Edmund Curll as publisher; the introduction and main text (containing a life of Nixon) were the work of John Oldmixon. Both author and publisher, of course, were lifelong adversaries of Pope, and both played a prominent role in the second book of *The Dunciad.* It can hardly be maintained that the poet had missed his targets or that there was no basis for his attack on popular millenary writing as this genre merged with routine anti-Catholic propaganda.

IV

Saints' days have a fixed term, but the calendar of heresy is one of moveable feasts, if only because the identity of heretics changes across time and space. To that extent, any historical interpretation of this phenomenon must involve a theory of relativity, to take account of the differing perspectives of participants and observers. It would be going too far to say that all heresy is a product of social construction. We might instance the mass suicide at Jonestown of 900 people, including 240 children, which the cult leader Jim Jones enforced in 1978. This offended the principles of almost every known religious group active around any part of the world in the past three millennia. Consequently, the action could reasonably be described as heretical in an absolute sense, that is, repugnant to the creed of every community outside this single cult. But in general the logic of this subject could essentially be conjugated, "I am a free spirit, you are a dissident, he/she is a heretic." Heterodox belief challenges the borders of normality as well as the definition of what is acceptable.

To some in the early eighteenth century, Roman Catholics themselves served as the arch-heretics. They too could be seen as looking towards a millennial future, especially when they espoused the cause of the Pretender. However, conservative theology (whether Catholic or High Anglican) drew the line at some things associated with messianic groups— for example, it was blasphemous to identify any other figure than Christ with the messiah. While Pope and his allies were willing to adopt the classical trope of the Golden Age for modern political purposes, as the entire design of *Windsor-Forest* confirms, they stopped short of any attempt to secularize the Second Coming. The monarchy was the instrument of restoration and rebirth, but did not ultimately constitute the spiritual essence of that process: individual monarchs were godlike only in a metaphoric and honorific sense. Nor, unlike Dryden, did Pope enlist astrological lore to vindicate his imaginative projection of a transformed and reinvigorated nation.[34]

One famous passage in the poem relates immediately to the issues discussed here. It shows that the future dreamed by the dunces resembles very closely the world turned upside down, as imagined by millenarian writers:

> Thence a new world to Nature's laws unknown,
> Breaks out refulgent, with a heav'n its own:
> Another Cynthia her new journey runs,
> And other planets circle other suns.
> The forests dance, the rivers upward rise,
> Whales sport in woods, and dolphins in the skies;
> And last, to give the whole creation grace,
> Lo! one vast Egg produces human race.

                                                      (3: 241-8)

Similarly, the tracts of the Ranters had proclaimed that high mountains would hide in the dust and the hills be levelled. This is perhaps a spiritual metaphor rather than a literal prophecy; but the belief that the Lord of Hosts would come as the great leveller and overturn the existing order was a more or less direct expression of political faith. Some Ranters, too, spoke of the "terrible" day of the Lord as appearing suddenly, leaving the believer intoxicated with happiness: "Whereupon being mad drunk, I so strangely spake, and acted I knew not what."[35]

What we have just seen indicates that Pope has a conscious rhetorical design: he figures his satiric victims as participants in a millenarian movement that is bent on destroying the great institutions of state in order to bring about the "new World" of Dulness. Some might be inclined to see this representation as a caricature of historical reality, with regard to these areas of belief. According to a scholar such as George Rudé, it is misleading to view crowds as the passive adherents of monstrous leaders along the lines in which Gustave Le Bon and Elias Canetti have variously depicted them.[36] Yet nobody could read Cohn's book without acknowledging that, historically, the messianic cults of medieval and early modern Europe did repeatedly exhibit just this pattern of charismatic Führer and a swarm of almost unthinking followers. Actually, *swarm* is not far from Pope's own word for it:

> None want a place, for all their Centre found,
> Hung to the Goddess, and coher'd around.
> Not closer, orb in orb, conglob'd are seen,
> The Buzzing Bees about their dusky Queen.

The gath'ring number, as it moves along,
Involves a vast involuntary throng,
Who gently drawn, and struggling less and less,
Roll in her Vortex, and her pow'r confess.

(4: 77-84)

The next couplet refers to "Not those alone who passive own her laws, /
But who, weak rebels, more advance her cause." This "motley mixture"
has already been anatomized earlier in the poem (2: 21): what produces a
more striking effect is the collapse of Dulness/Caroline into a queen bee,
regulating the lives of her dependent species as they instinctively attach
themselves to her person.

The plot of *The Dunciad* is such that any reading must appear over-
determined, since the action develops along so many parallel lines—
literary, mythological, political, and religious. Nevertheless, a cursory
examination of the argument to book 3 will show that Pope is seeking to
reattach visionary delusion to political troublemaking, disloyalty, and
cultural anomie. The new king of the dunces is laid to sleep in a temple, "a
position of marvellous virtue, which causes all the visions of wild
enthusiasts, projectors, politicians, inamorato's, castle-builders, chymists
and poets." He is carried on the wings of fancy to the banks of Lethe: here
he meets Settle, who takes him to "a *Mount of Vision*," from where he can
glimpse the past, present, and future triumphs of Dulness. Typically, the
scene blends allusions to the Bible (Moses on Mount Pisgah, in
Deuteronomy 3) and to Milton (Adam on the peak of a high mountain in
Paradie Lost, book 11). After witnessing the appearance of "miracles and
prodigies" that foretell the events of his reign to come, Cibber is shown
how Dulness will return all things to their original state of chaos. The
argument concludes with an assurance that the action of the poem is "but a
Type or Foretaste, giving a Glimpse or *Pisgah-sight* of the full glory of
Dulness."[37] It is safe to assume that this passage is the work of Scriblerus
or some other scholiast, who may be presumed to be on the side of the
Dunces and who greets this forecast of the future with every sign of
warmth. The great event announced at the start is an equivalent of the
great day of wrath, and it ushers in a kingdom of new saints, who turn out
to be the Dunces in this eschatology.

The evidence permits one further speculation at this point. Milton is
unquestionably present in the text as a source of allusion and analogy. We
have always known that the "Antichrist of wit" shares some of the
lineaments of Satan in *Paradise Lost,* and this has been all the more clear
since the appearance of Aubrey Williams's remarkable book on *The
Dunciad* in 1955.[38] The dreadful secret behind the poem may be that the

fierce campaign of Dulness could implicate Satan's creator, too. Pope loves his poetic father. Yet at the same time he fears Milton along with Cromwell among the ancestors of those who defined Catholicism as a heresy, rather than just the political threat it chiefly represented to the Elizabethans. If Christopher Hill has correctly described Milton's attitude to heresy and apostasy, then Pope can only have regarded his predecessor as theologically of the dunces' party.[39]

Today we are mostly on the side of the heresiarch, and perhaps that is for the good. Still, we need to remember that the blessed heretic of one man or woman may be another's oppressor. All three of the groups we have looked at had attributes in common—the medieval followers of Jack of Leiden, rampaging through Münster; the French prophets in London with their roots in violent Camisard protests; and the Protestant astrologers with their almanacs. Adherents of each sect considered themselves oppressed; each anticipated a great day of vengeance; all felt justified by their own inspiration and by mystical prophecies; and all made Catholicism a particular object of their fury. As *The Dunciad* reveals, the most marginal in society can find themselves targeted by cult and fringe groups who prove to be wholly intolerant when they achieve any sort of power—a lesson scarcely irrelevant to the course of twentieth-century history, even though that was a future into which neither the fictive Settle nor his creator could peer. With his life history as member of an embattled minority, Pope learned the lesson all too painfully: it is the dissidents whom dissidence often threatens.

Notes

[1] An earlier version of this essay was presented at a plenary session of the DeBartolo Conference at the University of South Florida in 1998. I am grateful to participants in informal discussion afterwards for suggestions and comments. The text followed is the four-book version of *The Dunciad* (1743), as reproduced in *TE* 5. References are by book and verse and, unless otherwise stated, refer to the "B" text.

[2] The most fully developed argument along these lines is that of Margarita Stocker, *Apocalyptic Marvell: The Second Coming in Seventeenth-Century Poetry* (Athens, OH: Ohio University Press, 1986). Stocker also provides (p. xii) a useful note on the terminology of the subject, distinguishing aptly between *millenarianism, chiliasm,* and *apocalyptic.* My use of these terms is broadly in line with that of Stocker.

[3] Keith Thomas, *Religion and the Decline of Magic* (Harmondsworth: Penguin 1978), p. 170. This seminal work is the most important general survey of the

historical issues underlying this essay, although I have also taken account of other scholars, including Christopher Hill and William M. Lamont.

[4] For the Ranters as pioneers of a "manic" mode of writing, see Clement Hawes, *Mania and Literary Style: The Rhetoric of Enthusiasm from the Ranters to Christopher Smart* (Cambridge: Cambridge University Press, 1996), pp 25-97. On the Fifth Monarchists, there is the more sober approach of B.S. Capp, *The Fifth Monarchy Men: A Study in Seventeenth-Century English Millenarianism* (London: Faber and Faber, 1972).

[5] Quoted by Thomas, *Religion,* pp. 488-9.

[6] See *TE* 1: 425.

[7] Thomas, *Religion,* pp. 459-514.

[8] Norman Cohn, *The Pursuit of the Millennium* (London: Oxford University Press, 1970), esp. pp. 19-36.

[9] Cohn, *Pursuit,* pp. 61-70: quotation from p. 63.

[10] Cohn, *Pursuit,* pp. 261-80.

[11] *A Tale of a Tub and Other Works,* ed. M. Walsh, *The Cambridge Edition of the Works of Jonathan Swift,* vol. 1 (Cambridge: Cambridge University Press, 2010), pp. 94, 109. Jack is also mentioned as one of the "late *Fanaticks* of Note" in "The Mechanical Operation of the Spirit," p. 185.

[12] See *Memoirs of Martinus Scriblerus,* pp. 63-5.

[13] Cohn, *Pursuit,* p. 267.

[14] Cohn, *Pursuit,* p. 273.

[15] Cohn, *Pursuit,* pp. 267-8, 278.

[16] Cohn, *Pursuit,* p. 274.

[17] This paragraph is based chiefly on Hillel Schwartz, *The French Prophets: The History of a Millenarian Group in Eighteenth-Century England* (Berkeley: University of California Press, 1980). The episode was first brought to general attention in modern times by James Sutherland, *Background for Queen Anne* (London: Methuen, 1939), pp. 36-74. On Jane Lead see also Paula McDowell, *The Women of Grub Street* (Oxford: Clarendon Press, 1998), pp. 167-79.

[18] Schwartz, *Prophets,* pp. 109-10.

[19] Schwartz, *Prophets,* p. 123.

[20] Schwartz, *Prophets,* pp. 75, 91.

[21] Schwartz, *Prophets,* p. 87.

[22] Schwartz, *Prophets,* p. 66.

[23] The best account of the loss of a paternal home is found in Paul Gabrinier, "The Papist's House, The Papist's Horse: Alexander Pope and the Removal from Binfield," in *Centennial Hauntings: Pope, Byron, and Eliot,* ed. C.C. Barfoot and T. D'Haen (Amsterdam: Rodopi, 1990), pp. 13-64. For the wider relevance of Pope's disabilities, see Mack, *Life,* passim.

[24] Bernard Capp, *English Almanacs 1500-1800: Astrology and the Popular Press* (Ithaca, NY: Cornell University Press, 1979), p. 178.

[25] Capp, *Almanacs,* p. 96.

[26] Quoted by Thomas, *Religion,* p. 407.

[27] The fullest modern treatment is Ann Geneva, *Astrology and the Seventeenth-Century Mind: William Lilly and the Language of the Stars* (Manchester: Manchester University Press, 1995).

[28] Capp, *Almanacs,* p. 252. For wider attitudes towards the millennium (e.g., regarding the conversion of the Jews), see Christopher Hill, *Antichrist in Seventeenth-Century England* (Oxford: Oxford University Press, 1971), p. 176.

[29] Capp, *Almanacs,* pp. 250-1.

[30] See Helen Mary Petter, *The Oxford Almanacks* (Oxford: Clarendon Press, 1974).

[31] See Patrick Curry, *Prophecy and Power: Astrology in Early Modern England* (Princeton: Princeton University Press, 1989).

[32] Capp, *Almanacs,* p. 252.

[33] In addition, Pope enjoyed playing with the formula "the Turk and Pope," sometimes with roguish self-reference: see his *Court Ballad* (1717), line 3, *TE* 6: 180.

[34] See Michael McKeon, *Politics and Poetry in Restoration England: The Case of Dryden's "Annus Mirabilis"* (Cambridge, MA: Harvard University Press, 1975).

[35] Quotations from Cohn, *Pursuit,* pp. 318-22.

[36] See for example George Rudé, *The Crowd in History* (New York: Wiley, 1964), as well as Rudé, *The Face of the Crowd: Studies in Revolution, Ideology, and Popular Protest,* ed. Harvey J. Kaye (Atlantic Highlands, NJ: Humanities Press International, 1988), p. 111. On the involvement of "fringe" religious groups in popular protest and insurrection, see Rudé's *Ideology and Popular Protest* (Chapel Hill, NC: University of North Carolina Press, 1995), esp. pp. 85-6 (on Ranters and Seekers).

[37] *TE* 5: 55-6. Here the slightly fuller 1729 text is quoted.

[38] Aubrey Williams, *Pope's Dunciad: A Study of its Meaning* (London: Methuen, 1955), pp. 131-58.

[39] See Christopher Hill, *Milton and the English Revolution* (London: Faber and Faber, 1979); as well as Hill, *Liberty against the Law: Some Seventeenth-Century Controversies* (London: Allen Lane, 1996), pp. 206-13.

CHAPTER THIRTEEN

THE DUNCIAD AND THE CITY OF LONDON

Alexander Pope had every reason to take note of the politics of the City of London. We may not think of him as primarily an urban writer, in the way of Ben Jonson, Baudelaire or T.S. Eliot. Yet Pope's origins lay in the London mercantile community and he kept up contacts with this group more than has been realised, even when resident in Berkshire or at Twickenham. Evidence of this fact is sprinkled through his poems and letters. His City friends included men like Slingsby Bethel, a prosperous African merchant who in the years immediately following Pope's death became warden of a livery company, alderman, sheriff and finally lord mayor.[1] A sign of the poet's continuing interest in London life can be found in his portraits of Sir Balaam and Sir John Cutler in the *Epistle to Bathurst*. However, the most telling literary exploitation of his commercial heritage occurs in *The Dunciad*.

Pope was born in the heart of the "square mile", during the same year that his father retired from his business as a linen merchant, 1688.[2] No evidence has come to light showing that the elder Pope served an apprenticeship or gained his freedom. Even if he did, as a converted Catholic, Alexander senior would have found great difficulty in swearing the oath of loyalty to the monarch, as freemen were required to do: within six months of the birth of the new son, William of Orange had landed at Torbay and within three more he had accepted the throne along with his wife Mary. By that time Mr Pope had given up trade, having made a sizeable fortune of around £10,000. He had run his export-import business from a narrow four-storey house at the foot of Plough Court, towards the eastern end of Lombard Street, long known as a hub of banking, close to where it meets Gracechurch Street. The area had been devastated in the Great Fire, and the Popes' plain but sturdy brick home must have dated from the period of reconstruction. It lay just a short walk from the newly rebuilt Royal Exchange, as well as from East India House, and not much further from the historic centre of municipal affairs, the Guildhall. In 1694-95 the newly founded Bank of England would open its doors first at Mercers' Hall and then at Grocers's Hall, off Poultry, both close to the

Exchange and a comfortable step from Plough Court. (Only in 1734 would the Bank acquire its more famous location in Threadneedle Street.) Further along Lombard Street to the west came the General Post Office, overseeing a significant sector of mercantile communications, and next door from 1691 Lloyd's coffee-shop, the home of the growing insurance industry. Across the road lay the entrance to Exchange Alley, which was to achieve a dubious fame as the epicentre of speculative activity at the time of the South Sea Bubble. Pope senior would not live to see that event or the erection of the new South Sea House in Threadneedle Street, though he would have known the old structure on this site. His son, an investor in the company, was undoubtedly familiar with both buildings. All in all, these institutions constituted the main locus of the Financial Revolution, a series of developments which dominated City life during the lifetime of Alexander Pope junior and which featured so prominently in his poetry.

It was in this house that young Alexander spent the first four or five years of his life – possibly even a little longer. The property stood in the small parish of St Edmund the King,[3] across the road from Plough Court, which Christopher Wren and Robert Hooke had rebuilt after the Fire. It belonged to Langbourn Ward, a narrow straggling area that extended from the eastern end of Fenchurch Street to the junction of Poultry and Cornhill – in very approximate modern terms, the stretch between the Bank and the Lloyd's Building. Like much of the inner city, the ward experienced several convulsions in this era, reflecting the nature of the divided society within its boundaries. The leading merchants and goldsmith-bankers mostly took a consistently pro-Whig position, while proportionately the smaller tradesmen and retailers harboured a stronger admixture of Tory sentiment. Matters came to a head at the aldermanic poll in 1712, when a fierce party clash led to uproar in the City's common council amid allegations of fraud and manipulation on behalf of the Whig Lord Mayor.[4] For much of Pope's lifetime the bigger battalions were able to have their way and the ward generally seems to have supported ministerial and court candidates against those allied with Tory and country interests.[5] The alderman so controversially elected in 1712 was Peter Delmé (d. 1728), a Levant merchant of Huguenots origins, and a director of the Bank, who would be knighted by George I as soon as he acceded to the throne – in short, a classic City plutocrat. Delmé became Lord Mayor in 1723, but not before a highly contentious election following a blocking manoeuvre by Tory councilmen in the previous year.[6] The newspapers were full of this episode and it would scarcely have escaped Pope.

I

Around 1692 the Popes moved out to Hammersmith, later to Binfield in Windsor Forest, and ultimately back to Chiswick. They never again lived within the historic confines of the City, as one of the earliest acts of parliament in the new reign (1 Wm. & M., c. 9) forbad anyone adjudged "a Popish Recusant Convict" to live within ten miles of London or Westminster. However, there are no grounds to assume that Pope forgot all about his first home or lost interest in the doings of his native city. Quite the contrary.

As often, Maynard Mack provides the most helpful pointer. He cites an excerpt from *The Dunciad Variorum* (1: 83-6) describing the installation of Sir George Thorold as Lord Mayor in 1720. We shall return to this passage, but Mack's remarks demand consideration at this juncture. He notes that the route taken by the minions of Queen Dulness in the poem "becomes a surreal rendering of the route by which the Lord Mayor and *his* minions journey on Lord Mayor's Day to pay their respects to the reigning monarch, and then return to the City." This much we behave understood since Aubrey Williams provided a classic reading of the plot of *The Dunciad* in 1955. However, Mack goes on to mention a manuscript version of the lines under review, suggesting that they may "point to residues of a more primitive response," reaching back into a child's mingled delight and terror at the sight of strange giant forms parading down the familiar streets.

The same scholar draws attention to another relevant issue. This has to do with a number of Pope-burning ceremonies of the 1670s and 1680s, before and after the Exclusion crisis, which were etched into Catholic memory for generations to come. He quotes a description of William II's return to the capital after the signing of the Peace of Ryswick in 1697. On this occasion the king was greeted not just by parliamentary officers and peers, but also by an elaborate retinue of City officials including marshals, aldermen, the recorder, sheriffs and many more. Their presence symbolises the crucial importance of London in affairs of the nation, a lesson which had become apparent in events during the later years of Charles II and the entire reign of his brother. Mack notes too that the most memorable figure of all for Pope in such assemblages may well have been the Lord Mayor, as he rode through the streets in his robes of rich fur and velvet.[7]

This commentary is, as we should expect, both aesthetically sensitive and psychologically shrewd. But more can be said. The single episode which may have impacted most deeply on the Pope family (although not

little Alexander, who was only sixteen months old) occurred at the Lord
Mayor's show of 1689. William's supporters determined to make this a
set-piece of unforgettable impact, and it was described at the time as
having outdone "all that has been seen before on the like occasion" – a
large claim, in view of the opulence of these affairs under the early
Stuarts. The show commemorated the installation of Sir Thomas
Pilkington, "perhaps the most acerbic of the Whig magistrates," and
spared little by way of expense or effort:

> [It] was celebrated by the Whigs as "London's Great Jubilee", a tribute to
> the Revolution and to the rescue of the City from oppression. The affair
> was rich with symbolism, studded with Whig talent, and most importantly,
> open to the people. . . .Participation was extended vicariously to the
> guildsmen, drawn up by company along the way, and to the people, who
> lined the streets and crowded the balconies. On his return from
> Westminster, the Lord Mayor officially reviewed four pageants presented
> in Cheapside and left standing until dark for the people's edification. An
> added attraction in 1689 was the stunning entrance of William and Mary in
> a cavalcade headed by the Earl of Monmouth.[8]

Three glosses are needed here. First, the title "Earl of Monmouth" had
only been recently bestowed: it covers the identity of a figure better known
as Charles Mordaunt, Earl of Peterborough (1658-1735), who had become
one of Pope's closest friends by the time of *The Dunciad*, and about whom
the poet told Joseph Spence a number of picturesque anecdotes. Second, it
is striking that in his draft version Pope imagined the menacing giants as
looming over Cheapside, where the pageants were staged in 1689 –
especially as he does not describe this section of the route in the published
poem. Third, we might stress the presence of the "guildsmen" in organized
blocks within the crowd lining the route, a testimony to the residual
strength of the livery companies in all official business within the City.
    This tradition of mounting the "triumphs of London" in the form of
allegorical carnival floats and pageants lapsed in the early eighteenth
century. The last known occasion was in 1702, when Elkanah Settle
contrived a show in the hopes of bringing back to life a festival said to be
"almost dropping into oblivion."[9] In fact one more pageant was devised
and fully choreographed in 1708, but for reasons to be explained the plan
fell through. However, the idea of reviving the tradition at least floated in
the head of Pope and in that of the incoming Lord Mayor as late as 1732.
On 24 August in that year Alderman John Barber wrote to Swift:

> The mayor's day is the 30th of October. . . .It would add very much to my
> felicity, if your health would permit you to come over in the spring, and

see a pageant of your own making. Had you been here now, I am persuaded you would have put me to an additional expense, by having a raree-shew (or pageant) as of old, on the lord-mayor's day. Mr. Pope and I were thinking of having a large machine carried through the city, with a printing press, author, publishers, hawkers, devils, &c., and a satirical poem printed and thrown out to the mob, in publick view, but not to give offence; but your absence spoils that design.

As David Woolley comments, citing Aubrey Williams' study of *The Dunciad*, "One recalls irresistably the *mise en scène* of Pope's great poem."[10] Barber, we shall see, was Pope's closest contact among the top political brass of the City. The point about the machines is that they express a *company* identity, for Barber was a Stationer; and municipal politics in the City always had much to do with the status of the livery companies. Equally, the progress of the Lord Mayor on his inaugural day was attended with the rites and symbols of the companies.[11] But the most significant aspect of the letter lies in its reminder of Pope's continuing absorption in the choreography of City pageants.

When *The Dunciad* first came out, John Barber had already been involved in the most recent show. Just after the accession of George II, the City fathers resolved to invite the entire royal family to the Lord Mayor's Day banquet. They also set up a small panel of alderman and common council members to seek permission from the King to erect his statue in the Royal Exchange and also portraits of George and Queen Caroline in the Guildhall – actions which would collectively bestow a symbolic blessing on commerce and civic pride. We may wonder what in what spirit three of the aldermen appointed – Barber, Humphrey Parsons and John Williams, strong Tories and probably Jacobites in every case – went about their task. All three men were also deputed to a larger committee to "take Care of the Entertainment" on the day itself. The show duly took place in its accustomed fashion, with the new Lord Mayor, Sir Edward Becher, a loyal acolyte of Robert Walpole, proceeding in the City barge to Westminster, "attended by the several Companies in their respective Barges."

Once their business was done there, the official party made their way back down the river to Blackfriars, and thence to the City. Although there were no pageants, the royal family watched the procession from a balcony overlooking Cheapside. At Guildhall the City fathers entertained the royal family with considerable state, after a greeting had been delivered in a speech by Sir William Thompson. He was Walpole's chief fixer in criminal matters, the man who decided whether individuals such as Jonathan Wild should live or die, and one who exerted great influence both in his parliamentary role and as recorder of the City of London. The feast was "very magnificent," and so it should have been, as it cost the civic authorities almost £5,000, with not far short of 300 dishes consumed at the royal table alone. (The table provided for the Lord Mayor and the aldermen got through only 130.) In its course the King proposed a toast to the health of Beechey, "and Prosperity to the City of *London,* and the Trade thereof." The Lord Mayor, aldermen and councilmen duly reciprocated.[12] Some of these goings-on seem to be recalled in *The Dunciad*, particularly during the scene in Book I when the new king of the dunces is installed, although Pope's major target is probably the coronation of George and Caroline, which had taken place less than three weeks before. Certainly the 315 dozens of bottles of wine, including champagne, burgundy, claret, malmsey, madeira, moselle, port, canary and hock, that went down the throats of the assembled guests at the Guildhall may have left them as stupefied as the dunces at the end of Book II.[13]

All the evidence indicates that Pope was in the throes of completing *The Dunciad* at this very moment. It would be extraordinary if a poem set on Lord Mayor's Day should contain no hint of the most recent celebration, especially as the ceremonial in 1727 was charged with unusual political import. Since the poem begins with the inauguration of a new leader of the dunces, it would have been difficult to suppress all recollection of this event, even if Pope had wished to do so. The accession of George and Caroline just four months before, their coronation even more lately, and the visit of the royal family to the Guildhall (something that only happened at the start of a reign in most cases) all gave the occasion a topical edge. But Pope had not suddenly become aware of this annual rite. He could have witnessed the carnival at first hand as a very small child: even if he did not, he obviously kept a close eye on its fortunes. This is made abundantly clear by the first note (1: 88) on Elkanah Settle, a key figure in *The Dunciad*, to be explored presently. The note provides an orderly and for the most part accurate chronology of events concerning the fortunes of the show. It does not suggest an author remote from his material or one who has had to carry out a great deal of "research." The information comes, as it were, from stock. A later note on Settle, at 3: 281, as well as some damaging thrusts in the text of the poem, will confirm this firmly based knowledge. In choosing the time and place of the action, consequently, Pope had not strayed far from his comfort zone. All he would have needed from Alderman Barber was, at the most, a piquant anecdote or two.

II

The Dunciad of 1729 does not wait long to address City affairs. Early in Pope describes the nerve-centre of Dulness, the "cave of Poverty and Poetry" (1: 32), which in the first version of the poem he placed at Rag Fair, annotated as "a place near the *Tower* of *London*, were old clothes are frippery are sold." The passage continues:

> This, the Great Mother dearer held than all
> The clubs of Quidnuncs, or her own *Guild-hall.*
>
> (1: 33-4)

It can scarcely be an accident that the Queen claims the Guildhall, the real-life nerve centre of London's local administration, as "her own." The cave houses the dubious activities of the print industry, represented by "Curl's chaste press and Lintot's rubric post," as well as "hymning Tyburn's elegiac lay" (1: 39-40). These two booksellers chosen to stand for "all the Grubstreet race" (1: 43) – the only individuals named – were both liverymen, Curll in the Cordwainers' company and Lintot in the Stationers'. Thus the poet shows Dulness as sponsor of a sort of corporate crime, leaving open the suggestion that the denizens of the cave are following in the wake of some bigger fish in the Guildhall.

The next verse paragraph alludes to four guardian virtues surrounding the Queen. As the Twickenham editor observes, such allegorical figures "were a recurring feature of the pageantry on a Lord Mayor's Day, and Pope may have associated them with the goddess for that reason" (*TE* 5: 65).[14] Only one example is cited, *London's Great Jubilee* – the festival held, as we have seen, in 1689 to greet William and Mary. It is true that the Coronation banquet in 1727 featured a similar array of allegories, but in this as in other respects the royal installation was mimicking the municipal ceremony. The last of the emblems is "poetic Justice, with her lifted scale; / Where in nice balance, truth with gold she weighs, / And solid pudding against empty praise" (1: 50). For "empty praise" Pope generally would need to look no further than Elkanah Settle, the epitome of vapid City panegyrics. In the "triumphs" Settle concocted for Sir Charles Duncombe, the goldsmith elevated to the post of mayor in 1708, the final pageant consisted of a tableau of "the Chariot of Justice," depicting Astraea carrying in her left hand "a Golden Balance with Silver Scales."[15] As already noted, this celebration was not actually mounted on the day; but Pope gave some of its main scenes a live performance thirty years later.

Shortly afterwards occurs a passage in which the action is tied directly to the City's great moment of the year:

'Twas on the day, when Thorold, rich and grave,
Like Cimon triumph'd, both on land and wave:
(Pomps without guilt, of bloodless swords and maces,
Glad chains, warm furs, broad banners, and broad faces)
Now Night descending, the proud scene was o'er,
But liv'd, in Settle's numbers, one day more.
Now May'rs and Shrieves all hush'd satiate lay,
Yet eat in dreams the custard of the day,
While pensive Poets painful vigils keep,
Sleepless themselves, to give their readers sleep.
Much to the mindful Queen the feast recalls,
When City-Swans once sung within the walls;
Much she revolves their arts, their ancient praise,
And sure succession down from Heywood's days.

(1: 83-96)

Pope's note to the opening line reads, "Sir *George Thorold* Lord Mayor of *London*, in the Year 1720. The Procession of a Lord Mayor is made partly by land, and partly by water." To be literal, the inauguration took place on 28-29 October 1719, with a swearing in held at the Guildhall on the Wednesday followed by the procession to Westminster Hall on the Thursday. The event was carried out "with the Ceremony and Formality that is customary in the like case, being attended to and from the Hall with the Noise, Pomp, Mob, and Show," as Nathaniel Mist's Tory *Weekly Journal* acerbically noted on 31 October.

What of Thorold? He may have been selected partly because his first name, George, set up possible connections with the new monarch in 1727. But he fitted the needs of the poem in broader ways. He came from a well-established family of Levant merchants, a "highly inbred and endogamous mercantile élite," and he had been given a leg up by his unmarried elder brother Charles, as regards both commercial and municipal advancement.[16] George was knighted in 1708, became an alderman in 1709 and a baronet (a comparatively rare honour for one of his breed) in 1709. He remained a solid Whig and managed to gain election as sheriff in 1710, a difficult year for all Whigs. In fact he and his colleague, representing "the Low-Church Party, carried it by a great Majority against *James Smith* and *John Hawkins*, who were put up by the High-Church Party, to the great Mortification of the latter."[17] As a result of his election he took over at a volatile juncture, in the wake of the Sacheverell riots which just three months earlier had convulsed the capital, including parts of the City, especially in Farringdon Ward Without.

It was part of his duties to preside over the controversial elections for the parliamentary seat and for the new Lord Mayor, both held in autumn. First came the mayoral election: on 29 September the sheriffs, including Thorold, declared a victory for the Whigs "by a great Majority," as the loyal *Daily Courant* reported next day, but the Tory candidate Sir Richard Hoare demanded a poll. Here the Tory strategy was to support the more moderate Whig, Sir Robert Beachcroft in the hope that he would oust a more senior figure, Sir Gilbert Heathcote. When the votes were counted, Beachcroft had prevailed by a considerable margin, 5092 against 2878 for Heathcote and 2506 for Hoare. However the court of aldermen overturned this result and installed his opponent, the doughty Whig Heathcote – a figure we shall encounter later in *The Dunciad*. Then when the parliamentary election followed on 9 October the sheriffs once more declared the Whig parliamentary candidates to be the winners, but a poll was demanded and a turbulent few days ensued.

One of the most notorious breaches of public order occurred as a mob encountered their *bête noire*: "Sir *Gilbert Heathcote*, one of the Whig Candidates, was going out of *Guild-Hall*, they not only insulted him by reviling Language, but one of them, more insolent than the rest, spit in his Face; an Affront which perhaps was never offer'd before, in any civiliz'd Nation, to a Person of his Character; he being the Lord Mayor Elect of the City of *London*, and as such, one of the first Magistrates in all *Christndom* (sic)."[18] Efforts were made on both sides to massage the figures to give them victory, but in the end the Tories were able to hold on to the lead they had gained in the ballot. Occurring in close succession, these marked two of many instances when, it was widely felt, the great autocrats of the corporate City had frustrated the will of ordinary citizens. The outcome took a form highly relevant to Pope's work:

> On the 30th of *October*, Sir *Gilb. Heathcote*, the new Lord Mayor, was, according to Custom, sworn at the *Exchequer*, in *Westminster*; but the Pageants, and some other Parts of the Solemnity of that Day, which used to be the greatest annual Festival in this Kingdom, were omitted; The Lord Mayor well knowing, that he was not acceptable to the common People, some of whom were so insolent, as to insult him in his Cavalcade.[19]

No one in future risked such treatment, as Heathcote was the last in this line to go to his inauguration on horseback. From now on every fresh incumbent rode in a carriage, normally drawn by four horses. Meanwhile the Queen declined to attend the Lord Mayor's feast and remained at

Hampton Court, a sign of the unpopularity Heathcote had incurred at court by his efforts to keep the failing ministry in power.

When Thorold was elected to the mayoralty in 1719, it meant that he held office during the Bubble year, so traumatic for a huge segment of the City of London. Pope could count on many of his readers to make this association. Just as the mayor's term was about to expire, a new threat arose, with news of the dread bubonic plague that was feared to be likely to spread from Marseilles. The bugs and bacilli that populate the bloodstream of *The Dunciad* may owe some of their subliminal effect to the race memory of this catastrophe, ever looming in the consciousness of Londoners in the early modern period. As for riches, Thorold was certainly among the wealthier potentates of the metropolis: he stood at the head of the "big lenders" who funded the land Tax in 1720, loaning the huge sum of £15,000. It was on men like him that the government relied for its ability to pay the national bills, whether short or long term. Thorold's commitment to the Whig ministry never wavered. In the aftermath of the trial of John Matthews, the teenage printer hanged for treason in 1719, he was asked by the authorities to clamp down on the hawkers and ballad singers, who were disseminating mainly Jacobite materials. He readily complied with the request.[20]

One other possible motive for the choice of Thorold has never been explored. His sister Prudence was the second wife of Sir George Browne, immortalized as "Sir Plume" in *The Rape of the Lock*. The couple's wedding took place on 5 February 1722 at Gray's Inn Chapel: the husband was marrying outside the faith of his forebears. By the time that *The Dunciad* appeared, Prudence Browne was no longer alive. Read's *Weekly Journal* recorded her death, which occurred in Covent Garden on 25 December 1725, with the name and office of her brother (who had died in 1723) included. It is virtually inconceivable that Pope did not know of this marriage: the Browne family was related to the Blounts, the Carylls and Englefields, to cite only three of the Catholic gentry with whom the poet had intimate links. It would be a stretch to remark that "Prudence" is one of the guardian virtues attending Dulness, listed in the verse immediately preceding Justice and her scales (1: 49). However, it involves no farfetched speculation to suppose that Pope may have deliberately given Sir George's former brother-in-law a featured role at the start of *The Dunciad*. By this means he could administer another light cuff on Sir George, the only individual who seems to have reacted badly to the *Rape*.

Another rumour surfaced shortly before the time when Pope, in all probability, began work on the *Dunciad*. Mist's fiercely Tory *Weekly Journal* reported on 24 October 1724, "It is said that Sir William

Thompson, Recorder of this City, is to be married to the Relic of Sir George Thorold, formerly Lord Mayor of London." In fact no evidence has come to light to confirm this story: Thompson had previously married one rich widow in 1710 as his second wife. But Pope was undoubtedly closely familiar with Mist's paper, and the tale, reliable or not, would have suited his purposes. Thompson had been the great scourge of the Tories since he took part in the prosecution of Dr Sacheverell and the trial of the Jacobite lords, and he now acted as Walpole's legal hatchet-man. In this very year he was awarded a pension of £1,200 a year, a sign of his closeness and his usefulness to the government. To relate the action of the mock-epic to Thorold, and now by implication the powerful Whig Thompson, was further to intensify the political colouring of the poem.

If we return to the passage describing Thorold's installation, it is clear that its main rhetorical energy goes towards an effort to link bad poetry with civic junketing. Pope uses language with his usual deadly precision. The first verb, "triumph'd" might suggest the reward for an ancient general: certainly Cimon gained renown by his double victory at the river Eurymedon in 466 BC, and the Athenians permitted him to erect "stone mercuries", monuments with inscription praising his heroic deeds (Plutarch, *Cimon* 12). Later, Pope may have recalled, Cimon's peace treaties with Persia were repudiated and led to his ostracism – a fate exactly parallel to that of Pope's friends Oxford and Bolingbroke, and one he must have wished on Walpole.[21] But the more obvious overtone here are with the "triumphs of London" Settle had devised. "Pomps", as the Twickenham editor observes, has the Greek sense of πομπή, a solemn procession – but again we are brought back from Athens with a pun on *guilt/gilt*.

There follows a list of the appurtenances of civic display, each by itself enough to serve as a metonym for the occasion and its participants. Pope's catalogue begins with the ceremonial sword which the Lord Mayor presented on his knees to the King when George entered the Guildhall in 1727, and which the outgoing mayor passed on to his successor along with the mace and other civic insignia as part of the installation ceremony. Then come the chains of office: Pope has a note attributed to Scriblerus concerning a misprint which occurred in one of the early editions in 1728, an error which showed "more regard for the metal of which the chains of Aldermen are made, to the beauty of the Latinism and Grecism, nay of figurative speech itself." The pedant as usual misses the poet's real intent, which is to reify classically based metaphors by substituting commonplace aldermanic props in which the "Ignorance of these Moderns" is revealed (*TE* 1: 89). As for the furs, Settle's account of the procession through the city informs us that it was headed by the wardens and assistants of the companies, "in Gowns faced with Foyns", followed by the liverymen "in Gowns with Budge" – two kinds of fur lining. In their wake came a varied retinue of henchmen, not least ushers bearing a number of banners, including "the City and Lord Mayor's Banner."[22] The "broad faces" are more of a generalized insult, suggesting flat northern countenances – perhaps indicating Dutch origin, as depicted in eighteenth-century caricature - as opposed to the Roman or aquiline features of their betters. Most overtones of the adjective invoke ideas of something blunt, clumsy, dull, inert or obtuse. The faces might belong to residents of Broad Street, a commercial hotbed in the heart of the City, home of the Drapers' Company, the Dutch church, and Old South Sea House.[23] Their owners might dispense "broad gold," the large old-fashioned pound coins that were being replaced by the more elegant milled guinea piece.

III

At this point Settle enters the text for the first time. He emerges from the group of "May'rs and Shrieves", satiated by the heavy meal they have enjoyed earlier in the day. As Vicesimus Knox recalled at the end of the eighteenth century, "One of the most common topics of common-place wit, is a jocularity on the lord-mayor and aldermen of London, as great eaters, particularly of custard."[24] Pope does not scruple to use the most hackneyed and vulgar forms of abuse when it suits his purpose. Aldermen are reduced to the level of engines of consumption. At this juncture the poet calls up the lineage of City poets gone by, a crucial element in a poem so concerned with the idea of succession: "Much to the mindful Queen the feast recalls, / When City-Swans once sung within the walls" (1: 93-4). There follows a roster of bad poets from Heywood to John Dennis – Pope's note confuses the Tudor poet John Heywood with Thomas Heywood, who had written pageants in the Jacobean and Caroline period. "City-Swans" is a nice touch, but it may have been prompted in part by recollections of moments such as the scene in Settle's *The Siege of Troy*, a tragedy much laden with special effects, where Venus descends in a chariot drawn by two swans. The play was turned into the most popular of all drolls, performed at Mrs Mimms' booth at Smithfield fair in 1707, and the stage direction survives in this version.

The long note attached to this passage carries many added thrusts. It begins:

Settle was alive at this time [notionally 1719], and Poet to the City of *London*. His office was to compose yearly panegyricks upon the Lord Mayors, and Verses to be spoken in the Pageants: But that part of the frugality of some Lord Mayors at length abolished, the employment of Settle ceas'd; so that upon *Settle's* demise, there was no successor to that place. This important point of time our Poet has chosen, as the Crisis of the Kingdom of *Dulness*, who thereupon decrees to remove her imperial seat from the City, and overspread the other parts of the town.

(1: 88 note)

We have some indication in Book III as to why Pope wished to remember Settle's fairground drolls, as they exemplify the theme announced in the poem's opening couplet: "Books and the Man I sing, the first who brings / The Smithfield muses to the Ear of Kings" (1: 1-2). But what of "his yearly panegyricks upon the Lord Mayors, and Verses to be spoken in the Pageants"?

Settle of course composed an endless stream of panegyric verses, mostly funeral poems and celebrations of happy events such as the union of the two East India companies. Some relate to public events, such as *Irene Triumphans*, occasioned by the Peace of Utrecht in 1713. Others simply lauded appropriate bodies or individuals, for example *Augusta Triumphans. To the Lieutenancy of the Honourable City of London, a Congratulatory Poem* (1711). In the last of the pageants he wrote which was actually performed, he celebrated the merchant who "digs the Oar," in contrast with the airy speculations of the book-learned: "They but read Worlds, He pushes to possess."[25] Given his political affiliations, Settle was happiest commemorating the protestant succession; he also took relish in heaping praise on members of the Whig establishment or City burghers, as in the case of a citizen and soap-boiler who died in 1719, in the form of *Augusta Lacrimans. A Funeral Poem to the Memory of the Honourable Sir Daniel Wray, Kt.* Under Anne he had been forced to adapt himself to the climate of the day, but after the Hanoverian accession was able to resume his more natural vein with items such as *Threnodia Apollinaris. A Funeral Poem to the Memory of the Right Honourable Joseph Addison, Esq;* (1719). This portrays the muses as equally ravished by "their own Patron *GOD*, and *BRITAIN's* Guardian LORD." The two "shining luminaries," god and king, appear as equally deserving glorification, Apollo "in the High'r Sphere, / And GEORGE in his lower Sphere." After such fulsome praise, a contemporary reader like Pope would not have been surprised (if he had got this far) to find Addison subsequently eulogized as a statesman fit to "disperse /The *Albion Fiat's* round the Universe," as well as a writer fit to rank with Virgil, Horace and Pindar. The final lines compare Addison with Alexander the Great in the role of one who had left a world to be shared out by his successors.[26] Even by the permissive standards of panegyric, it makes a startling conclusion.

We have already seen that Settle had written his last pageant for the ceremony on 29 October 1708. Its performance was cancelled owing to the death, two days earlier, of the royal consort, Prince George. However, the book for this occasion had obviously been set up in type in advance, and it was duly. published. The text shows just what Settle was capable of at the height of his career. It bears the title *The Triumphs of London for the Inauguration of the Right Honourable Sir Charles Duncombe, Knight. Lord Mayor of the City of London*. We are also promised a description of the pageants "and the whole Solemnity of the Day." The event was *"All set forth at the proper Cost and Charge of the Honourable Company of* GOLDSMITHS." This last follows normal custom, since Duncombe was a member of the Goldsmiths, one of the twelve great companies who dominated corporate life in the City.

The choice of Lord Mayor presented Settle with a number of problems. In the first place Duncombe was a Tory, although the unreliable one, who would decline to lend Harley's government the money they expected after coming to power in 1710. Moreover, he had a hugely controversial past. He was made free of the company as early as 1674 and served as prime warden in 1684. After that he held numerous offices and became an alderman in 1683. A client of the great Earl of Shaftesbury and the second Earl of Sunderland, he also occupied the important place of cashier of the excise: as a leading banker and government creditor, he stood at the centre of relations between the court and the City at the time of the Financial Revolution. However, in the mid 1690s he lost the confidence of Charles Montagu, the chancellor of the Exchequer, a main architect of the innovations, and probably of the King himself. Duncombe was implicated in financial scandals, and lost his post as cashier. Ultimately he was acquitted of the most serious charges by a less than impartial jury at the King's Bench, and promptly "staged a remarkable comeback with the support of the City Tories." Helped by some well placed and well timed donations while sheriff (he also freed fifty person from the debtors' gaol, and sent them home in his own coach), he regained his place on the aldermen's bench. By 1700 to all appearances he had completed his rehabilitation when he topped the mayoral poll by a wide margin, but as often happened the court of aldermen, inveterately Whiggish, elected his defeated opponent instead. Despite extensive protests, Duncombe was unable to prevail, and in the years 1701 and 1702 he stood no less than three times for the City in parliamentary elections – each time without success. It was not until 1708 that he achieved his ambition, as the senior alderman "below the chair" (i.e. not having served as Lord Mayor), in the face of opposition by "a furious Whig party." This was the situation, with Duncombe poised to take office, when the death of Prince George pre-empted his scheme for an especially sumptuous parade. It left Settle with a tricky task, since he had to eulogize a man widely distrusted an account of the unbridled use of his wealth and influence within the City.[27]

Indeed the dedication that Settle was now called on to address to Duncombe shows some awkwardness. Justly enough, he pays tribute to the unparalleled wealth, munificence and philanthropic zeal of the new mayor. At the same time, there are clear signs of embarrassment, marked by convoluted syntax, over Duncombe's chequered career and in particular his failure to gain the office in 1700. So grateful were the populace for his bounty, we are told, that he might have expected to have progressed rapidly in civic affairs, "as even by an unbroken Chain of Gold to have past your Lordship through the whole City-Honours in one continued Race." Instead:

> However, as the defeated Zeal in so warm a Cause, has been fated to wait Your Lordship's more slow Advance of a Lineal Succession to our Lordship's Consummation of those Honours; be it a part of Your Lordship's Glory to pass your Gracious Act of Oblivion; and look only forward to the growing Lawrels, You are now called to gather.

Such tortured prose did not often figure in the work of a practised panegyricist, but Pope might have been glad of the phrase about lineal succession. Settle seems much happier when he comes to address the Worshipful Company of Goldsmiths, rejoicing in the fact that under the auspices of its members "the antient Splendor and Magnificence, which formerly shined firth on this Solemn *City Festival*, now almost dropt into Oblivion, has taken this second Restoration among you. And indeed You answer the Crest of Your *Escotcheon*, you hold your own *Scales of Justice*." Previous pageants, notably one devised by the dramatist and poet Thomas Jordan in 1674, had incorporated elements of the arms and crest of the company, featuring an emblematic Astraea holding a golden balance.[28] Again we recall Pope's scornful line about Justice weighing gold against truth. The joke depends in part on the fact that the company had chosen this crest because they were keepers of the Troy weight, the standard measure of weight for gold and silver. Pope may have found it amusing that such a group should be designated arbiters of "true" worth.

The Triumphs of London continues with a description of the elaborate processions planned, but never realized in the event. Then come the pageants, with the first set in the Temple of Apollo. The second is built around the laboratory, with a key role for St Dunstan, "the antient Patron and Guardian of the Company" – a natural choice, since he was the patron saint of jewellers, metal-workers and artificers generally, and he figured in Jordan's pageant. Dunstan is enthroned on "a rich Golden Chair of State," and arrayed "in his Pontifical Ornaments, expressing his Prelatical Dignity." We are irresistibly reminded of the king of the dunces on his gorgeous seat at the beginning of Book II. But it is the final tableau which most pervasively recalls Pope's work, as it portrays "the Chariot of Justice." Astraea once more bears in her hands a touchstone and the scales of justice, just as she did in the company crest. In her speech the goddess informs the spectators that "the bright Justice of Great ANNA's Reign" had called her back to earth, a notion close to the central message of Pope's *Windsor-Forest* five years later. Addressing the Lord Mayor, she asserts, "Yes, Sir, my Sword and Scales are both your own, / Justice and her Great Lord shall fill one Throne" – a reminder that Duncombe was taking over as chief magistrate, and would for example preside in court at the Old Bailey.[29]

The question might arise whether Pope would know or care about any of this. His note makes clear that he was aware of the demise of the pageants, and Settle's role as the last of his line. But we have more explicit confirmation that the poet had his eye on the object. At the end of one of the finest among his imitations of Horace, the second satire of the second book (1734), he laments the transfer of property to unworthy hands:

> Shades, that to Bacon could retreat afford,
> Become the portion of a booby Lord;
> And Helmsley once proud Buckingham's delight,
> Slides to a Scriv'ner or a City Knight.

> (175-8)

The booby lord refers to a poetasting Whig MP, William Grimston, elevated to an Irish peerage in 1719. His fortune came from a rich great-uncle, an alderman of the City, and was compounded by his marriage to the daughter of a citizen of London, who brought with her no less than £20,000. More to the immediate point, the City knight is none other than Duncombe, who acquired the estate of Helmsley in Yorkshire, around 1695 after the death of the Duke of Buckingham. He planned an ambitious Vanbrugian mansion, but the house was not completed until after his death. For the estate he allegedly paid the extraordinary sum of £86,000, having bought out the Duke's executors, including the great City figure Sir Robert Clayton. (It has not previously been recognised that Clayton is the obvious, if not the only, candidate for Pope's "scrivener" here.) This transaction, allegedly the greatest purchase made by any English commoner up to this time, naturally "invite[d] much comment at a time of national hardship."[30] Among other things this acquisition gave the buyer considerable parliamentary influence in the rotten borough of Hedon. Pope may well have had knowledge of that last circumstance: about the same time as Duncombe's purchase of Helmsley, one of the seats at Hedon was taken by Sir William Trumbull, the poet's most important early patron,[31] and then a year later by Hugh Bethell of Rise, a Junto Whig related to Pope's close friends Hugh and Slingsby Bethel. In years to come, more transparently, the seat would be made over to Duncombe himself or his younger brother. Given that Pope was sufficiently well informed to craft this allusion to the banker's activities in the mid 1690s, it seems deeply unlikely that he could have missed the culminating event in Duncombe's public life, when he was elevated to the office of Lord Mayor in 1708.

At the end of his note on Settle, Pope holds out promise of further dirt to be dished: "For the latter part of his History, see the third Book, verse [291n}." But the wider intentions of the poem will become clearer if we follow the course of the main action. Soon afterwards, the new king, Tibbald, is introduced. Lewis Theobald had a relevant connection with Settle: he had produced the text for musical entertainments used in Settle's "comic-dramatick" opera, *The Lady's Triumph* (1718). The arch-dunce decides to set his books alight, after reflecting on the demise of Grub Street: "But see great Settle to the dust descend, / And all thy cause and empire at an end!" (1: 185-6). The fire is extinguished by Dulness, once more described as the tutelary goddess of the City: "Great in her charms! As when on Shrieves and May'rs / She looks, and breathes her self into their airs" (1: 219-20). Following this she anoints the new monarch, yet again linking the event to Lord Mayor's Day celebrations: "Know, Settle, cloy'd with custard and with praise, / Is gather'd to the Dull of antient days" (1: 247-8). Normally the grammar would suggest that Settle is cloyed with the praises bestowed on him, but the more subversive meaning here is that he has suffered panegyric fatigue in the wake of his activity as City poet.

IV

The poetic games in Book II begin outside the City limits, in the Strand, and then move back past Temple Bar into the heart of old London. As Aubrey Williams suggests, the setting of the opening contests "could mark the encroachment of literary dulness on Westminster."[32] A growing number of figures in the print trade, especially booksellers, had started to move westward from their historic centre near St Paul's, in search perhaps of the new market afforded by residents the legal, theatrical and entertainment district which stretched down Fleet Street and the Strand to Drury Lane, Covent Garden and Charing Cross. From the start we are made aware of the exact make-up of the group: "With Authors, Stationers obey'd the call, / The field of glory is a field for all" (2: 27-8). A complicated interplay of sneering innuendo is at work here, but the principal meaning runs along the lines, "Along with the writers who have traditionally been the chief agents of producing literature, the contests were open to their hangers-on, the tradesmen who have become more and more prominent in the generation of books."

Moreover, the word "stationers" has been carefully chosen. The predominant modern sense of the term, "A tradesman who sells stationery writing materials and similar articles," that is a purveyor of stationery, had not yet fully broken free, according to *OED*, sense 1(d), although as early as 1656 Charles Blount in his *Glossographia* had tried to distinguish between the stationer, the bookseller and the bookbinder . "Yet all three are of the Company of Stationers," Blount added. This provides the key to Pope's usage. It was the medieval guild, transformed into the livery company in 1556, whose identity is called up. In other words, *The Dunciad* treats members of the book trade as guildsmen, an incorporated group seeking monopoly power and trading, literally, on their established place in the City of London. As already mentioned, Curll belonged to a different livery, but many of the booksellers and printers who take part in the games were in the strict sense Stationers. They include Jacob Tonson, Bernard Lintot, William Mears, William Wilkins, John Dunton, Abel Roper, and Samuel Chapman. In the first book Pope had alluded to "mighty Mist!" (1: 194), glossed as publisher of a famous Tory paper", rather than as a printer. Likewise Roper figures in the notes (2: 141) as editor of the *Post-Boy*, rather than as bookseller, in which capacity he was clothed in 1693. John Dunton is called a broken Bookseller and abusive scribler" (2: 136).

He point seems to be that journalists, pamphleteers and newspaper proprietors have blurred the old distinctions: and yet they all serve the common cause. Amusingly, it is a Cordwainer who earns the highest accolade from the goddess, when she addresses Curll as her "son" skilled in perverting title-pages:

> Be thine, my stationer! this magic gift;
> Cook shall be Prior, and Concanen, Swift;
> So shall each hostile name become our own,
> And we too boast our Garth and Addison.

(2: 129-32)

Grub Street makes good its claim to high literary property by the hand of its officially appointed stationer.

In the course of the dunces' games, there are only a few glancing references to the City, as when Smedley describes how a branch of Styx, tinctured with the waters of Lethe, flows up into the Thames: "Each city-bowl is full / Of the mixt wave, all who drink grow dull" (2: 319-20). But a crucial passage in the middle of the book describes the last contest played out in the Strand, and the subsequent shift of venue to the vicinity of the Fleet Ditch. A "thousand tongues' compote to see who can make the loudest din, with hacks like Benjamin Norton Defoe and John Durant Breval in the lead. Then follows:

> As when the long-ear'd milky mothers wait
> At some sick miser's triple-bolted gate,
> A moan so loud, that all the Guild awake,
> Sore sighs Sir G **, starting at the bray
> From dreams of millions, and three groats to pay!

(2: 237-42)

The first question arising concerns the line about the guild. The Twickenham editor states, "Here "Guild" seems to mean nothing more than 'company' or 'fellowship'; i.e. the miser's neighbours in the City." Valerie Rumbold seems to get nearer the nub of the matter: "Associating the 'miser' and his neighbours with the tradesmen's guilds, and hence with the City of London, rather than with the wit and fashion of districts which considered themselves more refined."[33] It may be some even more specific overtones than that: the noise evidently carries to the heart of the square mile, to the residence of a former Lord Mayor and MP for the City. But before pursuing this lead, we need briefly to pick up another joke which seems to have gone unexplained. The asses' ears point unmistakably to Midas, the miser who prayed that everything he touched might be tuned into gold. It is one more clue pointing in the same direction.

Among the plethora of names in Book II, Sir Gilbert Heathcote (1652-1733) stands alone as the one figure who had nothing to do writing or publishing. He was the ultimate plutocrat, worth £700,000 at his death, according to the *Gentleman's Magazine*. His career embraced almost everything that the City stood for: an overseas trader on a grand scale, master of the Vintners' Company, government contractor, director of the East India Company, founder and leading investor in the Bank of England, as well as alderman, sheriff and Lord Mayor besides serving as MP for the constituency for almost ten years, president of the Honourable Artillery Company, colonel of the Blue Company of militia – the list could be extended. As "probably the most successful merchant of his generation," he bestrode the City as a genuine colossus of commerce.[34] When the South Sea Company faced disaster in 1720, it was Heathcote to whom the directors turned as their last hope of salvation: "The events of that dismal season signalled the complete triumph of Heathcote and whig finance over Harley's improvisations." He feared no one: "To the *Spectator* he was 'Sir Andrew Freeport,' the embodiment of what was best in English business; to his enemies 'the meanest man in England'. . . .When a hostile government curtailed his Lord Mayor's show on land [as we have seen, in 1711], he rode on horseback to the Mansion House [*recte* Guildhall] to be sworn and ordered the procession to follow him by water."[35] Again we are reminded of Pope's line about Thorold's double progress (84). Nor had Heathcote done with honours when the poem was written: a week before his death, Walpole's government granted him a baronetcy.

In fact Heathcote became a favourite butt of the poet. This may have had something to do with his close links to the dissenting community, especially presbyterians. However, these references mostly apply to personal qualities, especially his penurious nature. Thus, in the *Epistle to Bathurst*: "The grave Sir Gilbert holds it for a rule, / That 'every man in want is knave or fool'" (*TE* 3.ii: 99). In the prose satire *A Master Key to Poetry* (*c*.1732), he jokingly refutes the suggestion that a reference to "Sir Shylock's ill-got wealth to waste" in the earliest version of the *Epistle to Burlington* meant Heathcote: "There could not be invented a falser Scandal, or one that would *more hurt* this eminent Citizen, than to insinuate that he had *wasted his wealth*. . . .to say that Sir G---'s wealth is wasted, is to say that his parts are decay'd" (*TE* 3.ii: 182). Even the innocuous phrase "eminent Citizen" has its own charge here.[36] In the imitation of the second epistle of Horace's second book (1737) we find this:

> Heathcote himself, and such large-acred Men,
> Lords of fat *E'sham*, or of Lincoln Fen,
> Buy every stick of Wood that lends them heat,
> Buy every Pullet they afford to eat.
> Yet these are Wights who fondly call their own
> Half that the Dev'l o'erlooks from Lincoln Town.
>
> (*TE* 4: 181-3)

The last couplet plays on an old proverb which crops up in Swift's *Polite Conversation*: "as the devil looks over Lincoln," meaning to cast an envious eye on someone else's prosperity. In his will Heathcote left land in seven counties in addition to London, but Pope must have had in mind his purchase in 1729 of the manor of Normanton, where he promptly had a splendid mansion erected. The house survived until the 1920s, but most of the estate is now covered by Rutland Water, a reservoir constructed fifty years later.

Two features mark off the allusion in *The Dunciad*: its more oblique and less personal quality, and its symbolic resonance in political terms. The passage from Book II just quoted shows first that the sound of the dunces reached Heathcote, an alderman of the central ward of Walbrook - itself named after an underground tributary of the Thames. His home was in St Swithin's Lane, leading into Lombard Street about 75 yards west of Pope's family home as a child. Second, the lines politicize Heathcote's City connections. The slumbering guild points to the deafness of the City to popular feeling, except when animated by rabble-rousers such as the Sacheverell rioters or the dunces. In the Harley years, Sir Gilbert had led bitter City opposition to the government, especially the Tory peace. He even led a delegation from the Bank of England to the Queen in 1710, urging her to retain Godolphin in power, rather than appoint Harley, if the confidence of investors were to be preserved. Moreover, Heathcote was generally believed to have "abused his authority as returning office to frustrate open scrutinies" in a Broad Street ward election of 1711.[37] This was a charge regularly brought against the Whig-dominated Court of Aldermen, and reflected the polarization of the City between the smaller tradesmen and merchants (often members of the Common Council) and the great magnates who sat on the aldermanic bench. Pope's own memory went back at least far as the contested polls in 1710, in the wake of the Sacheverell affair, when (as we saw) his choice of a Lord Mayor – George Thorold – happened to be a sheriff enabling Heathcote's victory in the mayoral election.

All this helps to integrate Heathcote into the fabric of the poem, but a more particular ground may be found for Pope's decision to single out this individual. For this, we need to go back to the material described in Chapter 11. It will be recalled that the dunces foregather to play out their mock-epic contests "where the tall May-pole once o'erlook'd the Strand; /But now, so ANNE and Piety ordain, / A Church collects the saints of Drury-lane" (2: 24-6). The site was appropriate as it had long been the scene of May Day games, among the most widely celebrated festivities on the popular calendar. More important though this is the new "Queen Anne" church: this was St Mary le Strand, built by Pope's friend James Gibbs, and one of the fifty new structures planned to go up in the capital following an act of 1711 (9 Anne, c. 22). The initiative for this scheme came from the High Church, headed by another of Pope's close friends, Francis Atterbury, and they dominated the board of commissioners in its early years. Everything changed after the Hanoverian accession. Gibbs was ousted from his post as Surveyor to the project in 1716, and the board was packed with Whig loyalists. Men like Atterbury disappeared from the board, and the City men who had been among the original commissioners mostly went, too. They included a number of Tory aldermen: Sir John Cass, Sir Richard Hoare, Sir George Newland and Sir William Withers, the four candidates successful in the 1710 parliamentary election; Robert Child, who like Hoare was a warden of the Goldsmiths; Sir Thomas Crosse, who prevailed in an equally contentious poll for Westminster in 1710; and Sir William Stewart, Lord Mayor in 1721-22. When the commission was remodelled in 1715, all these individuals lost their place. In their place came aldermen with a reliable attachment to the government. They included Sir John Fryer, Lord Mayor in 1720-1, succeeding Thorold; Sir Randolph Knipe; Sir Harcourt Master; Sir Charles Peers, Lord Mayor in 1715-16; Sir John Tash, sheriff during Thorold's mayoralty, who succeeded Heathcote as alderman of Walbrook Ward; and Sir John Ward, who preceded Thorold and twice served as MP for the constituency. It was this set of men who kept the City safe for the ministry throughout the reign of George I. One name needs to be added to the list: that of Sir Gilbert Heathcote who, despite the doubts some harboured over his allegiance to the Church of England, took an active role when he became a commissioner.

Pope cannot have failed to know what was going on here, as indicated in previous chapters of this book. Apart from his links with Atterbury and Gibbs, he enjoyed an especially close friendship with another member of the Scriblerian group, Dr John Arbuthnot, formerly physician to the Queen. As described in Chapter 11, the doctor served as one of the commissioners, and along with other qualified individuals (including Wren, Vanbrugh and Halley) he was asked to "confer" about the new church in the Strand. He actually went with the Bishop of Hereford to the Queen, with Gibbs's design for a pillar at the front of St Mary's. Less than a month later Anne died, and soon Arbuthnot too found himself surplus to the commissioners' requirements.[38]

The winner of the braying contest that disturbed Heathcote's slumbers turns out to be Sir Richard Blackmore, with the most "sonorous" of all the entrants:

Walls, steeples, skies, bray back to him again:
In Tot'nam fields, the brethren with amaze
Prick all their ears up,and forget to graze;

Long Chanc'ry-lane retentive rolls the sound,
And courts to courts return it round and round.
Thames wafts it thence to Rufus' roaring hall,
And Hungerford re-echoes, bawl for bawl.

(2: 248-54)

Early on in this passage, the original reading (Tothill Fields in Westminster) might have made stronger sense, but they lay too close to Westminster Hall ("Rufus' roaring Hall") to convey the spread Pope wanted to achieve. As Valerie Rumbold indicates, the "brethren" refers to donkeys, "characterised as Blackmore's kin by virtue of his braying; but also suggesting the. . .dissenting sects, likely in Pope's view to be impressed by resonant nonsense." In the following couplet, Rumbold observes that "there may be a pun on 'Chancery Rolls,' the rolled documents which preserved its records."[39] There certainly looks or be a pun, and it may be still more cunningly contrived. The court records were held in the Rolls Office, on the east side of Chancery Lane; this contained a famous medieval chapel, where Atterbury had once held the place of Preacher at the Rolls, and Colen Campbell had restored the main house in Palladian guise around 1717. The Liberty of the Rolls lay right on the border of Farringdon Ward Without, where legal London and the commercial city abutted in often prosperous conjunctions.

The last allusion is to Hungerford Market, towards the western end of the Strand. The duces do not venture quite so far on their progress into Westminster, but the cavalcade of George and Caroline passed this way on Lord Mayor's Day 1727, with the streets lined from Temple Bar by the City militia. Moreover, a few days earlier, the usual partisan lection had been going on to choose members of parliament for the City. Supporters of the pro-ministerial candidates resident in Westminster were invited to meet at the Sun tavern in the Strand and then to make their way to the Guildhall for the vote (*Daily Journal*, 17 October 1727). The tavern lay opposite Hungerford Market, and the members would process eastward past St Mary's up Fleet Street towards the heart of the City. Here they joined the route of the duces, who at this stage are poised to go down past Bridewell to the spot "where Fleet-ditch with disemboguing streams / Rolls the large tribute of dead dogs to Thames" (2: 258-9).

This location gains in relevance because of a crucial change introduced in 1727. As the *Daily Journal* reported on 26 October, "For the more magnificent Procession of the Lord Mayor, the Aldermen and the Livery Companies through the City to Guildhall, on the Lord Mayor's Day, we hear that the new Lord Mayor, and the twelve principal Companies, will land at the Temple-Stairs, And not at Black-Fryars as heretofore." This

meant a change in the processional route on land, most likely by way of
Temple Lane , emerging into Fleet Street at Temple Bar. The route would
have been carefully chosen to avoid the squalid purlieus of Whitefriars and
Bridewell. But we ought not to forget that Bridewell, too, was to a large
extent a City responsibility, in practice though not in law. Its benefactors
were principally merchants, and in 1720 (as Pope could easily have learnt
from the new version of Stow), "the Governors of this Hospital . . .are
chiefly Citizens." A list published about 1726 showed that Alderman
Humphrey Parsons, the Tory brewer, served as president: the other
aldermen headed his colleagues, and as though by a law of nature the most
senior figure, Sir Gilbert Heathcote, comes first.[40] The aim of Bridewell
had been to educate poor children and apprentice them to become citizens,
but as time went on they were "taught different trades by certain persons
dignified by the title of arts masters, but who were merely so many poor
broken-down tradesmen."

After their aquatic sports the dunces are ready for a long rest. Before
the final game, Dulness moves slowly away from the "sable flood," that is
the Ditch, and attended by her priest moves back into the historic city
through "the gates of Lud" (2: 331-2) Pope's note on Ludgate quotes from
the 1720 edition by John Strype of Stow's *Survey of London*, another sign
of his preparations for writing the poem. By a nice coincidence – if
nothing more – the rector of St Martin's, the church directly abutting on
the ancient gateway was William Thorold. In August 1720 Sir George had
appointed this man to deliver a sermon on the anniversary of the Great
Fire, which he did in the Guildhall chapel (Mist's *Weekly Journal*, 10
September).[41] Across a small courtyard behind St Martin's stood
Stationers' Hall – so the dunces were truly returning home, as they entered
their own parish at Ludgate.

The assembled throng go in search of a bed at the end of the long
celebratory day, even if it should turn out to be no more than "some fam'd
round-house" - the parish of St Martin's in the Fields, in St Martin's Lane,
probably held the doubtful honour of owning the best-known of such lock-
up. Others find their refuge close at the hand in a city gaol – "the
neighbouring Fleet / Haunt of the Muses" (2: 395-6).

V

Settle has a prolonged and important part to play in Book III. However,
the satire bears chiefly on his role as a purveyor of spectacle in drolls
performed at St Bartholomew's fair. In a strict geographic sense
Smithfield lay in Farringdon Without, within the Liberty of London, and

the name certainly connotes low life in contrast to the entertainments of the fashionable parts of Westminster. Originally, too, the fair had been a huge trading market for cloth and other goods, a role that was receding by Pope's time, in favour of the freaks and sideshows Wordsworth evokes so vividly in Book VII of *The Prelude*. In a note to the opening couplet of the poem, Pope had referred to the "Shews, Machines and Dramatical Entertainments, formerly agreeable only to the taste of the Rabble" which writers like Theobald had brought to a new audience in the West End (1: 2). But for the most part the occasion had little direct bearing on the high politics of London.

For centuries the Lord Mayor conducted the official opening of the fair every August, stopping on his way at Newgate gaol, where the keeper gave him a glass of sack – in later times, replaced by a "lemonade." An account appeared in the *Daily Journal* on 24 August 1724, describing the "great state and solemnity" with which the party made their way to West Smithfield. A set protocol existed for this occasion, outlined in *The Order of my Lord Mayor, the Aldermen, and the Sheriffs, for their Meeting and Wearing of their Apparel throughout the whole Year* (1724). This required the aldermen to meet with the Lord Mayor and sheriffs at the Guildhall on St Bartholomew's eve, and after a service in the chapel all rode to Cloth Fair: they stopped at the "great gate" and the mayor read the proclamation. They returned through the churchyard of St Bartholomew the Great and Aldersgate to the mayor's house. On the feast day itself they were to dress themselves in their scarlet gowns lined, and ride with the Lord Mayor to the wrestling at the fair, again returning by Aldersgate. On the following day (or, if this fell on a Sunday, on the Monday) they were to attend "the Shooting."

Curious rituals like this enabled critics to portray the City as sponsors of mindless entertainment. Such a view elides the fact that the Lord Mayor and aldermen equally elected from their own number governors of St Bartholomew's hospital, which stood on a site immediately adjoining the fairground – but such things could easily be swept aside. When Pope consulted Stow's *Survey*, as edited by John Strype in 1720, he would have found page after page setting out the worthy benefactions of City fathers to a variety of charitable causes: the needs of his poem demanded that he ignore these aspects of their conduct. But he would have found too a dedication in the plan of London at the head of the first volume. The map is inscribed to Sir George Thorold - whose name also appears as an alderman among the collective dedicatees of the book. Here is yet another circumstance which could have factored into Pope's choice of the show in 1719 as the setting of his poem.

Apart from this, the civic bodies were involved in the fair chiefly as regulators of disorderly conduct. The proclamation at the opening ceremony had as its main purpose a requirement that all those attending should abide by the law: anyone committing a breach of the peace risked fine or imprisonment, "after the Discretion of the Lord-mayor and Aldermen." From time to time the City set out ordinances meant to restrict activities other than marketing, but by this time the junketing and stage-shows had become the main object of the exercise, and their efforts fell on deaf ears. Thus when Thorold performed the opening ceremony on 22 August 1719, he proclaimed the fair for three days, "for the sale of Cattle, Leather, and other goods, as usual, tho 'tis thought the Holiday Folks will keep it up beyond that time, as is usual also" (Mist's *Weekly Journal*, 29 August). The last act the corporation of London performed in its supervisory role was to close down the fair for good in 1855.

Settle's monologue occupies almost the whole of Book III – we generally forget that in the original version of the poem it is he who announces the apocalyptic future to come, with the restoration of anarchy, as "Art after Art goes out" (3: 346), a passage more familiar when uttered by the anonymous narrator in the new Book IV in 1743. In the 1729 text Settle addresses the politics of London only once, but it occurs in a passage central to the whole design. This section relates the themes of Book III back to the issues raised in the first two books, and connects Settle's now central role to what has been said about him earlier on. The key lines are these:

> In Lud's old walls, though long I rul'd renown'd,
> Far, as loud Bow's stupendous bells resound;
> Tho' my own Aldermen conferr'd my bays,
> To me committing their eternal praise,
> Their full-fed Heroes, their pacific May'rs,
> Their annual trophies, and their monthly wars.
> Tho' long my Party built on me their hopes,
> For writing pamphlets, and for burning popes;
> (Diff'rent our parties, but with equal grace
> The Goddess smiles on Whig and Tory race,
> 'Tis the same rope at sev'ral ends they twist,
> To Dulness, Ridpath is as dear as Mist.)

                                                        (3: 273-86)

The phrase about Settle's ruling over London through the patronage his "own" aldermen suggests not just the City poet but also the Lord Mayor himself – and even the King. We know that George, as Prince of Wales, paid a surreptitious visit to the fair in 1719, two months before Thorold's installation. He came there "incognito," at about ten o'clock in the evening, accompanied only by one nobleman and one footman (Mist's *Weekly Journal*, 31 August 1719). He went to a booth to witness of one of the theatrical shows, "and was very liberal to the Actors." Royal liberality, indeed.

Pope wrote notes to this passage that serve at once to elucidate and complicate the meaning. He says a good deal about Settle's activities in managing a pope-burning at the time of the Popish Plot, and at his booth in Bartholomew Fair. The modern historian David Cressy has remarked of the pope-burning ceremony, "On the streets but not of the streets, and hovering within the limits of control, it was more like the Lord Mayor's show than a popular protest" – an analogy that Pope may have intuited nearly three hundred years ago.[42] We are also reminded, too, that Settle ended up as a pensioner in the Charterhouse – an appropriate resting-place for a ruined veteran hack, perhaps, since the original charter provided a home for gentlemen by descent and in poverty, as well as merchants decayed by piracy or shipwreck. On top of this, the Charterhouse lay a stone's throw from Smithfield, and again the foundation relied squarely on City altruism and City money. Defoe considered its inception by the Jacobean merchant Thomas Sutton "the greatest and noblest Gift that ever was given for Charity, by any one Man, publick or private, in this Nation, since History gives us any Account of Things."[43] Once more, the details of Sutton's bequest were set out at great length in Stow's *Survey*, a work which we already know Pope consulted. The concluding lines offer in part an apologia for Settle's tergivisations: the note says that he, "like most Party-writers, was very uncertain in his political principles." In fact he remained obstinately Whiggish in his underlying principles, even if shifts in the complexion of the City's ruling elite meant that he had at times to make a show of glorifying men like Sir Charles Duncombe.

The drift of the passage, as the Twickenham editor noted, is to indicate how Settle's pageants for Lord Mayor's shows "had in a sense anticipated Theobald's pantomimes." For this to come across, Pope returns to his evocation in Book I of the City poet, with his base inside the old walls but claiming authority as far as Bow bells resound – the proverbial scope of Cockney identity is mixed here with recollections of the braying noises resounding through London. The brand of writing Settle represents is linked precisely to the municipality: his laurels are conferred by his "own" aldermen, who charge him with endowing them with "eternal" (enduring, but in Pope's formulation more like "incessant"). Their talent for consuming gargantuan feasts comes up again, as does their taste for pompous military exercises where they run no risk of getting hurt. The gloss to line 280 runs, "Annual trophies on the Lord Mayor's Day; and monthly wars, in the Artillery Ground." The City trained bands were so called from the instruction they received from the Honourable Artillery Company, an exercise which had delighted the satirist before. In addition the trained bands lined the streets when the new King made his way to the Guildhall in 1727 (*British Journal,* 4 November). As for the Company, their exploits at Moorfields often involved a preliminary salutation of the monarch, as on George I's last birthday in June 1727, while they were as prompt as the City itself to dispatch a loyal address to his son on accession. We recall that their president, appointed in the year of Thorold's mayoralty, was Sir Gilbert Heathcote, cementing his role as the burgomaster of all burgomasters.

VI

In 1735 Pope added to the preliminaries of *The Dunciad* a new "Declaration" by the author, printed in black letter. This took the form of mock-proclamation as issued by the king, and was sworn before "John Barber, Mayor." As we have seen, Barber had served in the office in 1732-33, and concerted plans with Pope for an imaginary Lord Mayor's procession featuring the Stationers. In some ways the document pardons the official licence granted by the secretary of state in 1722, when Barber was permitted to bring out Pope's edition of the works of the Duke of Buckingham. Given that the most notable aspect of the printer's term in office was his vigorous resistance on behalf of the City to Walpole's Excise scheme, we might anticipate that Pope would have held him in high regard – even more so, perhaps, because this did not prove enough to gain Barber election to represent the constituency in 1735 in the face of government pressure on floating voters. But the position is more complicated.

Scholars have never been able to decide exactly what the relations between the two men were. Pope never became as close a friend of Barber as did Swift. He may even have written an unkind epigram (or more than one) on the monument which Barber erected to the memory of Samuel Butler in Westminster Abbey. This was a favourite target for satirists: and at least one versifier was able to link Barber with none other than Settle. The lines appear in the *Daily Journal* on 21 March 1722 (repeated in Read's *Weekly Journal*, 24 March):

Castle Baynard's, March 20. 1721-2.
SIR, As I have lately set up a *Barber*'s Shop, I beg your Recommendation as a young beginner.

The first Customer I *Trimm'd* was a new Alderman, and he has promis'd to recommend me for the Lightness of my Hand. Yours, *Andrew Shaveclose.*
ADRICE (sic).
Let not the *Golden Chain* thy *Neck* adorn,
While *Portland-stone* sinks *Butler*'s Name to scron;
Rather let *Peru's Mines* his Ashes deck,
And hang the *Portland-Stone* about thy *Neck.*
Thy *grateful Bounty* let poor *Settle* share,
To whom *you owe* the *very Gold* you *wear.*

The point of the joke about Settle will emerge in a moment. Castle Baynard's was the ward where Barber was currently conducting an aldermanic election. It was widely suspected that Barber's gesture on behalf of Butler, coupled with a gift of £500 to found a charity school in the ward, was designed to ease his passage in a contest against the ministerial candidate.

Here lie the seeds of some equivocal attitudes on Pope's part. Barber had become heavily involved in municipal affairs. From 1709 to 1724 he had been City Printer, as well as holding the reversion to the post of King's Printer (a right he would never get to exercise). He served as Sheriff in 1729-30, and went to Westminster for his installation attended by sixteen Stationers in a barge pulled by the company's watermen. He gave the usual feasts during his tenure, and John Gay attended one such function in March 1730, which as he told Swift incorporated "a very fine dinner & a very fine Appearance of Company" (Swift *Corr*, 3: 297). When the City decided to build a grand new Mansion House in 1735, he was appointed to the committee to choose a site and obtain designs. Some of these events occurred just too late to have influenced the original *Dunciad*; but they show the way Barber's life was moving. What Pope would certainly have known is that Barber had been appointed to the committee to "approve and manage" the Lord Mayor's dinner in 1727, when the royal family came to the Guildhall (see above, pp. 267-8). The procession that year had a new feature: the aldermen and councilmen who had acted in this committee were directed to march that day, "with Gold Fringes on their Gloves, and rich Favours upon their Hats" (*Daily Journal*, 26 October). It is all uncomfortably close to the "Pomps" that Pope had described early in Book I of his poem.

Barber's career followed the pattern of the industrious apprentice. In the early 1720s, following substantial gains in the South Sea, he had bought a country house in East Sheen, as well as town house in Queen Square, Bloomsbury, later occupied by Charles Burney and his family. In a way Barber's move from the printing shop in Lambeth Hill, between St

Paul's and the river, to a fashionable corner of the West End enacts the very trajectory of dulness, as Pope plotted this in his work. Late in life Pope told Swift "I see J. Barber seldom," but he was aware of the other's whereabouts, for when "Alderman Barbars Relique" wrote to him in 1741 about the legacy he was to receive from the printer, he was able to pinpoint her whereabouts: "She lives in Queens Square where the Alderman livd, I suppose" (Pope *Corr* 4: 178, 367). It was at this house that Barber had mounted some splendid junketings, in the best aldermanic tradition.

For one reason or another a faint suspicion of coolness attends the relations of the two men, which makes Barber's legacy of £100 the more generous. Scholars have isolated one possible reason for this. The story, which allegedly goes back to a conversation between Pope and William Warburton, appears in Spence's *Anecdotes*:

> Mr. Pope never flattered anybody for money, in the whole course of his writing. Alderman Barber had a great inclination to have a stroke in his commendation inserted in some part of Mr. Pope's writings. He did not want money, and he wanted fame. He would probably have given four or five thousand pounds, to have been gratified in this desire: and gave Mr. Pope to understand as much, but Mr. Pope would never comply with such a baseness. And when the Alderman died, he left him a legacy only of a hundred pounds; which might have been some thousands, if he had obliged him only with a couplet.
>
> (*Anecdotes* 1: 161)

Whether this story has any truth in it cannot be proved now. In any case, a more solid reason for any possible loss of cordiality – and this bears directly on *The Dunciad*.

What all previous scholarship on Pope seems to ignore is the nature of the relationship between Barber and Settle. In fact, the City Poet was godfather to the City Printer, and a friend of Barber's own father. According to a biography published by Thomas Cooper in 1741, just after the alderman died, it was Settle who took the young boy into his home, clothed him and "put him to School at *Hampstead*." Through the influence of his mentor, together with a gift of twenty guineas, John was able to serve his apprenticeship in the Stationers' Company; and perhaps Settle brought him his first profitable job, a widely sold pamphlet by Dr Charles Davenant.[44] A different narrative appears in Curll's rival life, stressing the role of Davenant and not that of Settle; but the documents in the case establish that Cooper was right about the family link. In these circumstances it is hard to imagine that Barber felt anything but gratitude towards his benefactor. If that it so, we can easily conceive what must have been his chagrin and distress when Pope allocated Settle such a key role among the dunces, and picked out details of the old man's career with such cruel accuracy. Pope seems not to have cared too much about Barber's feelings – if he had not got wind of the relationship with Settle, then his normal intelligence gathering had suffered a severe breakdown. The poet in the *Daily Journal* certainly knew all about it. Perhaps, despite the political sympathy he felt with Barber as a tribune of the opposition, Pope had come to associate the printer with the corporate activity of the City. The gold fringes in 1727 might almost prefigure Barber's admission to the Goldsmiths' Company in 1732, to qualify as Lord Mayor.

Barber must have known of some of the adverse views his friends and fellow-Tories harboured, after his advancement to the pinnacle of City affairs. At the time of the Excise crisis, Swift wrote to him, addressing him as "My Lord," and mentioning "our friend Sr Gilbert" as a byword for avarice: the Dean's protégé Matthew Pilkington had become chaplain to the Lord Mayor, at the request of Swift, and he had evidently been telling tales out of school. Barber replied on 6 August from Goldsmiths' Hall: "I flattered myself with being very happy with you and some friends, on the important subject of the Cap of Maintenance, Custard, the Sword, and many more laudable things in the lord mayor's house" (Swift *Corr* 3: 655, 686). David Woolley suggests that Barber was remembering a plate to *A Tale of a Tub*, but the phrasing seems to indicate a more recent source – *The Dunciad*.

VII

In some ways Pope made it a goal of his life to distance himself from the mercantile background that he inherited on his paternal side. He could do this without reneging on the intense family piety he always displayed: "In a word, my Lord, I think it enough, that my Parents, such as they were, never cost me a *Blush*; and that their Son, such as he is, never cost them a *Tear*."[45] His father was in trade certainly, but not as the great princes of the City like Heathcote were in trade. The locus of their activities lay in the great public spaces of commercial London. They stalked the Royal Exchange, eulogized by Addison in the *Spectator*: "I look upon High-Change to be a great Council, in which all considerable Nations have their Representatives." They supplied the motor that powered "the great Hall where the Bank is kept," where Addison was pleased to find "the Directors, Secretaries, and Clerks, with all other Members of that wealthy Corporation, ranged in their several Stations, according to the Parts they act in that just and regular Oeconomy." It is no coincidence that the figure

of Sir Andrew Freeport, the "Merchant of great Eminence in the City of
London" who represents the acceptable face of trade, was seen by
contemporaries as based principally on Sir Gilbert Heathcote.[46] All around
stood the palaces of commerce, along with the solid brick mansions of the
goldsmiths in Lombard Street (like the one where the firm that became
Barclay's Bank was founded in 1690) and the impressive merchant's
house which had been converted into the Post Office. Nearby ran the
hidden back alley of Plough Court and the modest premises of Alexander
Pope senior.

Most scholars have analysed Pope's attitudes towards the moneyed
interest in moral terms. They have either deplored his views on the
Financial Revolution as backward-looking and snobbish, the product of a
cultural ideology perhaps misdescribed as the politics of nostalgia: or they
have applauded his principled denunciation of a corrupt and spiritually
bankrupt ruling elite.[47] In both cases, we fail to see how much of the poet's
outlook on such matters derived from his quarrels with the City of London
in the narrow sense – in other words, how thoroughly his attitudes were
shot through with intense personal feelings. His scorn for the burghers
rested on something more particular than dislike of "commercial values,"
or than opposition in terms of national politics – his treatment of the Tory
grandee Sir Charles Duncombe and his warm relations with the Whig
businessman Slingsby Bethel both point to this fact. Aldermen fall under
the poet's obloquy because they rigged elections, not just because they
embodied financial values. Mostly they kowtowed to Walpole, apart from
one brief episode, and even then the leader of City opposition, John
Barber, failed to get himself a seat at Westminster. The reason that Whigs
formed Pope's chief target was that they occupied the key role in City
affairs, and notoriously rode roughshod over the smaller businessmen –
people just like Alexander Pope, senior, in fact.

Notes

[1] Pope exchanged a number of letters with Slingsby, whom he probably got to
know through the merchant's brother Hugh, one of the poet's most intimate
friends. He also stayed at Bethel's house on Tower Hill. Slingsby was named after
the Whig republican and sheriff of London whom Dryden portrayed as Shimei in
Absalom and Achitophel. He procured Pope claret and madeira. A representative
excerpt from their correspondence occurs in Pope's letter of 31 October 1739: "I
have not been in London but one day these 3 months, & not one day in the City (I
think) since I saw you. This day I intended to have made you a Visit at Towerhill,
being to pass most of the day in the City upon business" (Pope *Corr*, 4: 197).

Bethel also acted as a kind of investment banker for the poet (Pope *Corr*, 4: 299, 365, 401, 447, 496-7, 513).

[2] Unless otherwise stated, details of Pope's early life are taken from Mack, *Life*.

[3] In 1679 Pope senior buried his first wife Magdalen at the church of St Bennet Fink, in Threadneedle Street, about a hundred yards north of his home. For details of the burial, see Mack, *Life*, p. 820. For St Edmund's parish, see *New Remarks of London. . .Collected by the Company of Parish-Clerks* (London: E. Midwinter, 1732, pp. 60-1. Even though it had been united in 1670 with the parish of St Nicholas Acons, destroyed in the Great Fire, there were still only 150 houses in the joint parish.

[4] See Gary Stuart De Krey, *A Fractured Society: The Politics of London in the First Age of Party1688-1715* (Oxford: Clarendon Press, 1985), pp. 232-6.

[5] "Club members were usually able to express their confidence in the outcome of elections for. . .Langbourn." See I.G. Doolittle, "Government Interference in City Elections 1714-1716," *Historical Journal* 24 (1981): 945-8 (947). Among the most regular attenders at the club were Sir Gilbert Heathcote and James Craggs, senior, sometimes described as "the minister for the City." He was father of Pope's good friend and later secretary of state, James Craggs, junior.

[6] A.J. Henderson, *London and the National Government, 1721-1742: A Study of City Politics and the Walpole Administration* (Durham, NC: Duke University Press, 1945; rptd Philadelphia: Porcupine Press, 1945), pp. 80-2.

[7] Mack, *Life*, pp. 34-7.

[8] De Kruy, *Fractured Society*, pp. 58-9.

[9] Walter Thornbury, *Old and New London: A Narrative of its History, its People and its Places*, 2 vols. (London: Cassell, 1872), 1: 322.

[10] Swift *Corr*, 3: 529. Swift replied on 11 September 1732, "I think I saw, in my youth, a lord mayor's show with all that pomp, when Sir Thomas Pilkington. . .made his procession" (3: 541). Significantly, this was the famous show of 1689, described above. The best short account of Pope's use of the Lord Mayor's procession remains Aubrey Williams, *Pope's Dunciad: A Study of its Meaning* (London: Methuen, 1955), pp. 29-41. On Barber, see Charles A. Rivington, *"Tyrant": The Story of John Barber, Jacobite Lord Mayor of London, and Printer and Friend to Dr. Swift* (York: William Sessions, 1989).

[11] Oddly Barber had to "translate" to the Goldsmiths' Company in order to qualify for election. Until the middle of the eighteenth century the Lord Mayor had to be a member of the "Twelve Great Companies," among whom the Stationers did not figure. During his year of office Barber lived at Goldsmiths' Hall.

[12] *The Historical Register...for the Year 1727*, vol. 12 (London: S. Nevill, [1727], 278-81.

[13] William Maitland, *The History of London from its Foundation to the Present Time*, 2 vols. (London: Osborn, Shipton and Hodges, 1756), 1: 542.

[14] For an abundant set of examples, see Robert Withington, *English Pageantry: An Historical Outline*, 2 vols (Cambridge, MA: Harvard University Press, 1918).

[15] Elkanah Settle, *The Triumphs of London for the Inauguration of the Right Honourable Sir Charles Duncombe, Knight. Lord Mayor of the City of London* (London: A. Baldwin, 1708), p. 5.

[16] De Kruy, *Fractured Society*, p. 143.

[17] Abel Boyer, *The History of the Reign of Queen Anne, Digested into Annals. Year the Ninth* (London: Thomas Ward, 1711), p. 420.

[18] *Daily Courant*, 30 September, 4 October, 1 October, 16 October 1710; Boyer, *History*, pp, 250-1. For the Tory strategy in these elections, see *The House of Commons 1690-1715*, ed. Eveline Cruickshanks, Stuart Handley and D.W. Hayton, 5 vols (Cambridge: Cambridge University Press, 2002), 2: 390-1.

[19] Boyer, *History*, p. 253.

[20] P.G.M. Dickson, *The Financial Revolution in England: A Study in the Development of Public Credit 1688-1756* (London: Macmillan, 1967), pp. 430-1; National Archives, SP 35/18/101, 102, 104.

[21] *TE* 5: 69 identified the double victory with the battle of Salamis in 480 BC, but this is incorrect.

[22] Settle, *Triumphs of London*, pp. 1-2.

[23] It was also the site of Pinners Hall, the best-known Independent conventicle in London, and the venue of the regular Merchants' Lecture, a sermon delivered to City worthies. In 1697 a recent Lord Mayor, Sir Humphrey Edwin, had caused a huge furore when he attended a service at Pinner's Hall accompanied by the official sword-bearer. More than any other event, this set off the long-lasting debate over occasional conformity.

[24] Vicesimus Knox, *Winter Evenings: or Lucubrations on Life and Letters*, 3 vols (London: Dilly, 1788), 1: 240.

[25] *The Triumphs of London, for the Inauguration of the Right Honourable Sir William Gore, Kt. Lord Mayor of the City of London* (London: Nutt, 1701), p. 6.

[26] *Threnodia Apollinaris. A Funeral Poem to the Memory of the Right Honourable Joseph Addison, Esq;* (London: printed for the author, 1719), pp. 3-4, 6, 8, 13.

[27] On Duncombe, see *House of Commons 1690-1715*, 3: 937-44; De Krey, *Fractured Society*, pp. 160-1, 195-6; and the entry by G.E. Aylmer for *The New Oxford Dictionary of National Biography*.

[28] Jordan was also responsible for mounting *London's Glory* in 1680, a set of scenes predictably directed against the Popish Plot.

[29] *The Triumphs of London for the Inauguration of the Right Honourable Sir Charles Duncombe* (London: A. Baldwin, 1708), pp. [ii, iv], 1-6.

[30] *House of Commons 1690-1715*, 3: 939.

[31] There are references to the various travails Duncombe endured in Trumbull's correspondence, now in the British Library.

[32] Williams, *Pope's Dunciad*, p. 36.

[33] *The Dunciad in Four Books*, ed. Valerie Rumbold (London: Longman, 1999), p. 184.

[34] *House of Commons 1690-1715*, 4: 310.

[35] Carswell, *Bubble*, pp. 22-3, 150-2. For Heathcote's associations with a group of presbyterian businessmen, see Richard Grassby, *Kinship and Capitalism: Marriage, Family, and Business in the English-Speaking World, 1580-1740* (Cambridge: Cambridge University Press, 2001), p. 308.

[36] A manuscript version of the third epistle in *An Essay on Man* reads: "The Fur that warms [a Monarch *deleted*] Sir Gilbert warm'd [an ermine first *deleted*] a

bear." See Maynard Mack, *The Last and Greatest Art: Some Unpublished Poetical Manuscripts of Alexander Pope* (Newark: University of Delaware Press, 1984), p. 257.

[37] Nicholas Rogers, *Whigs and Cities: Popular Politics in the Age of Walpole and Pitt* (Oxford: Clarendon Press, 1989), p. 20. For the delegation in 1710, see Bruce G. Carruthers, *City of Capital: Politics and Markets in the English Financial Revolution* (Princeton: Princeton University Press, 1999), p. 143.

[38] See *The Commission for Building Fifty New Churches: The Minute Books, 1711-27, A Calendar*, ed. M.H. Port (London: London Record Society, 1986).

[39] *The Dunciad*, ed. Rumbold, pp. 186-7.

[40] *The Governors of Bridewell and Bethlem* ([London], [1727?], p.1. The Guildhall is represented by Sir George Ludlam, who was City Chamberlain: his death in 1727, together with that of Sir John Ward in 1726, would set a terminus ad quem for this work. However, the presence of "Bishop Atterbury" in Westminster would suggest an earlier date. The evidence is contradictory, but 1725 seems a possible year. Under "the Exchequer" we find Dr Jonathan Swift, presumably as a relic of earlier days. Among the governors, amusingly, is Richard Blackmore; while Pater Noster Row is represented by Christopher Bateman, who was a member of the Stationers' Company.

[41] William Thorold graduated at Trinity College, Cambridge in 1694, was incorporated at Oxford in 1703, and became rector in 1717. I have not been able to discover his exact relationship to Sir George.

[42] David Cressy, *Bonfires and Bells: National Memory and the Protestant Calendar in Elizabethan and Stuart England* (Berkeley: University of California Press, 1989), p. 180.

[43] Defoe, *Tour*, 2: 120.

[44] *The Life and Character of John Barber, Esq; late Lord-Mayor of London* (London: T. Cooper, 1741), pp. 3-5; Rivington, *Tyrant*, pp. 5-6. The Cooper biography is not wholly reliable in detail, but the overall account is scarcely in doubt.

[45] Pope *Prose*, 2: 450.

[46] *Spectator* no. 69, 19 May 1711; no. 3, 3 March 1711; no. 2, 2 March 1711.

[47] For the first, see Isaac Kramnick, *Bolingbroke and his Circle: The Politics of Nostalgia in the Age of Walpole* (Ithaca: Cornell University Press, 1992), esp. Chapters 2, 3 and 8. For the second, see Colin Nicholson, *Writing and the Rise of Finance: Capital Satires of the Early Eighteenth Century* (Cambridge: Cambridge University Press, 1994). Nicholson, pp. 177-201, has many interesting things to say on *The Dunciad*; but unlike the essay here his account concentrates on Book IV, and isolates Colley Cibber as the key figure representing the new commercialism.

SELECT BIBLIOGRAPHY

This list is confined to (1) editions of the main primary texts used; and (2) printed secondary works which have been most regularly consulted and which have proved most immediately relevant to the issues discussed here. Standard reference works are omitted, such as the *Oxford English Dictionary*; the *Oxford Dictionary of National Biography*; *The History of Parliament*; *Grove's Dictionary of Music*; and *The Complete Peerage*.

Editions

J. Arbuthnot, *The Correspondence of Dr John Arbuthnot*, ed. A. Ross. München: Wilhelm Fink Verlag, 2006.

D. Defoe, *A Tour thro' the Whole Island of Great Britain*, in *Writings on Travel, Discovery and History*, ed. J. McVeagh. 4 vols. London: Pickering and Chatto, 2001.

The Letters of John Gay, ed. C.F. Burgess. Oxford: Clarendon, 1966.

J. Gay, *Poetry and Prose*, ed. V.A. Dearing and C.E. Beckwith. 2 vols. Oxford: Clarendon, 1974.

The Memoirs of the Extraordinary Life, Works, and Discoveries of Martinus Scriblerus, ed. C. Kerby-Miller. New York: Oxford University Press, 1988.

The Complete Letters of Lady Mary Wortley Montagu, ed. R. Halsband. 3 vols. Oxford: Clarendon Press, 1965-67.

The Correspondence of Alexander Pope, ed. G. Sherburn. 5 vols. Oxford: Clarendon, 1956.

The Dunciad in Four Books, ed. V. Rumbold. London: Longman, 1999.

The Prose Works of Alexander Pope. Vol. 1, *The Earlier Works 1711-1720,* ed. N. Ault. Oxford: Blackwell, 1936. Vol. 2, *The Major Works 1725-1744,* ed. R. Cowler. Hamden, CT: Archon, 1986.

The Twickenham Edition of the Poems of Alexander Pope, ed. J. Butt et al. 11 vols. London: Methuen, 1938-68.

The Correspondence of Jonathan Swift, ed. D. Woolley. 4 vols. Frankfurt: Peter Lang, 1999-2005.

Swift, J., *Journal to Stella,* ed. H. Williams. 2 vols. Oxford: Clarendon, 1948.

The Poems of Jonathan Swift, ed. H. Williams. 3 vols. Oxford: Clarendon, 1958.

The Prose Works of Jonathan Swift, ed. H. Davis et al. 14 vols. Oxford: Basil Blackwell, 1939-68.

Critical and Interpretative Studies

Ault, N., *New Light on Pope*. London: Methuen, 1949.

Erskine-Hill, H., *The Social Milieu of Alexander Pope: Lives, Example and the Poetic Response*. New Haven: Yale University Press, 1975.

Gerrard, C., *The Patriot Opposition to Walpole: Poetry, Politics, and National Myth 1725-1742*. Oxford: Clarendon, 1994.

Griffin, D., *Swift and Pope: Satirists in Dialogue*. Cambridge: Cambridge University Press, 2010.

Mack, M., *The Garden and the City: Retirement and Politics in the Later Poetry of Pope 1731-1743*. Toronto: University of Toronto Press, 1969.

Nicolson, M.H. and G.S. Rousseau, *"This Long Disease, My Life": Alexander Pope and the Sciences*. Princeton, NJ: Princeton University Press, 1968.

Rumbold, V., *Women's Place in Pope's World*. Cambridge: Cambridge University Press, 1989.

Williams, A., *Pope's Dunciad: A Study of its Meaning*. London: Methuen, 1955.

Cultural Studies

Hammond, B.S., *Professional Imaginative Writing in England 1670-1749: "Hackney for Bread."* Oxford: Clarendon, 1997.

Kramnick, I., *Bolingbroke and his Circle: The Politics of Nostalgia in the Age of Walpole*. Ithaca: Cornell University Press, 1992.

Levine, J.M, *Dr. Woodward's Shield: History, Science, and Satire in Augustan England*. Berkeley: University of California Press, 1977.

Todd, D. *Imagining Monsters: Miscreations of the Self in Eighteenth-Century England*. Chicago: University of Chicago Press, 1995.

Biographies of Scriblerian Circle

Beattie, L.M. *John Arbuthnot: Mathematician and Satirist*. Cambridge, MA: Harvard University Press, 1935.

Ehrenpreis, I., *Swift: The Man, the Works and the Age*. 3 vols. London: Methuen, 1962-83.

Mack, M., *Alexander Pope. A Life*. New Haven: Yale University Press, 1985.

Nokes, D., *John Gay: A Profession of Friendship*. Oxford: Oxford University Press, 1995.

Biographies of Others

Baines, P. and P. Rogers, *Edmund Curll, Bookseller*. Oxford: Clarendon, 2007.

Bennett, G.V., *The Tory Crisis in Church and State 1688-1730: The Career of Francis Atterbury Bishop of Rochester*. Oxford: Clarendon, 1975.

Deutsch, O.E., *Handel: A Documentary Biography*. London: Cassell, 1955.

Downes, K., *Sir John Vanbrugh: A Biography*. New York: St Martin's, 1987.

Dickinson, H.T., *Bolingbroke*. London: Constable, 1970.

Friedman, T., *James Gibbs*. New Haven: Yale University Press, 1984.

Grundy, I., *Lady Mary Wortley Montagu*. Oxford: Oxford University Press. 1999.

Paulson, R., *Hogarth*. 3 vols. New Brunswick: Rutgers University Press, 1991.

Plumb, J.H., *Sir Robert Walpole*. 2 vols. London: Cresset, 1956-60.

Rivington, C.A., *"Tyrant": The Story of John Barber 1675-1741*. York: William Sessions, 1989.

Politics

Bucholz, R.O., *The Augustan Court: Queen Anne and the Decline of Court Culture*. Stanford: Stanford University Press, 1993.

Hatton, R. *George I: Elector and King*. Cambridge, MA: Harvard University Press, 1978.

Monod, P.K.., *Jacobitism and the English People 1688-1788*. Cambridge: Cambridge University Press, 1989.

Rogers, N., *Crowds, Culture and Politics in Georgian Britain*. Oxford: Clarendon Press, 1998.

Thompson, E.P., *Whigs and Hunters: The Origin of the Black Act*. Harmondsworth: Penguin, 1977.

London

De Krey, G.S., *A Fractured Society: The Politics of London in the First Age of Party 1688-1715*. Oxford: Clarendon Press, 1985.

George, M.D., *London Life in the 18th Century*. New York: Capricorn Books, 1965.

Henderson, A.J., *London and the National Government, 1721-1742: A Study of City Politics and the Walpole Administration*. Durham, NC: Duke University Press, 1945.

Phillips, H., *Mid-Georgian London: A Topographical and Social Survey of Central and Western London about 1750*. London: Collins, 1964.

Economics

Carswell, J. *The South Sea Bubble*. Stroud: Sutton, 2001.

Dickson, P.G.M., *The Financial Revolution in England: A Study in the Development of Public Credit 1688-1756*. London: Macmillan, 1967.

Crime

Beattie, J.M., *Policing and Punishment in London, 1660-1750: Urban Crime and the Limits of Terror*. Oxford: Oxford University Press, 2001.

Howson, G., *Thief-Taker General: The Rise and Fall of Jonathan Wild*. London: Hutchinson, 1970.

Linebaugh, P. *The London Hanged: Crime and Civil Society in the Eighteenth Century*. Cambridge: Cambridge University Press, 1992.

Religion and Popular Beliefs

Bossy, J., *The English Catholic Community 1570-1850*. New York: Oxford University Press, 1976.

Capp, B., *English Almanacs 1500-1800: Astrology and the Popular Press*. Ithaca, NY: Cornell University Press, 1979.

Cressy, D., *Bonfires and Bells: National Memory and the Protestant Calendar in Elizabethan and Stuart England*. Berkeley: University of California Press, 1989.

Hutton, R., *The Rise and Fall of Merry England: The Ritual Year 1400-1770*. Oxford: Oxford University Press, 1996.

Thomas, K. *Religion and the Decline of Magic*. London: Penguin, 1991.

INDEX

Main entries are shown in bold type.